D0882545

98
52

From Friend to Comrade

This volume is sponsored by the
Center for Chinese Studies,
University of California, Berkeley

From Friend
to Comrade

The Founding of the Chinese
Communist Party, 1920–1927

HANS J. VAN DE VEN

University of California Press

BERKELEY   LOS ANGELES   OXFORD

University of California Press
Berkeley and Los Angeles, California

University of California Press, Ltd.
Oxford, England

Library of Congress Cataloging-in-Publication Data

van de Ven, Hans J.
   From friend to comrade : the founding of the Chinese
  Communist Party, 1920–1927 / Hans J. van de Ven.
    p. cm.
   Originally presented as the author's thesis (Ph.D.—Harvard
  University).
   Includes bibliographical references (p.   ) and index.
   ISBN 0-520-07271-5 (alk. paper)
   1. Chung-kuo kung ch'an tang—History. 2. China—Politics
  and government—1912–1928. I. Title.
  JQ1519.A5V36 1991
  324.251'075'09—dc20   91-13571
                                      CIP

Printed in the United States of America
9 8 7 6 5 4 3 2 1

The paper used in this publication meets the minimum requirements of
American National Standard for Information Sciences—Permanence of
Paper for Printed Library Materials, ANSI Z39.48-1984. ∞

Contents

Illustrations

Acknowledgments

This book began as a Ph.D. dissertation under the direction of Philip Kuhn. His wise counsel and prompt assistance I gratefully acknowledge here; this study would never have been written without him. Benjamin Schwartz also was generous with his time and advice. The intellectual debts I owe both will be obvious from the following pages.

I have relied heavily on new primary sources. I am grateful to all those in the People's Republic of China who provided access to the sources in their care. Their ready assistance and courage in making them available have been a constant inspiration.

Many of the ideas expressed in this study emerged first during discussions with my teachers and fellow students of Chinese history at Harvard University. Conversations with Timothy Cheek, David Ownby, Ding Xueliang, Joshua Fogel, and Roger Thompson were always stimulating. During a research year in Taiwan in 1983–1984, the members of the Modern History Institute of the Academia Sinica, especially Chang P'eng-yuan, Ch'en Yung-fa, Lin Man-hung, and Chang Yu-fa, offered many suggestions on sources for and interpretations of the republican period. John Fincher, Michael Schoenhals, Ch'eng I-fan, Yeh Wen-hsin, Edward McCord, and Joyce Kallgren added intellectual sparkle to the splendid environs in which the Center of Chinese Studies of the University of California at Berkeley is located.

Timothy Cheek, John Fincher, Robert Scalapino, Anthony Saich, Lawrence Sullivan, and Susan van de Ven all read the final dissertation in its entirety. Their comments and criticism opened up new perspectives and suggested areas for further research. I would also like to thank two anonymous readers for the University of California Press for their suggestions. The friendly and skilled editorial service delivered by Sheila Levine, Betsey Scheiner, and Robert Burdette is also much appreciated.

The following institutions provided financial support: The Harvard Club of the Republic of China made possible a research year spent at the Academia Sinica in 1983–1984. A grant from the National Cash Register Foundation financed a productive summer of research in the People's Republic of China in 1986. The National Graduate Fellowship Program enabled me to devote all my time to the dissertation during my final year at Harvard. A postdoctoral fellowship of the Center for Chinese Studies of the University of California at Berkeley provided the opportunity to begin the preparation of this book.

I should also like to thank my colleagues at the Faculty of Oriental Studies of Cambridge University as well as the fellows of St. Catharine's College. They have proved supportive company as this study was completed.

Acknowledgments of monographs like this have their history. A generation ago, scholars used to thank their wives for all they did at home to make it possible to spend their time in their studies. For good reasons this has gone out of fashion. But I should nonetheless like to thank Susan van de Ven for being willing to sacrifice much to accompany me wherever this study has required me to go and to bear with me in its writing.

Romanization

It is unfortunate that there are several transcription systems of Chinese characters in use and that in deference to entrenched usages in their own language, scholars do not apply the one they adopt with absolute rigor. The *pinyin* transliteration system is used in this study. However, in the case of geographic and personal names in the text, I have employed English transcriptions that were current in the 1920s and have remained so. For Chinese authors, I have used the transcriptions they use. Some inconsistency is unavoidable. In providing publication details in the bibliography I have applied the *pinyin* system in the transcription of all place names.

Introduction

Chinese communists have attracted scholarly attention in the past. Why, then, this study? In recent years, historians and archivists in the People's Republic of China (PRC) have produced a mountain of new primary sources on the early history of the Chinese Communist Party (CCP). What drew me to this mountain was the thought that a study of the organizational development of the early CCP had not yet been written. Past scholars have produced biographies of important Chinese communists, and they have examined ideological developments, CCP-Comintern relations, and the CCP's early peasant and labor movements. But none have put the CCP at the center of the story.

Previous writers have argued that Chinese communists established a true Leninist party with a centralized organization firmly asserting an ideology within a short time after the formal establishment of the CCP at its First Congress in July 1921. This study argues that this was a much more complicated process, which lasted until 1927 and involved deep changes in the norms of behavior and styles of action of CCP members. It was only in 1927 that they presented and treated the CCP as more than the sum of their total—as the Party. At the time of its formal inauguration, few CCP members had a firm concept of their party or what they wished it to stand for. Organizationally, it was a loose confederation of Marxist-Leninist study societies. In subsequent years, Chinese communists struggled to give meaning to the CCP while making it the framework of their political activities. They frequently collided over such issues as the distribution of authority, the correct attitude of individual members to the CCP, and the structure of their relationship with Chinese society. The CCP as a larger-than-life organization with its own culture was not a reality before 1927.

1

The first chapter places the spread of communism in China in the context of China's political crisis. While the 1911 Revolution had overthrown the dynastic order, the growing assertion of warlordism afterward and the spreading abuse of political power produced a situation in which many of China's educated elite expressed anger and frustration with what they saw as the brutalization of politics. The first chapter discusses the growing alienation from the Republic of those early CCP members for whom sufficient material exists to study the development of their thinking prior to the establishment of the CCP. Marxism-Leninism, with its depiction of politics as dominated by an exploitative elite, fitted their perception of politics as debased by elite profiteering, and they couched their decision to seek the ouster of political institutions of the Republic in its terms.

One of the principal attractions of Marxism-Leninism to Chinese communists was that it seemed to offer effective ways to confront China's political crisis. Most had been involved in study societies, which in the past had been used by elites as vehicles to promote political causes in the dynastic bureaucracy. Study societies had blossomed among China's new student population after the New Culture movement began in 1915. However, as the grip of warlordism on political institutions tightened and the republican political order showed itself impervious to calls for reform, debates in study societies broke out about the effectiveness of the societies to promote an honorable politics. The discussions dealt with such issues as whether society members should seek change by promoting new ideas or by seizing political power, whether participation in a political party would corrupt their moral integrity, and whether it was appropriate to combine on the basis of one ideology. In these discussions and in their writings of this time, future members of the CCP began to use Marxism-Leninism to formulate new political norms and advance new principles of political organization and action. It was as a result of this ferment that the first communist organizations were established.

The second chapter describes the activities of these organizations, which I call cells. The chapter discusses their formation and activities up to the First CCP Congress of July 1921. It suggests that the CCP was not the result of a central initiative but that in various places in China and abroad, Chinese established communist cells at more or less the same time, in some cases in ignorance of activities elsewhere. It also seeks to demonstrate that in general Chinese communists lacked a concept of a centralized leadership possessing ideological authority, or of a party having an exclusive claim on their time and their attachments. The chapter denies the centrality of Shanghai in the early CCP and emphasizes the relative autonomy of communist cells as well as the differences between them.

The CCP that emerged after the First Congress was fragmented. While the CCP's regional branches proved cohesive, its members looked toward CCP institutions and congresses in much the same way they had viewed those of study societies. Institutions lacked the power to enforce their decisions, and congresses were considered occasions for discussion and debate rather than mechanisms for drawing up plans of action and securing partywide implementation. Diversity of opinion existed about a range of topics, including the internal organization of the CCP and even whether it should develop a labor movement without procedures or shared norms providing ways to arrive at a settlement of the resulting conflicts. In 1923 central leadership collapsed completely in the CCP, in part as a result of the lack of organizational cohesion. At the same time, warlords and rural elites destroyed the CCP's labor and peasant movements, mostly because of the naiveté of CCP members about power relations in Chinese society and their vain confidence that workers and peasants would immediately grant them their allegiance. Chapter 3 first describes how the CCP nearly died a premature death between 1921 and 1923. It then analyzes how in the wake of these difficulties CCP members for the first time explored actively the organizational structures and techniques that Marxism-Leninism had to offer.

It was the May Thirtieth movement of 1925 that breathed life into the CCP. In 1925 CCP membership was still slightly under 1,000; two years later, it had grown to more than 57,000. CCP members had led huge mass movements, both in the city and in the countryside: the party had broken out of its social and urban isolation, its members came from all social strata, and it possessed an organizational presence in most urban centers and in much of the countryside of southern China. The same men who had still acted as modern Confuciuses in the early years of the CCP now could be found serving on committees with peasants and workers. They infiltrated gangs and Triads, and their long theoretical essays had made way for agitprop. They procured arms and instigated riots, and in public they all asserted one ideological line. It was a new world.

The fourth chapter seeks to demonstrate how CCP-society relations—and CCP conceptions of these—developed after the May Thirtieth movement. The movement was an open invitation for CCP members to create a "mass party," a party well embedded in Chinese society. To create a mass base, the CCP's challenge was to loosen Chinese from their existing social framework and tie them to CCP institutions. This was not an easy task. The CCP's first recruitment drives led to the incorporation into the CCP of gangs, bandit groups, Triads, and so on, which at times used the CCP for their own purposes rather than the other way around. It was because of problems like this that the CCP was unable to build a firm base and lost its struggle for power with the Nationalists, the Kuomintang (KMT), in 1927. Yet new approaches toward forming mass organizations were formulated, many of which became basic elements of the formula that in the end brought victory on mainland China to the CCP.

Chapter 5 examines the changes that took place in the 1925–1927 period within the CCP. The idea that the CCP was made up of friends who were equals in all respects made way for a central leadership that claimed it represented the correct party line and therefore possessed the right to direct CCP activities and give instructions to the party's members, who were, it was asserted, to accept its authority in all areas of life, including the intellectual realm. With CCP members possessing disparate social and cultural origins, the CCP needed to develop a new style of operation that was intelligible to all and also underscored their sense of distinctness. They did so on the basis of Marxism-Leninism, which became the fundament of a new mode of communication employed by CCP members on the one hand to cooperate in joint political activities and on the other to formulate new values and norms. They also employed the new mode of communication to promote their own ideas and represent their causes within their party. The August 7 emergency conference of 1927 was the first time all this came together. This is why this study ends with that event.

I do not mean to argue that Chinese communists ceased to debate the purpose and organization of the CCP after that date. The topics with which early CCP members struggled have emerged as issues of internal conflict again and again in the history of the CCP, as they did for example during the Long March, in Yan'an, during the Cultural Revolution, and in recent years. Not only has the CCP changed structurally over time, but at any given moment, different groups of members have attached their own meaning to it. However, it was in 1927 that the CCP became a centralized mass party, with its documents and its leading members asserting at least in public that the CCP was to be regarded as the source of all legitimate decisions and the institution that would deliver the future.

It is also not my belief that Chinese communists shed all traditional political norms and styles of behavior to acquire gradually the outlook, skills, and habits of real Leninists. Many fundamental changes had taken place in traditional Chinese politics before the establishment of the CCP. CCP members, in addition, produced their own organization, different from that of communists in the Soviet Union. Not all traditional norms or allegiances lost their value to Chinese communists, even if they were expressed in a different way.

This is an effort to analyze the founding of the CCP in terms of the

Chinese world. A background question that has constantly been on my mind is how one must understand the political transformation that occurred between the late Qing and the middle of this century. It is clear that a metamorphosis took place: the dynastic system made way for mass political parties asserting ideologies, and rebellions became mass movements involving students, urban workers, professionals, and the peasantry. Yet many aspects of this transformation have remained unexplored, and so far we have not moved beyond a choppy historiography of the period, with events following upon one another in a seemingly unconnected fashion. Of course, much that happened in this confused period was unconnected, and exigency and accident were important, something this book underscores many times. Nonetheless, the changes have been profound. By focusing on how one group structured its political activities during what seems an especially turbulent period, it is hoped that this study contributes to a better understanding of China's political metamorphosis.

The earliest generation of scholars to examine Chinese communism seriously did so in the context of the issue that framed much other research at the time—the intellectual and cultural continuity between traditional and modern China.[1] In Joseph Levenson's view, Marxist historicism provided Chinese communists with a way to combine an emotional attachment to their heritage and a rational commitment to modernity. It enabled them, he argued, to view their heritage as something of the past, but of their past.[2] Benjamin Schwartz argued that the relation with the West rather than Chinese tradition was uppermost in the minds of Chinese communists. According to Schwartz, Chinese communists found in Marxism-Leninism a theory that was Western yet critical of the West and spoke to their feelings of national inferiority. Rejecting the tradition-modernity dichotomy, Schwartz showed that they used Marxism-Leninism to draw insights into their own situation and that they developed it in the process.[3]

The issues that Schwartz and Levenson raised have continued to stimulate research on Chinese communism,[4] and in several aspects this book continues to deal with them. However, I differ from Schwartz and Levenson in that I am not interested only in issues of cultural identity and continuity but also in those involved in the evolution of the structure and the social background of political action, as well as in the conduct of conflict. In addition, my understanding of ideology is different from theirs.

It borrows from Clifford Geertz's definition. Geertz has written that ideologies are "schematic images of social order" that come into play when "a political system begins to free itself from the immediate governance of received tradition."[5] According to Geertz, received tradition—the religion, philosophy, and conventions of the past—loses out when it fails to provide ways of articulating new phenomena. In his view, ideology illuminates an unprecedented historical situation and functions as a road map in terrain that is emotionally and intellectually unfamiliar.[6] Marxism-Leninism, chapter 1 will argue, functioned in part as such a road map for Chinese communists.

Yet Chinese communists looked at this road map with their own considerations and objectives in mind. Following Philip Kuhn's approach to ideology in his study of the Taiping Rebellion of the mid-nineteenth century, I see Marxism-Leninism "fitting" the agenda of Chinese communists but also conflicting with norms of behavior and styles of operation to which they had adhered previously.[7] Both the fits and the contradictions sparked Chinese communists to develop new norms, institutions, and forms of communication and argument. This is not to argue that Marxism-Leninism and traditional Chinese forms of political action were exclusive entities. Communists were concerned with a number of issues with which political thinkers in China's past also struggled, and their behavior continued to display some traditional norms.

Perhaps the most significant way my view of ideology differs from earlier scholars' is that I stress its importance as a mode of communication and a legitimation device. Marxism-Leninism is a theory of history, politics, and economics, providing categories of analysis and policy prescriptions; at the same time the texts of Marxism-Leninism are a rich storehouse of symbols, mythologies, values, and norms. Marxism-Leninism shaped the thinking of CCP members, but they also marshaled its categories, values, and myths to articulate their thoughts, justify their actions, build coalitions, maintain their organization, and mislead others. This is why they could use it as a mode of communication. They also exploited Marxism-Leninism to maintain their organization, using it to sanction leadership selection and the exercise of authority within the CCP.

A second group of studies approached the history of the CCP from the perspective of social and political revolution, focusing on popular, especially peasant movements. The central issue in these studies—in which "revolution" was both a model of historical change derived from the social sciences and an explanatory metaphor—was why and how the CCP could mobilize the Chinese peasantry and so rise to power.[8] In an early attempt to provide an answer to these questions, Chalmers Johnson argued that the CCP rose to power not on the basis of its social and economic programs but by associating itself with a peasant nationalism evoked by Japanese rule.[9]

A number of authors based their interpretations of the relationship between the CCP and China's peasantry on the concept of the moral economy.[10] Ralph Thaxton, for instance, made the argument that economic dislocation caused by Western economic intrusion ruptured ties of reciprocity and fairness between landlord and tenant, leading landlords to exploit peasants to ever greater degrees during the Republic.[11] The CCP, according to Thaxton, mobilized the peasants by promising to satisfy their demand for justice against landlords.[12] In reaction to this view as well as that of Johnson, Ch'en Yung-fa has sought to put the revolutionary back into the story. In *Making Revolution*, he examined how local cadres both attempted to mobilize peasants by means of revolutionary programs and adjusted their policies to reduce their threat to rural elites.[13]

These studies and the questions they ask have also influenced this work, especially the fourth chapter. The revolution model, however, has tended to direct attention toward the relationship between the CCP and China's peasantry, assuming the CCP as a known factor. It has also tended to cast the changes that were taking place as essentially the ouster of a social class, the propertied elites, by a mass movement led by the CCP. While that is part of the story, it seems to me that China's revolution has run far deeper, involving nearly all aspects of Chinese life and bringing into question the most basic values and established forms of organization. Certainly the equation of the growth of the CCP with the maturation of that revolution seems a simplification. The idea that there was one revolution stretching back over a century and a half also suggests a cohesion among events that has not been spelled out.

1/Chinese Communists and China's Political Crisis

Writing several decades ago, Benjamin Schwartz and Maurice Meisner argued that the founding of the Chinese Communist Party was the result of the "messianic message" of Leninism.[1] The October Revolution, they maintained, dramatized to Chinese intellectuals the Leninist image of a global revolution giving birth to a new world, sweeping them from their feet. Leninism had the additional attraction of being critical of the West and catering to nationalist sentiments, important after the Treaty of Versailles in 1919 had granted former German rights in Shandong Province to Japan, an act that led to the famous May Fourth student demonstrations of that year in Peking and elsewhere.[2] Chinese historians have also insisted that it was the October Revolution that stimulated interest in Marxism-Leninism in China. They have maintained that it was the emergence of a working class in the 1910s that made Chinese receptive to Marxism-Leninism.[3]

Arif Dirlik has recently criticized the views of Schwartz and Meisner for overestimating the importance of the October Revolution. According to him, a great many ideologies found an enthusiastic audience in China in the late 1910s, anarchism being far more significant at first than Marxism-Leninism. The period was one of intense ideological debate according to Dirlik, Marxism-Leninism becoming a powerful ideological force only gradually. He is in agreement with Chinese historians that the emergent labor movement was the crucial factor in the process.[4]

This chapter places the spread of Marxism-Leninism in China in the context of China's political crisis. Those who were to join the CCP, I attempt to show, were enraged by what they perceived as the warping of the political realm in the Republic. Not only were they appalled by the despotic practices of the Republic's president, Yuan Shikai, and his successors, or the growing assertion of warlordism, but their feelings of frustration deepened in the late 1910s as they became convinced that Peking politics was a charade for warlord conflict. However, they were also disillusioned with local politics. Hailed only shortly before as the way to revitalize the nation, self-government institutions such as local assemblies were seen as instruments of bureaucratic venality and local elite exploitation.

The views of Chinese communists derived from their view of despotic actions as resulting from cultural backwardness, with those in power preventing the emergence of a new world. Their attitudes were also informed by their direct political experiences. A number had participated in the 1911 Revolution and the political institutions or parties established afterward. Many had involved themselves in one way or the other in efforts to reform the political world. There were those, like Mao Zedong, who were involved in local politics. There were also those who had participated in campaigns such as the New Culture movement that were designed to bring a halt to the debasement of politics in the Republic and to promote the crystallization of a modern one. By the end of the 1910s, despondency about the effectiveness of such efforts intensified.

What made the crisis run so deep was not only the concrete political situation and the ineffectiveness of reform campaigns but also the existence of profound doubts about the organization of the political realm and the reputability of various forms of political action. While by no means all traditional political norms had been abandoned and some still dreamed of a return to dynastic practices, many members of the ruling elites had come to see the traditional monarchy as outmoded, or they endorsed it instrumentally as a way to stem the slide toward chaos. By the late 1910s, as the Republic disintegrated, some also began to doubt the value of constitutionalism and republican political institutions, doubts that were all the more severe for the high hopes with which these had been invested earlier.

In this situation, Marxism-Leninism, this chapter argues, was interpreted by Chinese communists as suggesting a new way of looking at the political realities they confronted. It also provided them with a medium to articulate their anger with the perversion of politics during the Republic and to justify their rejection of established modes of political organization. Furthermore, they believed that Marxism-Leninism, with its primacy of politics, offered effective ways to confront the political crisis head-on, and this, in my view, was very important in their decision to make Marxism-Leninism the basis of their future political lives.

I begin with a discussion of the disintegration of the traditional political order and that of the Republic. My intention is not to argue that the founding of the CCP resulted in a direct and linear way from China's political crisis or that Leninism offered perfect solutions to it. Nonetheless, if in searching for the origins of the Chinese Communist Party we limit our view to the great events of the late 1910s inside and outside of China, it is not possible to secure a clear sense of the deeper historical trends to which CCP members responded.

CHINA'S POLITICAL CRISIS

Anxiety about the state of China's political system can be detected as early as the reign of the Jiaqing emperor (1796–1821) when rebellions, local government, flooding, and foreign encroachment made it clear to Wei Yuan that China faced unprecedented problems requiring innovative political solutions.[5] These worries intensified as internal domestic crises multiplied, foreigners made further inroads on Chinese sovereignty, and intellectual contacts with the West increased. At the same time that old political norms and values were challenged, new social groups began to carve out political roles, usually without official sanction. Because the population rapidly increased while the size of the establishment of local officials remained roughly the same, it was unavoidable that more and more tasks of local administration fell to local elites.[6]

The Taiping Rebellion of 1851–1864 formed a watershed. While it led to a short revitalization of the traditional system, the suppression of the rebellion to a large extent depended on the contributions of local elites, which raised militias and assumed local administrative functions.[7] After the rebellion, these elites sought to continue and strengthen their participation in the management of their localities. They tended therefore to be receptive to ideas endorsing their new roles.[8]

It was also after the rebellion that reform-minded officials and members of the educated elite for the first time began to study the West seriously in an attempt to find new ways to shore up the dynasty. While at first few wished to go beyond borrowing Western military technology, before long people like Yan Fu claimed that the strength of Western countries had more complex sources. As Benjamin Schwartz has written, Yan argued that the West's Faustian-Promethean spirit—the "exaltation of energy and power both over non-human nature and within human society"—and its liberal political institutions made Western societies powerful.[9] Yan concluded that the Chinese needed to transform their consciousness and their culture as a basis for political reform that would follow in an evolutionary fashion.

Yan was not the only convinced reformer in late-nineteenth-century China. Kang Youwei promoted the reform cause not just by introducing new ideas but also by involving himself directly in politics. He submitted his first plea for reform to the throne in 1888. Following China's defeat by Japan in the Sino-Japanese War of 1895, Kang led a protest movement of candidates for the metropolitan examination in Peking. In 1898 he induced the Guangxu emperor to promulgate a series of thorough political reforms, which if the Empress Dowager Cixi had not seized the initiative and quashed the reform edicts, would have resulted in the establishment of a constitutional monarchy, representative political institutions, a legal system based on Western models, and Western-style government ministries.[10]

Such governmental reform became increasingly acceptable to China's ruling elites as the ideological underpinnings of the dynastic system weakened. As Chang Hao has stated recently, central to the dynastic system was the assumption of a cosmic monarch whose authority to rule was thought to depend on the bestowal of a mandate on him by heaven. According to Chang, contact with the West and the introduction of science not only suggested an alternative epistemology but also undermined the idea that China was the center of the universe. The increasing familiarity with Western political institutions and political thought also challenged traditional conceptualizations of the political order, especially after Yan Fu postulated that these institutions were central to the West's strength.[11]

In 1902 the Qing court issued a set of decrees, known as the New Policies, that endorsed new political roles, especially for local elites. They provided for chambers of commerce, educational promotion agencies, and local assemblies, which local elites exploited to deepen their involvement in local society, using them to manage schools, levy local taxes, organize construction projects, conduct population surveys, and run police forces.[12] The New Policies were a recognition of the growing local elite involvement in politics. At the same time, they were an attempt by the state to bring local elite activism under its control or at least give local elites a stake in the continued existence of the dynasty.[13]

The New Policies dovetailed with the growing emphasis on local self-government in the reform movement. In 1897 Huang Zunxian had exhorted local elites to assume responsibility for the development of their communities. As a student in Japan, he had come in touch with local self-government notions, which had their origin in German political thought. He envisioned self-government institutions as mechanisms to mobilize local elite energies to strengthen the entire society. In 1902 Kang Youwei amplified Huang's ideas in his essay "On Citizen Self-Government."[14]

The abolishment of the examination system in 1905 fueled these developments; with it, the Qing discarded its right, of practical and symbolic significance, to license those participating in the world of politics. Public and political life ceased to be even formally coterminous as had been the case throughout dynastic times. Familiarity with Confucian texts was no longer an absolute requirement for public service. Rapid political change, in the social base and values, was unavoidable.

The 1911 Revolution was in part the product of the Qing court's attempts in the last years of the dynasty to turn back the clock on the changes that were taking place. However, it also resulted from the revolutionary movement pioneered by Sun Yatsen in the last decades of the Qing. Even the proponents of local self-government could find justification for their suggestions for political reform in a Confucian utopia of autonomous moral communities. Instead, appeals to nationalism and economic progress stood out in Sun's political platform. Sun was clearly oriented toward the West, adopting Western forms of bearing and dress. Lacking a traditional education but having earned a Western medical degree and influenced by China's coastal society, Sun sought to create a political base from parts of the population that had been ill represented in the official political world before, including the Triads of southern China and radical Nationalist students who congregated in Japan. Cultural as well as regional differences, besides divergent political outlooks, seem to have prevented China's revolutionaries from building a cohesive organization. The Revolutionary Alliance, the Tongmenghui, was set up in 1905 with Sun Yatsen as its focus, but by 1908 it already was past its heyday.[15]

The political order that emerged after the 1911 Revolution proved fragile from the beginning. The 1911 Revolution was the product of a short-lived coalition of various groups and organizations, including revolutionaries, elites centered around assemblies, and leading military figures and officials, finding a common cause in the overthrow of the Qing. Even the negotiations about the shape of the central government proved protracted and inconclusive. The debate centered on such issues as the power of the president, the independence of provincial and local assemblies, and the shape of the central government and representative organizations. The elections for the bicameral National Assembly held between December 1912 and April 1913 saw various groups that had participated in the Revolution, rebaptized as political parties, vying for power.[16]

Victory in the election went to the Nationalist party, the KMT, as the Revolutionary Alliance was renamed. The man who had led the KMT in the election, Song Jiaoren rather than Sun Yatsen, was assassinated on March 20, 1913, probably on the orders of Yuan Shikai, who had become president of the Republic as a result of the negotiations that followed the revolution. Song's assassination precipitated the Second Revolution, with KMT leaders, who were convinced that parliamentary methods would not work, taking up arms against Yuan Shikai. In control of the most important military forces in the country, Yuan Shikai suppressed the Second Revolution with ease.[17]

The result of these developments was that the exercise of authority came to lack the devices that normally serve to sanction and legitimize it. Yuan Shikai's effort to reestablish the dynastic system reflected, no doubt, his desire for power. However, given his support before the 1911 Revolution for important elements of the republican order, especially for local self-government institutions, it is unlikely that this was the only motivation for Yuan to seek the reestablishment of the monarchy. As Ernest Young has suggested, it may well have been in a desperate bid to stem China's slide into political chaos and moral anarchy that Yuan sought to revive old political rituals and in 1915 donned the imperial robes.[18] Whatever Yuan's motivation, the opposition to the monarchical movement was fierce. On March 22, 1916, Yuan declared that he would return to presidential procedures. Few were satisfied with this gesture, however, and a long period of negotiation and perhaps further warfare was prevented only by Yuan's death in early June.[19]

By 1916, all attempts to construct a cohesive political order had failed. It was at this moment, as the warlord period began, that the New Culture movement took off.[20] It resulted in a revitalization of political energies and the first modern student demonstration in China's history. Angered by what they saw as the usurpation of the political arena by men of mean and low character, the movement's founding intellectuals argued that nothing but the transformation of Chinese culture and the consciousnesses of individual Chinese could produce a new, prosperous, and fair society. An essential premise of the movement, therefore, was the idea that cultural reform was a prerequisite for the creation of a new political order. New Culture movement writers, including Hu Shi, Chen Duxiu, Li Dazhao, Wu Yu, and many others, carried out a devastating attack on the entire Chinese tradition, including Confucianism, the family, Buddhism, and Taoism. While they continued to advocate "Mr. Democracy"—the establishment of democratic and republican institutions—at the same time, they drew a clear line between themselves and those involved in existing political institutions. They either refused all contact with republican institutions, or when they did involve themselves directly in them, they treated the incumbents of republican offices as objects of reform.

The influence of the New Culture movement spread rapidly after Yuan Shikai's death as many of his political opponents and intellectuals persecuted by him returned from exile. In the more relaxed atmosphere that at first characterized the rule of Yuan's successor, Duan Qirui, they established study societies and published periodicals. Students at China's new institutions of higher education, which were in fact the result of Yuan Shikai's rule, proved an avid audience.

When they took to the streets during the May Fourth movement of 1919 in protest of the Treaty of Versailles, which granted German rights in Shandong Province to Japan rather than returning them to China, they initiated a tradition of student protest of high symbolic importance. Ever since the May Fourth movement, students in China have organized study societies, produced periodicals, and gone on protest marches, claiming to represent the very dignity of China. May Fourth students, asserting a passionate devotion to their country, electrified their countrymen at the same time that many New Culture authors, including Lu Hsun, expressed the darkest thoughts about the nature and future of Chinese society. The May Fourth movement created a general, if highly untargeted, sense of urgency to create a new China, with intellectuals duty-bound to point out the road ahead.

AGAINST THE REPUBLIC

It was in this context of intellectual ferment, alienation from the Republic, and an intense desire to assume a political role that in 1919 and 1920 Chinese intellectuals began to pay serious attention to the Russian October Revolution and Marxism-Leninism. Chinese communists depicted a world in which political institutions at all levels had been taken over by evil men, using them only for selfish ends. Their views reflected traditional expectations of the moral character of those wielding political authority, but they also derived from reformist thinking, which tested the validity of republicanism at the touchstone of its contribution to the creations of a strong, modern, and prosperous China.

The section below suggests that even if their criticism was in part infused by traditional concerns, it was with arguments and images derived from Marxism-Leninism that Chinese communists formulated their rejection of their previous political involvements. It illustrates that they were concerned with all levels of the republican political world and had long had considerable trouble in formulating their stance toward the Republic. In this, one is reminded of the equally complex deliberations in China's past of scholars and politicians who were ill at ease with the rulers of their time and had to come to a decision whether to withdraw their support from the reigning monarch. I focus here on the issue of how communists came to sever their last links with the coalition that had supported the 1911 Revolution and aimed to establish a republican order in China, as this was a first step in their decision to mount a revolution.

Chen Duxiu

In the first days after the 1911 Revolution, Chen Duxiu proved a firm supporter of the Republic. Chen, who gained fame as the editor of the *New Youth*, joined the Anhui provincial government and initiated educational reforms as part of the effort to bring constitutional procedures alive in the province.[21] Before the revolution, Chen was deeply involved in revolutionary organizations while abroad in Japan as well as in China. In his native Anhui Province, where his family was well connected, he organized a number of revolutionary organizations, belonging to that group of revolutionaries that sought to dislodge the Qing dynasty by assassinating its officials and organizing rebellions in the new military institutions of the late Qing. He shared many of the republican ideas of late Qing reformist thinkers like Liang Qichao and Yan Fu, and was closely connected with the radically nationalist student segment of the Tongmenghui, which had met in Japan and originated not just from Guangdong, as Sun's following did, but especially from central China and the Yangtze River area.[22]

Whatever Chen's hopes were at the time of the 1911 Revolution, they were dashed quickly when Yuan Shikai's troops reached Anhui Province in 1913, leading Chen to join the exodus of intellectuals to Japan.[23] While abandoning any direct participation in republican politics, Chen now became one of the main contributors to the New Culture movement. In a 1914 article entitled "Patriotism and Consciousness," Chen Duxiu asserted that China's problems were the product of misconceptions about the nature of the state and the relationship between state and individual. Nationalism, he argued, was made up of two ingredients. He asserted that its basis was an emotive pride in one's country but that it was to be checked by a rational understanding of the purpose of the state, which he defined as "an entity which works for the peace and prosperity of its citizens" and had "to protect individual rights."[24] According to Chen, China was in a state of malaise because Chinese failed to judge the government that ruled them—that of Yuan Shikai—by this standard.[25]

Like Yan Fu, Chen saw a close connection between politics and culture, and he argued that a cultural transformation which would release China from its "backwardness" and enlighten the Chinese to the values and attitudes proper to a liberal republic was a prerequisite for political and national regeneration.[26] Whereas Yan, endowed with a moderate temperament, professed an evolutionary view of change, Chen, a man of passion, called for immediate and total change, as Benjamin Schwartz and Lin Yusheng have argued.[27] He established the *New Youth* to make his message known among China's youth, who had access to the journal in school and university libraries in the larger towns and cities of China. In the journal Chen inveighed against Confucianism, especially denouncing the idea that it should become state doctrine, as Kang Youmei advocated. He argued that its ethical precepts, stressing obedience and hierarchy, could not form the basis for a modern political system that assumed equality between individuals. He also promoted the values he deemed central for the success of republicanism in China. In a 1915 article entitled "Warning to Chinese Youth," he defined these as individuality, independence, activism, cosmopolitanism, realism, and a scientific way of thinking. Science, for Chen, held the promise of helping Chinese to "cast off the Dark Ages."[28] He believed that, in the words of Schwartz, "science was a corrosive which could be used to undermine traditional values."[29]

References in Chen Duxiu's writings to the October Revolution or Marxism-Leninism remained cursory until 1920. In September of that year, in an article entitled "Talking about Politics," he abandoned the notion that the transformation of culture was a prerequisite for the transformation of the political order.[30] "The first need of our society," he wrote, "is to establish by revolutionary means a state of the working class (the proletariat), in order to create a government and laws which can put a stop to internal and external pillaging."[31] As we shall see, in the preceding summer months Chen had become deeply involved in the organization of a communist party.

In Chen Duxiu's writings predating "Talking about Politics" one can find many signs of deepening outrage at many aspects of the republican political world. While throughout 1918 and 1919 Chen continued to argue that a constitution, laws, and representative institutions arriving at decisions by democratic procedures should form the basis of China's political order, in his writings Chen expressed a mounting dismay at the growing stranglehold of militarists on republican political institutions, increasing bureaucratic venality, lack of government morale, and intensifying fragmentary tendencies.[32] In December 1918 he established the periodical the *Weekly Critic* (Meizhou Pinglun), devoted to the castigation of the Duan Qirui government, in which he criticized these tendencies. By the spring of 1919, Chen's writings sounded utterly despondent:

> Darkness will hem us in from all sides in these days of international powers, political horrors, the crime of private wealth, the darkness of war, the inequality of classes, . . . and of laws and ethics being divorced from reason and human nature. . . . It goes without saying that these evils have a long history and cannot be eliminated overnight. However, through individual effort and struggle, it is possible to use the bright side of human nature to improve its dark aspect.[33]

Under the influence of the French philosopher Bergson, Chen pinned his hopes now on the efforts of a few enlightened individuals.

Chen's faith in campaigns such as the New Culture movement also diminished. This was in part the result of the imperviousness of political leaders in Peking and elsewhere to the movement. The May Fourth movement also seems to have been a factor, however. Even though he was an inspiration to many students who joined the May Fourth demonstrations and his arrest on June 11 became something of a cause célèbre,[34] only two weeks after the demonstrations Chen Duxiu criticized the students for their naiveté. He depicted the demonstrations as a laudable outburst of patriotic sentiments but urged the students to temper their actions with reason. The issue, he wrote, was not whether the Duan Qirui government upheld Chinese sovereignty in Shandong but whether Duan's government was one that acted for the benefit of all Chinese.[35] When students took to burning Japanese goods, Chen issued a strong protest against blind nationalism:

> How must we deal with Japan, which now uses nationalism to encroach upon other people? In my opinion, we should not confront each other as two countries, but we must together with everybody (including the Japanese) who stresses right over might eradicate all people (including the Japanese) who emphasize might over right, basing ourselves on humaneness and love for what is right. . . . To destroy Japanese goods because they are made by Japanese is a dark movement in the history of human progress. . . . Our student circles should progress toward a deeper awakening; they must add a spirit of public-mindedness to their patriotism.[36]

Chen's faith in the New Culture movement also declined after the May Fourth movement dissolved into what he perceived as a general malaise. As the exaltation of the demonstrations ebbed away, pessimism gripped many students. In January 1920 Chen wrote a lengthy discussion of a suicide of a Peking University student who killed himself in November 1919, according to some because of despair about China's future.[37] The affair shocked Chen deeply. While he had been inspired by the new ideas, he was horrified that these same ideas had made "the youth feel that the world and life have no value and are not interesting. Such thoughts naturally create an outlook on life which is empty, dark, skeptical, tragic, and world-weary."[38] While Chen continued to argue for the need of a new culture as he had outlined, he also decried the youths who exploited his critique of traditional ethics as a defense of mere hedonism.[39]

The May Fourth movement is usually seen as leading in a direct and positive way to the founding of the CCP, by driving Chinese to explore all kinds of Western theories. By 1920, in addition to Chen, others of those who were to join the CCP expressed their doubts about it. Li Dazhao noted that the many student societies that had sprung up after the May Fourth movement were ridiculed as a "movement of constitutions" (*zhangcheng yundong*) since all of them made a great fuss about adopting constitutions and plans of action. The charge "was not without reason," Li commented.[40] Yun Daiying and Cai Hesen, two leading CCP members in the 1920s who will be discussed shortly, also came to speak negatively about the May Fourth movement.[41] The report of the Peking cell to the First Congress of the CCP in July 1921 expressed what seems to have been a general disillusionment with the May Fourth movement among those who were to join the Chinese Communist Party when it wrote that "the students exerted a great deal of effort, hoping to arouse the interest of the masses in political events. None of it bore any fruit."[42] The Chinese Communist Party, then, was not a straightforward continuation of the May Fourth movement.

Chen also became skeptical of the local component of the self-government movement. "The reason," he wrote in a December 1919 article entitled "The Basis for the Realization of Democracy," "that local self-government is a failure is because everybody allows a small group of gentry managers (*shendong*) to ensconce themselves in their localities and commit evil."[43] Arguing that democracy must have a basis in local practice and cannot be imposed from above, it was John Dewey, lecturing in China between May 1919 and July 1921,[44] who drew Chen's attention to local government.[45] Chen expressed surprise at the fact that people were somehow blind to the reality of elite behavior at the local level:

> The reasons for the unhappy political phenomena of today and the failure of democracy to be realized have many facets. First of all, our Republic is young. Secondly, we underestimated the difficulties in establishing a republic. . . . Thirdly, militarists control the armies of the Republic. . . . Fourthly, the two parties that uphold the Republic, the Progress Party and the KMT, do not understand the true nature of democracy. Both believe in the omnipotence of the government and put all their efforts into such issues as the constitution, the National Assembly, the cabinet, provincial autonomy. . . . In the fifth place, those few people who promote local self-government have no illusions about the central government but still make a fetish of large-scale provincial and county self-government. In reality, local self-government is no more than the separation of local government from the center. . . . It remains

government by bureaucrats, and this is entirely different from the
real basis of democracy—the direct and true association and
government of people by themselves.[46]

Chen Duxiu did not see existing local self-government institutions as a
nurturing ground for republicanism. His view of the Republic's history
was that its institutions had been invaded by men who abused republican
political institutions for purely private ends. Of course, in this Chen was
influenced by traditional criteria of political service, not by Western democratic ones, which do admit the representation of limited interests.

"Talking about Politics" formed Chen's farewell to the New Culture
movement and republicanism.[47] In the opening sentences of the article
Chen drew a clear line between current politicians—"those gentlemen
who are engaged in politics or hold offices just to make money"—and
himself to make clear that he continued to reject state-sanctioned politics
as then practiced in China. In the rest of the article Chen set forth basic
principles for a new but unsanctioned involvement in politics.

Chen Duxiu began the article by refuting arguments in favor of political
abstention. Most of those who made such a case, including intellectuals
and managers of chambers of commerce, Chen stated, did not reject politics
so much as the existing republican political practices in China. He also
denied the validity of what he deemed a more fundamental argument, that
all exercise of political power is inherently evil, as anarchists maintained:

> We must ask: Why can might produce evil? The reason is, I
> believe, that some people use it to uphold the powerful and the
> unscrupulous in order to oppress the weak and that which is right.
> However, if we turn this around and we use it to rescue the weak
> and righteousness, . . . obviously evil will not result.[48]

Later in the article Chen reiterated this instrumentalist view of political
power, which showed the influence of Dewey rather than Lenin, asserting
that "the state, the government, and the laws must be seen as instruments
to improve society; if they do not work well, we must improve them, but
we should not just discard them."[49]

Instead of arguing that republican institutions were good in principle
but China's backwardness had produced their corrupt use, Chen now stated
that an "indolent and wasteful bourgeoisie uses the instruments of the
organs of the state, the bureaucracy, and the laws to oppress the indus-
trious and productive proletariat, . . . treating them as less than machines
and beasts of burden."[50] He warned that the growth of political institutions and their penetration in the economic realm could only augment the
powers of "warlords and big officials."[51]

Clearly echoing Lenin, Chen rejected the suggestion that participation in the institutions of the Republic could lead to reform. He delineated two groups who had actively sought political involvement in the early Republic, one a group of ineffectual and naive traditionalists who believed in a "Chinese state of centuries of humaneness and benevolence" in which warlords "are not qualified to be involved." According to Chen, the second group, whom he called "Marxist revisionists," hoped to use representative institutions such as local assemblies to foster change. The result, Chen believed, was inevitably the reverse, as these groups would become assimilated to those who used these institutions for selfish ends and would become their accomplices; they would be tainted by them. Revolution, Chen Duxiu asserted, was the only method that could address China's problems:

> My conclusion is: I recognize that humans cannot divorce themselves from politics. . . . I believe that the state is only an instrument and not an ideology. In ancient times there were the city-states in which slaves were property, in the Middle Ages there was the state of feudal lords in which serfs were property, and in modern times there is the capitalist state in which the proletariat is property. All these states were states controlled by the propertied. The government and laws of these states were instruments of theft. . . . Even though I do not agree that we must totally reject the tools of the state, the government, and the laws, I do not believe that the current state, government, and laws of the bourgeoisie (the exploiting class) have the potential of eliminating social evil. I believe that revolutionary means must be used to establish a state of the working class.[52]

Chen's criticism of political realities during the Republic was in part moral. He condemned those controlling republican political institutions on the grounds that they acted on the basis of selfish motivations. Chen's moralism showed in his use of the words *gong* (public) and *si* (private). Already in the first decades of the twentieth century the lament was made that the elite's "private" interests had invaded the "public" realm.[53] In the last years of the Qing, as Mary Rankin has argued, the growth of elite participation in self-government institutions was often presented in the reverse way, as an expansion of the public (*gong*) realm.[54] In a 1923 lecture in Canton, Chen Duxiu applied the *gong* and *si* labels to capitalism and socialism:

> To simplify, the socialist system is (1) the concentration of capital and (2) the public ownership of property (*caichan gongyou*). It is certainly not the concentration of capital that socialists oppose in the capitalist system; it is private ownership. If we compare the

differences between the cornerstone of capitalism—the concentration of capital and private ownership of property (*caichan siyou*)—and that of socialism—the concentration of capital, with public ownership of property—the only difference is the character *si* as in private ownership and *gong* as in public ownership.[55]

Marxism-Leninism suggested to Chen ways of dealing with what he depicted as the immoralization and brutalization of the political realm. He had come to believe, to use his terminology, that the invasion of the *si* forces into politics rendered attempts to rid China of its backwardness by extrapolitical means such as the New Culture movement impotent. Marxism-Leninism, Chen seems to have hoped, offered a way of establishing a politics that was perhaps not ideal but would drive the *si* element back out of government, in which involvement would again be honorable and would promote the process of cultural and economic modernization.

Mao Zedong

Born in 1893 and nearly two decades younger than Chen, Mao set out his views of China in the summer of 1919 in "The Great Unity of the People." The article was published serially in the *Xiang River Review*, named after the river along which Changsha, the capital of Hunan Province, stands.[56] At the time, Mao was a student in the city. Past scholars have focused on "The Great Unity" for its negative remarks about Marxism, its laudatory statements about Kropotkinism, as well as the continuities between some of its ideas and Mao's Cultural Revolution thought.[57] The article also gives insight into Mao Zedong's motivations for the actions in which he was involved in the late 1910s, including his participation in a coalition led by Tan Yankai, a leading member of the Hunan Provincial Assembly, that sought to establish Hunanese self-government. In contrast to Chen Duxiu, Mao Zedong's attention was not focused on national but on provincial Hunanese politics.

"The Great Unity" argued that China was weak because autocratic dynasts had suppressed the ability of Chinese to form collective associations that were essential to making the country strong, an argument derived from social Darwinism that influenced many Chinese thinkers at the time.[58] This view was a common one at the time. The 1911 Revolution, Mao asserted, had removed the bars that had prevented people from setting up collectives. Evidence for their reemergence, he maintained, was the local and provincial assemblies, chambers of commerce, agricultural associations, and student associations. These associations, he wrote, "are very simple, and could be compared to a 'small association.' "[59] Mao declared that a strong China would emerge as people in one small association woke up to their shared interests with members of other associations and as they became accustomed to function cooperatively. They would then unite in ever-expanding circles until China was one "Great Union."[60] The existence of, for instance, the "National Union of Educational Associations" was a sign to Mao that China was already moving in this direction.[61]

While Mao was optimistic about the future, his assessment of the present was highly critical. He stated that some associations had come under the control of gentry (*shenshi*) and professional politicians (*zhengke*):

> Naturally it was unavoidable that numerous "gentry" and "professional politicians" have entered these associations, societies, organizations, and alliances. (Examples are the National Assembly, the provincial assemblies, provincial educational associations, provincial peasant associations. . . . They indeed are no more than associations of gentry or professional politicians).[62]

Echoing New Culture ideas, Mao also argued, in a nearly vindictive way, that Chinese lacked the appropriate cultural attitudes to manage collective organizations:

> People in our country have known only how to earn private profit, which in the final reckoning bears least interest. Businessmen don't know how to manage a public company, and workers don't know how to form a workers' party. Scholars know only the old way of locking themselves up in their studies. . . . We Chinese simply have no idea how to handle a coherent undertaking on a substantial scale. It is needless to talk about the mismanagement of politics. It is only because of foreigners that the postal system and the salt gabelle have their positive sides. . . . Schools are mismanaged, self-government is bungled, and even households and individual lives are mishandled.[63]

Mao made clear that he did not believe that an innate deficiency in the Chinese character was responsible for this situation. "We have lacked training," he stated.[64] Now that the political situation allowed for training in cooperation to take place, he believed, China stood on the brink of a bright future.

The Culture Book Society (Wenhua Shushe) was one vehicle that Mao, and others, used to promote this training in public-minded cooperation. Founded in July 1920, the society was financed by people who donated at least one *yuan*. Its purpose was the spread of New Culture ideas and values by making appropriate books and periodicals available. Regardless of the amount of the donation, which could not be withdrawn and on which interest or dividends were not given, each contributor possessed one vote at a semiannual "shareholders' meeting." At the meeting, investors elected one manager possessing full authority. The manager was obliged to keep daily and monthly accounts, and to report to the shareholders' meeting.[65] This was a model "small association." It did not recognize private property or profit; it had accountable executives and was to serve society at large.

Formed by Changsha students in 1917, the New Citizen Study Society was another "small association" in which Mao Zedong was involved.[66] Its purpose was to promote the norms appropriate to new public-minded citizens. The term *new citizen* referred to the journal the *New Citizen*, which Liang Qichao had founded in Tokyo in 1902,[67] and the society promoted new-citizen values. One reason the society is important for the study of early Chinese communism is that its members wrote each other frequently and distributed volumes of this correspondence within the society. These have now become available, providing us with a great deal of information about the thinking of Mao Zedong, for instance.[68] As I will attempt to show later in the chapter, the society played an important role in the lives of many of its members, who made it the base of their activities, intellectual as well as political.

It was his experience with Tan Yankai's self-government campaign that led to Mao Zedong's rejection of the local self-government movement and republicanism. Angus McDonald was the first to describe this episode in Mao's life.[69] Tan was an eminent scholar from Hunan—he had been a member of the Hanlin Academy, the highest imperial "think tank"—who after the 1911 Revolution served as president of the Hunan Provincial Assembly and also as Hunan governor.[70] In late 1919 he brought Hunanese elites together in an effort to drive the warlord Zhang Jingyao from the province. In the early months of 1920 Mao traveled to Peking and Shanghai to solicit support for the movement but also to push it in the direction in which he wished to see it go.[71]

Tan's coalition succeeded in removing Zhang Jingyao, principally by enlisting Zhao Hengti. Zhao, in possession of his own military base, was a Hunanese opponent of Zhang. Tan and Zhao, in control of the province, then declared Hunan independent, raising the slogan "Hunan for the Hunanese." This move raised the issue of who was to determine how Hunan was to be ruled. On September 13 Tan convened a self-government convention for which he picked the candidates.[72]

Those who were left out immediately responded, some charging that Tan's approach was more of the same—government by officials and not genuine self-government. Mao and several others, including Peng Huang, proposed that representatives for a Hunan constitutional convention be drawn from all public associations in the province.[73] They organized a meeting of representatives of these associations, which culminated in a march to the provincial government's offices to deliver a petition, which was received by Tan personally. Further meetings and demonstrations took place to promote the self-government cause, including a conference on constitutionalism, organized by various associations in Changsha, at which John Dewey and other leading Chinese intellectuals, including Cai Yuanpei, spoke. Although he showed some receptiveness to these pressures, rebellions and mutinies forced Tan to flee Changsha in late November 1920. He left the province in the hands of Zhao Hengti, who remained in control until the Northern Expedition of 1926.[74]

Disillusionment now overwhelmed Mao. He expressed this in a letter to Xiang Jingyu, a woman member of the New Citizen Study Society who had gone to France for study and became a women's-movement leader in the CCP. In a letter dated November 25, Mao explained to her that

> in the past year, I, and others such as Peng Huang, have worked hard in direct ways to achieve something, but we have nothing to show for it. Education did not work, the people have remained unenlightened, and most Hunanese continue to be blind. . . . Few people even knew about it when Peng Huang and I advocated that we should make Hunan into an independent country, divorce ourselves from the backward provinces in the North and those in the South that have very different conditions in order to break away from this empty and unorganized China and link up directly with the awakened peoples of the world. It hardly created a stir when the issue of self-government came up. . . . Most people could not make head or tail of our proposal . . . or they thought it entirely strange. . . . Hunanese have no brains, no ideals, and no basic plan. Politics is shrouded in dark clouds; it is corrupt, and there is no hope for the path of political reform.[75]

Only a month later, in a letter of December 1, 1920, to New Citizen Study Society members in France, Mao Zedong declared: "I believe a Russian-style revolution offers a solution where all else has failed."[76] In explaining this new view, Mao took as point of departure comments made by Bertrand Russell at the conference on constitutionalism in Changsha:

> When Russell lectured in Changsha, he advocated communism but opposed the dictatorship of the proletariat, saying that it would be better to use education to awaken the bourgeoisie, as then one might preserve freedom and avoid the bloodshed of war and revolution. My view can be summed in the following phrase: "It sounds good in principle, but it won't work." For education one needs money, people, and institutions. In today's world, all money

is in the hands of capitalists. Those in charge of education are capitalists or their slaves. Capitalists control completely the two most important educational institutions in the world today—schools and the press. . . . The reason for this is that capitalists control the "assemblies" that enact laws that protect them and keep down the proletariat. They have "a government" that enforces these laws. . . . They have "armies" and a "police" that on the one hand safeguard their well-being and also keeps down the proletariat. . . . They have "banks" that serve as the storehouses for the wealth and the properties they circulate. They have factories as institutions to monopolize their products.[77]

Mao eagerly seized the arguments and the vocabulary of Marxism-Leninism to articulate his anger at the abuse of political institutions in China. As in the case of Chen Duxiu, Marxism-Leninism suggested to him that political power was a prerequisite for reform, not its goal.

Li Dazhao

As early as 1913, in a highly emotive poem, "My Great Lament," Li Dazhao decried the Republic as a thin veneer barely covering the greedy machinations of selfish officials and merchants.[78] Born in 1889, Li Dazhao was twenty-two at the time of the 1911 Revolution. Like Chen Duxiu, Li fled to Japan soon after Yuan pressed his claims to power. Even if he was an outspoken opponent of the Republic at this point, I argue that Li nonetheless had difficulty in defining his political stance and that his interest in the Bolsheviks and in Marxism-Leninism resulted in part from this. His support for the formation of a communist party, I suggest, was in part similar to that of Chen Duxiu, seeing it as a way to sweep away the evil forces that controlled political power. Li also saw a communist party as a means to take the construction of cooperative institutions in hand and so to achieve a strong China.

Li was the first leading Chinese intellectual to announce his support for a Leninist world revolution publicly in 1918 and its most effective early propagandist in China.[79] Meisner and Schwartz have both emphasized the differences between Chen Duxiu and Li Dazhao. While Chen and Li shared a hostility to what they described as China's backwardness, Li Dazhao's "thought remained on the cosmic level, looking forward to some cosmic act of liberation," as Schwartz has written.[80] Chen Duxiu did not believe that such an event was about to occur, and in fact, as Meisner has stated, Li was temperamentally of an optimistic bent, rejecting Chen's pessimism.[81]

Chen and Li held fundamentally different views about what attitude to adopt toward the Republic, as Meisner has mentioned.[82] Unlike Chen, Li

Dazhao did not renounce direct involvement in republican politics. After returning from exile in Japan, Li participated in the reformist Progress Party (Jinbudang), founded by Liang Qichao.[83] During his stay in Japan, Li's reading of John Stuart Mill, Montesquieu, and Voltaire only strengthened his faith in the political ideas on which the Republic was founded.[84]

In "Pessimism and Self-Awareness," published in August 1915, Li defended his participation in republican politics. The article was a response to Chen Duxiu's "Patriotism and Self-Awareness."[85] He praised "intellectuals" (*wenren*) who "come out in response to their time and with their lively pens ring the alarm bells, thus preventing the eternal obstruction of the human mind."[86] This, I believe, was genuine praise for Chen Duxiu.

However, Chen's article had argued that Chinese served their government for the wrong reasons, not understanding the nature of the state and motivated by a naive desire to see their country attain glory. In his article, Li retorted that mere pessimism had led some people to withdraw from engagement in public and official life—a clear attack on Chen Duxiu's abstention from direct involvement with republican institutions.

Li's vision of the Republic at the time of the beginning of the New Culture movement was similar to that of Chen Duxiu. Both believed that the political realm was controlled by people who lacked understanding of the true purpose of politics. In Li's view, however, it was a sacred duty of those who did possess such an awareness to develop an active political involvement. Li Dazhao, it appears, wished to be both a *wenren*, sounding the alarm bells, and a political leader. This conception of the role of the intellectual is in part traditional but also seems influenced by romanticist ideas.

In 1916, shortly after the exchange with Chen Duxiu, Li Dazhao discovered in a personal way the problems of reconciling engagement in political action and being an intellectual true to one's convictions when the leaders of Li's party refused to let him publish a piece critical of Duan Qirui.[87] When Duan cracked down on political opposition in Peking, Li again fled the city, this time seeking safety in the Shanghai Concessions.

Li sang the praises of the October Revolution shortly afterward. In November 1918 Li Dazhao described the October Revolution as an event that had unleashed forces that would bring about a new age in the present, one in which the natural harmony of all people in the world would be restored and governments would cease to oppress the vitality and energies of the general population. "The victory of Bolshevism," he wrote, "is the victory of the new spirit of a shared awakening in the minds of each individual in the twentieth-century world."[88] He stated that the October Revolution heralded a world in which weak nations would regain their lost independence, peasants would rid themselves of landlord exploitation, and women would find their liberation from the shackles put on them by men. Li envisioned a society in much the same way as Mao: it would consist of voluntary and self-governing units, cooperating with each other in ever-larger bodies.[89] Li associated the October Revolution with everything that was good and would produce a cooperative world; it had opened up "a thoroughfare to world unity [datong]."[90]

Believing that China had an important contribution to make to the postrevolutionary world, "nationalism was very much involved in [Li's] interpretation of Marxism-Leninism,"[91] as Maurice Meisner argued. Li was not a nationalist in the narrow sense of the word, interested only in seeing the glory of China asserted in the international arena. He also did not show any inclination to articulate a Chinese national myth, recording the common descent and history of the Chinese people in their struggle to become one country. He placed the October Revolution in the context of the First World War, arguing that it had emerged out of the desire of "the common people" to break down national boundaries and to eliminate national governments used by a few to exploit the rest of humanity.[92] Li's faith in the emergence of a new China was part of a view of history as a process of global redemption.

In Li's view, the world revolution had a cultural agenda, as it was the event in which China would shed itself from its cultural backwardness. In 1918, in an article entitled "The New! The Old!," Li pictured his own time as one in which the old and the new were in constant struggle. He gave examples from the contemporary scene: the old nightwatch as well as a modern police force patrolled the streets; monogamous marriage was the law, but concubinage was widespread; cars and rickshaws crowded the same streets; and a constitution had been adopted at the same time that Confucianism was made into a state religion.[93] Li compared the world revolution to the biblical flood that would wash away everything and reveal a new age.[94]

In January 1921, Li published "Training in Cooperation and the Business of Reform," the article in which he spoke in dismissive terms of the May Fourth movement and called for the founding of a communist party in China. Only recently reissued, it surveyed modern Chinese political history, showing Li's disenchantment with the Republic:

> After the Xianfeng emperor [reigned 1851–1861] of the Manchu's Qing dynasty removed the prohibition on sea trade, two large parties arose who were Europeanized to some extent. One was the Tongmenghui, and the other was the Qiangxuehui [the Study Society for the Promotion of Self-Strengthening, founded by Kang

Youwei in 1895]. The 1898 reform movement was the latter's accomplishment, while the first achieved the 1911 Revolution. . . . As to the political parties that have come forth since the founding of the Republic, they simply have used the outbreak of a fire to loot: they set up cliques for their own selfish interests.[95]

In this article Li Dazhao argued, as he and others had before, that China was weak because its people were unable to cohere, because "our organizational capabilities have regressed in the deadly apathy resulting from thousands of years of dictatorship, shackles of thought, and infection with theories stressing passivity, laziness, and pessimism."[96] It filled him with shame, he wrote, to know that Chinese were not even able to overthrow the current government, which, foreigners had told him, was so weak that less than one thousand revolutionaries would be enough for the task. He endorsed a communist party, he stated, in admiration for the vigor and energy that communists around the world displayed in forming social organizations. Befitting his internationalist orientation, he also praised their establishment of the Comintern to achieve cooperation across borders.[97]

An interesting aspect of this article is that Li's commitment to a communist party was not exclusive. For him it made sense as a means to promote "social cooperation" and to oust the political authorities of his day. This view implied that he believed that in the course of time all kinds of associations would emerge. Li did not assert that the party was to be the sole focus of activities of its members. While Li was to be an influential CCP member for the rest of his life—he was executed in April 1927 in Peking—he did not concern himself deeply with CCP organizational matters and did not develop a substantial role for himself in the CCP outside Peking, where the CCP grew little during the 1920s.

Li continued to seek cooperation with other forces in China. In 1922 Li Dazhao used his connections with Wu Peifu, the dominant warlord in north China at the time, to help CCP members organize workers along the Peking-Hankow Railroad, an enterprise that resulted in a violent crackdown on the union in February 1923. Li was also an important supporter of KMT-CCP collaboration in the first united front and after 1925 sought to bring about an alliance between the CCP and Feng Yuxiang. Li seems to have remained wedded to his hopes of forming a society consisting of an alliance of voluntary cooperatives, seeing the CCP as a means to prod China in that direction.

In short, Li Dazhao supported the formation of a communist party in China as a way of attacking the abuse of political institutions and promoting cooperation, which he continued to see as essential to producing a prosperous society. Li wrote with hot-blooded conviction about the October Revolution and the coming world revolution, deploying images of the Bolshevik Revolution creating a new age to their maximum agitational effect. It was because of this that he could inspire many at a time when the euphoria of the May Fourth movement had ebbed away, a fact he noted in the same article that called for a communist organization in China.[98] In this way Li Dazhao found a way to achieve what he thought a *wenren* should do: he sounded the alarm bells and so spurred his audience to action. Marxist-Leninist ideas and imagery, as well as the role of the propagandist of the revolution, offered him new ways of giving political meaning to his life.

Yun Daiying

Yun Daiying was a leading figure in Wuhan student circles in the late 1910s. He became a driving force behind the Communist Youth League in the early twenties, editing *China Youth* (Zhongguo Qingnian). In 1925 he was instrumental in bringing about antiforeign student strikes in Shanghai. He subsequently taught political thought, probably interpreted as Marxism-Leninism, at the famous Whampoa Military Academy near Canton and helped organize uprisings in Shanghai in 1927.[99] Despite his importance as a leading CCP member in the early history of the CCP, a collection of his writings appeared only a few years ago.[100] Yun's diaries covering the 1917–1919 period and a selection of his correspondence from 1917 to 1924 have now been added.[101]

After having been involved in the May Fourth movement in the Wuhan area, Yun became a proponent of the New Village movement (*xincun yundong*). Its goal was the formation of self-sufficient cooperatives in the countryside where people jointly worked, studied, and supported one another in moral cultivation.[102] Yun's New Village was a radical attempt to bring about moral self-ruling collectives, which, it was hoped, would prove infectious examples.

Yun was highly critical of the intellectual reform currents of his time and asserted that students had been naive in their association with what he vaguely termed "existing forces." He quoted Zhang Taiyan, a revolutionary most known for his anti-Manchuism and a scholar of great prestige, with approval:

> Mr. Zhang Taiyan has said that "a weak point of today's youth is their illusion that they can depend on any existing force." . . .
> There is no force in China upon which we can depend. Because they have been infected by millennia of absurd theories and

customary habits, if one depends on them, they will use you. They are all the same: the Northern and Southern warlords, the old and new assemblymen, the bureaucrats and returned students who treat civil service as a business, as well as the professional politicians and representatives of student associations, who only want to stir up protest in the streets, and the National Essence scholars and the New Thought specialists whose only ideology is to make a name for themselves.[103]

The National Essence movement included scholars and political activists who hoped to locate roots for modern nationalism in China's past.[104] "New Thought" (*xin sixiang*) refers to Western theories.

The New Village was for Yun a solution to the problem of how to protect and nurture the good moral instinct, which he believed most people possessed innately, and "an evil social system" that forced people to go against that instinct.[105] While people were naturally inclined to act morally, Yun argued, the economic pressures of daily life forced them to violate their moral nature. He hoped that collective life would not so much strengthen the moral resolve of individuals—that was strong enough—as secure a stable economic base so that they could live by its guidance.[106] To Yun's mind, cooperation was essential to the preservation of one's moral integrity.

Yun Daiying never succeeded in building a New Village. He served as a teacher in a number of schools but became disappointed when he found that students wished only to obtain a diploma to advance their careers and that most teachers quickly lost their idealism.[107] Other ventures, including a bookstore, also proved unsuccessful.[108] In a letter of June 1921 Yun complained of depression, stating that he could think of no way his actions might truly contribute to society.[109]

Yun Daiying was a member of the Young China Study Society, to which a number of future CCP members, including Li Dazhao and Mao Zedong, belonged, like other young and progressive intellectuals of the time. The society convened a meeting in early July 1921 to debate whether it should become a communist organization. The minutes of the meeting indicate that Yun was sympathetic to the idea but continued to have his doubts, especially about whether China had a man like Lenin in possession of the appropriate moral and intellectual leadership qualities.[110]

In a letter written shortly afterward, Yun wrote that "my own idea is, and I really hope this, that the society will become a Bolshevist body; this is a great change in my thinking that occurred after the annual conference."[111] In a long letter offered to the society in explanation, Yun explained himself in detail. Economic determinism fitted his earlier conviction that economic pressures prevented a principled life. He emphatically declared that "the evils of the old society are all the result from the evil economic system."[112] The essential reality of contemporary life, he stated, was exploitation: "In this economic system, all of humanity depends on extortion and theft for a living. . . . The aristocracy and the bourgeoisie must do so, but even people subject to them must use all kinds of tricks to mislead and cheat."[113] This reality, Yun asserted, left no endeavor untouched. "The political world is naturally controlled by the third class," [114] he declared. Activities that many believed to be above politics or to possess some sort of redeeming social value, Yun now argued, should be seen as part of the same system of exploitation."Even in the case of education," he wrote,"while normally people regard it with esteem and as valuable, in the current system it is only for sons of the aristocracy."[115] Yun drew the conclusion that revolution, the total eradication of the present system, was the only course left.[116] He no longer believed that it was possible somehow to separate oneself from society, an idea that had been fundamental to the New Village movement. He wrote that "it is necessary that we enter the old society, and use all opportunities" in order to "generate a fundamental and effective attack on the present evil economic system."[117]

In the letter in which he explained his views to the Young China Study Society, Yun, like other future CCP members, depicted republican political institutions as instruments used by one class to exploit the other. He also used Marxism-Leninism to set out a new political role. He no longer saw his task as fostering moral forces in society through education and practice but as shouldering the awesome task of leading the revolution. "Our responsibility," he wrote, "is to lead the masses in a coolheaded, thoughtful, alert, and decisive way."[118]

Cai Hesen

New Citizen Study Society members, according to the recollection of one of them, said of Cai Hesen and Mao Zedong that "Hesen is the theorist and Mao the realist."[119] Together with other New Citizen Study Society members, Cai traveled to France for study in late 1919 and set out on what he intended to be a five-year course of study of socialist movements in Europe.[120] During the voyage from Shanghai to Marseilles, Cai met and fell in love with Xiang Jingyu, the woman to whom Mao Zedong poured out his heart in November 1920. In the spirit of the times, Cai and Xiang maintained, as Cai Hesen informed Mao in a letter of May 28, 1920, "a union of real love (*lian'ai*)."[121] Soon after his arrival in France, Cai became enthusiastic about the October Revolution and began a career as a communist agitator and organizer that ended in 1931 after the British police in Hong Kong arrested him and handed him over to the KMT in Canton. [122]

In a July 1919 letter to Mao, Cai Hesen stated in a typically dramatic fashion that he saw an irreconcilable conflict, given China's conditions, between the imperative to live the life of a moral man and the desire to effect change of benefit to the entire society: "In the situation of our country today, in this vile world of evil and degeneration, if one must be a just and moral man, how can one found a new world?"[123] Cai was a student of Yang Changji, a specialist in neo-Confucianism and Western ethics in Changsha who became a professor at Peking University in 1918. Yang, who also taught Mao Zedong, exhorted his students to strive for moral self-perfection and integrity. He counseled his students to forgo the lure of office or salary to maintain their independence and their moral purity, serving society in this way. [124] Cai Hesen's remark above was the result of a clash with Yang Changji. Yang had been asked to serve as academic editor of a new periodical but had refused on the grounds that association with the journal might taint him. Cai Hesen wrote Mao that he had disagreed, arguing that "in my view, for true humaneness and courage, in order to help the people reach a better life, one must descend into hell."[125]

In emotional language, Cai Hesen declared that the Confucian insistence on a public stance of uncompromising moral integrity and withdrawal from active involvement in politics in a time of pervasive evil produced a situation in which many of China's best and brightest refused to join battle with the "immoral" forces that he believed ran wild in Chinese society. In an August 1918 letter, Cai, "increasingly afflicted by the darkness and backwardness of society," condemned "these *junzi* indignant about their times" for standing idly by when "evil men perpetrate disaster." The *junzi* was the Confucian ideal of the morally upright man, thought to be able to bend the world toward the good by his moral force. Cai declared that *junzi*

> are bound by all kinds of public and moral strictures and so are able only to perpetrate acts of false goodness and not of false evil. What I advocate is to commit wrongs in order to achieve a greater good. In my view, it is impossible to be completely good without any evil. Even if the evil of the just man hides goodness, to demand perfection nonetheless easily leads to hypocrisy. [126]

Cai asserted that Lenin had made the truly heroic sacrifice of forgoing a posture of public integrity, committing evil for the future benefit of society. "It is he whom I want to take as my model," he declared. [127] The justification, he argued, was the ultimate good of society: "The *junzi* can commit any good and any evil. He takes into account only the utility for the whole, not his own selfish one."[128] He believed that Lenin was a man who did that.

Cai Hesen, as the above suggests, was most concerned with developing a new political role. He rejected the Confucian ideal of the *junzi* as well as the Confucian injunction that in times of pervasive evil the moral man retreats from political service after having exhausted all avenues to counsel the ruler to change his ways. He stressed the good of society as the ultimate criterion for political action, a value that reformist thinkers of the late Qing increasingly asserted to form the purpose and justification of political service, as Ch'eng I-fan has argued.[129]

Cai's new views led him to consider the Republic from a new perspective. In an August 1920 letter to Mao Zedong in Changsha, Cai Hesen described the world as caught in the throes of a world revolution, with Russia, "the place where the proletarian revolution has succeeded," as its epicenter.[130] The point of the letter was to warn Mao not to be misled by the outward attractiveness of reformist ideas and politicians, and not to involve himself once again in an initiative that would not last:

> In China now, these chameleonlike professional politicians and military men . . . are getting themselves ready to become a Lenin. I estimate that in the next three to five years, China will see the emergence of a Kerensky government. In other words, there will be a revolution like Russia's February Revolution. The man in charge will be an old warlord, a professional politician, or a capitalist donning yet a new guise. Some youths, I am sure, will get involved, but I hope that you will not. You must prepare for our October Revolution.[131]

Cai rejected self-government approaches to reform, as Chen Duxiu had. In a follow-up letter to Mao a month later, Cai took on Zhang Junmai, better known as Carsun Chang, the famous advocate of constitutionalist ideas. Cai wrote that

> Zhang Junmai views the Russian Revolution with the reactionary eyes of the bourgeoisie. . . . His proposals, in eight items, are half-baked. . . . The result of class struggle must be the dictatorship of the proletariat; otherwise we cannot reform society or protect the revolution. Class struggle is really a political struggle because politics today is bourgeois politics. The bourgeoisie is able to suppress the workers only because it employs political power, the laws, and the army. . . . We must destroy the bourgeoisie's state

structure (whether that of a constitutional monarchy or parliamentary democracy).[132]

Cai Hesen too used Marxism-Leninism to sever the last strands of his allegiance to the Republic.

Cai's letters are of special importance in the history of Chinese communism because they seem to have reached Mao at a crucial stage in the development of his thinking. Their impact is clear from the fact that Mao's December 1, 1920, letter, in which he declared his support for a Bolshevik-style revolution in China, was written in response to one of Cai's. To a follow-up letter of Cai Hesen, which outlined the organization of the Bolshevik Party and its basic strategy, Mao Zedong responded on January 20, 1921, with a short comment that said of Cai's letter that "there is not one word with which I do not agree."[133] Given the dates of Mao's responses, it seems probable that Cai's letters arrived in Changsha shortly after the Hunan self-government movement had collapsed, which led Mao to write his despondent letter to Xiang Jingyu. It was Cai's letters that led Mao to picture Hunanese politics as controlled by a selfish bourgeoisie and to announce his support for the Leninist revolutionary strategy.

The concrete political experiences of those who were to join the CCP were closely connected with their adoption of Leninist views. They viewed the political realm of their country as run over by men of mean character who selfishly abused political power. Marxism-Leninism suggested to them an explanation for this situation, as well as what they saw as the futility of their past efforts to produce change by means of such campaigns as the New Culture movement and the New Village movement or the participation in local self-government. They used it to justify not their rejection of the goals which they had sought to achieve but attempts to do so without political power, by means of education and persuasion alone.

Even though there were bleak aspects to the thinking of Chinese communists, this should not obscure that in Marxism-Leninism they found new grounds to be optimistic and to take action, something they passionately desired to do. They asserted a renewed faith in a better future for China and in the possibility of what they thought of as an honorable way of engaging in politics. It was this faith that led them to set off on a new road.

FORMING A PARTY

The locution "*junzi* do not form parties" (*junzi budang*) encoded a not entirely unambiguous elite rejection of political alliances in traditional China. In his essay *On Political Cliques*, Ouyang Xiu (1007–1072) of the Song dynasty had in fact argued that *junzi* should be permitted to form political groups. In contrast to lesser men, he argued, *junzi* would join together in "allegiance to a common tao."[134] However, as Frederic Wakeman has discussed, in 1652 the Qing prohibited the formation of elite political organizations: "Licentiates are not allowed to form parties (*dang*) of several people or to take oaths and form clubs. Nor can they influence local officials nor arbitrarily mediate local disputes. Any literary works that they write cannot be freely printed."[135] The Yongzheng emperor (1723–1735) went so far as to rebut Ouyang Xiu in a piece also entitled *On Political Cliques*.[136]

It was a memorial by Yang Yongjian that set out the arguments for the prohibition. According to Yang, Frederic Wakeman has shown, elite political alliances depended on friendship ties, teacher-student relationships, and bonds of common geographical origin.[137] In addition to cultivating contacts at court, Yang argued, these alliances were used by their members to counter Qing encroachment on their local positions. Parties, then, were seen as combines used by regional elites to advance their own interests, thus corrupting the whole purpose of political action.

In this section I describe how future CCP members came to defend their decision to form an insurrectionist political party. The organizational antecedents for the CCP were not, as might be thought, the political parties that had emerged around the 1911 Revolution but study societies, connecting the CCP to an important semilegitimate elite tradition of political protest. Western political theories endorsed political parties. Some were founded in the years before the 1911 Revolution, and afterward their numbers increased. However, Chinese communists saw these parties as "old-style" political combines used by elites to amass and exploit political power.

It might be useful to set out here, in cursory form, the principal aspects of Lenin's party concept, as I will refer to them below. In chapter 3 I give a more detailed exposition of the organizational concepts that were transmitted to China by Comintern agents as well as by Chinese communists who studied in France, like Cai Hesen. I should state that in my view it is wrong to speak of "the" Leninist party concept. Not only did party concepts change over time, but among CCP members there have always been different attitudes toward their party, and debate about the nature and purpose of the party has at times been intense. Before the ascendancy of Stalin, this was true even in the Soviet Union.

Lenin wrote *What Is to Be Done?* to wrestle with an issue that did not exist in an urgent form for Marx or Engels and that they did not discuss extensively, namely, how to build a political party with a mass following drawn from different segments of the population that was capable of mobilizing this following to capture political power. He confronted these issues in the first years of this century when his party, then still called the Social Democrats, proved unable to profit from widespread labor unrest in Russia and was paralyzed by interminable disputes. His principal opponent was Bernstein, a socialist leader in Germany who proposed that the Social Democrats should join the parliamentary process, abandoning violent revolution. In a way that was to become typical of Marxist-Leninist parties the world over and was completely alien to Chinese intellectuals, Lenin made his case in an argumentative fashion, denouncing his opponents by name and on doctrinaire grounds.[138]

To strengthen the Social Democrats, Lenin outlined a restructuring of their party that aimed at forming a "charismatic" institution. To achieve this, the Social Democrats, until then fragmented into groups of intellectuals preoccupied with theoretical debates, were to form a small and secret insurrectionary party in which all members were subject to strict discipline. "The thing we need," Lenin wrote, "is a military organization of agents all lending their attention to the same cause."[139]

A central element of Lenin's strategy was to build up among the population an image of the Social Democratic Party as a strong, dedicated, and altruistic leader. Internal discipline, the public display of unity, one clear set of policies, and members unselfishly but competently working day and night for their party and the proletariat all aimed at this. Lenin's strategy as articulated in *What Is to Be Done?* was to seize power by having a tight core of party leaders employ the charisma of the party to lead an amorphous mass of workers.[140]

According to Marxist theory, the urban proletariat is the motive force of history. Noting the lack of results of "spontaneous" labor unrest, Lenin argued that workers could not achieve a proletarian consciousness by themselves. Communist intellectuals, usually from a bourgeois background, had the task to inject a proletarian consciousness into the proletariat. An essential element in this was the creation of labor unions containing workers, regardless of their convictions and their geographical origins. The Social Democratic Party was to remain a small party but to have its members dispersed throughout workers' organizations.

In *What Is to Be Done?* Lenin did not reject argument within the Social Democratic Party, and communist parties have always exhibited a great deal of dispute. What he did oppose was deviance from dogma and the subordination of party interests and party discipline to one's own theory. Lenin abhorred open-ended debate, declaring that "freedom of criticism often means the freedom of ideas altogether,"[141] and he believed that the effort to derive one's views from Marxist theory was the only way to generate "consciousness" and that this enabled one to overcome the flaws of "spontaneity." What was wrong with spontaneity in Lenin's eyes was that it was often no more than an overestimation of the worth of one's pet theories and one's actions. For Lenin, argument about dogma was a way to cleanse the mind from the confusions and misconceptions caused by alienation.[142]

The effort to overcome these confusions and arrive at the "objectively" correct policies also served, according to Lenin, to unify the party and prevent differences of opinion from paralyzing it, as they had done in the past. If policies were to be articulated in terms of dogma and backed by party institutions, it was more difficult for individual claims of unique insight to undermine its stability.[143]

Lenin was convinced of the primacy of politics. He believed that without the seizure of political power, no reform program could be effective, an idea that appealed to Chinese communists. The way to achieve that power, according to Lenin, was to organize a small and centralized party that would establish labor unions among the urban proletariat and foster an image among it of the party as the all-knowing leader. The party itself was to function like a well-trained army in the hands of its leaders.

From Study Societies to Communist Cells

It was within the framework of study societies (*xuehui* or *xueshe*), as Arif Dirlik has noted,[144] that Chinese communists for the first time considered the implications of basing their political actions on Leninist principles. Almost all of them were deeply involved in these societies, and early CCP cells developed directly out of them. In a 1926 history of the CCP, Cai Hesen described study societies as the organizational antecedents of the CCP. "They were not," he wrote, "fully communist, . . . they lacked a national umbrella, but they were the rudiments [of our party]."[145]

Three factors contributed to the revival of study societies in the late Qing. In the 1880s U.S. and British missionaries, safe from prosecution thanks to extraterritoriality, set up the Chinese Education Society (Zhongguo Jiaoyuhui) and the Society for the Spread of Learning (Guang Xuehui) to support translation activities of religious texts and the publication of articles promoting reform on the basis of Christian principles.[146] Involving many Chinese, these organizations fitted the study-society tradition.

When Kang Youwei and Liang Qichao began their reform campaigns, they used a study society, the Self-Strengthening Study Society (Qiang Xuehui), as their vehicle. In 1895 Kang defended this act in a memorial, stating that in the Ming, study societies had hurt the powerful but helped the country. Their society enjoyed official patronage as it was formally under the leadership of a metropolitan official.[147] In the wake of Kang's memorial, Chinese reformers created a series of study societies. Some were devoted to a broad reform program, and others pursued limited objectives such as the abolishment of foot binding or opium smoking.

A second wave of study societies resulted from an edict issued in 1906 announcing plans for the establishment of local self-government institutions, as Roger Thompson has shown.[148] Reform-minded elites organized self-government study societies in their home regions. Their members included degree holders, but also leaders in commerce and industry. Usually a provincial official acted as overseer, tying the study societies to the official political system. Their activities included census taking, surveys of local customs, promotion of new industries, and the discharge of certain local government tasks. Admission requirements included financial and educational standards, as well as an oath swearing compliance to certain standards of behavior. To some Yang Yongjian's fears may well have seemed prescient.

After 1915 the New Culture movement gave rise to yet another round of study-society foundings. The recent publication of *Societies and Leagues of the May Fourth Period* has made it possible for scholars to examine New Culture study societies.[149] Vera Schwarcz used this source to examine the New Tide Society (Xinchaoshe) for its contributions to what she has termed the Chinese Enlightenment, the intellectual rejection of China's traditional culture and thought. Based at Peking University, it produced a host of cultural luminaries, including the literary scholar Yu Pingbo, the historians Feng Youlan and Gu Jiegang, and the philologist Fu Sinian.[150] John Leung discussed the study-society connections of Chinese students who traveled to France in the late 1910s and 1920s as participants in the work-study movement, using two documentary collections that deal with the movement.[151] In addition to the sources used by Schwarcz and Leung, I have used other collections of primary material, including *Sources for the New Citizen Study Society*,[152] the society in which Mao Zedong and Cai Hesen were involved.

New Culture Study Societies

Vera Schwarcz has noted that study societies depended on regional, friendship, and educational ties rather than a shared commitment to one intellectual position, as their participants have claimed.[153] At Peking University, students from one region usually resided together. When a student set up a study society to promote one aspect of the New Culture movement, he or she usually drew in his or her friends. Hence students from Shandong at Peking University dominated the New Tide Society.[154] Traditional student-teacher relations were also important. A 1920 New Citizen Study Society report explained that "one reason [for the founding of the society] was that almost all of us are students of Mr. Yang Changji."[155] Yang Changji was the teacher of ethics in Changsha who reprimanded Cai Hesen. His daughter was to be Mao Zedong's first wife.

Even if this was the reality of the study societies, the 1920 New Citizen Study Society report suggests that its members (see figure 1) seriously aspired to discard what they saw as traditional ideas and that they thought of binding together in a study society as a liberating act of rebellion against tradition. In recounting the reasons for the founding of the society in 1918, the report stated: "At that time the New Thought and the New Literature had already begun. In our eyes, the old thought, the old ethical principles, and the old literature had been eliminated in one fell swoop. We suddenly realized the falseness of a solitary life of quietude and in a complete contrast, pursued a life of action and cooperation."[156]

Symbolizing the desire to live by new values, study-society constitutions stipulated criteria of admission, provided for accountable society officers, guaranteed equal rights for all members, and laid down procedures for internal discipline.[157] They prescribed certain attitudes and rules of behavior deemed essential for a new culture. The constitution of the Young China Study Society stipulated that members were to display "determination, realism, perseverance, and simplicity" in their daily conduct.[158] Gambling, visiting prostitutes, and the entertainment of links with political parties were also proscribed.[159] While preparations for the society began in 1918, its founding meeting convened on July 1, 1919. It was the Nanjing conference in July 1921 of this society that played such a role in the development of Yun Daiying's thought.

The New Citizen Study Society constitution, translated in part below, was adopted at the founding meeting of the society held on April 17, 1918, in Cai Hesen's house on Yuelushan Mountain just outside Changsha. It indicates the ideas its members pursued and the importance with which they viewed the society:

1.   The name of this society is the New Citizen Study Society.

2.   The aim of the society is the renewal of learning, the steeling of character, and the improvement of the minds of the people and their customs.

3.   All those who are introduced by at least five members and are approved by a majority of the membership can become a member of the society.

4. All members must accept the following principles:
    a. No dishonesty;
    b. No laziness;
    c. No wastefulness;
    d. No gambling;
    e. No visiting of prostitutes.

5. All members of the society have the duty to communicate by letter at least once a year with the society, to report on themselves and the areas where they live, as well as on the fruits of their studies. This is to assist one another.

6. The society has one general manager who presides over the management of the society's affairs, and several officers who assist the general manager in a specific aspect of the society's affairs. The period of incumbency is three years, and posts are filled by general ballot. . . .

10. If a member behaves incorrectly and on purpose violates this constitution, then a resolution by a majority of the membership expels him.[160]

Defiance of tradition was not the only reason that motivated the establishment of study societies. Study-society members pictured themselves as involved not only in the propagation of new ideas but in a quest that would lead toward a new culture and produce new communal forms of social and political organization. They lacked faith, however, in the capacity of the individual operating singly to precipitate change, a topic on which Yun Daiying was most clear. This perception contrasted with the traditional view of the Confucian *junzi*, whose solitary stance was perceived as essential to his moral integrity.

This view of the fragility of the individual reflected the notion that the transformation of the self and of the world were inextricably linked and that the acquisition of the ability to live communally was essential to both. Members of the New Citizen Study Society, according to its 1920 report, had founded the society to assist each other in "remolding their own nature."[161] The report stated that the aim of the society was to foster "the progress of the lives of all individuals and all humanity" by "gathering together those with the same ambition (*tongzhi*) and establishing a new environment to cooperate."[162]

The above conceptualization of the purpose of study societies was central to the justification of endowing them with the right to lay down ethical norms and impose rules of conduct, as most of them did, including the New Citizen Study Society. The constitution of the Young China Study Society defined the expected conduct of its members more carefully than that of the New Citizen, and it included arrangements for a special office of the society, the Criticism Department, to investigate violations of the constitution:

> Item 14: If a member commits any of the following acts, the Criticism Department will issue a statement of warning and send it to the member in question to encourage him to repent speedily and change his ways:
>   1.   To gamble or visit prostitutes or engage in any other immoral activity;
>   2.   To be suspected of maintaining relations with any political party and so to harm the society's reputation; . . .
>   3.   To violate the creed of the society;
>   4.   To lack concern for society affairs;
>   5.   To be careless in recommending members.
> Item 15: If a member commits any of the following acts, he will be expelled after an investigation of the Criticism Department has verified the allegations and a vote has been taken at an extraordinary meeting:
>   1.   Violation of the society's general principle;
>   2.   Use of the name of the society for private profit;
>   3.   Joining another party or group after joining the society and so to harm the society's reputation. [163]

Work-study mutual-aid societies exemplified the basic aspects of New Culture study societies in the most extreme form. In the spring of 1920, students in various major cities set up these societies as small cooperatives where they studied, worked, and lived entirely communally. One participant explained that a work-study mutual-aid society was the way to "create a new life and a new organization for all young men now buried under the evil system of the old society."[164] A future leader of the Socialist Youth League, Shi Cuntong, stated that work-study mutual-aid societies "had resolved six issues," in which he included the family, education, cooperative production, and prejudices about the importance of manual labor and intellectual activities.[165] The constitution of one work-study mutual-aid society defined its purpose and organization as follows:

> 1.   General principle: on the basis of the spirit of mutual aid we will practice joint work and study.
> 2.   All those who are introduced by one society member and receive the approval of all can join.
> 3.   Each member must work four hours every day. . . .
> 4.   The society will provide all necessities of life, including clothing, food, and lodgings. All educational fees, medical charges, and

the costs of books will be borne by the society, with books commonly owned by the society.

. . . .

6.   All income gained from labor is property of the society.

. . . .

8.   Organization: all members together form the Society Meeting. It elects manager members, and discusses all important affairs and evaluates all new members. . . . On the last day of each month a new manager will be elected.[166]

The yearning for new arrangements for even the most fundamental aspects of life found a reflection in the attitude of Chinese communists, even if they acceded to the idea that change might not come in such an immediate or voluntary fashion as they once as study-society members had hoped. Zheng Chaolin, head of the CCP Publications Department in the late 1920s,[167] recently recalled the morning of June 18, 1922, when he and others met in an open spot in the Bois de Boulogne in Paris to form a communist cell.[168] After everybody had sat down on rented chairs, Zhou Enlai suggested that each take an oath. "Almost everybody," according to Zheng, "opposed. Why would we have wanted to adopt such a 'religious ritual'?"[169] Both religion and taking an oath of loyalty were apparently considered signs of backwardness.

New Culture study societies provide a clue why Chinese communists could come to see a political party as an organization that safeguarded rather than undermined their integrity. They believed that combining into a group of like-minded people was absolutely essential to withstand the corrupting pressures of society. They had little faith that they could maintain their integrity alone and believed that cooperative action would not only result from reform but was essential to achieving it. While for Yang Yongjian membership in an elite association was a sign of corruptness, for New Culture study-society members it was the opposite.

New Culture study societies were something of a preparatory ground for early Chinese communists. Whatever the reality, as study-society members they were introduced to the idea of making decisions in committees, developing action plans, abiding by a constitution, and subordinating their moral conscience to a criticism department. While the step from study society to CCP cell was large, it was not as large as it would have been had Chinese communists not been part of study societies.

Study Society Debates About Leninism

While the New Culture movement had led to the establishment of a great many study societies, by 1920 skepticism about their suitability as vehicles for reform had become widespread. As mentioned, Li Dazhao found himself forced to agree with ridicule of study societies as producing little more than paper constitutions. The late-1920 report of the New Citizen Study Society stated that academically the society had remained shallow, that many members remained "immature in their thinking and actions," and that internal relations were often weak, thereby leaving one of the central purposes of the societies unfulfilled.[170] Many of their members had been involved in reform activities, but few had produced any results. At the same time, the May Fourth movement had heightened the sense of political responsibility and mission.

A debate in the spring of 1920 in the pages of the *New Youth* about the work-study mutual-aid societies for the first time raised the issue of whether study societies could lead to significant change and saw Chinese intellectuals adopt Marxist-Leninist arguments in the discussion of the issue. The work-study mutual-aid societies that had been established all had collapsed within a few months, leading New Culture luminaries—including Hu Shi, Li Dazhao, and Chen Duxiu, who had supported their founding—to comment about the reasons for this. Hu Shi, the advocate of pragmatism and a student of John Dewey at Columbia University, stated that work-study societies were uneconomical and that the internal tensions and organizational work they created interfered with the academic work of the students.[171] At this time still adhering to his New Culture ideas, Chen asserted that "the lack of a strong will, the habit of work, and productive skills" accounted for the collapse of the societies.[172] Dai Jitao and others, however, made the argument that the societies were bound to fail because "in a social organization" predicated on "capitalist productive methods," "the attempt to engage in production and at the same time to attain academic goals cannot succeed."[173] Dai was a KMT member who for some time participated in the discussions of early communists in Shanghai. His thinking was influenced especially by Marxist economic views, but he rejected Leninist political propositions.[174]

This section covers the debates in study societies about Marxism-Leninism. The next chapter discusses the formation of communist cells. It should be mentioned that it was also by 1920 that disagreements began to deepen among those who had supported the New Culture movement. The discussions, as we shall see, focused on the usefulness of ideology. In August 1919 Hu Shi fanned the flames of the discussions when he published an article that argued that Chinese should tackle problems in a pragmatic fashion, one by one, on the basis of a scientific spirit, and rejected any attempt to find a total solution on the basis of an ideology.[175]

New Citizen Members Vote for "Radical Communism" In the case of the New Citizen Study Society, a majority of the membership at a meeting held January 1–3, 1921, agreed with the idea that the society's strategy was wrong, and a vote resulted in the declaration that the society would adopt a Marxist-Leninist strategy. According to minutes of the meeting, Mao Zedong, having declared himself in favor of the Bolshevik Revolution in letters to Cai Hesen, seized the initiative when the floor was opened for discussion. According to Mao, the following were the major strategies by which one could pursue change: "1. a social policy; 2. social democracy; 3. radical communism (Leninism); 4. moderate communism (Russellism); 5. anarchism."[176] Mao explained his choice for the third:

> A social policy is a stopgap measure and does not add up to a method. Social democracy uses parliament as a mechanism for change, but in fact the laws enacted by parliament always protect the bourgeoisie. Anarchism denies political power; I am afraid that it is completely unrealistic. Moderate communism, like Russell's propaganda of extreme freedom, will give free rein to capitalists and hence is also unrealistic. Extreme communism, that is, the so-called worker-peasant-ism (*laonongzhuyi*), uses the method of class dictatorship; it can be expected to deliver results. Hence we should adopt it.[177]

In the discussion that followed, most society members expressed their agreement with Mao's views. While different arguments were presented, those who agreed with the idea of basing the study society on Marxism-Leninism usually listed the ineffectualness of education. A woman member, Tao Yi, said: "In the past, I too had this fantasy of effecting change through education. However, in China's present economic situation, we absolutely cannot accomplish anything with education."[178] Another member focused on Bolshevik success in Russia: "I approve of implementing the Russian method. The reason is that of all the methods with which people in the world now propose to achieve reform, only the one adopted in Russia has survived the test of reality. Others, such as anarchism, unionism, syndicalism, and so on, all have not been realized on any scale."[179]

The idea that the Bolshevik Revolution had shown the practicality of Marxism-Leninism, while study societies had achieved little, was an important reason for some to support Marxism-Leninism. Yi Lirong echoed Yun Daiying's statements about the need of unselfish revolutionaries: "Society must be transformed, and that can only be achieved by revolution. After the revolution, we of course must have a dictatorship of leaders.

Of course, this dictatorship will not be as it is commonly thought of; it must be one with a goal."[180]

Opposition came from those who remained committed to education. As one New Citizen Study Society member stated, "I have serious doubts about using the method of the Russian Soviet government. I believe that Russell's moderate methods are best. We must start with education and transform the individual. Once most people have gained a new understanding, we can then achieve the transformation of the whole."[181] Another made the case as follows: "I have doubts about bolshevism [*guoji-zhuyi*]: It restricts freedom, which goes against human nature. It is better to use education for gradual progress and gradual reform."[182]

After the discussion had gone on for some time, "the chairman submitted the issue to a vote," according to a society report probably written shortly afterward, with the result that "twelve supported Bolshevism. . . . Two favored democracy, . . . and one favored moderate communism."[183] The society had voted itself an organization committed to Marxism-Leninism.

The New Year's Conference of New Citizen Study Society members convened in the aftermath of a meeting of the members in France. Many Changsha students had used the society to travel to France for study. They were part of a contingent of two thousand students who went to France during and after the First World War. Cai Hesen had played an important role in establishing a link between the New Citizen Study Society and the organizers of the program in Peking.[184] In France, students belonging to the society studied in various places. After having been dispersed, they decided to meet from July 6 to July 10, 1920, in Montargis, a city south of Paris.

At this meeting, Cai Hesen collided with Xiao Zisheng. Xiao had been the first society member (see figure 2) to arrive in France and had developed a strong affinity with the views of the organizers of the program.[185] These included Cai Yuanpei and Li Shizeng, both of whom professed a Kropotkinist ideology, arguing that China's progress depended on cultural change to be achieved by education and training in a new communal lifestyle. The students who participated in the program, like those who joined work-study societies, were required to live cooperatively and combine manual and intellectual labor.[186] Once students arrived in France, however, they found that France's economic crisis made it impossible to find work, and unrest broke out among them when they discovered that neither the Chinese legation in Paris nor the program organizers could support them. In short, the program had collapsed quickly.[187]

During the Montargis conference, Cai Hesen attacked the work-study philosophy; Xiao Zisheng defended it. The issue that divided them, as it would the Changsha members, was the possibility of achieving reform through education, without the employment of force. Following the meeting, Xiao Zisheng sent a long letter to Changsha, explaining the rift within the society and expounding his own views. He attacked Cai Hesen as follows:

> Cai Hesen advocated the formation of a communist party to establish the dictatorship of the proletariat. Its doctrine and method are to be like the one of Russia today. I argued that because progress of the world is a never-ending process and because revolution is also an endless enterprise, we should not agree to the sacrifice of a minority for the welfare of the majority. I proposed moderate revolution—a revolution by means of education, one that serves the welfare of all—with labor unions and cooperatives as its methods of implementation. I truly do not believe that a Russian-style—a Marxist—revolution is right, but tend toward anarchism—without force—a Kropotkinist-style revolution. This is more peaceful and perhaps slow; but even though slow, it is peaceful.[188]

Cai Hesen was not influenced only by the fate of the work-study movement. In June 1920 he wrote a long article on workers' strikes organized by French syndicalists in the spring of that year. The strikes had led to massive work stoppages and had paralyzed the country. However, the French government had succeeded in defeating the strikes by mobilizing the legal system and the army, and syndicalists had shown themselves unable to mount effective measures against the government's tactics. In the article, Cai Hesen mentioned that a number of socialist groupings in France had decided to join the Communist International in Moscow. Cai's support for Leninism, the article suggested, was at least in part the result of his study of political development in Western Europe. He also discussed recent revolutionary failures in Germany.[189]

Debate on Ideology in the Young China Society   In May 1919 Wang Guangqi began preparations for the founding conference of the Young China Study Society, which at that point had already operated informally for some time. From the beginning, the society proved a battleground for the different forces involved in the New Culture movement. The society was the largest one, with some 120 members drawn from various regional centers that had important institutions of higher learning. Its founding was an attempt to bring the main figures of the New Culture movement together in one organization and generate a cohesive movement.

During a January 1919 meeting of society members in Shanghai, Wang tried to formulate a broad platform for the society to forestall its fragmentation. He noted that "among our society members, there are estatists [*guojiapai*] as well as cosmopolitanists, and there are also anarchists. They cannot agree, and should not be forced to do so."[190] Wang then outlined four points that, he argued, were shared by all members. They included the commitment to combine learning and practice, to focus study on concrete reality, to develop social activities, and to fight the "fin-de-siècle atmosphere."[191] Wang argued that in comparison, "so-called isms are entirely secondary" and that at least for the near future, the society should stress academic pursuits.[192]

While some agreed,[193] members studying in France produced a letter that took issue with Wang's views on a number of points. It argued that ideologies derived from learning and like science could be used in the "elimination of darkness."[194] They expressed doubts about Wang's suggestion that in the future a "complete and wise ideology" would present itself as learning progressed. However, their most important complaint was that acceptance of Wang's ideas did nothing to help them in bringing about political change; it would reduce them to mere inaction, they argued.[195]

The Nanjing Conference of the Young China Study Society, which lasted from July 1 to July 3, 1921, saw members debating this issue. This meeting was perhaps at least as important as the First Congress of the Chinese Communist Party, which opened only weeks later in Shanghai. The meeting was a milestone, for instance, in the development of Yun Daiying's thought. Besides Yun Daiying, many other early CCP members were involved, including Deng Zhongxia, one of the architects of the CCP's early labor movement, and Liu Renjing, who was present at the CCP's First Congress, and several others.[196] After the meeting, the society's journal published minutes of the discussions as well as a number of articles about ideology, thus further enhancing its impact.[197]

Deng Zhongxia, these minutes suggest, was the most vociferous defender of Marxism-Leninism as the society's ideology. He did not plead for its immediate adoption but argued that it was a requirement for effective social action: "The reason that the society's social activities in the past bore little fruit is that we lacked a common ideology." He denied that an ideology would produce a schism. It provided a standard by which to judge the actions of members, according to Deng, and therefore increased the society's cohesion. Ideology, he stated, made it possible to "divide labor and help each other."[198] After the discussions had gone on for some time, he stated his case unambiguously:

If we can determine an ideology, our attitudes about whether we belong to the third or the fourth class [the bourgeoisie or the proletariat] and whether we advocate private property or joint property will be concretely expressed. Only then can all our activities be brought into harmony. Education will then no longer be just the nurturing ground of inhumanity; literature will no longer be only the plaything of the rich; and enterprises will not just nurture the new capitalists.[199]

Like the communists discussed earlier, Deng saw ideology as fundamental to the development of political action and an essential instrument in the attack on the old economic and political order. Gao Junyu phrased this idea succinctly when he stated that "my opinion is that an ideology is not a religion. It is a method with which we can transform all kinds of areas."[200]

The minutes of the Nanjing meeting suggest that fears of compromising one's integrity by participating in politics were deeply rooted. Deng Zhong-xia argued that "we must enter the political world in order to create a new politics, and therefore we must accept the leadership of officers (*ganbu*)."[201] Deng, then, thought that members could safely enter the treacherous realm of political action as long as they were part of an organization based on ideology, with officers holding members to that ideology.[202]

Some of those who participated in the conference objected to Deng's proposals on the ground that an ideology was imperfect as a worldview and would be restrictive intellectually. Those at the meeting in favor of the adoption of an ideology denied this. Liu Renjing stated that "an ideology of course is not set for all time."[203] He made the case that ideology was to action what theory was to learning. One would base one's actions on it but change it as one learned from practice.[204] The instrumentalist attitude toward ideology fostered such a view.

As in the case of the New Citizen Study Society, eventually the decision whether to adopt an ideology was reached on the basis of a vote. Seventeen were in favor; six were against.[205] An interesting aspect of the Nanjing Conference is that its members were less concerned with which ideology they would adopt than with the fact of adopting an ideology. It was decided to thrash out the first issue by holding further meetings and debating it in the pages of *Youth*, the society's journal. The meeting, then, did not lead to the transformation of the society into a communist organization.

In October 1921 Wang Guangqi wrote an article about the issue. "Those who believed in reform based on politics," he stated, "hold two basic ideas: one is that if one wants to change society, one must travel the road of political power, and the second is the almightiness of bureaucracy."[206] He then wondered what would happen if a study society adopted an ideology and became a political party but was unable to seize power. "If one succeeds in taking power," he went on, "what measures will be necessary to stay in power?"[207] "If one succeeds in maintaining power, what will it take to enforce one's reform policies in a country as large as China and with a backward population?"[208]

The society's members never did reach an agreement about what ideology to install as the society's orthodoxy. The society continued to exist after 1921, with the participation of a number of CCP members. Ideological conflict became increasingly sharp, with some of the most important anti-communists coming from the society's ranks. After 1925, the society ceased to exist for all intents and purposes.[209]

Chinese communists stood Ouyang Xiu upon his head. They asserted that it was not just that their own integrity justified the formation of a party but that only such a party could safeguard their integrity. It was the commitment to an ideology that made it possible to avoid becoming like "old" political parties and to organize cooperative action against the evil forces to which politics had fallen prey.

The complex discussions of communists about political action and organization make clear that even if they were inspired by the idea of a world revolution and were convinced that a new world was to emerge in their time, they were not simply swept from their feet by the October Revolution. In their ruminations they showed hesitations and doubt, as well as the enduring influence of past political norms. Rather than simply setting out to replace one regime by a new one, or installing a political system that they knew beforehand, they continued to think of themselves as involved in a quest in which the shape of the future would reveal itself as they moved forward and in which they would be transformed.

Study societies may well have formed one of the origins of the "work unit," the *danwei*, of contemporary China. Based on socioeconomic or geographic ties rather than kinship, the *danwei* is a basic unit in Chinese society today that is responsible for distributing many commodities and housing and whose members must meet regularly to discuss matters of ideology and politics. Even though work units have come to function as an extension of the state and are often riddled with conflict, in conception they are the basic unit of society, trusted by each member.

The State and the Masses

The assumption of a political role requires decisions about many basic issues, not just about the permissibility of participation in a political party.

Others include a definition of the true source of political power and the justiciability of the use of violence. Problems of self-definition, the significance of the individual, and the malleability of society are also involved. In the discussion so far, many of these topics have been touched upon in passing. While this is not the place for an exhaustive treatment of all issues, which would take us deep into political theory, I present below in brief form the thinking of those who were to join the CCP about the use of the instruments of the state and the population as the fundamental source of power. The purpose of this is to spell out further their political attitudes.

The Use of Force   Just prior to the 1911 Revolution, the reformist newspaper the *Times* (Shibao) of Shanghai had written, "If the affairs of the empire are managed only by officials, there is no way that they will succeed. If citizens capable of constitutional government manage the public affairs of their areas, how can one fear that they will not succeed?"[210] For Chinese communists, as Chen Duxiu's thought has suggested, the repudiation of the Republic entailed a rejection of the drift toward local autonomy. They called again for a strong state, with Marxism-Leninism suggesting to them the necessity of backing up the transformation of society with state power. "Not to look at how and why governmental power is used," Chen Duxiu argued in "Talking about Politics," "but to close your eyes and oppose all power is just like refusing to eat for fear of choking."[211]

Mao Zedong believed that. He argued that without state power, the propagation of new values "would be, as Zhu Xi termed it, 'learning of no more use than support given to a drunken man: he swings to the right and left, and still falls.' "[212] Moral drive, Mao argued, required the support of a strong political system to flourish and to be brought into play, an idea that is not at all in contradiction to certain strains in the Confucian tradition.

Mao also endorsed the aggressive use of political power. "To want a capitalist to become a communist is impossible," he asserted; "human life is highly habitual, and this constitutes a psychological force, working in the same way as the gravitational force in physics that forces something on an incline to go down."[213] In a December 1, 1920, letter to Cai Hesen and other New Citizen members in France, Mao described how the political realm was occupied and exploited by the bourgeoisie. Showing himself in agreement with the core of Leninism,[214] perhaps without being entirely conscious of this, he concluded that the first step in the revolution was to be the seizure of state power and its aggressive deployment against what he called the bourgeoisie: "I believe that a Russian-style revolution forms a strategy that can reach where no other road has reached before and that we will have to use. It is not that I would abandon it in favor of a better method; we simply must have this Reign of Terror."[215]

Even if Mao was more blunt than others, none of them disagreed. Chen Duxiu argued in "Talking about Politics" that only violence could wipe away the ingrained habits and attitudes of the past.[216] So did Li Dazhao, depicting the violence of his time as a cleansing process from which a new world would emerge.[217] The statements of Deng Zhongxia and Yun Daiying discussed previously also implied approval of the ruthless exploitation of state violence.

Population and History   It is not difficult to demonstrate that Chinese communists viewed the population as uneducated and politically apathetic. Mao Zedong's despairing comments about the Hunanese population are a case in point. Yun Daiying pictured the population as lazy, spurred to action only under extreme conditions.[218] Revolutions, he wrote, were "violent outbursts of mass emotions," adding somberly that "it is safe to say that reason rarely controls the outbreak of revolution."[219] With the Taiping and Boxer rebellions in the not too distant past, such a remark displayed a deeply embedded suspicion of popular upheaval.

At the same time, Yun Daiying also wrote in his letter to the Young China Study Society to explain his support for Marxism-Leninism that "nothing in the world can oppose the force of the masses once they are united."[220] In 1914 Li Dazhao argued that "the people's will creates history."[221] The common vision of hierarchical associations too was premised on the idea that involving the masses in politics was the way to create a vigorous society.

Nationalist notions of the source of political power had already become widespread in the late nineteenth century, and in this respect the republicanism of the New Culture movement brought nothing new. However, a great difficulty existed in reconciling the common elite perception of China's population as usually apathetic but given to moments of irrational and usually destructive outbursts with the idea that the population was the central force in history. Yun Daiying argued that the October Revolution had succeeded because a group of revolutionaries had been able to exploit an emotional outburst of the masses. In October 1920 Yun wrote that "revolutionaries with minds that are as sharp and cool as they are enthusiastic and ready for sacrifice" were essential to direct the rare "outbursts of mass emotions."[222] These masses, he stated in his letter of explanation to Young China members, naturally tended toward coordinated revolutionary action, as they were motivated by economic exploitation and their shared situation made them sympathetic to one another.[223]

Chinese communists could find in the concept of the revolutionary a way of reconciling the idea that history is propelled by the population and what they saw as that population's backwardness. While by themselves masses would achieve little, Yun argued, revolutionaries could direct them: "The masses are a force, which we employ. While the masses might be enthusiastic, we must be calm. The masses are simple, but we must be subtle and comprehensive. We must use the masses to the extent of our abilities. . . . We must compel the masses to accept our leadership."[224] Communists surrounded the concept of the revolutionary with a grand mystique, as Lenin had done. Cai Hesen's portrayal of the revolutionary whose commitment was so large that he was willing to toil without recognition and to enter "hell" was one aspect of this. The whole development of parties, with their special terminology and rituals, was another. The complex deliberations of communists about political action suggest that the psychology of a revolutionary is no simpler than that of any other political actor.

By the late 1910s, the attachment of many Chinese intellectuals to the Republic had been stretched to a breaking point. Before they began to set up communist organizations, communists had been involved in politics at the central as well as the local level. They had sought to stem the decline of the Republic, either by participating in its institutions directly or by mounting campaigns to promote what they saw as norms and practices essential to the Republic's proper functioning, again as defined in their terms. This chapter has suggested that what pulled them toward Marxism-Leninism was its suggestive depiction of an evil elite dominating and abusing political power, blocking the natural flow of history and the emergence of a new world. It also suggested concrete ways to confront the corruption of the political order, which, in the eyes of Chinese communists, had shown itself to be practical in Russia and which they believed would be more effective than any known alternative.

In severing their ties with the Republic, communists used Marxism-Leninism to define new norms and principles to structure their political activities. However, they were not dismissive of all traditional values, somehow swept from their feet by the message of the October Revolution. The image of the moral man remonstrating in vain with evil rulers found an echo in the deliberations on their attitude toward the Republic. Study societies connected communists with a long tradition of elite protest in China. The revolutionary organizations and movements of the last two decades of the Qing were also part of the background to the deliberations of communists about political action.

Chinese communists were not ignorant of events outside of China, and most asserted a sense of being participants in world events. Li Dazhao wrote at length about the October Revolution. Political events in France formed part of the background against which Cai Hesen, and probably other Chinese communists in Europe, considered strategies for change in China. However, all shared a rage against the debasement of political life in the Republic.

In rejecting republicanism and declaring that they would base their actions on Marxism-Leninism, Chinese communists seem to have experienced a sense of liberation. It also led them to reassert their belief that a new world was about to be born, and they were convinced that they were to play a leading role in its delivery. Yet they had only vague ideas of the shape of the future. Communists had no deep or consistent understanding of the Leninist party, Marxism-Leninism, or a revolutionary strategy. The idea that Chinese communists founded the CCP after a long period of study of Marxism and Leninism and fully cognizant of all its implications is false. They built the CCP, and gave it meaning, as they went along.

The discussions in study societies do not suggest that Chinese communists were concerned with the emergence of an industrial proletariat, as Dirlik and Chinese historians have maintained. The interest they developed in a workers' movement was a result and not a cause of their interest in Marxism-Leninism.

2/The Founding of Communist Cells and the First Congress

Most scholarship on the Chinese Communist Party has portrayed its organizational establishment as the result of the efforts of a few individuals who, inspired by the October Revolution and assisted by representatives of the Communist International, built a Leninist party in China. It has argued that Chen Duxiu and Li Dazhao were the CCP's undisputed leaders; that CCP members were committed to Leninist values and forms of organization from the beginning, attaching an importance to their party that transcended all else; and that Shanghai was the center of organized communism in China. Histories of the CCP produced in the People's Republic of China portrayed its founding in this light; historians elsewhere have adopted essentially the same view. [1]

The purpose of this chapter is to suggest a different understanding of the CCP's early organizational history in which the following points are central. First, there was no core group of leaders, and there was no central leadership organization. The CCP emerged out of a number of autonomous communist organizations, which had come about both inside and outside of China and were closely linked to study societies. Not all of these became part of the CCP, and some resisted incorporation into the CCP actively. Those that did not, retained and continued to guard their independence even after the First Congress. While the idea of a unified party under one leadership existed, when Chen Duxiu sought to assert his authority as CCP leader, he aroused passionate opposition. Cell members did not easily accept the idea that somebody they considered an outsider should exercise authority over them. The integration of the CCP's cells into one unit and the development of shared institutions, as the rest of this book will show, was a highly complex process.

Second, CCP members were not instant Bolsheviks. Study-society ties, friendships, regional bonds, and so forth were not immediately supplanted by a shared commitment to "the Party" and a joint communist ethic. This chapter will emphasize the differences between the CCP's early regional units and will suggest that the vitality of each depended to a large extent on their embeddedness in local society—by which I mean their attachment to existing local social structures, whether elite or not—rather than on the degree to which they had adopted Leninist principles of organization. The CCP's formal leadership, which the First Congress entitled a secretariat, seated in Shanghai, was a facilitating agency rather than a leadership body like the Politburo of later days.

Third, even though a number of those involved in the early CCP, like Mao Zedong and Cai Hesen, were familiar with some of the basics of a Leninist Party, among early CCP members there was no agreement about how the CCP was to be organized, what policies it should follow, what its basic values and norms were to be, or how authority was to be distributed. Chinese communists did not begin their lives as CCP members with a strong personal commitment to the CCP. This developed only over time, the August 7 emergency conference forming a milestone in the process. Similarly, they created procedures and developed shared values and norms only over time as they tried to come to terms with the problems facing them, dealt with the conflicts about these matters among themselves, and studied Marxist and Leninist writings.

Finally, while agents of the Communist International—or Comintern, as the joint organization in Moscow of various communist parties subscribing to Marxism-Leninism is usually known—did play a major role in the history of the CCP, this chapter argues that a number of early communist organizations emerged independently of Comintern efforts and that a number of these possessed greater vitality than those in which Comintern agents were influential. The next chapter will suggest that CCP members were not simply the obedient executors of Comintern policy or its agents. Comintern efforts to expand the forces of communism into East Asia were not a sine qua non for the founding of the CCP.

CCP CELLS

This view of the founding of the CCP is radically different from that presented by Arif Dirlik in *The Origins of Chinese Communism*. Like most previous authors, Dirlik has argued that the formation of cells meant the assumption by Chinese communists of a full Bolshevik "radical identity." He did not mean that they understood or accepted all aspects of Marxist doctrine but that they embraced the basic principles of Leninist organization, especially the idea that they had to form a "tightly organized

Communist party with a tightly defined organizational ideology."[2] This, according to Dirlik, included the acceptance of a strong central authority; the adoption of ideological standpoints and political programs as determined by the party leadership; the subordination of all other attachments, including those created by kinship, study society, and friendship, to the party; the subordination of all personal desires and private interests to the party; a commitment to political action and class struggle; and an identification with China's proletariat.[3]

Dirlik is entirely correct in arguing that the acceptance of Marxist views does not automatically result in membership in a communist party and that therefore we must examine not just what Chinese communists saw in Marxism but also why some chose to set up a party organization.[4] Restricting myself to Dirlik's views about the founding of the Chinese Communist Party, I believe that his conceptualization of what a communist party is and how the CCP emerged is wrong. He understands the CCP as possessing a number of immutable qualities invulnerable to the impact of history or manipulation by its members. He also argues that such a party had come about in 1921 and that the founding of the CCP consisted essentially of the process of CCP members' committing themselves to it. This book argues that it is certainly incorrect to speak of the CCP as a Leninist party before 1927, that the motivation of Chinese communists was more complex than Dirlik believes, and that the CCP changed as its members altered their expectations of it and their attitudes toward it.

In accepting the notion that Leninists have an all-transcending loyalty to their party and that obedience to central leadership is complete, Dirlik accepts an important element not only of the model image of the relationship between the member and the institution as depicted in communist propaganda but also of the totalitarian understanding of communist parties. In truth, few communists live up to the Bolshevik ideals that Dirlik identifies as characteristic of them. Not all sacrifice their private interests, ignore kinship ties, or subordinate themselves completely to the party. In practice, communist parties do not impose such high standards of commitment on all their members. One of the reasons for the CCP's ultimate victory—and the Bolshevik Party's in Russia—was its ability to incorporate large numbers of people with strong outside commitments. After 1925, as chapter 4 will suggest, CCP members abandoned the elite conception of party membership. The ultimate goal remained to make all members conform to Leninist ideals, but the idea was let go that only those who already conformed to these ideals should be allowed to join the CCP.

Even higher-level CCP members were not perfect Bolsheviks. Of course, many no doubt felt a genuine compulsion to adhere to a norm such as conformity to party discipline. However, such norms do not preclude differences of opinion, and clearly there has been much internal struggle within the CCP in which less than perfect communist motivations played a role. Furthermore, we should not forget that norms such as party discipline or a display of doctrinal orthodoxy are political assets or resources that can be mobilized in internal party disputes.

As he acknowledged, Dirlik's account depended entirely on memoirs.[5] Drawn mostly from a recently published collection of source materials entitled *At the Time of the First Congress*,[6] these are problematic not only for the usual reasons that memoirs are often difficult to use as historical sources. While a number were written after 1978 and appear to have been the result of historians asking people who participated in a cell to write down their recollections or to narrate them orally, others were written in the 1950s and 1960s in circumstances that are not clear and may well have been part of one political campaign or another. For the survivors, they also provided the opportunity to settle scores or to assert their own communist qualifications, an opportunity that Li Da, for instance, seems to have seized with both hands.[7] It would be dogmatic to argue that memoirs are entirely useless. Certainly those published in China provide illustrative detail and give insights into personal relations that primary documents often do not. In the discussion below of the founding of the CCP, I have used them for these purposes but only when I knew something about the author and was able to place him in context.

A number of new document collections do provide primary documents, and I have relied essentially on these. The important one is *Archival Sources for the First Congress of the Chinese Communist Party: Revised and Enlarged Edition*, edited under auspices of the CCP Central Committee Archives and printed in 1984.[8] For our purposes, the most significant element of the collection is the reports of regional communist organizations at the First Congress, which convened on July 23, 1921, in Shanghai, and to the Comintern. The editorial introduction states that most documents in the collection are Chinese translations of Russian originals held in the Comintern Archives. Since the CCP did not maintain archives at this point, these documents form the most solid base upon which to study the activities of Chinese communists up to and including the First Congress. Other important primary document collections are *Sources for the New Citizen Study Society, Societies and Leagues of the May Fourth Period*, and *Source Materials for the Work-Study Movement in France*.[9]

Chinese historians refer to communist organizations in China before the First Congress of 1921 as cells (*xiaozu*). This is a misnomer, as the word implies tight organization and a connection to a central leadership institution. To comply with common usage, I nonetheless use the word *cell* in this chapter to refer to any communist organization before the First Congress. In 1920 and 1921, Chinese communists referred to their local organizations by a variety of names, including "communist cell" (*gongchanzhuyi xiaozu*), "small group" (*xiao zuzhi*), "communist organization" (*gongchanzhuyi zuzhi*), or simply "communist party" (*gongchandang*).[10]

Shanghai

The idea that the Shanghai cell functioned as a Politburo *avant la lettre* in Chinese communism before the First Congress is an idea that stands up to scrutiny only to a very limited degree. The sources make clear that the Shanghai communist cell nearly ceased all activity once its coagulant, Chen Duxiu, departed for Canton in 1920 to join the regime of the "socialist" warlord Chen Jiongming as head of his Education Bureau. Following Chen's departure, the cell became dominated by communists who envisaged a party that was decentralized and involved only in propaganda activities.

In the early decades of the twentieth century, the French and International Concessions of Shanghai provided a safe haven for Chinese intellectuals who had run into trouble with the authorities. The city was a gathering point for students leaving for or returning from study abroad. A host of publishing houses could be found in Shanghai making money out of producing translations of Western books and publishing progressive and conservative periodicals. At some point in the spring of 1920—the exact date is impossible to determine—intellectuals in the city began to meet to discuss Marxist theory. The names mentioned in the memoir literature include Dai Jitao, Shi Cuntong, Zhang Dongsun, Chen Wangdao, Shen Xuanlong, Li Hanjun, Li Da, Yu Xiusong, and Shao Lizi.[11] These men were intellectuals, interested in Marxism as a theory. With the exception of Shi Cuntong, none remained with the CCP once it imposed demands on members as a political organization, and even Shi withdrew in 1927.

Nonetheless, it was in these circles that the Shanghai cell emerged. Chen Duxiu played a leading role in this process. A 1921 CCP report to the Comintern wrote: "At first the organization in Shanghai had only five people. Its leader was the well-known editor in chief of the *New Youth*, Chen Duxiu."[12] Recollections confirm Chen's eminence in the earliest history of the CCP.[13] Chen Duxiu injected himself into the world of Shanghai intellectuals after his release from a jail in Peking on September 16, 1919. After the May Fourth demonstrations, Peking authorities had imprisoned Chen for fear that he might incite further student protests.[14]

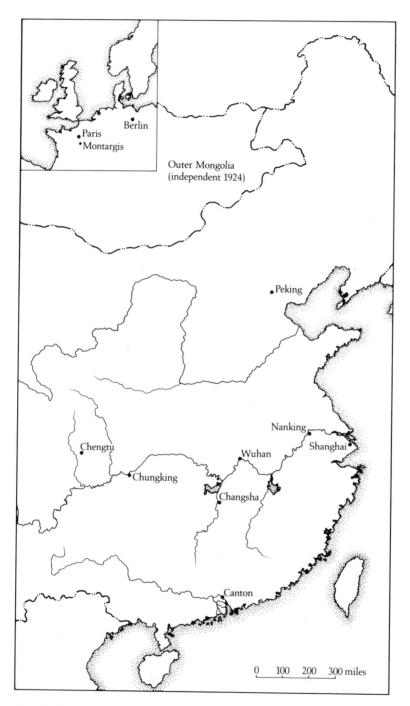

Map 1. Birthplaces of the CCP.

Upon his arrival in Shanghai, Chen Duxiu did not immediately undertake the formation of a communist organization. In Shanghai he initially reconstituted the editorial group of the *New Youth* into the New Youth Society and continued to cooperate even with the liberal Hu Shi.[15] As discussed in chapter 1, at this point he still expressed non-Marxist arguments in the debate about the failure of work-study societies. However, in his memoirs, Zhang Guotao, a man who played a leading role in the formation of the Peking cell and challenged Mao Zedong in the 1930s for CCP leadership, claimed that in July 1920 he had found Chen busily organizing a communist cell in Shanghai.[16] And on September 1, 1920, he published "Talking about Politics," in which, as we have seen, he announced his support for a Leninist seizure of power in China.

It seems likely that Gregory Voitinsky, an emissary of the Comintern, played a considerable role perhaps not in Chen Duxiu's abandonment of republicanism but in his decision to take the initiative in the construction of a Leninist party in China. Voitinsky was the head of a delegation dispatched by the Comintern in the wake of the May Fourth movement and arrived in Shanghai in April or May 1920. Hatano Ken'ichi suggests that Voitinsky's threefold brief consisted of investigating the possibilities of setting up a communist party, beginning a labor movement, and recruiting Chinese youths for study in Moscow.[17] Voitinsky traveled with two Russian aides and a translator, Yang Mingzhai. Setting out from Vladivostok, the delegation arrived in April in Peking, where Voitinsky established contact with Li Dazhao with the help of two Russian teachers at Peking University. Li pointed Voitinsky in the direction of Chen Duxiu.[18]

By November 1920, Chen Duxiu and Voitinsky were well on the way toward establishing a communist organization in Shanghai, their activities reflecting Voitinsky's brief, if that indeed existed. In November, "The Manifesto of the Chinese Communist Party" saw the light of day.[19] It outlined some of the most fundamental concepts and aims of Marxism-Leninism, including the dictatorship of the proletariat and class struggle. It also discussed the significance of the October Revolution as an event that would affect the struggle against bourgeois hegemony throughout the world. The text appears to have been intended as a declaration of principles on which to base a communist party in China.

In the same month the first issue of the *Communist Party Monthly* rolled from the mimeograph. This and the five issues that followed introduced Leninist ideas, critiqued anarchism, and explained how one organizes a labor union. It also contained articles on the history of various communist parties, especially the Bolshevik Party, and on the international labor movement. According to some memoirs, cell members also published *The Salesclerk* (Huoyou) and an illustrated magazine for work-ers.[20] Like the *Communist Party Monthly*, this periodical did not last long.[21]

Despite some assertions to the contrary, the *New Youth* was not a CCP organ at this point.[22] While the magazine contained articles on commu-nism, these were theoretical discussions, and the journal continued to publish numerous contributions by non-communist authors, including Hu Shi and Cai Yuanpei.[23] A note by Maring, a Dutch Comintern agent who arrived in China in 1921, suggests that Chen Duxiu wanted to make the *New Youth* a CCP journal, but that it was not within his powers to do so. "T. S. Chen wants to make the organ property of the party," Maring wrote with reference to the *New Youth*, "but at this moment property right not clear [sic]."[24]

A further activity that communists in Shanghai undertook was the operation of the Foreign Languages School. Voitinsky's wife and Yang Mingzhai, a Russian-born Chinese,[25] jointly operated this school to pre-pare students, of whom Liu Shaoqi was one, to go to Moscow for study.[26] Contemporary newspaper accounts state that Chen Duxiu assisted Shang-hai labor organizations in preparing for a "world labor commemoration day" on April 18, 1920. This did not mean that Chen had set up a CCP labor union. In Shanghai a host of institutions, including the YMCA, ran labor organizations, and Chen may well have spoken at the invitation of one of these.

It was at this point, when the Shanghai cell seemed ready to take off, that Chen Duxiu received Chen Jiongming's invitation, and he left the city in December, accompanied by Voitinsky.[27] No document reveals con-clusively why the two abandoned Shanghai, but if their expectation was that they could use Chen's position of power in Chen Jiongming's regime in Guangdong, they were to be disappointed, as we shall see.

In a July 1922 report to the Comintern, Maring described the circum-stances in which he had found the Shanghai cell upon his arrival in the city on June 4, 1921. All activities outside the cell had ceased, he wrote, and even attempts to recruit new members among the city's intellectual circles had stopped:

> The great excitement among the intellectuals that followed the
> Versailles peace treaty has disappeared entirely. The leaders of the
> student movement were given the opportunity by the Chinese
> government to continue their study abroad. . . . The old forms of
> labor organization that exist in Chinese society, guilds and secret
> societies such as the gangs in Shanghai. . . are more of a hindrance
> than a help. While Comrade Voitinsky was working in Shanghai, a

group of Chinese communists was formed under the leadership of
Comrade Chen Duxiu. . . . When Comrade Voitinsky left, the group
found itself without financial means and had to stop its activities.[28]

The decline of the Shanghai cell had several causes. As Maring indicated, underworld organizations like the Green Gang, ubiquitous in the
Shanghai society of the 1920s, made it very difficult for the CCP to develop
activities in the city. The departure of Chen Duxiu and Voitinsky was a
serious loss; Chen was a vigorous and well-respected figure to whom
Voitinsky contributed both organizational expertise and probably financial
resources. Recollections by Li Da—whose reliability is not beyond doubt,
as mentioned earlier—indicate that following Chen Duxiu's and Voitinsky's move to Canton, a quarrel erupted between Chen and Li Hanjun, the
man who had assumed responsibility in Shanghai,[29] involving Li Hanjun's
negligence in editing the *New Youth* and Chen Duxiu's failure to organize
payments to Li.[30]

Perhaps the most important reason, however, was Li Hanjun's vision
of the CCP, radically different from Chen Duxiu's. Zhang Guotao has
written that Li Hanjun was the best Marxist theoretician among early
Chinese communists,[31] and Cai Hesen too has praised Li for his knowledge
of Marxism.[32] Li grew up in Japan, where he studied civil engineering at
Tokyo Imperial College and developed an interest in Kawakami Hajime, a
leading Japanese Marxist and a professor in the Department of Political
Economy at Tokyo Imperial College. Li might have taken some of Kawakami's classes.[33] Back in China, Li translated Kawakami's *Introduction to
"Das Kapital."*[34] After his graduation in 1919, Li first moved to Wuhan,
the capital of the province of his birth, and then to Shanghai, where he
joined the staffs of the *New Youth* and Dai Jitao's *Weekly Review* (Xingqi
Pinglun).[35]

According to Cai Hesen's 1926 history of the CCP, the vision of the
CCP that Li Hanjun promoted was that of a decentralized party that engaged only in advocating communism among intellectuals. Li, Cai wrote,
opposed the idea that its members should engage in covert labor-movement activities and objected to a rigorous implementation of party discipline, favoring a decentralized organizational structure.[36] Various recollections provide supporting evidence for Cai's contention,[37] and a few years
ago a leading historian of the early CCP, Shao Weizheng, also argued that
Li made such arguments.[38]

Li received support, according to Cai Hesen's history, from Chen
Wangdao, a philologist and translator of *The Communist Manifesto* who

later became president of Fudan University in Shanghai, and Shen Xuanlu, an editor of the *Weekly Critic* and the first man associated with the CCP to organize a peasant association.[39] This group of "intellectualist" party members was not without influence, as the next chapter will indicate. However, Li Hanjun terminated his membership shortly after the Third Congress, at which he was still elected alternate Central Executive Committee member.[40] Shen joined the KMT in the same year,[41] and Chen Wangdao, according to Cai Hesen, became increasingly passive and withdrew from the CCP in 1923.[42]

This description of the Shanghai cell suggests that while Chen Duxiu and Voitinsky had been busy creating a Leninist organization in the city and conceived it as the seed for a nationwide one, the Shanghai cell disintegrated following their departure. The cell was not a proto-leadership body, and to the extent that leadership existed, it consisted of Chen Duxiu's. In addition, powerful forces in Shanghai opposed the construction of a centralized party, and therefore no firm conceptual ground existed on which Shanghai communists could build a centralized party. In contrast to places where cells developed "naturally" out of study societies, communists in Shanghai also lacked strong personal bonds or a basis in local society.

Canton

According to a report delivered at the First Congress by a delegate from Canton, two Russians named Peslin and Minor arrived in the city in late 1920, perhaps directed there by Voitinsky to pave the way for Chen and himself. Peslin and Minor established contact with a man named Huang Lingshuang, a former Peking University student of Chen Duxiu's,[43] and they proceeded to build a communist cell. Huang was an anarchist.[44] In Canton, anarchism possessed a strong following because of the influence of Liu Shifu—a promoter of Esperanto—who had founded the Study Society for Cocks Crowing in the Dark (Huimin Xueshe) after the 1911 Revolution and published *The Voice of the People* (Minsheng).[45] As a result of Huang Lingshuang's introduction, the Canton report to the First Congress explained, the efforts of the two Russians had resulted not in a communist but in an anarchist organization:

> Comrade Huang Lingshuang introduced [the two Russians] to
> Canton revolutionary circles, and thereby they were immediately
> surrounded by anarchists. Even though they organized a com-
> munist party, it would be better to call this an anarchist
> communist party. Of the nine members of its executive committee,
> only Comrades Peslin and Minor were communists.[46]

When Chen Duxiu and Voitinsky arrived in Canton in January, they immediately set out to remove anarchists from the Canton cell.[47] Chen presented himself as the leader of the Socialist Youth League and during a meeting of the Canton cell demanded that it establish a central organization and accept his leadership. This is clear from a March 13, 1921, letter by an anarchist named Guan Qian in which he reported information received from Huang Lingshuang. According to Guan, Canton anarchists responded in the following way to Chen Duxiu's demand:

> The initial idea of the majority of comrades here was to join forces with the Socialist Youth League to overthrow the present government and all evil systems. . . . Several times we consulted with Chen Duxiu, the leader of the Socialist Youth League. He was ambitious and dictatorial, however, asserting that to unite our generation, we had to obey his commands and that everything should be carried out according to the centralism of the league. . . . We all were extremely mad at him and refused.[48]

The effort to purge anarchists from the Canton cell was successful. As the Canton report to the First Congress stated, "The anarchists withdrew from the party. Thereupon we began building a real communist party."[49] This rebuilt cell had nine members, "including Chen Duxiu, Minor, and Peslin."[50]

The price the Canton cell paid for the purification was the loss of its base in Canton society. Cell members used Chen Duxiu's position in the Canton government to expand its influence. They set up a school for workers, issued a periodical, and ran a Marxism research society to develop interest in Marxism among the student population.[51] However, the Canton report to the First Congress makes clear that as in Shanghai, financial shortages forced its members to abandon most of these activities and that they were unable to counter the opposition not only of the anarchists in Canton but also of KMT followers.[52] While communists in Canton had very little time to make something of their efforts, the lack of some sort of basis in Canton society, which the anarchists and KMT both did possess, hindered the growth of a communist presence in the city not only before the First Congress but, as the next chapter will show, for several years after it as well.

Hunan

In his July 1922 report, Maring testified to the importance of study-society backgrounds for communist cells. In December 1921, he left Shanghai to visit Sun Yatsen, then residing in Guilin, the capital of the southern China province of Guangxi. With his translator, Zhang Tailei, he sailed up the Yangtze River, went through Hunan, and then traveled through Guangxi and Guangdong before sailing back to Shanghai from Canton. In his report Maring contrasted the desperate situation in Shanghai with the vigor and enthusiasm that he found in members of study societies in the hinterland. He depicted these members as discussing social issues and socialist ideas with passion and possessing a genuine drive to develop social and political activities rather than just publishing journals as in Shanghai.[53] This is an indication that the CCP had considerable roots in China's hinterland.

Maring specifically mentioned Changsha. The New Year's Conference of the New Citizen Study Society, it will be recalled, had resulted in a declaration stating that the society based itself on Marxism-Leninism. Historians in the People's Republic of China have argued that after the New Year's Conference a cell was set up in Changsha in addition to the New Citizen Study Society. This assertion probably derived from the need to sustain the view that CCP branches resulted from initiatives developed in Shanghai with the aid of Comintern agents.[54]

There is no evidence of a cell besides the New Citizen Study Society. There was little need for it. On January 3, during the third day of the New Year's Conference, the society's participants discussed the question of how to give concrete expression to their new commitment to seeking change on the basis of Marxism-Leninism. The result was a surprisingly moderate plan of action:

1. Study and cultivation
   A. Ism
   B. Various fields of learning. . . .
3. Propaganda
   A. Education
   B. Periodicals and pamphlets
   C. Lectures
4. Contacting comrades
5. Funds: Organizing a savings society
6. Basic Activities
   A. Schools (also an evening school)
   B. Expansion of New Culture Book Society
   C. A press
   D. An editorial committee
   E. A periodical in the vernacular
   F. A lecture group
   G. A vegetable garden[55]

It is unclear what motivation lay behind the idea of cultivating a vegetable garden, the last item. The program does make clear that the creation of a new form of life remained a basic desire of New Citizen Study Society members.

Writings by Cai Hesen and Mao Zedong indicate that the modest ambitions of the program were the result of the expressed consideration that China was not ready for a full-fledged Leninist party. Cai Hesen's letters of August and September 1920 to Mao Zedong provided a basic exposition on Marxist-Leninist organizational principles. In his August letter, Cai wrote that the Leninist party made use of "four tools": the party—"the nerve center of the proletarian movement"; labor unions; cooperatives (mentioned in the society's plan of action); and soviets.[56]

In his September letter, Cai went into the details of Leninist organization. Crucial to the success of the Bolsheviks, he stated, had been their adoption of strict recruitment standards and the subjection of new members to rigorous training and testing. Upon admission, Cai noted, members had to declare that they accepted "iron discipline."[57] "Centralism," he wrote, was also essential in the internal organization of the Bolshevik Party, enabling it to wage campaigns "under the direction and supervision of the Central Committee; nobody is allowed to act freely on his own authority."[58] In setting out the basic framework of the Bolshevik Party, Cai wrote that "the highest organization of the party was the Central Committee," with departments for "propaganda, organization, research and statistics, and labor duty."[59] He suggested that the last was intended to organize the membership's obligatory participation in manual labor, a point worth noting, given Mao Zedong's later policies in this regard.[60]

Outlining Marxist-Leninist revolutionary strategy, Cai Hesen wrote that "the indispensable methods of socialism [are] class struggle and the dictatorship of the proletariat. I believe that they form the only way a revolution in the world of today can achieve victory."[61] He described class struggle as "simply a political struggle, designed to smash the scaffolding of the bourgeoisie (the National Assembly) and to establish that of the proletariat—the soviets."[62] Soviets, Cai explained, were organizations of workers stacked vertically in geographical hierarchies so that the central soviet would be the government of the country.[63] This was the institutional expression of the dictatorship of the proletariat, necessary according to Cai because "without political power . . . production cannot be socialized . . . nor a counterrevolution resisted."[64]

In his September letter, Cai Hesen outlined for Mao the stages he believed needed to be passed through before a true communist party could be established in China:

(1) We gather all people who have the same understanding and ideas as I just set forth into one association for research, propaganda, and for publishing. (2) We establish contacts everywhere and conduct a campaign demanding freedom of congregation, association, and publishing. . . . (3) We select carefully all real party members, and distribute them among various occupational institutions, factories, farms, and assemblies. (4) We publish a strong and visible periodical, and then in full daylight we officially establish the Chinese Communist Party.[65]

While Cai knew the basic elements of the Leninist strategy, he did not believe that China was ripe for it. This feeling was perhaps even stronger in China. Mao Zedong, in his response, wrote that he agreed with the assessment, stating that he envisaged a "purely preparatory period" lasting at least until "the thirtieth year of the Republic," that is, 1941.[66] Writing from France, Cai told Mao that he would "research the Soviet Union and the situation in other countries; you in China can perhaps investigate the situation in various provinces and collect statistics on population, land, production, communications, the situation of labor, the economy, and education."[67]

A number of the plans of New Citizen members became a reality. Mao established the Self-Study University (Zixiu Daxue) in August 1921 as an institution where people had the opportunity to read and discuss socialist theories.[68] Society members published the *New Age* (Xin Shidai), a periodical geared toward an intellectual audience, discussing various socialist theories and expositions on Chinese society. They also succeeded in forming contacts with others in China who identified with Marxism-Leninism. Mao Zedong's letter to Cai Hesen of January 21, 1921, which mentioned Chen Duxiu's effort to organize a communist party,[69] suggests that Mao Zedong corresponded with Chen. It may be that Maring visited the society on his way to Sun Yatsen. Mao Zedong's participation in the First Congress was probably a culmination of these efforts and probably an attempt to strengthen and expand contacts with other Chinese communists.

The development in Hunan of an organization with members asserting that they favored the adoption of methods pioneered by the Bolsheviks in Russia makes clear that the role of communists in Shanghai or of Comintern agents was not a determining factor in the rise of communist cells in China. In the first few years of the CCP, the Hunan communist organization developed rapidly. It was the hotbed of Chinese communism with a membership larger than that of other places, even on such a late date as May 1924, the first time for which regional membership figures are extant.[70]

The Hunan case also suggests that an embeddedness in local society and in the study-society tradition, rather than simply the commitment to Marxism-Leninism or the adoption of Leninist organizational forms, was vital in the emergence of durable communist cells in China. I do not mean that cell members had established institutions in rural villages or labor unions in the cities. However, members of the Hunan cell were connected to Hunan society through their families, their schooling, their publication activities, and so on. They were considered insiders and treated as such.

Even though the New Year's Conference brought important changes to the New Citizen Study Society, there were continuities with the past, first in that its members remained focused on their own collective. In addition, the meeting's members asserted, as they had before, that only collective action could produce change. Collectives continued to be thought of as essential to sustaining the commitment to change oneself and to change China.

Peking

While it is true that the Peking cell's founding was connected with developments in Shanghai, the members of that cell acted very much on their own authority. According to the report of the Peking cell to the First Congress, a communist cell was established in Peking "only ten months ago," hence around October 1920.[71] An important binding element among its members was a common reverence for Li Dazhao. Zhang Guotao claimed in his memoirs that his visit to Chen Duxiu in Shanghai in July 1920, probably organized with the help of Li Dazhao, who had also sent Voitinsky on to Chen Duxiu, prompted him to suggest to Li Dazhao that they organize a communist cell in Peking.[72] Even if Zhang Guotao's memoirs are self-serving on many points, his claim that he took the initiative in organizing the cell while Li Dazhao acted as a supportive patron and facilitator may well be correct. Meisner too depicted Li Dazhao acting as a benign father to early members of the CCP in Peking rather than as institution builder.[73] When Voitinsky came to China, Li Dazhao sent him on to Shanghai, and in the early CCP it was very much Zhang Guotao who proved the active organizer in the CCP and especially in its labor-union activities.

Nonetheless, Li Dazhao's role in unifying the members of the cell, mostly drawn from three study societies,[74] was no doubt significant in sustaining the cell. Memoirs make clear that cell members treated Li as somebody to whom they owed respect, who infused their meetings with a significance they otherwise would have lacked.[75] Li's generous financial contributions strengthened his stature as a fatherly patron but naturally also had pragmatic value.[76]

The report of the Peking cell suggests that members operated in highly unfavorable conditions but that they nonetheless enjoyed some successes. They set up a Remedial School for Workers (Laodong Buxi Xuexiao) in Changxindian, the site of an important railroad workshop near Peking where Deng Zhongxia and Zhang Guotao had already approached workers as members of the Normal People's Education and Lecture Society.[77] In the school, three cell members gave instruction in reading and writing, using such ideas as capitalist exploitation and the history of the labor movement as lesson material. As part of their class assignments, workers were to write reports on their lives and their living conditions.[78]

The adoption of an educational role by CCP members in their first labor-union endeavors fitted the premium on education in Chinese society and was a strategy to which they were to resort frequently. Schoolteachers were less likely to arouse the immediate suspicion of the authorities than plain union activists, and because of public opinion, the authorities were less prone to take suppressive action. It is probably also true that workers found it easier to accept young intellectuals as teachers than as union organizers.

Even so, the strategy had serious shortcomings, of which Peking cell members were well aware. Its report stated that schools could do nothing to break the hold over workers of traditional labor organizers, the foremen (*gongtou*) who brokered employment in Chinese society for a considerable fee.[79] Foremen usually possessed a strong hold over the workers who used their services, and they were frequently connected to underworld groups.

Tight government control was a further problem for Peking cell members, which hindered them especially in their efforts to recruit new members from the city's substantial student population, or "intellectual elements" (*zhishifenzi*), as they called them.[80] According to the report, it was impossible for communists in Peking to print pamphlets or periodicals: "These days all printing shops are watched. . . . We translated some small pamphlets like *The Russian Revolution and Class Struggle* and *The Communist Party Program*, but we still have not been able to print them. We only distributed *The Communist Party Manifesto* and *Talks on Economics* printed in Shanghai."[81]

In Changsha and Canton, and obviously in Shanghai, government suppression seems to have been a less serious issue. One way Peking cell members sought to overcome this obstacle was throwing themselves into public debates. Bertrand Russell's lectures formed an excellent opportunity:

> When Professor Russell lectured in Shanghai and advocated guild socialism, we organized public disputations and announced ideas opposing his. It was unavoidable that we carried on arguments in meetings with anarchists as well as with people from the Social Party. We rarely joined in written polemics; these were mostly public debates or personal conversations.[82]

The Social Party (Shehuidang) was organized by Jiang Kanghu in 1914. Not much is known about him. While the Russians courted him for a while, they dropped him in circumstances that still await investigation.[83] In May 1922, Jiang was in Paris and criticized the Soviet Union fiercely in a public lecture.[84]

Despite the obstacles in their way, Peking cell members managed a May First demonstration in 1921 in which, the Peking report to the First Congress claimed, some fifteen hundred workers chanted slogans like "Raise Wages, Shorten Work Hours."[85] They also produced a few publications aimed at workers, bearing titles such as *Workers Weekly* (Gongren Zhoukan) and the *Voice of Humanity* (Rensheng). These did not last very long. The first "was closed by the government," and the second was abandoned after some time because of a "lack of funds."[86]

An interesting aspect of the Peking report is that it began with an analysis of the makeup of Peking society. It pointed out that of the two hundred thousand remaining Manchus in the city, many still refused definite employment out of loyalty to the Qing dynasty.[87] It described the city's population as dominated by small-time civil and military officials and a sizable group of modern professionals. "One can roughly say," the report asserted, "that more than half of Peking's population, no greater than 900,000, belong to the leisured strata."[88] It also mentioned that a modern labor movement would be difficult to organize because the city lacked large modern industries or enterprises.[89]

While its activities were not of earthshaking proportions, it is clear that the Peking cell was anchored in the shared study-society background of its members and their common veneration for Li Dazhao. Even if Zhang Guotao and Li Dazhao were on amicable terms with Chen Duxiu at the founding of the Peking cell and coordinated their activities with his, the Peking report indicates that they acted on their own initiative, basing their actions in the cell that they constructed. That the relationship between Chen Duxiu and the Peking cell was not hierarchical is also suggested by the fact that following the Second Congress of the CCP, Zhang Guotao organized a "small group" in which Li Dazhao was involved. The incident will be considered later.

Wuhan

Wuhan, an important industrial and trade center on the Yangtze River, played an important role in early CCP labor-organization efforts and in 1923 became the scene of the first violent clash, resulting in casualties, between the warlord in control of the city and a union in which the CCP was heavily involved. Wuhan communists did not produce a report to the First Congress, although two representatives did attend the congress, and therefore the emergence of communist organization and activities in Wuhan must be reconstructed entirely from memoirs, to the extent that this is possible.

According to a recent memoir published in Wuhan, it was Li Hanjun who sparked the founding of a communist cell in Wuhan. Li Hanjun, according to this memoir, contacted a friend and acquaintance named Dong Biwu, suggesting that he do so.[90] Dong, who was to become one of the most senior CCP members,[91] became acquainted with Li Hanjun in Shanghai in 1919 when he returned to China from Japan, and therefore it is certainly possible that Li Hanjun was in a position to approach Dong once he became involved in the Shanghai cell. A recent scholarly article supports this theory.[92]

Other memoirs suggest that a contact of Chen Duxiu's took the initiative in setting up the Wuhan cell. Liu Bochui, a lawyer, visited Chen in Shanghai; Chen then asked him to establish a cell in Wuhan with Dong Biwu.[93] Chen is said to have given Liu a party program, perhaps "The Manifesto of the Chinese Communist Party."[94] Most accounts agree that whoever took the initiative, Liu Bochui, Dong Biwu, and several others met as a communist cell in Wuhan. However, no source suggests that this cell generated much activity.[95]

Wuhan was also the city of Yun Daiying. According to one memoir, on July 16, 1921, only weeks after the Nanjing Conference of the Young China Study Society and a few days before the opening of the First Congress, Yun and other members of Wuhan study societies held a joint meeting that ended in the formation of a "Boshe," a Bolshevik society, named the Coexistence Society (Gongcunshe), that enshrined in its platform as its guiding principle "to prepare actively and earnestly for the realization of a Soviet government by means of class struggle."[96] Given what we know about Yun's thinking and his future involvement in the CCP, it is entirely within reason that Yun set up something like a cell. There are no documents describing its planned activities or its structure.

An interesting aspect of Yun's cell is that it was founded in the presence of a New Citizen Study Society member. Perhaps, then, New Citizen members had established links with Yun or with people connected to Yun in their efforts to contact like-minded students. This is likely because Changsha and Wuhan were well connected by rail and waterways.[97] The section below on the spread of Marxism-Leninism in China also makes clear that both Yun and New Citizen members ran bookstores to give currency to New Culture literature. This too may have formed the basis of contact between the two groups.

Chungking and Chengdu

Memoirs have been silent about the existence of a Chungking cell, and no participant in the First Congress was from Chungking. Nonetheless, the collection of archival sources that forms the documentary backbone for this account of early communist organizations in China contains a report from a Chungking cell depicting a thriving communist community in that city.[98] The collection was published under the auspices of the CCP Central Committee Archives, that is, by people who know most of CCP history. Like the other documents in the collection, the report of the Chungking cell is presented as a translation of an original in Russian held in Moscow. Its existence was confirmed recently in private by a Russian scholar, and therefore its authenticity is highly probable.

The document raises a number of important questions, such as why no mention has been made of it elsewhere if it existed and whether there are other "undiscovered" CCP cells. First, however, consider the issue of what the document actually reveals. Undated, it describes the organization and activities of a communist cell in Chungking, formally established on March 12, 1920. It discusses the event as something that happened not long ago and was the result of the activities of Chungking students and workers who had participated in strikes. The Chungking cell (if a reality) had four departments: a secretariat, a propaganda department, a finance department, and a publications department. There were forty regular and sixty candidate members, and the cell had four branches outside Chungking, according to the report. The report stated furthermore that cell members confined themselves to making propaganda, but it did note that workers in Chungking's textile industry were a promising target for unionization efforts, given the fact that they struck frequently. Two cell members, according to the report, were learning Tibetan with a view to translating communist literature into Tibetan and establishing a branch in Tibet.[99]

The report's last paragraph states that the Chungking communist organization dispatched a four-man delegation with the aim of contacting Chinese communists elsewhere in China and gathering communist scriptures:

We four were selected in Sichuan and entrusted with the following tasks: . . . (1) To link up with communist organizations in all provinces; . . . (2) To travel to the Soviet Union to investigate how members of the Russian communist party build their society and to obtain precious books that China lacks. We really need to understand communism completely from the books written by members of the Russian communist party or from the Russian comrades so rich in knowledge. Even though the journey from Sichuan to Russia is very long and totally exhausting, it is worth risking. . . . Without doubt, when we return in the future to Sichuan and apply the knowledge gained in Russia to our organization, it will be much improved.[100]

It would certainly not be strange if a communist cell existed in Chungking. Sichuan was a rich province, and while somewhat separate from the rest of China, it was not intellectually isolated. Many students from Sichuan were involved in the Young China Study Society, and a 1921 article by Zhou Enlai, in France at this point, stated that more students from Sichuan participated in the work-study movement than from any other province.[101] While this may be an exaggeration, it is clear that Sichuan was not an isolated backwater province.

A possible reconstruction of events is that a Chungking cell did exist and that a delegation was sent to Shanghai—the report stated that the delegation had purchased a printing press and type in the city with a considerable amount of money[102]—with the idea of establishing links with other communists and traveling to the Soviet Union. It is possible that when they did establish contact, conflict prevented the incorporation of the Chungking communist organization into the CCP, or into the structure headed by Chen Duxiu. The polite phrases about Russia in the document might indicate that the report was a briefing by the delegation to Russians.

The feasibility of this scenario is enhanced by the fact that another communist organization in Sichuan, located in the province's other big city, Chengdu, remained outside the CCP's orbit, at least until 1925. The cell grew up around Wu Yuzhang. Wu had studied in Japan and in France, where he was one of the leading organizers of the work-study movement. In Yan'an, Wu later headed the Lu Hsun Arts Academy.[103] Before involving himself in communism, Wu was a KMT member. In 1922 he returned to Sichuan as director of the Chengdu Higher Teachers College,[104] where he organized the Communist Party of the Chinese Youth in 1922 or 1923,[105] with a branch in Peking. According to his own account, Wu visited Peking in 1925, and when he then learned of the existence of the CCP, he agreed immediately to fuse his organization with the official

CCP.[106] More likely, Wu gradually moved closer to the CCP, perhaps committing himself fully only after he involved himself in the Nanchang uprising of August 1927 that was to lead to the founding of the Red Army.

Many questions remain unresolved about communism in Sichuan. But what is known illustrates very clearly some of the major points I am seeking to make in this chapter. It suggests that there was a great diversity among early Chinese communists; that not all were connected to Chen Duxiu, who had decided to establish himself as China's Lenin; and that not all wanted to be so connected.

Europe

In the late 1910s and early 1920s, more than two thousand Chinese students traveled to Europe, predominantly as participants in the work-study movement organized by Cai Yuanpei, Wu Zhihui, Li Shizeng, and other Chinese anarchists. The philosophy behind the movement was that Chinese students would acquire the mental outlook and intellectual skills proper to a modern culture most effectively where such a culture was firmly established. Chinese anarchists like Cai Yuanpei and Wu Zhihui held that modern culture was essentially cooperative and that it combined mental and manual labor. Therefore, two important features of the work-study movement were the insistence that students work while they studied and that they live cooperatively. An advantage the program was believed to possess was that it provided a cheap way for Chinese to pursue study abroad.[107]

Cai Hesen, Zhou Enlai, Zhao Shiyan, Li Lisan, Nie Rongzhen, Chen Yi, and Deng Xiaoping were only some of the more prominent Chinese communists involved in the movement. It was not until early 1923 that a cohesive organization of Chinese communists in Europe was formally created, as chapter 3 will discuss, and even at that time, its link with the CCP in China was not entirely free of tension. Even before a unified cell came into existence, however, there was considerable communist activity among Chinese students in France, with an important early strain, the one in which Cai Hesen played a leading role, having no connections with developments in Shanghai.

Zhang Shenfu, a Peking University professor, figured prominently in the one that was directly linked to the Shanghai cell, or more precisely, to Chen Duxiu. According to interviews conducted with Zhang in 1979 and 1980 by Chinese researchers, Chen Duxiu wrote a letter to Li Dazhao and Zhang Shenfu in August 1920 requesting the assistance of both in the organization of a communist party. In September, Zhang traveled to Shanghai to meet Russell, staying in Chen Duxiu's house. In November he left for France with Cai Yuanpei to take a teaching post at the China Academy of Lyon University, an academy set up by the Sino-French Educational Association that included the organizers of the work-study movement that brought Chinese students to France.[108]

After his arrival in France, the China Academy was not ready to open its doors, and Zhang lived in Paris.[109] In the interviews, he claimed that he recruited for the CCP such people as Zhou Enlai and Zhao Shiyan in the spring of 1921, published *Youth*, and formed the Young China Study Society.[110] According to PRC historians, this was the beginning of a Chinese communist cell in Europe.[111]

While containing inaccuracies and requiring qualifications, Zhang's assertions contain elements of truth. It was Wang Guangqi who founded the Young China Study Society, as we have seen. However, it is distinctly possible that Zhang was active in the distribution and publication of *Youth*. Wang Guangqi moved to Germany in 1920, later becoming a teacher at Bochum University and producing an important study of Chinese music.[112] *Youth* became an important journal among Chinese students in Europe, especially among communists. A March 1923 report of the communist cell that had then just been established mentioned that *Youth* was the cell's organ.[113]

It is unlikely that Zhou Enlai and Zhao Shiyan became part of a real communist cell in 1921, as Zhang seems to imply in his recollections. However, they did do so later, and it is highly plausible that both Zhou and Zhao did so while in close contact with Zhang, and perhaps under his influence. Zhou Enlai expressed his commitment to Marxism-Leninism in a March 1922 article, writing that he was "late" in accepting the Marxist-Leninist worldview as his own because of "my natural tendency to seek a harmonious solution and secondly because I always have a deep desire to seek the truth."[114] Zhao Shiyan discussed communism and a communist organization in letters dated April 1922 to a friend in China.[115] Zhao's letters confirmed his contact with Zhang Shenfu and mentioned that he corresponded with Chen Duxiu. Clearly, Chen and some Chinese communists in Europe were in touch and discussed communist organization. However, the letters also make clear that it was only in the spring of 1922 that Zhao began to think about organizing a communist organization and that he had very little idea what that meant.

According to Zhang Shenfu, he, Zhou Enlai, and several others moved to Germany in February 1922 after he resigned from the faculty of the China Academy at Lyon University, thus losing his salary. His action was precipitated by Chinese student demonstrations against the academy, an event that will be discussed. He claimed as reason for the departure from

France that life in Berlin was cheaper than in France. They supported themselves, Zhang stated, by writing articles for the Chinese press.[116] In an April 25, 1922, letter to Li Lisan, Zhao Shiyan mentioned that two members of the Berlin group were planning to go to Russia to serve as "representatives to the Fourth Congress,"[117] presumably the Fourth Comintern Congress that convened between November 7 and December 5, 1922, which Chen Duxiu attended.[118] It is possible that the Berlin group received financial assistance from the Comintern and that they moved to Germany upon the Comintern's suggestion as the prospects for a communist revolution were bright in Germany at the time.

Chinese historians have emphasized this cell—again, probably because it supports the theory that the Shanghai cell took the initiative in setting up other cells. However, before Zhang Shenfu's cell became active, New Citizen Study Society members under prompting by Cai Hesen had already developed a communist cell independently of Chen Duxiu or the Shanghai cell. Even if Zhang Shenfu began organizing a communist cell in Europe, the Chinese communist organization that eventually developed there did not have its origins only in his activities but also in those of Cai Hesen.

During the Montargis Conference of the New Citizen Study Society, as we have seen, Cai Hesen attacked the Kropotkinist thought of Xiao Zisheng and others, challenging the fundamental purpose of the work-study movement. A number of society members moved to Montargis, where Cai Hesen lived, probably not because of a great affinity to Cai's ideas but because the town had a sizable Chinese population and the local shoe factory provided employment. One man who moved to Montargis was Li Weihan. Li had sided with Xiao Zisheng against Cai Hesen during the Montargis Conference. Like Xiao and Cai, he had set out his reasons in a letter addressed to Mao.[119]

According to Li Weihan, later a leading CCP member, who recently published a book combining his recollections with the results of research conducted in CCP archives, he set up his own study society among Chinese students in France, called the Work-Study World Society (Gong-Xue Shi-jieshe), which involved study-society members who engaged in manual labor, something most did not. If Li Weihan's recollections are correct, the first organization of Chinese students in Europe that identified itself with Marxism-Leninism came about when in September or October 1920 Cai Hesen gave a presentation to a meeting of Li Weihan's group, with the result that "most members approved making the belief in Marxism and the implementation of a Russian-style social revolution our general principle."[120]

As Paul Bailey showed in his recent survey of the work-study movement, student demonstrations in 1921 gave Cai Hesen and others involved in the communist cell the chance to expand their activities. Cai, Xiang Jingyu, and four hundred other students joined in a protest in front of the Chinese legation in Paris to vent their frustrations with the work-study movement. Its organizers had declared that they were not capable of finding employment for all Chinese students who had now arrived in France or of supporting them. The protesting students demanded that the Chinese government finance their studies.[121]

Zhao Shiyan and others, including Li Lisan, refused to participate in this demonstration. At this point they favored continuation of the work-study movement, therefore rejecting the demand made by the demonstrators that the Chinese government finance full-time study. They protested that Chinese students should not depend on the tainted money of the Peking government.[122]

It did not take long for Zhao Shiyan and Cai Hesen to put their differences behind them and begin to cooperate. In the spring of 1921, the news leaked of a loan deal between the Chinese and French governments. Chinese tobacco, alcohol, and stamp duties, as well as the printing tax and French railroad construction rights, were to form the security for the loan. In response, Cai, Zhao, and other Chinese students in France formed a Reject-the-Loan Committee (Jukuan Weiyuanhui) that incorporated representatives of various study societies.[123]

Chinese students in France became even more agitated when the organizers of the work-study movement decided to sever all remaining ties between them and Chinese students already in France. At the same time, however, they had set up the China Academy in Lyon in cooperation with Lyon University and were bringing new students from China to study at that institution. The academy was scheduled to open in September 1921 with a new group of students recruited in China. On September 20, 104 students, including Cai Hesen and Zhao Shiyan, descended upon Lyon and occupied the China Academy. After negotiations between the students, the directors of the academy, Chinese diplomats, and French authorities broke down, French authorities expelled the students. Zhao Shiyan avoided returning to China by escaping from the detention center where he was held.[124]

It was Zhao Shiyan who was to fashion a communist cell out of the remnants of the student demonstrations. After escaping from French authorities in Marseilles, Zhao first kept a low profile, working in the north of France, cleaning up battlefields of the First World War.[125] In February

1923 Chinese communists from various places in Europe gathered near Paris, finally to establish a joint organization, attached to the Socialist Youth League rather than the CCP.[126] One of its acts, significantly, was the impeachment of Zhang Shenfu, who was accused of neglecting his duties and sowing discord.[127]

On April 26, 1922, Zhao wrote to a friend in China, stating that some Chinese students in France had decided to form a Youth League that he stated would in fact be "a Communist Party of Chinese Youths [Zhongguo Shaonian Gongchandang]."[128] Zhao explained that this group could count on twenty members in France, seven or eight in Belgium, and six or seven in Germany. The purpose of his letter was to ask how a Socialist Youth League should be organized and what its relation with the CCP should be. He requested his friend to mail him articles about communism and party organization.[129]

Another letter written by Zhao at the same time makes clear that Chen Duxiu had written Zhao with the request that Zhao return to China to assist with the CCP. Zhao wrote in response that "even though I do believe that the plan to establish a Bolshevik Party in China brings a ray of hope, at present I truly do not have any expectation that I could achieve much, and so I will not come back for the moment."[130] This was nearly a year after the CCP's First Congress. Zhao clearly did not think that he needed to obey Chen Duxiu's leadership, and like Mao Zedong and Cai Hesen, he believed that he should continue with his studies and reading rather than plunge headlong into the building of a Leninist party.

The European branch of the CCP possessed a complex genealogy. As in Chungking and Hunan, developments in the world of Chinese students in France seem to have been more germane to its emergence than the activities of the man who possessed a clear link to Chen Duxiu. The European case also makes clear that the emergence of cells did not suddenly stop at the eve of the First Congress or that the establishment of cells after that time was the result of CCP initiatives without also having local histories. The European cell also remained ill integrated into the CCP for a long time after the First Congress.

It is because Chinese students remained socially and intellectually preoccupied with the situation in China that they are a central topic in the study of the emergence of the CCP. Their period abroad was for few a time off from their worries, their social attachments, or the political battles in which they were involved. They did not develop a distance from the political conflicts or ideological polemics raging in China; in fact, many remained active participants, and they approached what Europe had to offer intellectually from that perspective.

As in China, communist cells among Chinese in Europe were most vital when building upon the study-society tradition. However, even though this took time, ultimately students with different study-society backgrounds combined into one organization. This process in Europe was no doubt stimulated by the fact that students from different regional and study-society backgrounds were thrown together as well as by demonstrations against the Chinese government and the occupation of the China Academy at Lyon University. It was in these events that Marxism-Leninism provided a basis for cooperative political action that study societies could not. In the end it was the ability of Marxism-Leninism and the CCP to incorporate as well as transcend such connections that its success in China depended on. In this way, the history of Chinese communism in Europe foreshadowed events in China. There it was only in the years between 1925 and 1927, when large demonstrations and mass movements held the country in their grip, that Chinese communists from various places were brought together, the CCP showed itself to be an institution capable of sustaining large-scale and nationwide political action, and study-society and regional attachments were finally transcended.

The 1922 report to the Comintern on the First Congress mentioned that delegates from Ji'nan, the provincial capital of Shandong, and from Japan attended the congress.[131] It seems that Zhou Fohai, the supposed Tokyo representative, was invited to join in the First Congress simply because he was present in Shanghai at the time. In Ji'nan there were two communists, and they appear to have had contact with Li Dazhao and others in Peking. Ji'nan was connected to Peking by rail. However, even memoirs do not suggest that there was a well-developed and active communist cell in Ji'nan before the First Congress.[132]

A number of conclusions emerge from the above account. First, the idea that the Shanghai cell, under Chen Duxiu's leadership and supported by Voitinsky, was the CCP's founding cell is false. Cells emerged in several places around the same time. Members of cells were oriented toward their own organizations and did not accept the Shanghai cell as a central leadership organization. There was a strong desire for coordination but not for subordination.

Second, study-society ties and personal relations in general were of great importance. The formation of cells was not the result of all those committed to Marxism-Leninism joining a cell, regardless of previous experiences, geographic location, education, and so on. Instead, people previously connected to each other on the basis of study-society or school ties set up a cell. The contacts between cells also depended on personal links that had previously existed. As mentioned, in Europe the establishment of an organization based on one ideology fitted the dissolution of study-society ties that was taking place and provided students with new ways of organization and political protest. Even in Europe, however, the emergence of a communist organization combining members with different backgrounds was a slow process that was not consummated until 1923. In addition, there is no evidence to suggest that Chinese communists in Europe formed a cell under tight control from Shanghai.

The formation of a unified communist party in China was to prove a complicated task. It required individual cells to hand over authority to the central leadership. The evidence presented above makes it clear that Chinese communists in general did envision a unified party but that in practice they were oriented toward their own cells. Even if Marxism-Leninism pushed them to create a centralized political party, existing values as well as social and political divisions in the country all hampered the realization of this. In addition, some expressed the idea that China was not yet ripe for a nationwide, centralized mass party.

A final point is that the advice of Voitinsky seems to have been of considerable importance in convincing Chen Duxiu to seek to unify communist cells in China into one centralized party. While it is probable that without Comintern agents a unified party would eventually have emerged in China, it undoubtedly would have taken longer.

MARXISM RESEARCH SOCIETIES AND THE PROPAGANDA OF COMMUNIST THOUGHT IN CHINA

The first reference to Marx in Chinese occurred in 1899 in a publication of late Qing reformers. In the first decade of this century, Liang Qichao and other exiled Chinese intellectuals paid some attention to Marxism.[133] Nonetheless, the spread of Marxism-Leninism was slow in China. Not only did few Marxist or Leninist writings find their way to China before the October Revolution, as has often been remarked,[134] but it was only after the creation of communist organizations that the audience interested in Marxism-Leninism rapidly increased. Rather than to say that the Chinese Communist Party was the product of the spread of Marxist and Leninist writings in China, it is far more accurate to argue the reverse.

One reason to make this case is that the important vehicle for the distribution of Marxism-Leninism—Marxism research societies—came into existence only after communist cells were set up. Of course, some Chinese did study Marxism and Leninism before the establishment of the CCP, as the first chapter has argued. After the October Revolution, Li

Dazhao produced many articles expounding his interpretation of the significance of the October Revolution, and under his editorship the *New Youth* devoted a special issue to Marxism.[135] Nonetheless, Li found his audience only in 1920 and 1921. In 1918 he had approached friends and students at Peking University in the hope of forming a group to study Marxism, but few showed enthusiasm.[136] He attempted to set up a Marxism study society again in the spring of 1920 after the collapse of the work-study societies, and this time he was more successful. Still, it was not until November 1921, more than three months after the First Congress, that the Marxism Research Society was officially established (see figure 3). It remained active until 1925.[137]

Meetings of Marxism research societies were occasions for communists to study Marxist thought. However, they treated Marxism as an academic topic, and as Dirlik has made clear, an academic interest in Marxism does not make a Leninist. A February 1922 announcement of the Peking Marxism Research Society that listed the materials it had available showed that the interests of its members were not restricted to Marxism-Leninism. Titles in Chinese in the original are presented here in transliteration, followed by my translation in square brackets; those originally in English are repeated as they appeared in the announcement; authorial information in rounded brackets is as it appears in the announcement:[138]

Communist Manifesto	(Marx and Engels)
Socialism, Utopian and Scientific	(Engels)
Ethics and the Materialistic Conception of History	(Kautsky)
. . . .	
Anarchism and Socialism	(Plechanoff)
The Origin of Family	(Engels)
Bolshevik Theory	(Postgate)
The Infantile Sickness of ⟨⟨Leftism⟩⟩ [sic] in Communism	(Lenin)
. . . .	
Militarism	(Liebknecht)
. . . .	
Dao Ziyou zhi Lu [The Road to Freedom]	(Yanbing, Lingshuang, Songnian Gongyi) [Translated by Shen Yanbing, Huang Lingshuang, and Chen Songnian]

Gongtuanzhuyi [Unionism]	(Li Ji Yi)
	[Translated by Li Ji]
Boehm-Bawerk's Criticism of Karl Marx	(Rudolf Hilferding)
. . . .	
Progress and Poverty	(Henry George)
. . . .	
General History of Civilization in Europe	(Guizot)
. . . .	
The 18th Brumaire of Louis Bonaparte	(Marx)
. . . .	
The International Relations of Chinese Empire (2 vols.)	(Morse)

In order of appearance, the full names of the authors in the announcement are Karl Marx, Friedrich Engels, Karl Kautsky, Georgi Plekhanov, Karl Liebknecht, François Guizot, and Horse Ballou Morse.

It should be noted as well that it was not only Marxism research societies that contributed to the spread of Marxist or socialist thought in China. More instrumental in the promotion of Marxist theory in Hunan was the aforementioned Culture Book Society.[139] Basically a distribution organization, it was started in August 1920 to import books not available in Hunan. It had distribution points in most major cities in Hunan.[140] A list published in November 1920 showed that at that time, before the New Year's Conference, it sold New Culture periodicals and major Chinese newspapers besides books on anarchism and Darwinism; books by Dewey, Russell, Hu Shi, and Cai Yuanpei; and so on. The topics that stand out are New Culture topics: the history of Western philosophy, Western ethics, scientific methodology, love, "new life," "the female sex," and so on.[141]

Shortly after the New Year's Conference, the Culture Book Society published a new list. This one showed that items on the previous one continued to be sold, although now it had many more books on Marxism. The list is interesting as it formed something of a best-seller list, stating how many copies had been sold of each book in the half year before.[142] Dewey did best, although in the aggregate Marxist books were by far the most popular:

Magesi Zibenlun Rumen [Introduction to Karl Marx's *Das Kapital*]	200 copies
History of Socialism	100
Dao Ziyou zhi Lu [The Road to Freedom]	60

Gongtuanzhuyi [Unionism]	60 copies
. . . .	
Pragmatism	100
Duwei Wuda Jiangyan [Five Great Lectures by Dewey]	220
. . . .	
Chenbao Xiaoshuo Diyiji [Novels of The Morning Post, vol. 1]	200
Kelubaotejin de Sixiang [The Thought of Kropotkin]	200
Xin Eguo zhi Yanjiu [Research on the New Russia]	80
Laonung Zhengfu yu Zhongguo [Soviet Government and China]	80
Tuoersitaizhuan [Biography of Tolstoy]	100
Shixian Lunlixue [The Logic of Pragmatism]	250
. . . .	
Zhongguo Zhexueshi Dagang [Outline of the History of Chinese Philosophy]	80
Zhongguo Wenfa Tonglun [General Discussion of Chinese Grammar]	60
Xin Biaodian Rulin Waishi [New Punctuated Edition of *The Scholars*]	140
Derwen Wushi Yuanshi [Darwin's *On the Origin of Species*]	30
Luosu Zhengzhi Sixiang [Russell's Political Thought]	70

Despite the fact that the Culture Book Society was run along modern lines and made its officers accountable, there is no guarantee that the above sales figures are fully accurate; the figures were at least rounded off.

In Wuhan too, it was not a Marxism study society but a book society that was most instrumental in introducing Marxism. This society distributed other Culture literature, and it published two journals, *Ours* (Womende) and the *Wuhan Weekly Critic* (Wuhan Xingqi Pinglun).[143] It had contacts with the Culture Book Society, and the two exchanged members. The society, based on work-study principles, also managed a library.[144] As in Hunan, many forms of socialism received attention. Yun Daiying himself translated Kautsky's *Class Struggle*.[145]

It was only with the emergence of communist organizations in China that an infrastructure developed for the spread of Marxism-Leninism in China. Marxism research societies were institutions where communists and others could gather to study Marxist-Leninist thought. They probably also provided Chinese communists with the opportunity to attract and vet recruits. Of course, as many have shown, including Stuart Schram in the case of Mao Zedong, the important question is not so much what socialist material was available or who read what, but what people made of it.

THE FIRST CONGRESS

Not all existing Chinese communist organizations were represented at the First Congress of the Chinese Communist Party. At the same time, those who were present had come to Shanghai, where the congress convened, out of their own and their constituency's desire to establish a nationwide party and cooperate in one organization. It was on the basis of this wish that the CCP was built.

While the commitment to the idea of a nationally coordinated communist movement might have been strong, many issues remained that few Chinese communists had thought about in a systematic way. What kind of party the CCP was to be, what activities it was to engage in, how authority was to be distributed, and what it could demand of its members were among the most important of these. The answers, never permanent, took shape in practice, through discussion and struggle.

A report produced shortly after the First Congress surveyed the debates the issues mentioned above generated at the First Congress. The report was probably submitted to the Far East Bureau of the Comintern in Irkutsk.[146] A representative from the bureau, Nikolaevsky, was present at the meeting, and he suggested that participants produce a report for the Irkutsk bureau.[147]

The report noted that the congress had been scheduled to open on June 12, 1921, but that it opened on July 23 because only then had the representatives from the communist organizations of Peking, Wuhan, Canton, Changsha, Ji'nan, and Japan all assembled in Shanghai.[148] Two people represented each locale according to an article by Zhao Bu, a historian working in the CCP Central Committee Archives, with an additional participant bringing the number of Chinese to thirteen.[149] The Comintern agents were Maring and Nikolaevsky.[150]

The available sources do not provide conclusive evidence about how the congress was prepared. According to one memoir, it was Li Hanjun who took care of the concrete preparations, probably with the assistance of Li Da's wife, Wang Huiwu. This is likely, as Li Hanjun was the man in charge in Shanghai and the congress convened at his home.[151] The idea for the congress itself probably came from one of the Comintern agents. A number of attendants at the congress were there, it seems, by virtue of a connection with Chen Duxiu, who himself did not attend. This was the case for Zhang Guotao and Mao Zedong. Zhang, it will be remembered, had stayed with Chen Duxiu in Shanghai. In a January 1921 letter to Cai Hesen, Mao Zedong mentioned that Chen Duxiu was organizing a party and was publishing the *Communist Party Monthly*. Thus, Chen and Mao were in touch.[152] No doubt, Chen also was instrumental in arranging the presence of Chen Gongbo, who represented Guangdong.

Zhang Guotao chaired the meetings of the congress. In his opening remarks, Zhang stated that the purpose of the meeting was to determine a party program and to draw up a plan of action. After this, the congress settled in to a day of listening to cell reports. The opening statement of the Peking report—delivered by Zhang Guotao or Liu Renjing, the other Peking representative—gives a sense of the atmosphere of the congress's first day:

> Those who joined our young organization are none but a few intellectual elements, most of whom lack revolutionary experience. Because of changes in the current situation, all our activities have run into problems, and so the results of our efforts are little to brag about. . . . We hope sincerely that this congress can enrich our experiences and provide us with principles and instructions for the conduct of future activities.[153]

The self-deprecatory statements did not reflect an honest assessment of the difficulties facing the CCP; they were polite phrases, made to display that the speaker approached the meeting as a solemn occasion.

The second day was taken up with speeches by Maring and Nikolaevsky. Maring spoke about his experiences as a communist organizer in Java, the main island of what was then the Dutch Indies, and in the labor movement. Nikolaevsky discussed the situation in Russia and reported to the meeting on the Far East Bureau of the Comintern that had been set up in Irkutsk. Maring suggested that the meeting appoint two committees, one to draft a party program and another to compose an action plan. These committees met during the next two days.[154] It is not clear whether the two Comintern representatives rejoined the congress when it reconvened or decided to remain in the background.

It was at this point, when they had to come to an agreement on basic issues such as the organization of the CCP and what activities they would undertake, that all the latent conflicts among those who attended the First Congress exploded. The disputes involved several interconnected issues. The most important one was whether the CCP was to be a decentralized party, restricting its activities to propaganda among intellectuals, or should be a centralized one, engaged in covert activities among urban workers. The report did not provide names, but as mentioned, the sources are unanimous in attributing the first view to Li Hanjun and his supporters, the second to Zhang Guotao. The third, fourth, and fifth days of the congress saw heated debates about these issues, which in the end remained without a settlement. The report to the Comintern noted that "after some issue had been discussed for a very long time, a final resolution was proposed, but only with the point that had generated so much contention left out."[155]

A related point of debate was whether CCP members should take official positions. Especially because the relationship between the two was probably strained, it is difficult to avoid the thought that Li Hanjun raised the issue in criticism of Chen Duxiu, at this point heading Chen Jiongming's Education Bureau. No matter what the personal background was, the issue cut through to basic problems involved in attitudes of CCP members toward their party. One side, the report indicated, argued that membership in the CCP, and subordination to leadership exercised in its name, removed the danger that involvement in the political system at a high level would corrupt one's revolutionary commitment. Opponents lacked the faith in the ability of the CCP to keep its members on the right path. The meeting did not resolve the issue, and it was shelved until the next congress. The report to the Comintern, however, did mention that there was a general consensus that CCP members should not take any official posting that gave them important executive powers.[156] At the time of the First Congress, the CCP was far removed from being a centralized Bolshevik organization with all members firmly attached to the CCP. These issues, it will be remembered, had produced debate at the Nanjing conference of the Young China Study Society only weeks before the First Congress. The participants in the First Congress had not entirely put the world of study societies behind them.

A third point of debate was whether the CCP should engage in what the text called "secret work" (*mimi gongzuo*).[157] One side, probably Li Hanjun's, argued that the CCP should fight for freedom of the press and freedom of congregation and association, as this would enable the CCP to conduct propaganda. Secret work was understood, it appears, not as the construction of an underground system of agents but as the establishment of labor unions that would eventually come to serve as the basis for antigovernment political action.[158] The defenders of secret work, no doubt including Zhang Guotao, argued that public activities be combined with covert ones, since

> if we do not believe that within twenty-four hours we can destroy the state, or . . . if we do not believe that a general strike can continue to be suppressed by capitalists, political action is mandatory. Opportunities for an uprising are few. . . . However, in times of peace, we must make solid preparations for it.[159]

They also argued that "the plan of trying to establish a new society within the confines of the old one is useless and that even if we try this, it would be futile."[160]

As is well known, the session of the congress held at the sixth meeting day was disturbed by a police raid. Soon after it convened, in the evening, the police entered Li Hanjun's house, probably by mistake as the report argued.[161] Nonetheless, it was decided that the congress should hold its final meeting outside Shanghai. The last session of the congress took place in a boat on South Lake.[162] Debate erupted once more, centering on the question whether CCP members should ally with other parties or political factions. This issue can probably be traced to Maring. Before the congress, he had suggested that the CCP join into an alliance with the KMT.[163] A number of those present at the congress opposed Maring's suggestion, arguing that "in theory and practice, the proletariat must always struggle with all other parties and factions."[164] Others were in favor of the idea that the CCP cooperate with others against a common enemy, which the report identified not as international imperialism but as China's warlords. As long as the CCP criticized all other political groupings in its periodicals, they stated, collaboration did not violate party principles.[165]

Given the circumstances of the meeting, it was difficult for participants in the First Congress to drag out the discussion on this point, and the meeting decided to approve the plan of action that had been compiled in committee during the third and fourth days. A copy of this is available, and its relevant section makes clear that the anticollaboration faction had prevailed: "With regard to other parties," it wrote, "we must follow a policy of complete independence."[166] The report to the Comintern stated that the participants in the congress also decided to concentrate their efforts on organizing workers,[167] something the plan confirms.[168] Maring's report to the Comintern corroborates this.[169] On this important point, then, the Li Hanjun faction had to give way. This did not mean, as chapter 3 will indicate, that his ideas lost all their influence.

The meeting ended with elections. The report stated that three men were elected to fill executive positions in a "secretariat" (shujichu).[170] It does not give the names, but all sources agree that Chen Duxiu was elected to head the secretariat, Zhang Guotao organization, and Li Da propaganda.[171]

Several reasons can be marshaled to account for Chen Duxiu's election to the CCP leadership. The divisive debates among the participants in the First Congress, as well as the personality conflicts which had come out into the open, made the congress turn toward Chen Duxiu as a man who could unite the divergent constituencies of the CCP and give it immediate national prestige. Chen was the eminent former dean of humanities at Peking University, the editor of the *New Youth,* an esteemed philologist, and the man who with his articles had done much to create the New Culture movement. He possessed an implacable revolutionary record, having opposed the Qing, Yuan Shikai, and Duan Qirui, and having risked his life on more than one occasion for his ideals. He was recognized by all for his uncompromising moral courage and scholarly commitment, stating in June 1919 that "world civilization has two sources: one is the laboratory, the other is jail. We youth must go from laboratory to jail, and from jail to laboratory."[172] Chen was deeply involved in organizing the CCP in both Shanghai and Canton. In addition, he was tagged by Voitinsky as the man he wished to work with in China, and this gave Chen the stature of somebody deemed capable by Bolshevik leaders of carrying the revolution to China.

Li Dazhao was the only real alternative to Chen Duxiu, but as mentioned, he was not interested in organizational affairs and restricted his activities to the Peking area. When Voitinsky came to China, Li sent him on to Chen Duxiu in Shanghai. One consideration might have been that Shanghai was a safer place from which to direct Comintern activities in Asia. They also may have thought that as China's most industrialized city, Shanghai formed the logical base of activity for a communist party in China. Like Chen, Li did not attend the congress.

Even if Chen Duxiu was generally respected by early Chinese communists, that does not mean that they therefore accepted Chen as their Lenin. As the next chapter will attempt to demonstrate, CCP members did not accept his every word as command. The expectation of at least a number of them appears to have been, as the next chapter will suggest, that Chen would act as a benign, somewhat paternalistic and distant leader who was not to exert day-to-day control over the organization but whose reputation could be employed by CCP members in advancing their cause.

The congress proceedings underscored the fact that CCP members had not yet developed a consensus about what type of party the CCP should be and that they lacked mechanisms to settle conflicts. Not surprisingly, the deliberations between the two groups of opinion reflected the concerns about political action with which CCP members were grappling at this point. They confirm that their hesitations did not vanish once they made the decision to base themselves upon Marxism-Leninism and form a party and that they saw the congress much as they had seen study-society meetings.

If the CCP remained infused with aspects of the study-society culture, there was one important difference between the CCP and the study societies of the New Culture period. The members of the Chinese Communist Party were committed to the violent removal of all who possessed power, be they republican politician, warlord, magistrate, or assemblyman, and to the fashioning of an entirely new political system. They laid the first plans to do so at the First Congress. Study society members may have been deeply critical of many aspects of the political world and society, but their strategy nonetheless was based on the hope that in some way or another—by example, by demonstration, or by the written word—those who held positions of power could be influenced. The First Congress consummated the severing by those who joined the CCP of their links with the Republic.

1. New Citizen Study Society members in Changsha.

2. New Citizen Study Society members in France.

3. Peking Marxism Research Society.

4. A consumer cooperative of Anyuan railroad and mine workers.

5. Demonstration in Shanghai during the May Thirtieth movement.

6. Demonstration in Shanghai during the May Thirtieth movement.

7. Members of the Shanghai Executive Branch of the KMT. Mao Zedong is second from the left in the last row, under the U.S. flag.

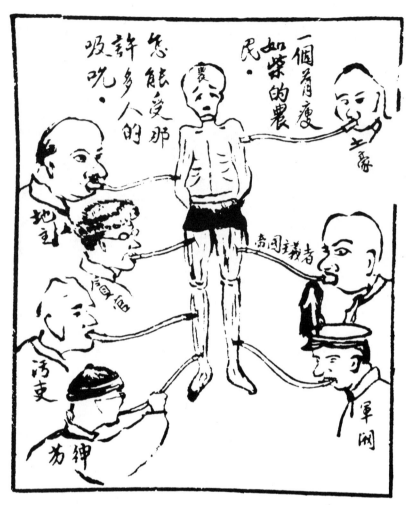

8. An example of CCP propaganda: a peasant has the life sucked out of him by, clockwise from top right, a local bully, an imperialist, a warlord, evil gentry, a corrupt clerk, a greedy official, and a landlord.

海豐縣農民協會減租證

海豐縣第九區大夫寮の鄉

會員姓名 黃義合

非有此證不得減租
借給別人當爲無效

民國十五年六月 十二 日

9. Haifeng peasant association certificate entitling the holder to rent reduction. The certificate was issued on June 12, 1926.

10.   Meeting place of the Fifth Congress.

3/Hesitant Beginnings, 1921–1925

After returning to Shanghai in August 1921 to assume his position as the head of the CCP's secretariat, leaving his post in Chen Jiongming's regime, Chen Duxiu confronted the task of fashioning a unity from the various Chinese communist organizations. He declared in his June 1923 Third Congress report that "party members often do not have complete faith in the party."[1] His efforts had reaped little reward.

After the First Congress, the atmosphere among the CCP membership soured quickly. If at the time of the First Congress personality problems had existed, most CCP members no doubt entertained expectations of communists cooperating harmoniously and enthusiastically with each other, considering themselves friends among whom pettiness had no place. A variety of conflicts destroyed such illusions in a short time. Serious differences of opinion about policy proved difficult to settle. Chen Duxiu clashed with a number of regional CCP leaders about issues involved with the centralization of authority. Zhang Guotao was found to have organized a "party within the party" in an attempt to maneuver around opposition to his labor-movement activities. The Comintern agent Maring seems to have aroused the animosity of all CCP members because of what they perceived as his high-handedness.

Even if until the Third Congress the CCP remained an extremely loose organization in which confusion about the distribution of authority was rife, this did not mean that Chinese communists were not active individually. Individual members produced labor and peasant movements of some size soon after the First Congress. These activities took place without the assistance, or the coordination and supervision, of a strong central leadership.

However, these endeavors soon ran into problems. In February 1923, for instance, the Peking-Hankow Railroad strike, in which the CCP was deeply involved, was ruthlessly suppressed by Wu Peifu, a northern warlord. Activities undertaken by communists in the countryside suffered the same fate. The lack of success was due, besides the strength of the forces opposed to the CCP, to scant knowledge among CCP members of power relations in Chinese society and a belief that China's population would flock to support them as soon as they made their presence known. As a result, they failed to generate an identification of labor-union and peasant-association members with the CCP's cause. In short, the CCP was in no position to marshal the resources, military or otherwise, by which to overcome warlord or gentry attack.

The Third Congress of June 1923 represented a nadir in the early history of the CCP. As a result of internal chaos and strife, as well as setbacks in labor and peasant movements, CCP membership actually may have plummeted from a high of over 400 to somewhere between 100 and 250.[2] During the Third Congress, CCP members and Comintern agents all criticized one another, and a sizable number of Chinese communists, Mao Zedong included, declared they had given up on the idea that the Chinese people could organize their own revolution.

The conflicts at the Third Congress were perhaps intense, but the congress nonetheless formed a turning point in the history of the CCP. Its clashes were settled in a resolution, and even though the losers continued their opposition for some time after the congress, they did not cause the CCP to splinter. While Chen Duxiu was no doubt correct in arguing that until the congress few CCP members had a strong sense of identity with the CCP as a whole, the discussions at the congress suggest that such an attitude was beginning to develop. The congress was a turning point also because it resulted in the creation of central institutions. Arrangements were made for representatives of the CCP's regional units to meet regularly, and the peasant and labor movements were placed on a different organizational footing. Not all of these reforms became a reality before the Fourth Congress of 1925, and none were tested in practice, since between the Third and Fourth congresses, the CCP by and large withdrew from active involvement in society. Nonetheless, the Leninization, so to speak, of the CCP had begun.

THE CCP'S LEADERSHIP CRISIS BEFORE
THE THIRD CONGRESS

Chen Duxiu's report to the Third Congress of June 1923 makes clear that in practice the CCP lacked a well-articulated central leadership structure.

Lack of personnel, frequent relocations, and political suppression were one set of reasons, as Chen explained:

> The Central Committee had too few members and therefore could not collect materials. . . . When repression intensified in Shanghai, we moved to Peking, thinking that the political situation in that city might still allow us to carry on there, and we then began to reform our institutions. However, even before we had begun to implement our plan, the wild reactionary clique forced us to leave Peking after the Peking-Hankow Railroad strike and to return to Shanghai. We still were unable to realize our plans for the reform of our institutions because repression in Shanghai was fierce and we wanted to prepare for the next party congress. We therefore moved the Central Committee to Canton, but there the situation also was not stable.[3]

Not only what communists would call "objective" forces played a role in the failure of CCP members to produce a strong central leadership. Many actively resisted the growth of central institutions. Chen Duxiu suggested the enlargement of the Central Bureau by two members to a CCP leadership meeting of August 1922, which convened in Hangzhou, a city to the southwest of Shanghai. But Li Dazhao, the delegate from Peking, and the representative from Shanghai protested, and the proposal was not carried.[4]

The centralization of authority within the CCP was resisted for several reasons. In chapters 1 and 2, I have described the plans of Mao Zedong and Cai Hesen about communist organization in China, emphasizing that they believed that it would take some time in China before a true Bolshevik Party could be established. Li Hanjun expressed his strong support for a decentralized party at the First Congress. While some supported the rapid centralization of authority, including Chen Duxiu, even a Comintern agent, Maring, did not believe that the time was ripe.[5]

Another reason was the continuing influence of regionalist attitudes and study-society modes of operation. While most communists were committed to cooperation in a nationwide CCP, they remained strongly wedded to their regional organizations, on which they had depended in the past. Regionalist tendencies were enhanced by past elite political practices and by the lingering suspicion of the centralization of authority.

In addition, Chinese communists were not familiar with Leninist ways of doing things, and as the case of Zhang Guotao's small group suggests, some may have seen Chen more as a patron than as CCP secretary general and the CCP as a convenient framework in which to develop their activities rather than as an organization that required them to report all their actions to its leadership and obtain authorization before undertaking any activity.

The first two CCP constitutions, adopted at the Second and Third congresses of July 1922 and June 1923, respectively, underscored the disjointed structure of the early CCP. They provided only for an annual national congress. They did not contain regulations for mechanisms to integrate regional organizations. They also did not outline bureaucratic pyramids culminating in central offices in Shanghai. The second CCP constitution, passed by the Third Congress of June 1923, strengthened the power of the regions by stipulating that a CCP congress was to be convened if just a third of the regions requested this.[6] It was only with the Third Congress that regulations were formulated to govern a permanent central leadership organization, called the Central Bureau (Zhongyangju).[7] To keep matters simple, I refer to the CCP's leadership elected by a congress as the Central Bureau in this and the following chapters.

Regionalist Resistance to Centralization

Several conflicts illustrate the fact that despite the desire to construct a unified party, CCP members found it difficult to shed regionalist and study-society attitudes. One case involved the Central Bureau in Shanghai and the Guangdong Regional Executive Committee, which ended in a complete breakdown of trust in the relationship and appears to have come close to a formal breakaway from the CCP by Guangdong communists. Writing in 1926 when a strong central leadership institution was vigorously promoted by all leading CCP members, Cai Hesen stated that communists in Canton had objected to a Central Bureau instruction to cut all relations with Chen Jiongming, the dominant Guangdong warlord. They refused to implement the order, even after an August 1922 meeting in Hangzhou of CCP leaders had decided that communists in China were to support Sun Yatsen. At this time, Sun was in the process of constructing a government in Canton, proceeding against the wishes and interests of Chen Jiongming.[8]

The Central Bureau dispatched an emissary to investigate the situation. The resulting report, Cai Hesen argued, stated that the *Pearl River Review* (Zhujiang Pinglun), a publication of Canton CCP members, was financed by Chen Jiongming. It also mentioned that Chen Gongbo—a leading CCP member in Guangdong who later joined the KMT and subsequently the Japanese puppet government of Wang Jingwei for complicated but not merely opportunistic reasons—served as Chen Jiongming's Labor Bureau chief and that he "opposed the Central Bureau's policy toward Chen Jiongming and planned to withdraw from the party and organize the Communist Party of Guangdong."[9] Acting on the basis of this report, the Central Bureau expelled Chen Gongbo. According to Chen Gongbo, when he informed other communists in Canton of this, they all favored cutting their links with Shanghai. Chen himself, he stated in his recollections, had become so disenchanted with the behavior of communists that he refused to have anything to do with whatever organization they might set up.[10]

There is no doubt about the existence of a sharp conflict between the CCP leadership in Shanghai and communists in Guangdong. In his report to the Third Congress, which was held in June 1923, Chen Duxiu confirmed its existence, stating that "comrades in Canton have made very serious mistakes with regard to the issue of Chen Jiongming."[11] It is not clear whether the Guangdong branch actually severed its ties with Shanghai. According to Cai Hesen, the relationship improved only after the Central Bureau moved to Canton in 1923 in preparation for the Third Congress.[12] Chen Gongbo's 1946 recollections of the incident are in agreement on the main facts with Cai Hesen's 1926 account.

Yet there is an important difference between the two versions, one that illuminates the deeper issues involved in the conflict. In 1946 Chen Gongbo declared that he had left the CCP not so much because of his opposition to the Central Bureau's policy toward Chen Jiongming but because he believed that its dispatch of someone to spy on him was something that "should not happen between people in general, let alone between friends."[13] He also wrote that he was disgusted with the internal bickering in the CCP and the high-handedness of some of its members. Chen Gongbo's memoirs suggest, then, that he had seen the dispatch of an investigator from Shanghai—a normal leadership prerogative in centralized systems—and the strife among its leaders as something that undercut the moral base of relations in an organization he thought to be composed of people who were morally equal, who had identical rights within the organization, and who would voluntarily cooperate. Writing in 1926, Cai Hesen used the fact that somebody remained loyal to regional connections and resisted central authority as a way of smearing the reputation of Chen Gongbo. By 1926, CCP leaders vigorously promoted the norm of party discipline, and disobedience to the central leadership had become a serious charge. Of course, the ideal that the CCP was a group of equals voluntarily thinking and acting in the same way remained powerful, and this was no doubt one reason why Chen Gongbo chose to emphasize the CCP's deviance from it in 1946 when he had become one of the CCP's main opponents.

A second case involved Chen Duxiu and Chinese communists in Europe. Here too we find the dissonance between an ideal image of the party and the infringements that the requirements of a tightly organized and centralized organization threatened to make upon it. It will be remembered that by the end of 1922, Zhao Shiyan had succeeded in bringing various groups of Chinese communists in Europe together into one organization called the Communist Party of Chinese Youth. The incorporation of this group into the CCP was one of the subjects of a report written by Zhou Enlai in March 1923 as a member of the Communist Party of Chinese Youth.[14] In November 1922, this group had sent a letter to China, according to Zhou's report, that had expressed the desire to establish a link with Chinese communists in China. Shortly afterward, and perhaps the two communications crossed in the mail, a letter had come back to France that ordered the Communist Party of Chinese Youth to rename their party the French Branch of the Chinese Communist Youth League and to rename its Central Executive Committee the Executive Committee.[15] The Youth League was the CCP's youth organization. The required changes were obviously intended to delineate a hierarchical relationship.

These events are confirmed by Zheng Chaolin's memoirs, which provide the additional information that it was Chen Duxiu who produced the letter and that he did so in Moscow, where he was attending the Comintern's Fourth Congress. Zheng, an active participant in the emergent Chinese-communist organization in Europe and an important propaganda worker in the CCP in the late 1920s,[16] also stated that Chen requested Zhao Shiyan not to focus solely on Chinese workers in Europe—the Allies had brought between 100,000 and 200,000 Chinese workers to Europe to make up for labor shortages at the time of the First World War[17]—but to go to Moscow for a brief period of study and then to return to China.[18]

Zhou Enlai's report indicated that he and his fellow party members had taken offense at the high-handed tone of the letter from Shanghai. Besides giving the above orders, it had set out in detail all the ways they had misunderstood the Youth League's platform. While Chinese communists in Europe, maybe under Comintern pressure, accepted Chen Duxiu's instructions,[19] Zhou's report—resulting from the Communist Party of Chinese Youth meeting that decided that the party would become a Youth League branch—makes clear that like Chen Gongbo, they continued to see themselves as a closely knit organization of friends, loyal to each other rather than to a faraway leadership. Zhao Shiyan himself, as mentioned in the previous chapter, refused to accept Chen Duxiu's entreaties in the belief that he could not contribute to activities in China and preferred to stay in France. While Chinese communists in Europe wished to be part of the CCP, it is clear that at the same time they did not believe that all initiative and authority therefore rested with Chen Duxiu.

The contentiousness of the leadership issue among Chinese communists in Europe is also evident from an incident involving Zhang Shenfu. According to Zheng Chaolin, "Zhang Shenfu continuously interfered in our organization and activities on the basis of his status as correspondent [of the CCP]. The reason was that we did not carry out his orders, which made him very angry, and this aroused our animosity."[20] The minutes of the February 1923 meeting of the Communist Party of Chinese Youth stated that the issue had its origins in Zhang's refusal to accept its decisions and that he had balked when a meeting in Berlin sought to force him to accept them.[21] The meeting decided that it was not in their powers to expel Zhang and that they therefore would not take any action, but instead report the matter. Zheng Chaolin's recollections note that the issue was especially sensitive because Zhang Shenfu had supported Zhao Shiyan's and Zhou Enlai's applications for CCP membership. Zhou defended him, Zheng Chaolin wrote, while Zhao at first refused to continue to preside over the meeting. After the meeting, Zheng suggests, Zhang provoked even further anger when he wrote a letter accusing Zhao and Zhou of scheming against him and asserted that his position in Europe was like that of Chen Duxiu in China.[22]

The incidents in which Chinese communists in Europe were involved highlight the difficulties Chinese communists had in forming clear lines of authority and establishing firm organizational patterns. It is clear that Chinese communists in Europe strove to form a unified organization, that they did wish to be a part of the CCP system, and that they wanted to operate according to its rules. At the same time, they did not treat Chen Duxiu's instructions as orders they had to accept and implement. Even if they did accept the idea of a unified organization run on the basis of regulations, they found it difficult to accept any one person's actually assuming the post of leader and exercising its functions. Personal obligations remained important, and they continued to value a harmonious atmosphere among the membership. Zhang Shenfu's actions were resented because they were seen as high-handed and as spoiling relations. Chinese communists were thought of as a group of natural friends cooperating with understanding and forbearance, in which organization was to exist to promote coordination but not to ensure the implementation of decisions taken at the central level.

Opposition to the Bloc-within Policy

An attempt of Maring to have Chinese communists accept and implement not only a policy of cooperation with the KMT but a program that required all CCP members to enter it formed the most ambitious attempt of the CCP to enforce a central policy. The bloc-within policy, as Maring's program is known, was widely unpopular with CCP members. It required them to join the CCP individually and obey KMT rules. The policy remained operative until 1927 and throughout its existence generated sharp disagreements among CCP members. Its implementation and consequences for the CCP form a major theme in the rest of this study. Here I will use the issue to illustrate the significance of regionalism in the early CCP.

An April 6, 1922, letter from Chen Duxiu to Voitinsky, then in Moscow, spelled out the objections of CCP members to the policy when Maring first pressed them to implement it. Chen wrote this letter in the hope of persuading Voitinsky to have Maring's bosses in the Comintern instruct Maring to withdraw the policy. According to Chen, the CCP's regional branches had discussed Maring's proposal, and all objected to the KMT, for the following reasons:[23]

> 3. The KMT has never published a party program; as the people in the provinces outside of Guangdong see it, it is still a political clique out for power. If the party entered it, it would damage our social reputation (especially among youth societies . . .).
> . . . .
> 5. The Sun Yatsen faction in the KMT in the past never accepted suggestions of new members or gave them power.[24]

Maring continued to push for the policy. In August 1922 he returned from a visit to Moscow armed with a Comintern instruction ordering CCP members to implement the bloc-within policy.[25] Maring wrote in a 1923 letter that Karl Radek, a member of the Comintern Executive Committee, had written the instruction in the name of that committee:[26]

> 2. The Comintern's Executive Committee believes that the KMT is a revolutionary political party . . . that aims at the establishment of an independent Chinese republic.
> 3. In order to complete their task, communist-party members must establish their own blocs [*tuanti*] within the KMT and labor unions.[27]

Upon his arrival in Shanghai, Maring convened a meeting of top CCP members, which was held in Hangzhou on August 29 and 30.[28] All accounts agree that the debate between Maring and CCP leaders—Chen Duxiu, Li Dazhao, Cai Hesen, Zhang Guotao, and Gao Junyu—was passionate, but in the end Maring achieved his purpose.[29] As Chen Duxiu commented about the meeting in his report to the Third Congress in June 1923, "While at first most people opposed our entrance into the KMT, the representative of the Comintern Executive Committee convinced the participants in the [Hangzhou] meeting. We decided to persuade all party members to join the KMT."[30]

Maring acted on the supposition that acceptance of the bloc-within policy by the CCP leaders would produce partywide implementation and that the formal agreement at a meeting meant a hard commitment of those who attended to work for its realization. This would have been entirely logical if the CCP had been a centralized Leninist party. However, the CCP leadership did not control institutions capable of enforcing central decisions. In reality, a policy achieved implementation only if members of regional units supported it and if they possessed the means to realize their goal.

It is first not clear that even those who attended the Hangzhou meeting worked hard to implement the meeting's decision. Shortly afterward, a CCP delegation, including Chen Duxiu, set off for Moscow, officially to attend the Fourth Comintern Congress, which opened in November 1922.[31] Liu Renjing, a member of the delegation, addressed the congress. Apparently attempting to offset raving comments about Sun Yatsen in Maring's reports, he stressed Sun's weak military position and the traditional aspects of Sun's political vision. Liu also suggested that the CCP was not quite as isolated as Maring had argued. Liu made much of "the growth of the influence of our party among the masses."[32]

Probably as a result of this delegation's protests, the Comintern in January 1923 produced an instruction to the CCP that affirmed the bloc-within policy, writing that "under present conditions, it is appropriate for the Chinese Communist Party to remain in the KMT" but also stating that the CCP was to retain its own organization and conduct its own propaganda campaigns, and that "the important and special responsibilities of the CCP are the organization and education of the masses of workers."[33] "The price" of CCP members entering the KMT, it stressed, "must not be the elimination of the CCP's independent political posture."[34] When he heard of this, Maring "immediately returned to Moscow in order to defend the continuation of the policy adopted in August [1922 at the Hangzhou meeting],"[35] as he stated in a letter to Comintern leaders shortly after the Third Congress.

We know of the failure of regional executive committees to implement the bloc-within policy from reports made by regional representatives and central CCP leaders in November 1923. Such meetings became a regular occurrence after the Third Congress of June 1923. The report from the Peking representative to the November 1923 meeting commented on CCP collaboration with the KMT in the Peking area, stating that "at first it was ineffective because many members had doubts about the policy and also because they had arguments with nationalist comrades and because some people in the KMT branch used comrades to create disturbances."[36] The report mentioned that it was taking measures to bring about improvements. The Hubei Regional Committee stated that "as for the Nationalist movement, the patriotic movement that erupted suddenly has now dissipated."[37] It mentioned that a number of organizations that had been set up in Wuhan to further the Nationalist cause had been closed down.[38] The report on the situation in Shanghai argued that communists in the city had been unable to begin a nationalist movement because most of its members were from outside the city.[39] The Hunan Regional Committee's report did not even mention the topic. The Central Bureau's report summarized the situation with the statement that

> with regard to our relationship with the KMT, we have still not been able to carry out the resolution of the congress because (1) comrades have quite a few doubts about it; (2) the KMT's management of its affairs is far from perfect; (3) our comrades and the members of the KMT are suspicious of each other, and their ideological concepts are not the same; and (4) our own financial problems.[40]

The congress referred to in the quotation above is the Third Congress of June 1923, which formally endorsed the decision of the Hangzhou meeting to commit the CCP to the bloc-within policy.[41]

As late as November 1923, more than a year after the August 1922 Hangzhou meeting, regional executive committees did not implement the policy. As the above quotes indicate, one reason was the fact that the KMT itself had not yet been firmly established in many areas. At the same time, the reports of the regional executive committees and the Central Bureau also make it clear that the dislike among CCP members of the policy and their unwillingness to cooperate with KMT members prevented the policy's implementation. There was little that the Central Bureau could do, given this attitude among CCP members and the lack of powerful central institutions, to pursue the bloc-within policy with any determination.

Zhang Guotao's Small Group (Xiaozu)

Before the First Congress, Zhang Guotao set up the Secretariat of China's Labor Federation (Zhongguo Laodong Zuhe Shujibu) with the help of Maring as an umbrella organization to coordinate CCP labor-movement activities in various regions.[42] At the First Congress, Zhang Guotao had pushed hard for a labor movement and what was called covert activity and so had won himself the dislike of Chen Gongbo and Li Hanjun, both of whom saw him as quarrelsome, domineering, and ambitious.[43] Personal antagonism against him, as well as the fragmented state of the CCP, prevented Zhang Guotao from pursuing a labor policy through existing channels. As a result, he turned the Labor Secretariat into a "party within the party." This "small group" illustrates Zhang Guotao's lack of a strong CCP concept and respect for formal procedures.

According to Zhang Guotao's own memoirs, the secretariat began to function in this way at the time of the Second Congress of July 1922. Those who attended the congress met frequently in small numbers in separate locations for security reasons. Zhang's group was made up of people who belonged to the secretariat. After the Second Congress, instead of disbanding, its members continued to meet as an independent caucus.[44] When Maring returned from Moscow in August, he discovered that a storm had broken out in the CCP about the existence of Zhang's small group. He found that four of the five Central Bureau members, all but Chen Duxiu, belonged to the small group and that Chen Duxiu had resigned from the leadership when he had learned about its existence.[45]

Comments by Chen Duxiu and Maring at the Third Congress suggest that they believed that Zhang had not acted to set up an opposition faction in the CCP but simply to maneuver around opposition to a covert labor movement. Chen Duxiu stated that he had confidence in Zhang's overall good intentions, remarking that "Comrade Zhang Guotao is no doubt sincerely faithful to the party, but he is terribly narrow-minded in ideology and therefore has committed grave errors. His organization of a small association within the party is an example."[46] Maring stated that Zhang "divided the comrades into good and bad, and aimed to strengthen the party by means of the small group."[47]

Members of communist parties are of course not supposed to keep information from the formal leadership or establish organizations within their party without central approval. Chen Duxiu's and Maring's reactions at the Third Congress suggest that they believed that misconceptions about the nature of party organization were to be expected and that violations of internal discipline were pardonable on this ground.

The depiction of Zhang as innocently perpetrating violations of party discipline did not necessarily form the whole truth. His behavior when he organized the Peking cell, as well as his management of the Labor Secretariat, indicates that he saw the CCP as a useful device in which to undertake his projects, which included the organization of a labor movement in northern China, as I describe in the next section. But Zhang did not believe it necessary to obtain permission from Chen Duxiu for these activities.

Zhang's small group also formed a response to the fragmented nature of the early CCP. In order to pursue a labor movement, it was necessary for Zhang to establish an organization on a national scale, or at least one that transcended existing regional boundaries. He decided to work around formal CCP channels and institutions, it seems probable, not just because of the opposition to a secret labor movement by people like Li Hanjun but also because the CCP did not possess the institutions he could have exploited to construct a strong labor movement.

Of course, in organizing a small group, Zhang added to the fragmentary forces in the CCP. It may be doubted that the small group had no history preceding the Second Congress, and the issue stayed with the CCP at least until the November 1923 Central Executive Committee meeting. Zhang lost his leadership position at the Third Congress, but as the report of that meeting and a letter by Zhang to Voitinsky make clear, Zhang did not abandon his efforts to promote his policies at that point, even when this divided the CCP membership.[48] The small group was not a minor affair. It raised in a concrete fashion the complicated issue of how the CCP was to deal with internal disagreements. The early CCP, Zhang's small group illustrated, was ill equipped for this.

Before the Third Congress, Chen Duxiu was unable to integrate the CCP's regional organizations or to expand the scope of CCP activity. Its organization did not branch out substantially from the areas in which CCP members were active at the time of the First Congress. The conditions under which CCP members operated were in part responsible for this. In this section I have also adduced a number of reasons for this state of affairs, which were of the making of CCP members themselves and related especially to their attitudes toward organization. At the central level, the CCP was fragmented, with a minimal leadership without the institutional or symbolic resources necessary to realize its own policies. Communists remained influenced by study-society traditions, and regional patterns of association continued to be strong. Attitudes toward the CCP were characterized by confusion and disagreement about the proper allocation of power and the purpose of the CCP. Not all CCP members were familiar with Leninist procedures, and some possessed what can be called a traditional instrumentalist view of the CCP. It is clear that Chen Duxiu was correct when in his Third Congress report he asserted that few CCP members had complete faith in the CCP. "Serious individualistic tendencies exist within our party," Chen Duxiu stated, and he lamented that "internal relations in the party are not at all close, and everybody is suspicious of one another."[49] He criticized several of those present at the congress by name, including Zhang Guotao and Deng Zhongxia.

CHINESE COMMUNISTS IN ACTION:
THE FIRST LABOR AND PEASANT MOVEMENTS

The program of action adopted at the First Congress stipulated that CCP members were to concentrate on organizing a nationally coordinated labor movement. The initial strategy of Zhang Guotao's secretariat was to recruit high-level officers of traditional labor associations, including gangs, and on this basis to form a national workers' alliance.[50] In this context, Chen Duxiu instructed regional executive committees to begin forming labor unions in November 1921.[51] This approach broke down when Shanghai authorities found Li Qihan, a secretariat officer with good contacts in the dominant Green Gang of Shanghai, inciting worker agitation. They arrested him and closed the secretariat.[52]

Despite these setbacks, CCP members did bring off important labor movements before the Third Congress. However, these were not centrally coordinated or planned. They resulted from the pioneering efforts of individual CCP members, usually sustained regionally with the help of the members of a regional CCP branch. The same is true of the CCP's earliest peasant-movement activities.

Zhang Guotao's Labor Union Activities at the Peking-Hankow Railroad

CCP historiography maintains that Chinese communists directed the Hong Kong seamen's strike of the first weeks of 1922.[53] This is unfounded. None of the strike leaders were involved in the CCP at the time; rather than CCP members, it was British Labour Party members who first set up a seamen's union among Chinese in London.[54] Moreover, the support of money and lodgings in Canton from the KMT and the Canton government were no doubt more significant for the strike than the three thousand fliers the CCP contributed.[55]

Communists did play a crucial role in the workers' strikes that ended, disastrously for them, in the February 7 incident of 1923. After he abandoned the grand scheme of a national general union, Zhang Guotao refocused his labor organization's efforts on Changxindian, near Peking, where he had opened an evening school for workers during his study-society period. Here he hoped to expand among the workers of the Peking-Hankow Railroad.[56]

From one perspective, the workers seem a heterogeneous group: They consisted of bankrupt former landlords and officials, small merchants, and peasants, all in need of money.[57] But the workers were in fact tightly organized, as most belonged to a *bang*. A *bang* was an association of people who traced their origins to a common area. Originally local elites set up such *bang* to mobilize local surplus labor for projects or enterprises outside their home area. *Bang* managers provided transport and lodging, and paid salaries. In time, the *bang* in reality became labor rackets, with foremen (*gongtou*) acting as middlemen with a monopoly over labor and employment. As recent work on China's urban industrial workers has shown, factory managers often lacked control over the recruitment of workers in their own factories.[58]

Several *bang* provided the labor for the Peking-Hankow Railroad. In the workshop in Jiang'an near Hankow, for instance, workers belonged either to the Hubei, Tianjin, or Guangdong *bang*.[59] It was the contacts of *bang* bosses that determined which *bang* linked up with the railroad. The Peking-Hankow Railroad for some time had been in the control of the Communications Clique (Jiaotongxi), a warlord clique that involved, besides military men, Peking politicians, financiers, rich entrepreneurs, and the like.[60] Communication Clique associates involved in running the line hired laborers through their *bang*. This was one way warlordism in China possessed thick social roots.

The reason that communists believed that they could challenge the *bang* of the Peking-Hankow railroad was that they had concluded a pact with Wu Peifu. Wu was a warlord competing with the Communications Clique, which he had just defeated on the battlefield. Part of his booty was the Peking-Hankow Railroad, of great strategic value because it connected his base in Hunan and Hubei with Peking and because it connected the British Kailuan Mines with industrial centers.[61] To help cleanse the railroad from the influence of the Communications Clique, Wu agreed to appoint six CCP members as investigators who roamed the line on a free travel pass with the task of suggesting candidates for dismissal among managers of the railroad tied to the Communications Clique.[62] Chen Duxiu acknowledged the existence of this arrangement in June 1923 when he stated at the Third Congress, "We have consistently opposed warlords. Once, however, we were busy organizing workers of the Peking-Hankow Railroad and wanted to fight the Communications Clique. Since Wu Peifu also opposed the clique, we stopped opposing him."[63] Zhang Guotao also described the deal in his memoirs, identifying Li Dazhao as the man who had set up the pact.[64]

Enjoying Wu's backing, it was easy for communists to build unions among the railroad workers.[65] The result was, Zhang claimed in 1925, that during the spring of 1922, the Labor Secretariat formed sixteen separate labor unions in various locations along the Peking-Hankow Railroad.[66] The first step toward a unified union of all workers attached to the line was taken in April 1922 when the secretariat convened a meeting in

Changxindian of the representatives of the existing unions. In August a second meeting was held in Zhengzhou, located between Hankow and Peking along the line, where regulations were discussed and a preparatory committee organized. Shortly afterward, the workers of the northern section went on strike for a wage hike of three *yuan*, which they obtained after the members of the other unions of Peking-Hankow Railroad workers also walked off their jobs.[67]

This brought home to Wu Peifu the danger and the high cost of using communists to fight the Communications Clique. The Peking-Hankow Railroad employed twenty thousand workers; a pay raise of three *yuan* made a noticeable impact on his budget. The strike also alerted him to the fact that he was replacing one threat to his power with another.[68] At the same time, the success of the strike led workers to believe that Zhang Guotao and his allies had something to offer. The stage was set for a confrontation.

On January 5, the Preparatory Committee of the General Peking-Hankow Railroad Union met again in Zhengzhou and determined that a founding conference was to convene on February 1. After sixty-five representatives of the sixteen union branches had already convened in Zhengzhou for the conference, the Zhengzhou chief of police closed the offices of the committee on January 28, seizing the ritual presents and placards the branches had sent. Wu Peifu personally met with union representatives three days later, informing them that the union was disbanded.[69] It was up to the union, and its CCP leaders, to buckle under or fight back.

When the sixty-five representatives returned to their bases, they did so committed to a strike for union rights. The union's headquarters were relocated to Jiang'an. On February 4, the workers laid down their tools, paralyzing all traffic along the line. The strike demands, as issued from Jiang'an, included the sacking of the director of the railroad; an indemnity for damages suffered in Zhengzhou; one day off per week and an annual vacation of one week, both with pay.[70] On February 7, Wu's troops took action, crushing the union and in the process killing several dozen workers and wounding several hundred.[71] More than one thousand workers lost their jobs.[72]

The strategic mistake of Zhang Guotao and other CCP members was to take on the man they depended on for their power. In attacking Wu Peifu, they removed the ground from under their own feet. Only if the CCP had been able to establish a firm following among the railroad workers would they have been able to create an alternative base of support, although even then it is not likely that they would have been successful in resisting determined action by Wu Peifu. However, CCP members did not succeed in replacing the *bang* with unions under their control. It was the other way round. The *bang* replicated themselves in the union. The leaders from different *bang* who joined the union negotiated who would occupy what position.[73] After the beginning of the strike, Zhang Guotao quickly lost prestige. Documents in the Maring Archive suggest that Zhang counseled against a large-scale strike, and the day after the beginning of the strike he proposed "to take strike order back," thereby "losing trust workers [*sic*]."[74] CCP control over the strike seems to have been limited.

The Peking-Hankow Railroad workers' strike may well have been in part an attempt by threatened *bang* officers to shore up their positions, threatened by Wu Peifu's efforts to establish his control over the railroad. In any case, a wage raise would profit workers as well as *bang* officers, as these would increase their income by raising their "fees." With regard to the CCP as an organization, what stands out is the fact that Zhang ran the union as his own affair. All pamphlets and all communications went out in the name of the secretariat. No steps were undertaken to induct workers into the CCP or to make propaganda for the CCP among workers.[75] As a result, few workers could have been aware what the goals of communists were. The failure to acquire the allegiance of the railroad workers was also one reason why the CCP was unable to establish firm control over the strike.

Failure in Shanghai

CCP members were well aware of the anomaly that they were least successful in forming a labor movement in Shanghai, China's most industrialized city. A November 1923 report by Shanghai members attributed this failure to the following four reasons:

1.   Communications are good, and therefore the supply of labor exceeds the demand. The competition among those working in one industry is intense, so nobody dares to compete with those who do the hiring.

2.   The women workers employed in silk filatures, cotton mills, and tobacco factories form more than the majority of all Shanghai workers. This too is a reason why the Shanghai labor movement has not gone anywhere.

3.   The workers come from many different places. Regionalism is a factor preventing worker unity.

4.   The original Red and Green Gang not only surreptitiously prevents worker unity but has also drawn in police detectives who now keep a close watch over each and every movement of workers.[76]

Numbers 2 and 4 require some background information. In her study of Shanghai women workers, Emily Honig has noted that regionalism and gender solidarity were reasons for the CCP's inability to establish labor organizations in Shanghai in the 1920s and 1930s. For the CCP, gender was indeed a problem, as gender-based social divisions divided its labor unions, which incorporated both men and women workers. A Third Congress resolution on the women's movement made clear that male sexism of the crudest sort seriously undermined the stability of labor unions.[77] CCP members considered setting up separate unions for men and women, but they rejected the idea on the ground that this "created institutions dividing the proletariat."[78] The Fourth Congress of January 1925 resolved that women's liberation was a part of the class struggle.[79]

Besides the strength of these traditional ties, the Red and Green Gang, or simply the Green Gang as it was usually referred to, impeded the CCP's ability to establish labor unions. The Green Gang was a criminalized association of *bang*. According to Chesneaux, it had its origin in the Anqinghui, the Society for Peace and Happiness. In order to combat crime, ironically enough, in 1725 several gentry established this society among the transport workers of the Grand Canal who moved grain up the canal to Peking. They divided the workers in 128 *bang*, using Buddhism to enhance their cohesiveness. The *bang* were organized like religious sects. When the significance of the canal as a grain-transport route decreased in the late nineteenth century, the Green Gang diversified into Shanghai, providing a work force to the new industries which sprang up after the 1895 Treaty of Shimonoseki granted foreigners the right to erect factories in China.[80] The city administration of Shanghai was superficial, in part because of the city's sensitive international position and in part because of its rapid expansion. The Green Gang exploited the vacuum, ruling much of the lower strata of Shanghai society and forcing many others to accept its "protection."

As the CCP report quoted above indicated, the gang and Shanghai authorities developed a symbiotic relationship.[81] The Green Gang controlled labor supply and employment by the contract-labor system, in which gang members forced employers to hire only through them. They brought labor from the countryside into the city, taking a substantial cut from the "contracts" they offered. The system was backed by intimidation, kidnapping, assassination, blackmail, and other forms of violence.

The literature usually describes the Green Gang as a dark but highly cohesive and well-organized force in Shanghai society. However, it remains vague what the Green Gang actually was. Rather than a tightly controlled organization, for instance, it might well be that it was a loose association of various criminal organizations operating in Shanghai that continuously contested one another's sphere of influence. The gang's connections with other elements of Shanghai society have also remained obscure. Of course, it may well be that at times one man, or one subsection, dominated the whole Green Gang. In the late 1920s, the legendary Du Yuesheng, for instance, seems to have become the unchallenged Green Gang leader.

There was little place in Shanghai society for CCP labor organizations. Gangs possessed a monopoly over employment in Shanghai, and they had industrial workers and many of the unemployed in their grip. Communists had no means of cutting into gang turf, making a labor movement an impossible area of activity for them in Shanghai. Communist membership in Shanghai also suffered from frequent changes, so that no cohesive group could emerge with a solid organization, and it was difficult to form solid contacts with Shanghai society. The report of the Shanghai representative to the leadership meeting of November 1923 argued that these two problems had hampered Shanghai communists:

> After the congress [of June 1923] we focused all our attention in this area to rectify our internal situation in Shanghai, because before this, we were internally fragmented, to the extent that there was no organization at all. Even though Shanghai is the largest city in China, our activities have seen hardly any progress. Because most of our members come from outside the province and are unemployed, they are cut off from local society, and therefore it has been impossible to conduct the nationalist movement.[82]

The Hunan CCP

In contrast to Zhang Guotao, CCP members in Hunan succeeded in forming a strong workers' organization and conducting a victorious strike. In doing so, they employed traditional elite roles and made sure to maintain good relations with various local power groups. The strategies they employed were radically different from those used by Zhang Guotao.

With Changsha lacking a sizable modern proletariat, Hunan CCP members developed labor-organization efforts among workers employed by the Anyuan Mines and the Zhu-Ping Railroad in Kiangsi Province.[83] The mines were located some fifteen miles to the south of the Pingxiang County capital in the Anyuan Mountains, renowned for their rich coal deposits. They were part of the Hanyeping Iron and Steel Company, headquartered in Wuhan, the *ping* of Hanyeping being the *ping* of Pingxiang County. The Zhu-Ping Railroad connected the mines to Zhuzhou, located south of Changsha on the Xiang River. From Zhuzhou, boats carried the coal to Wuhan. Anyuan fell within the natural sphere of action of CCP members reporting to the Hunan Regional Executive Committee.

A report from the Anyuan Local Committee, attached to the report of the Hunan Regional Committee to a May 1924 meeting of regional and central CCP leaders, provides insight into the situation communists faced in Anyuan when they began to set up a workers' organization there. It made the point that Triads were deeply entrenched in the area.[84] According to Triad lore, lodges were founded after the Manchus destroyed Shaolin Monastery in Fujian Province, famous as a center of martial arts, despite the assistance monks had provided them when they founded the Qing dynasty. Five surviving monks established one lodge each in the five major southern China provinces. Triads asserted an ideology of overthrowing the Qing and restoring the Ming.[85]

Whatever the true history of Triads, lodges were held together by pseudokinship ties, with members swearing oaths of brotherhood for mutual assistance and protection.[86] While lodges may not have been well connected with each other, each one possessed a hierarchical structure, control of which was at times probably contested. Triads were a southern Chinese phenomenon where bandits, smugglers, and settlers resorted to lodge formation when they found themselves thrown together in a harsh situation where none of the traditional forms of social organization provided a common framework. Kuhn and Mann suggested that beginning in the 1840s, Triads penetrated settled society in southern China when increasingly sharp economic competition forced especially the poorer lineages to expand their scope of cooperation.[87] When modern industries emerged at the turn of the century, lodges easily branched out into this new area of economic life.

Opium dens and gambling rings were a feature of Anyuan society heavily stressed in CCP documents. Triads were no doubt involved in their operation, and they therefore took with one hand what the other gave.[88] Li Lisan—famous for promoting or being forced to promote a disastrous insurrectionist strategy when he was CCP general secretary in 1929 and 1930[89]—moved cautiously when he arrived in Anyuan, exploiting roles sanctioned by tradition. Li arrived in Anyuan in November 1921 and as his first act petitioned the authorities for the right to establish elementary schools. This was granted, and after some time he also set up schools for workers.[90]

As a next step, communists in Anyuan established cooperatives, for which capital was raised from the workers. Besides selling salt, oil, liquor, and food, the cooperatives exchanged copper and silver (see figure 4). Manipulation of the exchange rate between copper, the currency of local society, and silver, used in higher-level transactions and the currency in which taxes were assessed, was an established means of fleecing the population.[91] While mounting this challenge to entrenched commercial interests of the Triads and the more orthodox elites, Li attempted to disguise the CCP's threat to the dominant elements of local society as much as possible. He asked one of the lodge members to introduce him to the lodge head. Bringing along gifts, Li visited the man and drank chicken blood, thus performing a rite signifying his participation in the lodge.[92]

There is no doubt that Li was opposed to Triads and their practices. At the same time, it is possible that in the early 1920s he and other CCP members had hopes that they could establish working relations with such organizations and gradually convert them into labor unions tied to the CCP. As we shall see, while some realization that Triads or gangs were not the CCP's natural allies in Chinese society emerged among CCP members soon after first attempts were made at arousing labor and peasant movements, hopes to the contrary were not dashed until the incorporation of vast numbers of Triad and gang members in CCP unions during the May Thirtieth movement of 1925 backfired on the CCP. It was after this that the CCP devolved policies aimed at weeding out their influence in the CCP and attacking them in Chinese society.

In the spring of 1922, the Anyuan Railroad and Mine Workers Club (Anyuan Lu-Kuang Laodong Julebu) was formed. Li claimed in his memoirs that it achieved successes in reducing opium smoking, gambling, and crime among workers.[93] While the results of his efforts should not be overestimated, in September 1922 the Workers Club did conduct a campaign that obtained higher wages for Anyuan workers.

Mine workers in Anyuan had not received their wages for some time. On September 11, 1922, the Workers Club dispatched a letter to the manager of the Anyuan Mines. It opened with the statement that the club had worked to improve the "ethical conduct" of workers and was recognized as legal by the authorities. It then noted that workers had become severely agitated by rumors that mine officials planned to bring in outside help to close down the club. The letter demanded that the manager, jointly with the head of the Zhu-Ping Railroad, request the government "to announce clearly support for the club in order to halt the fabrication of rumors."[94] It also asked both companies to contribute one hundred *yuan* per month to support the club's leisure, educational, and mutual-aid activities, the latter referring probably to the cooperatives. The last but clearly most significant item on the list of demands was that all salary arrears were to be cleared within seven days.[95] On September 14, the club sent a note to the Hanyeping Company, announcing that because workers did not receive their wages, "they cannot live, and therefore they now have abandoned their jobs."[96] On October 5, the club was able to announce an agreement with the company that basically met all its demands.[97]

Several things stand out in Li Lisan's approach to the formation of the Anyuan Railroad and Mine Workers Club and the management of the strike. First, he was careful to fit the club into the social system. Officials could not protest openly the efforts of Chinese youths to teach workers and their children, and at least in public they had little option but to suggest that they welcomed attempts to set up organizations that undermined the control of Triads. In his relationship with the Triads, Li Lisan conducted himself as the follower of a Triad head, and Triad leaders no doubt relished the wage increase, as a substantial portion was bound to find its way into their purses. The language of his correspondence with Hanyeping officials was conciliatory and appealed to the moral sensibilities to which Hanyeping officials in public had to display sensitivity. Instead of talking about the oppression of the proletariat by evil capitalists, Li pointed out the civilizing effect the club had on workers and argued that workers were not disloyal or rebellious but that desperation had driven them to "abandon" their jobs.

While this strategy was initially effective, it could not remove the fact that the Workers Club had no real power. The club continued to function even after Wu Peifu's suppression of the Peking-Hankow Railroad Union, which had led to what Chesneaux has termed "two years of retreat" in the Chinese labor movement.[98] One reason for this was that Hanyeping officials, or their warlord supporters, did not want to take the trouble to move troops to Anyuan, which they could have done by using the railroad, to quash a workers' organization that to their minds might have held the promise of serving as a counterweight to Triad power. However, as a CCP resolution of 1925 explained, after the strike the Workers Club increasingly provoked local conflict. It reduced the financial opportunities of local officials and Triad leaders alike. When in 1925 during a period of national labor unrest company officials decided to move for the closure of the club—and by this time events like the February 7 incident had created a popular image of Chinese communists as fanatical labor agitators—they encountered little difficulty.[99]

Peasant-Movement Failures

The first peasant association set up by a CCP member was the Yaqian Peasant Association in Xiaoshan District near Hangzhou in Zhejiang Province. It was not the much-vaunted Haifeng Peasant Association formed by Peng Pai. The moving spirit in Yaqian was Shen Xuanlu, a typical well-meaning son of a rich local gentry family who had edited and contributed to the *Weekly Critic* (Xingqi Pinglun) during the New Culture movement and had joined in the discussions of the Shanghai cell.[100] Returning to Yaqian, his place of birth, in the summer of 1921, Shen set up a free school for peasants in his house. In public speeches in which he reputedly dressed in peasant clothes, Shen declared in August 1921 that the family would not collect rents.[101] In September 1921, he formed the Yaqian Peasant Association, publishing its declaration and regulations in the *New Youth*.[102] The association quickly spread to include some eighty villages. In the fall, Shen headed up a rent-reduction campaign, angering the local elite.[103] The association was easily destroyed by prefectural troops called up by district officials.[104]

Peng Pai's involvement with the Guangdong peasantry has received much scholarly attention. Most of this has focused on his activities during the Guangdong peasant movement of 1925 and 1926 and his creation of a soviet in Hailufeng comprising two counties, Haifeng and Lufeng, on the east coast of Guangdong where Peng was born and raised.[105] Here I want to draw attention to the fact that Peng's first attempt at setting up a peasant association followed the same broad outline as that of Shen and possessed the same traditional features of a gentry son trying to do good. Peng failed in part because of the interference of Chen Jiongming but also because he was unable to establish a reliable social base and acted in flagrant disregard of the realities in which the Haifeng peasantry lived. In November 1923, Chen Duxiu explained the quick suppression of the first Haifeng Peasant Association as follows:

> 1.   Our comrades did not possess deep roots in peasant villages, and when they continuously stirred up economic conflict, this attracted opposition of the majority of middle peasants. These linked up with warlords and officialdom, and then suppressed them militarily.
> 2.   Huizhou [near Haifeng] was under the influence of the reactionary forces of Chen Jiongming. . . . Thus politics was also a reason.[106]

Peng Pai belonged to a rich and influential local family, as did Shen Xuanlu.[107] As a student in Japan, Peng came into contact with socialism and participated in a rent-reduction campaign in the Japanese countryside.[108] After returning to Haifeng, one of the two counties that make up Hailufeng, he joined the government of Chen Jiongming. Chen's reformist standing as well as Peng's roots in the Haifeng elite, his popularity among Haifeng students, and his political and educational background made him a perfect candidate for the job of head of the Haifeng Education Promotion Agency.[109]

Peng resigned from his education job in May 1922.[110] In August, he formed a peasant association,[111] urged on by his close friend Yang Sizhen, also a native of Haifeng, who had studied with Peng in Japan.[112] A September 1923 report to the Youth League Central Executive Committee presented the association's activities as follows:

> We plan to undertake the following twelve items: (1) preventing landlords from letting land lay fallow to guard against hardship in peasant lives and prevent the gradual decline of productivity resulting from a lack of fertilizer application; (2) in times of poor harvest or excessive lifestyles [of landlords], the society will investigate and apply to the landlord for rent reduction; (3) in case of trouble between members, we will do our utmost to solve the issue peacefully . . . ; (4) prohibit members from taking opium or gambling; (5) manage various levels of peasant schools . . . ; (6) organize agricultural affairs such as . . . afforestation, fertilizers, seeds, plowing methods, implements . . . ; (7) manage irrigation . . . ; (8) establish rural hospitals . . . ; (9) conduct surveys of peasant households, land use, harvest production . . . ; (12) set up a peasant militia to eradicate theft and robbery and protect agricultural products.[113]

As Robert Marks has pointed out, Chen Jiongming was widely hailed as an enlightened reformer.[114] The *Lu'an Daily*, distributed in Haifeng and neighboring Lufeng, suggests that local self-government was pursued vigorously in the county; there was a self-government bureau as well as elections for the presidency and vice presidency of the Haifeng District Assembly. Meetings of the assembly dealt with issues such as the destruction of the city wall, road construction, and relief granaries. It issued prohibitions of the sale of spoiled pork, revenge killings by the wife's family in case of suicide, and so on.[115]

Despite the reformist rhetoric, Haifeng society neared a state of anarchy. A chronology published in 1922 covering August 1921 to May 1922 repeatedly mentioned bandit attacks on transports, incidents of piracy and highway robbery, and police breakups of opium dens and gambling houses.[116] Given this situation, Peng's decision to form a peasant association might well have been the result of mounting disgust with the way Haifeng elites failed to use their new powers to rebuild local society. His decision to cut his relations with Haifeng elites seems to have sprung from the same discontent that led Mao Zedong and other communists to abandon their involvement in local elite political institutions.

Yang Sizhen recounted in a February 1923 letter how the association decided to move the local sweet-potato market to a new place so that it could levy its own market fees, with which it intended to finance a pharmacy. The landlords living near the old marketplace boycotted the move, for some time importing potatoes from elsewhere. In the standoff the association held firm, even though peasants feared the collapse of the new market.[117]

The peasant association quickly ran into entrenched local forces. It was shut down after it championed a rent-reduction campaign in August 1923. Association leaders appealed to landowners to accede to the campaign after two typhoons wrought damage in the area. The gentry, combined in an Association for the Support of Agriculture (Liangye Weichihui), refused any lowering of harvest rents, and their collectors beat up nonpayers and threw them in jail. The magistrate assisted the gentry. He closed down the association's headquarters, seizing all its property and documents. In the following days, its health clinic was also sealed up, and the police went into the countryside to collect membership cards from peasants.[118]

In setting up labor unions and peasant associations, CCP members constructed political and social institutions they hoped would replace existing power structures. Their activities illustrate that they viewed the entire social system as their target. Zhang Guotao sought to attack the warlord- and *bang*-dominated world of the Peking-Hankow railroad; Peng Pai and Shen Xuanlu attacked the rural political institutions in the control of traditional landholders and reformist elites.

The first attempts by CCP members to construct a new social and political order failed because they had few resources at their disposal. They lacked the organizational strength and capacity to coordinate their activities that might have enabled them to make better use of what was available. In addition, they expected that peasants and workers would immediately become their avid followers and that existing institutions would easily crumble away.

THE THIRD CONGRESS

In what was probably a draft of a speech to the Third Congress, Maring asserted that Mao Zedong—the man usually painted as possessed with an indefatigable faith in the powers of the Chinese—had expressed to him in the days before the congress a complete disbelief in the possibility of a revolution in China without assistance from Soviet communists (the English is as in the original): "Comrade Mao told me that Hunan has 30 millions population and 30 till 40 thousand modern workers. He is at the end of his Latin with labour-organization and was so pessimistic that he saw the only salvation of China in the intervention by Russia."[119] In Dutch, the phrase "to be at the end of one's Latin" means to be at a total loss about what to do after making numerous efforts.

If Mao Zedong had found in Marxism-Leninism at first a cause for new hope, by the time of the Third Congress, this had dissipated. He was not alone. Mao's despair was shared by the entire delegation from Hunan. In a letter to Comintern officials written shortly after the congress, Maring stated that the Hunan delegation had told him that "a mass party in China is impossible not only for Communists but also for the Nationalists."[120] Chen's comments in his Third Congress report also were not enthusiastic about the CCP's past.

The previous pages have indicated that CCP members had many reasons to be demoralized. The Third Congress may well have been intended as an occasion to heal wounds. Even if Chen's report was critical of the past, it spoke with acceptance about the bloc-within policy and asserted that the issue of Zhang Guotao's "small group" was now a matter of the past. Maring appears to have gone to the congress in the expectation that the congress would without further ado confirm in a resolution the approval of the bloc-within policy that CCP leaders had given at the Hangzhou meeting of August 1922. After Chen's speech, Maring even sought to soften its critical nature, "pointing out that [Chen Duxiu's] report was extremely pessimistic; with respect to the labor movement and political activism, there were achievements."[121]

However, before long, Maring himself launched into a tirade against the deficiencies of the CCP and a number of its members. The congress quickly turned into a scene of bitter struggle. What prompted Maring's change of attitude was that Cai Hesen and Zhang Guotao submitted a resolution to the congress designed to transform the bloc-within policy. In contrast to Mao Zedong, Chen Duxiu, and Maring himself, Maring's comments at the congress and letters by him to Comintern leaders in Moscow make it clear that the strike of Peking-Hankow Railroad workers was evidence to Zhang Guotao and Cai Hesen for the opposite idea. They believed that the strike had shown that in China a large labor movement was about to erupt and that the CCP could seize power if it would throw itself behind it.[122] On the basis of this conviction, they submitted to the congress the resolution reproduced in part below. It paid lip service to the bloc-within policy but was designed to strengthen the CCP as an independent organization and to have it undertake a labor movement separate from the KMT.

1. The third congress approves the thesis decided by the E.C.I. on the relation of C.P.C. to Kuomintan. . . .

2. The 3 congress acknowledges chinese proletariat occupies the important position in the national movement. In other words, the chinese proletariat in the future revolution will be at least one of factors in its leading.

3. Therefore chinese communist party in the recent period should with the proletarian independent flag organize labour mass and peasants, on the one side leading them to make national revolutionary movement. . . .

4. The third congress sees that under the present condition it is expedient to join Kuomintan. . . .[123]

ECI stands for Executive Committee of the [Communist] International. A copy of this resolution can be found in the Maring Archives. In the margin of the second item, the perplexed exclamation "What is this?" was written. (The English is as in the original.)

No doubt to Maring's great frustration, in support of their resolution Zhang Guotao and Cai Hesen quoted the January 1923 Comintern instruction to the CCP, the one that had resulted from Chen Duxiu's and other CCP members' visit to Moscow. We know this from Maring's speech to the Third Congress, which accused specifically Zhang Guotao of utterly misrepresenting this instruction, stating that "the interpretation of Chang Ko Tao [Zhang Guotao] . . . is absolutely wrong."[124] Since the Comintern instruction affirmed the importance for the CCP to maintain its own organization and construct a labor movement, Zhang and Cai could present it as supporting their resolution with some justification.

The opening paragraph of his draft speech suggested Maring's bewilderment. "Wanting to understand the minds of Chinese communists," he stated, "I put the question to Tschue Tsze Bo [Qu Qiubai]: please tell me in which way I must develop the viewpoint of the theses of Komintern and my interpretation in the conference [*sic*]."[125] With his authority and prestige at a low, Maring launched into a blistering attack on Zhang Guotao and Cai Hesen. In his tirade he first exclaimed that it was beyond his comprehension that CCP members suspected that his true aim for the bloc-within policy was the dissolution of the CCP in the KMT. He angrily rebutted the charge, pointing out that he of all people wanted to see Chinese communists succeed and that he had worked hard for this.[126] Here we may well have a basic reason for the clash between Maring and Zhang Guotao and Cai Hesen. The latter feared that the bloc-within policy would eventually result in the disappearance of the CCP, and they thought that Maring wanted this. For Maring, the seasoned revolutionary, the bloc-within was no more than a strategy, of no threat to the CCP. He may not have fully appreciated Zhang and Cai's anxieties.

The argument Maring put forth against Zhang and Cai's resolution was that "the exaggeration of our results in labourwork is ridiculous."[127] Referring to his conversations with Mao and with other CCP members involved in the labor movement, Maring remarked in his draft speech that China's workers were interested only in improving their economic positions and were not prepared to wage revolution, as they lacked class consciousness and political awareness. This is what he wrote about the Peking-Hankow Railroad workers (the English is again as in the original): "Even about the results in Hupeh [Hubei] we should not mislead ourselves. How we organized the railway union? What were these comrades appointed by the Communications department. . . . Why we went to workers under the flag of the Laboursecretariate and not of the Communist party?"[128] By "Communications department" was meant the Communications Clique. Besides calling into question Zhang Guotao's successes among Peking-Hankou Railroad workers, Maring pointed out that in Shanghai and Tianjin, with their large populations of industrial workers, the CCP had been unable to set up unions. He also warned that Chinese communists should not confuse union building and party building.[129]

Maring did not leave it at this. He first accused Zhang Guotao of unconstructive behavior by dividing CCP members into "leftists" and "rightists," a reference to Zhang's small group. He castigated Zhang's submission of his resolution as a contemptuous attempt to twist the meaning of the January 1923 Comintern directive. In apparent frustration, Maring remarked that the Comintern "supposes that even in CP of China there is something like discipline and cannot make its resolutions for China in such a way that some or other ingenious inventor manufactures arguments to make passive resistance . . . possible."[130] ("CP," also frequently used in CCP documents of the 1920s, refers to Communist Party.) Cai Hesen, he noted, "cannot analyze the conditions dialectically," and both Zhang and Cai, according to Maring, "base the tactic of our party on illusions and dreams."[131]

Despite these harsh statements, the draft speech also mentioned that he was not so pessimistic as Mao Zedong and that he did believe that in the future a labor movement under CCP control would indeed be possible in China. He remarked further, "I don't fear the contact of Chinese communists inside KMT with other tendencies. . . . I believe in our spiritual power."[132] CCP members, as Chen Duxiu remarked, did not yet possess great faith in their party; Maring, the seasoned Bolshevik, had lived by such faith for a long time.

Chen Duxiu and Maring won this battle, although not by much. In his postcongress letter to Comintern leaders, Maring revealed that the bloc-within policy, as expressed in a resolution submitted in the name of Chen Duxiu, had been passed 21–16. In elections for the Central Executive Committee, Zhang Guotao obtained only six votes, therefore losing his leadership position in the CCP.[133]

Despite the fact that the Third Congress degenerated into acrimony, when one steps back, it is clear that the idea of the party had in fact begun to take on a life of its own. Chen insisted that CCP members should have faith in their party and argued that Zhang Guotao was in fact loyal to it. Zhang and Cai Hesen followed Leninist procedures; they did not simply develop their activities as they deemed fit but submitted their ideas in the form of a resolution to be ratified by a party congress. The Third Congress adopted measures, as we shall see, to expand the CCP's central leadership institutions and to integrate the CCP. The idea that the CCP was to be a decentralized organization was no longer mentioned. Its supporters, including Li Hanjun, left the CCP.[134]

THE TRANSMISSION OF LENINIST CONCEPTS OF PARTY ORGANIZATION

Several authors have dealt with the impact of Soviet communists in China. For the early CCP especially, Alan Whiting's *Soviet Policies in China* is important. Whiting analyzed conflicts within the Comintern, pointing out the tension between Soviet national-security objectives and the Comintern's aim of promoting the world revolution.[135] Conrad Brandt dealt with the effect on China of the factional struggle between Stalin and Trotsky in 1926 and 1927; his points I discuss later. In this section I discuss the organizational concepts Comintern members transmitted to China. Using the case of Maring, I also analyze the personal dimension of the Comintern presence in China, in which half-articulated cultural values were not unimportant.

Information about Leninist organizational practices reached China not only from Moscow but also via Chinese students studying in Europe. The importance of this channel is suggested by the effect of Cai Hesen's letters on Mao Zedong. Mao Zedong gave wide currency to Cai's ideas when he printed three volumes of correspondence of the New Citizen Study Society, distributing them through the Culture Book Society.[136] The three volumes were organized to suggest that Cai's letters formed the grand climax in the debate on the reform of China waged in the New Citizen Study Society.

Cai Hesen himself made an impact upon his return to China. He arrived in Shanghai in November 1921 and at the Second Congress was elected the head of the CCP's Propaganda Department. He was editor of the *Guide Weekly* and was put in charge of the Education and Propaganda Committee established in November 1923.[137] As such, he was in a good position to exert influence in the CCP, and given his knowledge of Leninist organizational practices, to which his letters to Mao testified, it is likely that Cai contributed significantly to the Leninization of the CCP. Especially the Education and Propaganda Committee played a considerable role in this process, as the next section discusses.

Cai Hesen was not the only Chinese who studied in Europe and made an impact on the course of Chinese communism. One volume of a collection of primary documents concerning Chinese students in Europe reprinted nearly four hundred pages of writings by these students about Marxism-Leninism.[138] While written in Europe, many of these were printed in China in such leading periodicals as the *Morning Post* (Chenbao), the *Youth* (Shaonian), the *Improve the World Journal* (Yishibao), the *Times* (Shishi Xinbao). Zhou Enlai wrote "The October Revolution" and "The Religious Spirit and Communism" in the *Youth*.[139] Zhao Shiyan produced "The Lesson of the Russian Revolution" under the pseudonym "F," standing for the French *feu*, or "fire," an allusion to Lenin's *Iskra*, literally, "the spark."[140] He discussed such ideas as the proletariat, revisionism, and the Leninist party in "Chinese Students in France Should Wake Up."[141] Someone using the pseudonym Rui ("sharp") wrote "The New Soviet Republic and Imperialism."[142] Zhang Shenfu published "The Political Standpoint of People like Hu Shi and Us," in which he argued for a centralized Leninist party.[143] This list could easily be extended.

An important difference between the Comintern's depiction of communist parties and Cai Hesen's understanding of them was that despite his emphasis on the international aspects of the proletarian revolution, he did not locate authority in Moscow. For him, the Bolshevik Party was a model the Chinese should imitate but they themselves, not people in Moscow, should run. It was probably not coincidental that he figured prominently in Third Congress opposition to Maring, an opposition that was conducted in ways Cai no doubt understood as properly Leninist.

Even if it is clear that not only the Comintern documents and representatives transmitted Leninist organizational precepts to the CCP, it is undeniable that the Comintern affected the CCP profoundly. The First Congress made the CCP a branch of the Communist International.[144] Founded in March 1919 in Moscow, the Comintern was set up as a "communist party of communist parties." In the Comintern scheme, communist parties attached to it were the Comintern's branches. They sent delegates to

Comintern congresses in Moscow where they deliberated on and passed resolutions, and they elected an Executive Committee to form the leadership organization of the international communist movement.

As part of the Comintern's efforts to promote revolution around the globe, it produced manuals for communist party organization. An example of this is *An Outline for the Organizational Establishment, Work Methods, and Contents of a Communist Party* (Gongchandang de Zuzhi Jianshe, Gongzuo Fangfa, he Gongzuo Neirong).[145] There is no positive evidence that this blueprint found its way to China, even though this is likely, as I found it in a recent Chinese collection designed to document the Comintern's impact in China. However, the idea of the party as set out in the booklet was known to at least a number of CCP members, as several of them were present at the Third Comintern Congress of July 1921 that endorsed it.[146]

The booklet assigned considerable attention to democratic centralism (*minzhu jizhongzhi*) as the basic principle underlying party organization.[147] In institutional terms, according to this document, democratic centralism meant that party members in each area elected their own officers. The election did not take effect, however, until a higher-level leadership approved its outcome.[148] Democratic centralism, the booklet stated explicitly, also meant that members recognized the right of higher-level party functionaries to supervise and inspect their activities.[149] In turn, party members possessed the right to appeal to any higher-level unit in the party, including to the Comintern Central Executive Committee.[150] In justifying this arrangement, the Comintern explained that "centralism" was essential in "the creation and maintenance of a leadership which is strong and combative as well as resourceful and agile."[151] "Democracy" was regarded as a way of preventing the hegemony of a small group within the party.[152] Marxists, of course, do not admit to democracy as an end in itself.

Lenin had not paid much attention to democracy inside the party, depicting an ideal of the party as a Prussian army unquestioningly executing the orders of party leaders. Democratic centralism reflected Lenin's insistence on central leadership but also suggested a tension between the idea that a party member was a cog in the party's machine and that each communist was a new man, transformed and enlightened by a proletarian class consciousness and part of the vanguard that would bring about the new age. The Comintern booklet stated that within the party, members could say what they wished under the condition that they obeyed party discipline and in public supported party policy:

All party members must always show that they are a member of a combat organization obeying discipline when they speak among the masses. If differences of opinion emerge about whether or not the approach is correct about a certain issue, they must as much as possible carry out discussions within the party organization before speaking out among the masses. . . . If the resolution of a party organization or leadership institution follows the views of other members—or worse, is wrong—when they speak among the masses, these members should never forget, weaken, or break the unity of our ranks; this would constitute an extremely undesirable violation of party discipline and a highly undesirable mistake in revolutionary struggle.[153]

Lenin had emphasized the importance of a centrally controlled party press to foster an esprit de corps among the diverse constituencies of the party and promote the charismatic image of the party in society. The blueprint described in great detail how a party press should be organized, what kinds of topics should be covered, and how articles should be written.[154] It noted that party papers should jealously guard their financial independence and that while propaganda was to be as appealing to workers as possible, it should remain serious and dignified: "Our party papers ought never to cater to 'the masses,' publishing news or diversions they would find merely pleasant."[155]

Lenin did not address issues involved in basic party organization and party units' forming an alternative type of social order. The blueprint did describe in detail the functioning of party cells. They were to be set up in factories, labor unions, army troops, and so on,[156] in places in the existing social and economic structure where party members had accumulated, and they were to constitute the "kernels" of the party, responsible for carrying out the "daily activities of the party such as house-by-house propaganda, . . . service in party periodicals and papers, the sale of books, information gathering, and liaison."[157]

Two comments must be made. First, handbooks such as the one described were not simply technical instruction manuals. They reflected the images and ideals their authors had of their party, and to some extent they served propaganda purposes. The handbook was suffused with the idea that workers would naturally swarm to communist party institutions. Its description of democratic centralism emphasized the democratic rights of party members, which probably were not a reality in the Bolshevik Party, even before the days of Stalin. Cai Hesen and Zhang Guotao may well have believed that they acted as good Leninists when they opposed Maring, and Maring equally may have thought that they subordinated his higher authority in a way that revealed their ignorance, especially of what "party discipline" meant.

Second, even though Maring and CCP members were all communists, they were imbued by different cultures and had different institutional allegiances. Like all such relations, cultural values and misunderstanding affected the impact of the Comintern in China. Maring's involvement in the CCP highlights the intricacy of the relationship.

When Maring arrived in China, he at first made little impact. However, he was a determined man, one who was fully confident of the correctness of his own prescriptions for the CCP. He clashed with CCP members, but the result of this was that Chinese communists did begin to treat the Comintern in Moscow as a higher authority. Even if regionalism allowed Chinese communists to avoid the bloc-within policy, one result of Maring's persistence in its promotion was that Chinese communists went over his head, appealing to Maring's bosses in Moscow. In other words, they treated the Comintern as something like an adjudicatory agent.

When CCP leaders accepted the bloc-within policy at the Hangzhou meeting but then immediately traveled to Moscow, they may have thought that they were acting with circumspection and with a degree of respect for Maring. However, it evoked bewilderment and anger in Maring. For CCP members, party members were supposed to be "friends," even if reality was not like that, and meetings had the purpose in part of displaying and celebrating mutual respect. Maring, on the other hand, approached meetings very differently. For him, they were to be conducted with the focus on the issues and in a frank and open atmosphere, so that things could get done; anything else he probably saw as a display of petty backhandedness that could indicate only that one was not a mature communist.

Such different perceptions of meetings and of the proper way to settle conflicts likely contributed to Maring's difficult relation with Zhang Guotao. Their problems were not confined to the Third Congress. One reason for Maring to convene the Hangzhou meeting was to deal with Zhang Guotao's small group. Maring raised the issue of the small group in one of the Hangzhou sessions, and at one point, according to Zhang Guotao, pulled a resolution out of his pocket that warned about unwitting factionalist tendencies of some CCP members. This was aimed at Zhang's small group. Maring may well have intended this as a way of clearing the air in the CCP, but Zhang's memoirs suggest that he felt mortally insulted at being made the butt of public criticism. The small group was of course no secret to any of those who attended the Hangzhou meeting. In the end, one of the Chinese participants suggested that there was no need for Maring's resolution. But according to Zhang, those present at the meeting also refused to vote it down out of respect for Maring and adopted the solution to ''let it lie where it was'' without any action.[158]

Maring left China shortly after the Third Congress, first traveling to Moscow and then to the Netherlands. Documents in the Maring Archive suggest that he ran afoul of Comintern leaders, in part because they objected to his incessant demands for special favors.[159] They also may have worried about the antagonism he evoked among CCP members. After the Comintern turned down Maring's requests to be sent back to China, he wrote Sun Yatsen and Chiang Kai-shek independently, proposing that the KMT hire him directly. He suggested that among other things he could help them in writing propaganda.[160]

Comintern agents were important in many ways. They transmitted funds and literature, provided concrete organizational advice, and contributed to the formulation of strategy. In addition, they exemplified, consciously or not, organizational attitudes and styles of behavior that diverged from those of their hosts. Even if relations between CCP members and Comintern agents were explosive, by the time of the Third Congress, all CCP members were in a position to know a good deal about how a Leninist party was run, and their contacts with Comintern agents might have alerted them to some of the ways their attitudes toward meetings, workers, or central leadership were ''un-Leninist.'' Combined with the return of students from Europe, this meant that a base for the Leninization of the CCP was in place.

FIRST STEPS TOWARD CENTRALIZATION, 1923–1925

In the year and a half between the Third Congress of June 1923 and the Fourth Congress of January 1925, the CCP undertook few eye-catching activities. There were no large-scale demonstrations or major attempts to set up labor unions or peasant movements. Even within the KMT the CCP's activities remained limited, in part because the KMT was still organizing itself.

But beneath this calm surface important organizational changes took place in the CCP. Beginning with the Third Congress, CCP documents began to envision a unified party under homogeneous leadership, with a local structure based on cells. Documents outlined systems for internal supervision and communication, and provided for a number of centralized task-oriented bureaucracies. They also formulated new methods of constructing labor unions and announced a new labor-movement strategy. A leadership meeting of May 1924 formed an important watershed. The

Fourth Congress of January 1925, on the whole, did no more than endorse resolutions taken at this meeting.

Concrete results were achieved at the central level, most notably in devising ways to bring regional representatives together. Although after the Fourth Congress leadership strife would break out once more, at the time of the congress itself, it seemed that leadership conflict was a thing of the past. In other areas reforms were announced but failed to lead to actual changes in the operation of the CCP. Even if the new party had not become a reality, the reforms reflected a new attitude, at least among those CCP members who produced the documents announcing the reforms, one in which study-society relations were no longer essential and in which the party, rather than individuals or a regional group of communists, assumed a far greater role. An important bridge was crossed.

The Central Executive Committee

Until the Third Congress, the CCP had been a regionally fragmented party whose leaders rarely met, and when they did so, they ended up fighting each other. In response, the Third Congress first established a Central Executive Committee. The "Rules for the Organization of the CCP Central Executive Committee" provided for a Central Executive Committee of nine members.[161] These were to meet immediately after a party congress to elect from among themselves a five-member Central Bureau, and subsequently they were to convene a meeting every four months.[162] The remaining four were each assigned to a regional executive committee to supervise CCP activity under that committee's jurisdiction,[163] thus establishing an institutional link between the center and local CCP units.

Central Executive Committee Meetings Three Central Executive Committee meetings took place between the Third Congress of June 1923 and the Fourth Congress of January 1925. The first was held in November 1923, the next in February 1924, and the last the following May. The reports and resolutions of the first and third are extant; one resolution is available for the second.[164]

Central Executive Committee meetings lacked the emotional altercations that characterized CCP congresses. The reports and resolutions of the meetings give the impression that they were businesslike affairs in which the participants gave frank accounts of the party affairs for which they were responsible and problems were dealt with in a constructive way.

To give a few examples, the November 1923 Central Bureau report straightforwardly explained the bureau's difficulties in publishing the party's periodicals on schedule.[165] It also analyzed internal CCP resistance to the bloc-within policy and examined in detail the failure of the early labor and peasant movements.[166] The report also noted that the *Guide* had achieved some popularity, with the result that "after the congress, the anti-imperialist atmosphere slowly thickened."[167]

The reports from the regional delegates were also candid. In November 1923 the Shanghai delegate to the Central Executive Committee reported on the fragmented condition of his committee and examined at length the reasons for the inability of communists in Shanghai to bring about a labor movement.[168] The Peking representative brought up the wrangling between KMT and CCP members, and he admitted that CCP work among students and workers had failed to generate any response.[169] A delegate from Hankou revealed that few of the forty-seven local members paid much attention to shouldering organizational tasks or conducting propaganda. "Students like to criticize," it stated, referring to a constituency that probably accounted for the vast majority of party members, "but they do not work very hard, while workers are too immature in their ideology and cannot take responsibility for activities by themselves."[170] All reports to both the November 1923 and the May 1924 Central Executive Committee meetings were filled with no-nonsense comments.

Opposition to the Bloc-within Policy   The bloc-within policy had exactly the opposite effect on the CCP as the one Zhang Guotao and Cai Hesen feared. Instead of dissolving the CCP in the KMT, it provided its members with an object against which to define themselves and thus served to strengthen the identification of CCP members with their party as a whole. This happened because the bloc-within policy forced the leaders of the CCP's regional units to cooperate and to develop ways to safeguard the unity of CCP members active in the KMT and to exploit their positions to maximum advantage.

It was in Central Executive Committee meetings that CCP leaders formulated a common strategy toward the KMT. After the Third Congress, Zhang Guotao continued to mobilize support for his position. In November 1923, he wrote a letter to Voitinsky in Moscow in response to Voitinsky's request for Zhang to give his view on rumors that he had attempted after the Third Congress to stage a coup within the CCP. Zhang explained: "Immediately after the closure of the congress, its errors were revealed. In several CCP branches, opposition strengthened about the issue of our relation with the KMT; a majority probably opposed. Next, such large branches as those of Changsha, Hankow, and Peking devised a way to convene immediately a party congress to resolve the issue."[171] Statutorily, such a congress would have to be convened if a majority of regional com-

mittees demanded it.[172] The above-mentioned regional executive committees desisted, according to Zhang, because of his intervention.[173]

What happened in reality was that regional and central CCP leaders
used Central Executive Committee meetings to develop a joint strategy
toward the KMT. It was the issue of the bloc-within policy that provided
the substance of most of their meetings. The November 1923 meeting led
to a resolution that ordered CCP members to recruit into the KMT as
many people as possible who would be sympathetic to the CCP. It instructed them to focus on workers, students, and professionals—most
likely to oppose traditional gentry, bureaucrats, and warlord elements in
the KMT.[174] At the same time, it instructed "CCP members active in the
KMT to form one secret organization, and in all political statements and
actions they must follow the leadership of this party."[175] This instruction
was issued in anticipation of the First Congress of a reorganized KMT,
held in January 1924, to make sure that its elections and resolutions would
be as favorable to the CCP as possible.

The policy brought results. During the KMT's First Congress, CCP
members succeeded in obtaining election to the highest KMT bodies, and
CCP members were placed in charge of the crucial Organization Department as well as the Peasant Department. Moreover, the congress resulted
in an overwhelming defeat for those elements in the KMT that opposed
the CCP.[176] In its report to the May 1924 meeting, the Central Bureau
claimed that organized opposition to the KMT had now disappeared:

> Serious wrangling arose at the time of the congresses of the C.P.
> [*sic*] and the S.Y. In recent months it gradually eased, and after
> the publication of the resolution of the second Central Executive
> Committee at the end of February, it completely died out. The
> Central Bureau can guarantee that the so-called small group
> association no longer is a reality, and from now on comrades
> should not indulge in wild speculations that hamper the
> development of the party.[177]

Within the KMT, the success of the CCP's strategy produced a backlash,
however. Strong voices called for the curtailment of the activities of CCP
members in the KMT. In response, the May 1924 Central Executive Committee, at which Voitinsky was present,[178] produced a policy that divided
the KMT into a left and a right wing and declared that the CCP supported
only the left wing. It also declared that the CCP's task now was to establish
an independent CCP base among urban workers by organizing unions
under direct CCP control and not in the name of the KMT.[179]

The May 1924 "Resolution on Issues in the CCP's Work in the KMT" analyzed the future of the KMT and the United Front on the basis of a class analysis of the KMT's constituency. It noted that the KMT had strengthened as a party and also that workers' unions had begun to re-emerge following the setback suffered in the aftermath of the Peking-Han-kow Railroad strike. According to the resolution, "A large part of KMT members in fact clearly tended to be part of the industrial and agricultural bourgeoisie and sidestepped the anti-imperialist struggle; their class inter-est and those of the working people will in the future of course not be identical."[180] This KMT constituency, the resolution argued, would tend toward compromise with imperialist forces. Within the KMT, it stated, two factions had coagulated: the left wing, under Sun Yatsen's leadership, which was committed to a national revolution, and the right wing, with members who were too attached to foreign and warlord interests to "strug-gle until the Chinese people reach complete independence."[181] The resolu-tion also argued that "we will be of most help to the KMT if we first set up labor unions for pure class struggle."[182] "Our party serves the KMT best," it stated, "not by assisting them to set up KMT unions. . . . They would simply disappear in the KMT and lose their class nature."[183]

Two comments should be made here. First, this was by and large the policy Zhang Guotao and Cai Hesen had proposed to the Third Congress. It was designed, it seems, to cater both to those who wanted an independent CCP and those who favored a bloc-within policy. Second, it presented the change in CCP policy, as announced in CCP documents, as the result of changes in class relations and their impact on the KMT. This was an important innovation in the way CCP members made their arguments. The development signaled a growing familiarity of Chinese communists with styles particular to Leninist parties. Its timing, as well as the fact that it was the participants in Central Executive Committee meetings who took the lead, suggests that the language of Marxism-Leninism began to be used as a basis for communication and cooperation, when CCP members could easily have fallen back on regional or study-society modes of behav-ior, and the CCP began to function as a unified organization.

According to the Russian historian Glunin, Voitinsky was in part re-sponsible for the May 1924 reformulation of the bloc-within policy and had the support of Comintern leaders.[184] Chinese communists could refer to the January 1923 Comintern instruction that Zhang Guotao and Cai Hesen had quoted. However, they knew that Maring had opposed Zhang and Cai's interpretation of it in the name of the Comintern. Voitinsky's support was probably important to the adoption of a limited concept of the bloc-within policy at the May 1924 Central Executive Committee meeting; however, CCP members had already been moving in this direction. A month before the congress, Chen Duxiu had outlined a concept of the KMT as consisting of a right wing and a left wing, stating that the CCP should support the "real" KMT, the one consisting of the left wing.[185]

The Central Bureau

Besides setting up the Central Executive Committee, the Third Congress adopted regulations for a Central Bureau. At its first meeting after a congress, the Central Executive Committee was not only to elect five of its members to the Central Bureau, which "exercises authority in the name of the Central Executive Committee,"[186] but also to appoint three of the five to specific Central Bureau offices. There was a chair (*weiyuanzhang*), a secretary (*mishu*), and a financial officer (*kuaiji*). The chair's responsibility was to preside over all Central Executive Committee and Central Bureau meetings; the secretary handled communications; and the financial officer looked after the CCP's coffers.[187] After the Third Congress, the Central Executive Committee returned Chen Duxiu to the chairmanship, Mao Zedong became the secretary, and Luo Zhanglong was placed in charge of finances.[188]

Following the Third Congress, the Central Bureau established its offices in the Zhabei district in Shanghai, in a building its inhabitants referred to as the Three Household Mansion (*Sanhulou*).[189] Here lived Luo Zhanglong, Mao Zedong, and Cai Hesen, all Central Bureau members, together with their families, including Mao's two children. They operated under the cover of being an Assistance Bureau for Customs Declarations (*Baoguanhang*). In Shanghai, the foreign Inspectorate of Customs had since 1854 handled China's customs, forcing Chinese to seek assistance in filling out forms.[190]

At the Three Household Mansion, Central Bureau officers drafted CCP documents, prepared meetings of the Central Executive Committee, and put together CCP periodicals, including the *Guide*. It was the place where Central Bureau members met for their statutory weekly meetings.[191] Chen Duxiu lived elsewhere, but a bed was kept ready for him in case he was forced to spend the night. The Central Bureau was also an information-gathering unit. Besides receiving whatever reports were sent in, the Central Bureau subscribed to a variety of newspapers and magazines, including the *News* (Xinwenbao), the venerable *Shanghai Herald* (Shenbao), the *Shanghai Citizen Daily* (Shanghai Guomin Ribao), and, of course, Comintern periodicals.[192]

After the establishment of the Central Bureau, an internal-communications network developed in the CCP. Central Executive Committee announcements (*zhongyang tonggao*) were essential in this. In accordance with its power to act for the Central Executive Committee, officers of the Central Bureau could issue announcements in the name of the Central Executive Committee. Central Executive Committee announcements required the signature of the chair and the secretary. According to Luo Zhanglong's recollection, some twenty-five announcements saw light of day between the Third and Fourth Congresses; in other words, they were produced at the rate of two per month on average.[193] For the period of June 1923 to January 1925, eight of these are extant.[194]

Announcements usually went out after each Central Executive Committee meeting to parlay its decisions in short form to the membership. Announcement 13, of December 1923, detailed the November Central Executive Committee's measures altering the CCP's approach to the bloc-within policy.[195] The Central Bureau staff also used announcements to instruct CCP members on how to respond to sudden events. Announcement 17 outlined the CCP view on the event of an outbreak of warlord fighting.[196] Announcements were targeted usually to a specific audience in the party hierarchy, such as all regional committee members or cell heads. They were short and carried concise instructions for one or more (sometimes unrelated) tasks.

In May 1924, the Central Executive Committee revamped the CCP's central institutions. Three departments were set up within the Central Bureau, one for propaganda, one for organization, and one for workers and peasants. The change was to be carried out throughout the CCP, with chairs taking charge of propaganda departments (*xuanchuanbu*), secretaries becoming the heads of organization departments (*zuzhibu*), and the directorships of the workers and peasant departments (*gong-nongbu*) going to the financial officers. It may be that the earlier terminology—chair, secretary, and financial officer—resulted from the influence of traditional British organizational nomenclature, which may have been strong especially in the lower Yangtze area.

The same meeting created labor union movement committees (*gonghui yundong weiyuanhui*). At the central level, the committee was situated within the Workers and Peasant Department, and it issued instructions directly to lower-level committees. This created a separate hierarchy in the party apart from local, regional, and central executive committees.[197]

The post of inspector (*xunxing zhidaoshi*) was another innovation of the May 1924 Central Executive Committee meeting. An inspector was a roving commissioner who filed monthly reports on the central and regional CCP institutions he visited. They were intended to increase Central Bureau information about CCP affairs and to strengthen its control over regional CCP units.

Formally the Central Executive Committee was the policy-making body, but in a time of crisis it was difficult for Central Executive Committee members to be convened. Announcements gave Central Bureau members a tool to direct CCP activities centrally. Once Central Executive Committee meetings had resulted in a degree of commonality among the regional power centers in the CCP and internal communications networks had grown up, the Central Bureau made a first attempt to act entirely on its own initiative. Sun Yatsen's departure from Canton on November 13, 1924, to participate in a warlord reconciliation conference provided a suitable crisis.

Sun's participation in the conference required an immediate CCP response since a settlement between Sun and the warlords was bound to lock out the communists.[198] While CCP members in the KMT were first told to oppose the move, a November 1924 Central Executive Committee announcement retracted this. It instructed CCP members to form "national congress promotion associations" (*guomin huiyi cuchenghui*) around the country and to have the members of these associations send letters to Sun exhorting him to adhere to the KMT's First Congress platform, which precluded any compromise of its nationalist program or its cooperation with the CCP.[199] This, then, was a CCP attempt to influence the agenda of the conference. In the end, CCP fears did not materialize because Sun's death on March 12, 1925, created an opportunity for strong left-wing KMT leaders to seize the helm of their party.[200]

Internal Propaganda

After the Third Congress, CCP leaders set up a system of internal propaganda, using it to promote Leninist organizational procedures and attitudes. In the first years of the CCP, the idea was prevalent that even if not all members knew a great deal about Marxism or Leninist organization, they were all revolutionaries who would cooperate smoothly with each other. If friction occurred, it was understood as resulting from a lack of knowledge about doctrine or the procedures and attitudes proper to a communist party. This is how Maring and Chen Duxiu explained the behavior of Zhang Guotao.

The installation of an internal-propaganda system entailed an important departure from this concept of the party. At first, internal propaganda may well have been conceived of as no more than a simple measure to ensure that understandable holes in the knowledge of Marxism-Leninism among CCP members were filled. However, before long, a subtle but decisive change occurred when CCP documents began to picture a membership in which some required education but others were regarded as mature members. This formed the conceptual base, on the one hand, for mass recruitment, as the idea was abandoned that all CCP members were to be perfect communists and, on the other, for the creation of institutions designed to enforce internal discipline.

The November 1923 Central Executive Committee meeting passed the "Resolution on Education and Propaganda,"[201] and it was this resolution that started the CCP on the road toward a party with strong disciplinary institutions. As mentioned, it was Cai Hesen who headed the committee. The resolution contained detailed prescriptions on CCP opinions on a range of important issues and made some provisions for "internal education." It was quickly followed by a letter from the Central Bureau to all CCP units in which the organization of a propaganda system was laid out. At the central level, the CCP and the Youth League were to constitute a joint Committee on Education and Propaganda.[202] The regulations for the committee envisioned five departments—editing, printing, mail, translation, and editorial reference.[203] The November 1923 resolution also directed local CCP and Socialist Youth League members to convene joint sessions to discuss the contents of CCP periodicals, resolutions, the CCP constitution, and important articles, and to listen to lectures on CCP policy and organization.[204] The local representative of the Committee on Education and Propaganda was to report on the proceedings of these meetings.[205]

To convey its documents to the rank-and-file membership, the Central Executive Committee (CEC) set up the *Party Journal*, thus distributing the documents to be discussed by the joint CCP and Youth League meetings. Besides the reports to and resolutions of the November 1923 meeting, the journal's first issue, dated November 30, contained a piece entitled, significantly, "The Reasons for the Existence of the Chinese Communist Party."[206] It disputed the idea that "since the present situation in China today is that of cooperation between various classes for the national revolution, . . . there seems to be no need for the CCP,"[207] an idea of which Cai Hesen lived in fear. Issues of the *Party Journal* appeared after each CEC meeting.[208] All members received one copy gratis.

The May 1924 CEC meeting abolished the joint Youth League and CCP sessions, instructing CCP cells to take over their function.[209] Until the May 1924 meeting, the Youth League and CCP were not clearly separated, and therefore the distinction was irrelevant. However, a May 1924 resolution separated the two, setting an upper age limit for Youth League members of twenty-five. It also stated that the task of the Youth League was to create a youth movement among workers and peasant youths as well as students.[210]

Party Cells (Zu) *and Party Blocs* (Dangtuan)

Cells and party blocs were to become the basis for the CCP's penetration of society. An important point about cells, as the Comintern handbook pointed out, was that they should be formed not on the basis of geographic proximity, friendship ties, or educational achievement but should be made up of CCP members in one socioeconomic unit. Two effects seem to have been intended. First, in grafting the CCP directly onto the socioeconomic system, the party maximized its leverage in society. For instance, if communist teachers in a school set up a cell, they immediately formed a powerful bloc within a much larger institution because party discipline compelled them to act as one unit. Even if only a few penetrated that school's ruling bodies, a cell could affect a great many people. Second, by combining party members with different tasks into one cell, divisions along functional lines were weakened. Zhang Guotao's small group had shown the dangers of this.

The terminological history of cells is as follows: The first CCP constitution of July 1922 stipulated that party members living in one peasant village, working in one factory, or studying at the same institution should form "groups" (*zu*).[211] The Third Congress redefined these as "cells" (*xiaozu*), and the Fourth Congress rebaptized them as "branches" (*zhibu*).[212] In order to follow CCP usage and yet not create too much confusion, as mentioned, I use *cell* in this chapter; in chapters 4 and 5, I switch to *branch*.

To base the CCP on cells, it was necessary to remove CCP members from their original social networks and have them adopt their cells as the central unit in their lives. This was by no means easily achieved. It was probably not coincidental that cells were first set up in the city where few traditional ties bound communists together. CCP members in Shanghai drew up membership lists for cells for the first time in July 1923.[213] In allocating members to cells, the principle was still "to place into one cell all members living closely together,"[214] as a recent scholarly article based on materials in Shanghai archives stated.

In May 1924, the Central Executive Committee released a "Resolution on Problems of Internal Organization and Propaganda." It was this document that for the first time called on all CCP members to construct cells. An important task of the cells was the instruction and supervision of new CCP members. However, they also were to serve expansionary purposes. The resolution stated that "besides recruiting and educating party members, cells must frequently undertake propaganda activities among the masses of workers."[215] A Central Committee announcement of November

1924 made cells responsible not just for instilling CCP values and organiza-tional forms in the membership but also for the allocation of tasks to the rank-and-file party member.[216] The cell, then, was to be the point of connection between party members and the CCP as a whole, as well as between the CCP and Chinese society.

The difference between a CCP bloc and a CCP cell was that a bloc combined party members in one type of activity, such as making propa-ganda. Even if communist parties were designed to avoid functional spe-cialization, which would endanger the identification of the party member with the party as a whole, it was expedient if not crucial also to create mechanisms that could bring members engaged in one type of activity into one unit. However, each member of a bloc was also a member of a cell—the opposite is not true—and blocs were to take their orders from the primary CCP hierarchy of cells, local committees, regional committees, and the Central Committee.[217]

The word *bloc* was first used in the "Resolution on Organization" of the Fourth Congress, which stated that "in the Kuomintang and in other significant political entities the party must form party blocs and so control their activities."[218] CCP members operating in the KMT formed a natural bloc; a resolution of the November 1923 Central Executive Committee stated that "our party members working in the KMT must form secret groups and must accept CCP guidance in their political utterances and actions."[219] In June 1924, one Comintern agent noted the problem of maintaining the allegiance of CCP members in the KMT to the CCP when he stated that "after the CCP had joined the KMT for three months . . . we noticed the mixing in of a good many right-wing KMT people, and therefore we had to organize party blocs."[220] In this way, the bloc-within policy stimulated CCP members to define their own identity and to set up institutions strengthening it.

Blocs were also essential in making the most out of the CCP presence in the KMT. The CCP bloc in the KMT was soon used for such offensive purposes. The February 1924 "Resolution on the Attitude and Activities of Our Comrades in the KMT" directed CCP members in the KMT to acquire KMT posts "in order to help with and supervise the conduct of KMT affairs."[221] Central Executive Announcement 15, of July 1924, in-structed CCP members operating in the KMT to take action against the KMT right wing.

While the bloc of CCP members in the KMT was more or less a reality, this was not the case for cells, at least outside Shanghai. In November 1924, just two months before the Fifth Congress, CEC Announcement 21 still had to set out the basics:

1. Cells and local committees must convene meetings in accordance with the regulations, and without interruptions.

2. At meetings, you must frequently raise concrete political issues for discussion. . . .

3. Those in charge of party branches and cell heads must draw up plans of action and allocate responsibilities to each member to train each comrade to become a truly capable party member.

4. Whenever you receive Central Bureau documents, you must present them for discussion to your meetings; you must carry them out to the extent of your capabilities, and you must report at appropriate times whether you encounter difficulties and what results you have achieved.

5. Committee chairs and cell leaders must report at least once a week to the Central Bureau.[222]

Union Cells (Gonghui Xiaozu) and a New Labor-Movement Policy

Union cells, cells of workers in one factory, were the result of the realization of communists that *bang*, gangs, and Triads were not the CCP's natural allies. Even before the disaster of the February 7 strike, a CCP plan of action for the labor movement had already commented that "only a system of committees in factories that eliminates obstacles created by such middlemen as foremen . . . can succeed in extending the force of workers into units of production themselves."[223] A May 1924 CEC resolution stated unambiguously that "the party and the unions must attack regionalist and secret-society concepts among workers."[224]

The May 1924 CEC resolution on the CCP's labor-union activities called on CCP members to create union cells from small groups of workers. A union cell was to be confined to one section of a factory and could be further subdivided into "leagues of ten" (*shirentuan*) if necessary. Union cells were regularly to conduct meetings—flash meetings if security reasons prevented more elaborate ones—to discuss concrete labor and wage issues as they existed in the factory, opportunities the CCP members in the cell were to use for the promotion of CCP policies as well.[225]

A further change in the CCP's labor-movement strategy was its relocation to cities with heavy foreign influence. In 1923, members of the CEC decided to focus labor-movement activities on railroad, water transport, and mining industries[226]—all areas of economic activity in which foreigners were highly visible. A resolution of the May 1924 CEC meeting explained: "The power of foreign capitalists is greatest in the shipbuilding industry, railroads, and sea and river transport. To organize these workers is the most suitable way of fighting the power of foreign capital and opposing imperialism."[227] The change fitted the CCP's loudly proclaimed anti-imperialist rhetoric. It also minimized the risk of conflicts with domestic industrialists, thus diminishing the likelihood of friction with the KMT.

Cells enabled the CCP to restructure the relationship of its members to one another and to society. Party cells embedded CCP members in a network of other CCP members, thus fostering identification with the CCP. They were efficient ways of recruiting and training new members, as each cell could be under the control of a few "seasoned comrades." In calling for the creation of union cells, the May 1924 CEC resolution in fact moved toward a system of intermeshing networks, one consisting of CCP members and one of workers in labor unions. This system made optimum use of the CCP's limited manpower, and it reduced problems of security due to the insularity of cells. The great advantage of this new method of implanting the CCP in Chinese society was that it made the CCP independent of traditional social forces like warlords or gangs. It was for an organization without any independent source of power the best possible means of penetrating the social structure.

Fourth Congress resolutions made clear that the reorganization of the labor movement had not progressed far. Besides blaming increased imperialist and warlord repression, and reiterating the powers among workers of traditional labor organizations like gangs, the resolution on the labor movement stated the following about the CCP's activities:

> In the past our activities have been too technical. We were pure union secretaries. Now we must immediately begin with the real work of the party: the political education of the masses of workers, as well as the organizing of the party among them. . . .
> The enlarged Central Executive Committee (May last year) has already pointed out the imperfections in our previous methods of union organization and also resolved to engage in the task of "factory cells." However, the results have been minimal.[228]

While many of the reforms did not become a reality, especially not those designed to alter the fundamental structure of the CCP and its interaction with Chinese society, the proceedings of the Fourth Congress suggested that at least at the central level, Leninist organizational ideas had taken hold.

The congress was originally planned to begin on November 15, 1924. In August, the Central Bureau sent a letter to all party organizations and cells to compile reports containing an evaluation of all policies and programs conducted in the preceding year. These reports were to be discussed by the appropriate meetings of party members and then forwarded to the Central Bureau. If individual members wished to do so, they could ask the committee chair or the cell leader to forward a letter expressing their views. On September 15, the Central Bureau issued the formal congress announcement, which made clear that congress delegates would represent regions rather than a number of members. Each place where the CCP was active was instructed to elect one representative to attend the congress. The Soviet Union and Europe each was also to send a delegate, and the Socialist Youth League and the Comintern were represented. The congress was postponed to January when it became clear that it would be impossible for the Comintern delegate to arrive in time for the original opening date.[229]

The above suggests that external circumstances were responsible for the fact that the congress opened half a year after it should have done statutorily. In this half year there were no CEC meetings, probably for the same reason. No major institutional changes were introduced between the May 1924 CEC meeting and the Fourth Congress. The congress by and large restricted itself to approving and reformulating resolutions of the May 1924 CEC meeting. In this period the CCP's most visible activities were restricted to dealing with Sun Yatsen's participation in the reconciliation conference and the CCP's attempts to influence its outcome by setting up national congress promotion associations.

From January 11 to January 22, the congress met in a schoolhouse located in the Zhabei section of Shanghai on the border of the International Concession, so that neither the Concession police nor the Chinese police would feel eager to intervene. The participants were instructed to be prepared to act like students in case a police raid should take place. The congress was well prepared and smoothly executed. A drafting committee had prepared resolutions in advance, which at the congress were discussed in specially designated committees. The old Central Bureau had put together a slate for the new Central Executive Committee.[230]

One witness of the congress, Peng Shuzhi, had returned from Moscow just before its opening. He was elected by the congress to the CEC. He saw in the smoothness of the congress proceedings a sign that the CCP had overcome the problems of the past and was solidly set on the way to becoming a Leninist party. With apparent relief, he wrote to friends in Moscow on February 2, 1925: "The atmosphere at the congress was excellent, displaying a spirit of close unity. The delegates from all places manifested a loyal as well as enthusiastic acceptance of the congress's lessons. We can say that having gone through this congress, our Party has moved from the stage of a small association into that of a real Party."[231] Zhang

Bojian, another student who had returned from Moscow just before the congress, agreed that "we can believe that the CP . . . is moving towards Bolshevization."[232]

Peng and Zhang spoke of their hope that the CCP was changing. They did not say that the process was completed. Fourth Congress documents sharpened the distinction between fully mature CCP members and ones who had yet to be educated in the CCP's ideology and organization, and they presented the realization of the new party model as a struggle of CCP leaders against the backwardness and inertia of the general CCP membership. The "Resolution on Organizational Problems" stated:

> The congress on the one hand approves in general the resolutions on organizational issues passed by the enlarged Central Executive Committee meeting of May 1924. On the other hand, it also must acknowledge that before August of the same year most were not put into practice either at the central or at the local level. Besides objective reasons (lack of personnel and financial shortages; warlord oppression; arrest of several cadres), . . . we must point out another reason, namely that cadres at all levels of the party neglected the implementation of these resolutions, and that local party members really did not understand them very well.[233]

"Cadre" here translates *fu zeren zhi tongzhi* (a comrade with responsibility). It should be kept in mind that the CCP had only a thousand members; it was not yet a mass party.

The persistence of traditional habits was not, as these documents suggested, simply the result of CCP members blindly clinging to outmoded ways. CCP members, especially those operating in local society, were no doubt conscious of the dangers involved in cutting their old attachments and staking their lives entirely on what at the time was a young party with very few successes to its name, as CCP documents insisted that they should. No matter what the level of ideological commitment of these members was, most were probably quite hesitant to take such a serious step. Inspired by the communist vision of a better society, some probably took the step with enthusiasm. Others may have done so with some hesitation, but no doubt there were also those who played it safe. The next chapter will describe how the CCP itself withdrew from this radical demand on CCP members, drawing the distinction between Chinese society and the world of the CCP in a less radical way.

However, at the time of the Fourth Congress, CCP leaders had declared war on all aspects of the old society. CCP documents suggested not only that the CCP should fight "backwardness" but that the success of the CCP depended on this. It was not simply one of the tasks CCP members had set themselves; its accomplishment was portrayed as a prerequisite for the CCP's survival. No wonder there was a tone of urgency and anxiety in Fourth Congress resolutions.

4/The CCP as Mass Party: Tapping the Power of the Masses

On May 30, 1925, some two thousand Chinese students took to the streets of Shanghai in protest of the killing of a Chinese worker in a Japanese-owned cotton mill and the imprisonment of several others who had launched a strike for a wage increase. As students demonstrated within the International Settlement, antiforeign sentiments ran high. The protest turned into an uncontrollable riot, leading the settlement police to open fire, killing several of the students. The following day, a general strike began in Shanghai, involving many segments of society, including students, workers, shopkeepers, and businessmen (see figures 5 and 6).[1]

The response around the country was immediate. In Peking, students massed in Tiananmen Square on June 3.[2] In Wuhan, stone-throwing workers and students threatening to enter the foreign concessions precipitated further killings, with marines landing from gunboats to come to the assistance of a beleaguered foreign volunteer corps. Similar events took place in Kiukiang, Chungking, and many other cities.[3] In Canton on June 23, a huge noontime rally in front of the British Concession on Shameen Island led to an exchange of gunfire in which at least fifty-two Chinese died. This sparked the eighteen-month-long Canton–Hong Kong strike aimed at blockading the "fragrant harbor" (the meaning of the city's name in Chinese) with the aim of turning it into the "stinking harbor."[4]

The May Thirtieth movement, as these events are usually called, initiated a two-year period in which mass demonstrations swept through cities and peasants rebelled in the countryside. Chinese communists had always thought that enormous powers were embedded in China's society. The movement not only confirmed this but also suggested that now these powers were coming to the fore. If Yun Daiying was waiting for an "emotional outburst" of China's population, here it was.

147

The May Thirtieth movement disproved the pessimism about the prospect of a revolution in China that had taken hold of a substantial number of CCP members at the time of the Third Congress. But now they faced the problem of how to tap the energies released by the May Thirtieth movement, or, as Yun Daiying would have said, how to be cool-headed revolutionaries employing the population's outburst. They faced the issue while they were still in the process of building their party.

In the 1925–1927 period, CCP members attempted to mobilize China's population by establishing mass organizations in several major cities and in the countryside first of Guangdong Province and later several other southern Chinese provinces. But these efforts failed to create a reliable mass base for the CCP, and when in the spring and summer of 1927 the KMT attacked the CCP to seize power, it was in no position to defend itself. Nonetheless, the efforts of CCP members to establish a mass base had important results for the CCP.

CCP members first gained a much better understanding of power relations in Chinese society, and this translated into a different approach to the construction of a mass-based party. Whereas CCP members had first sought to impose new anonymous institutions from above, they now shifted their attention to creating a close personal relationship between CCP members and the general population. A campaign was conducted to foster attitudes designed to establish such a relationship, and CCP members were told to focus their organizational activities at the lowest level of the social hierarchy rather than at higher levels as they had done so far.

In addition, a number of CCP members developed an appreciation of military power and its revolutionary potential. For its strategy of imposing institutions from above on the population to have succeeded, the CCP needed the backing of military power. It could not count on this. In Shanghai, the CCP's labor unions were destroyed almost before they had been set up by those whose interests they threatened, including the Green Gang. In Guangdong, the KMT at first provided support for the CCP, including military backing for peasant associations. For the KMT, the associations were initially important to the subjugation of local opposition to its rule and extending the reach of the KMT government based in Canton. However, they evoked much opposition, and after the opposition had mobilized significant segments of the KMT, on March 20, 1926, Chiang Kai-shek threw himself behind it. He cracked down on CCP influence in the KMT and withdrew KMT military support from peasant associations, thus causing the collapse of the Guangdong peasant movement.

As a result of these experiences and similar ones that followed, CCP members began to abandon the idea that they could rise to power simply by mobilizing China's masses. It was in this context that Mao Zedong declared that "power comes out of the barrel of a gun." Party control of military power was especially important in China, where there was no centralized government and society was severely fragmented.

I proceed chronologically. I first describe the response of the CCP to the challenge of the May Thirtieth movement in Shanghai and Canton, and then examine the Guangdong peasant movement. Following Chiang Kai-shek's crackdown on the CCP in Guangdong Province in March 1926, CCP leaders initiated a campaign to change the attitude of CCP members, and they made a serious study of the reasons for the CCP's failure to institutionalize the mass party, which I discuss. Finally I examine the CCP's experiences during the Northern Expedition. Despite the tense relations between the CCP and the KMT, in July 1926, the two set out jointly on a military campaign against warlord forces, with the aim of unifying China. When it became clear in the spring of 1927 that this campaign would succeed, Chiang ended the CCP's aspirations for power by doing what he had done in Guangdong earlier, but in a much more radical fashion, cracking down hard on the CCP and its ancillary organizations.

Even if the period ended in disaster for the CCP, it did succeed in becoming an indelible part of Chinese society. At the eve of the May Thirtieth movement, it existed in political and social isolation. By 1927, the CCP had broken out of its confinement: its membership had grown from 1,000 to 57,000; it had conducted large-scale labor and peasant movements; it had set up mass organizations involving millions of people; and its activity came to encompass most major urban centers and much of the southern Chinese countryside. Even if Chiang Kai-shek's White Terror made deep inroads into the CCP's ranks and its mass following, it was not able to expunge the CCP from Chinese society. In 1925, this would have posed no problem.

THE CCP AND THE MAY THIRTIETH MOVEMENT

In 1925, CCP members responded vigorously to the challenge of the May Thirtieth movement in two cities, Shanghai and Canton. In Shanghai, they contributed significantly to the transformation of instances of labor unrest into a strike with wide nationalistic appeal. However, they were not able to translate their agitational and propaganda successes into firm institutional gains, and soon after the movement began, the CCP's labor union was destroyed.

In Canton, the political situation was different from that in Shanghai. Here Sun Yatsen and the KMT were in the process of constructing a government. The importance of Soviet aid and CCP personnel to the ability of the KMT's Canton Government to consolidate its position in the province enabled CCP members in Canton to set up, together with the KMT, a powerful labor union. It maintained an economic embargo of Hong Kong for the next year and a half with some success and was able to consolidate its hold over union members.

Shanghai

On the eve of the May Thirtieth movement, CCP members in Shanghai concerned themselves not so much with building labor unions as with the implementation of the bloc-within policy. The Shanghai Executive Branch of the KMT (Guomindang Shanghai Zhixingbu) had been set up in 1924 in the French Concession, with a French policy inspector receiving bribes for passing on any information of French action against the KMT in Shanghai. Chinese communists occupied leading positions in the branch: Mao Zedong was its secretary; Yun Daiying, Shi Cuntong, and others staffed the Propaganda Department; Luo Zhanglong served in the Organization Department; and Deng Zhongxia and Li Lisan worked for the KMT's Department for Workers and Peasants (see figure 7). CCP strategy in Shanghai was to help the KMT in setting up a base in the city and to obtain as much influence in it as possible.[5]

CCP members did not completely neglect workers. Several CCP branches existed in Shanghai's industrial districts.[6] The total membership in Shanghai, however, was no more than 220, with the largest branch (from now on, I speak of *branches* rather than *cells*) having no more than 46 members.[7] Li Lisan's Anyuan strategy provided the model for CCP labor organizations in Shanghai prior to the May Thirtieth movement. In the second half of 1924, Deng Zhongxia and others set up workers' clubs that organized cooperatives, ran savings societies, provided relief, and offered leisure activities.[8] The scale of these activities was limited. In each of the two important workers' districts of Yangshupu and Xiaoshadu, the CCP reached only around one thousand workers with the workers' clubs.[9]

On February 2, a wildcat strike erupted in West Shanghai in a cotton mill belonging to the Japanese Naigai Wata Kaisha firm after a Japanese manager beat a Chinese worker and sacked several others. The atmosphere in Shanghai's industrial world was tense not only because of nationalistic passions but also because factory managements as well as foremen and the Green Gang sought to increase their control over workers.[10] After February 2, labor unrest increased rapidly.[11]

CCP members were in a quandary as to how they should respond to these strikes. The minutes of a Shanghai Local Committee meeting of May 8 reveal that Li Lisan, transferred to Shanghai in November 1924, wanted to discontinue them. The reason he offered was that he feared that the CCP's limited control over the workers' clubs would make worker rioting inevitable. This, Li argued, could only provoke suppression:

> In the process of agitating for a strike at the occasion of May First celebration and promoting the issue of wages, in some factories the union organizers have done all right, but in others they did not put the unions together well. This has caused disorderly conduct. The capitalists have been unsuccessful in using foremen to put the trouble down. . . . There is now no real need for strikes. We should resolve to use the power of unions to settle the turmoil to demonstrate that their strategy of employing foremen is a failure and to make capitalists realize the real power of our labor unions.[12]

On May 15, Li once more counseled the Shanghai Local Committee "not to cause the expansion of the strike to avoid political repression and economic panic."[13]

That same evening, the committee received the report that Japanese had shot two workers dead.[14] One of them was Gu Zhenghong, whose death quickly became the symbol for Japanese violation of Chinese nationalistic pride. It is unclear whether indeed there was a second casualty. CCP members now faced a difficult situation. They could not very well do nothing and urge workers not to respond.

In conformity with the declared CCP policy of a nationalistic movement not just of workers but of all Chinese against imperialism, CCP members established links with other social and political entities of Shanghai society and called for a general anti-Japanese protest campaign. CCP archival documents suggest that the CCP was successful in this and that even if its endeavors were of an ad hoc nature and did not flow from a previously established and consistently pursued program, its efforts were nonetheless crucial in the creation of the student demonstration of May 30 that led to the May Thirtieth movement. However, CCP members in Shanghai resisted the escalation of the movement. They were overwhelmed by the successes of their own efforts and soon lost control over the course of events, reacting to them rather than directing them. Of course, the KMT, the Green Gang, Chinese businessmen, compradors, and so on had their own reasons for joining what was presented as a nationalistic strike.

The CCP's mobilization for anti-Japanese protests depended to a large extent on its contacts in the KMT. As mentioned, CCP members occupied important positions in the KMT's Shanghai Executive Branch. The CEC Announcement of May 19 instructed CCP members to convene meetings with the Youth League to launch a joint protest movement by means of demonstrations and public lectures. KMT members were to be involved in these meetings.[15] KMT and CCP propaganda workers distributed large numbers of fliers, sent telegrams, organized meetings, and dispatched student groups to lecture on the streets of Shanghai.[16]

This collaboration produced the student demonstrations of May 30. Yun Daiying, working in the Propaganda Department of the Shanghai Executive Branch of the KMT, reported to a joint meeting of CCP and KMT propaganda workers of May 28 that he had arranged for students of Shanghai University to go to schools, accompanied by workers, with the aim of arousing students from all over Shanghai to join in an anti-Japanese demonstration in the International Concession area on May 30.[17] With some four hundred students mostly from outside the city, Shanghai University was a center of KMT left-wing and CCP activity.[18] On May 29, Yun reported to a meeting of the KMT's Propaganda Department that student agitators had succeeded in securing the participation of four hundred to five hundred students.[19]

The CCP not only called on the KMT to participate in an anti-Japanese protest movement, but appealed also to the Shanghai Chamber of Commerce and other associations of the Shanghai elite.[20] Supported by industrial and commercial leaders and by *bang* and other such organizations, the Chamber of Commerce carried out the civil administration of Chinese parts of Shanghai. The CCP also sought to involve other civic bodies, instructing CCP members to pressure those organizations of which they were members to issue public denunciations of Gu's killing. [21]

Despite these preparations, the CCP remained unwilling to escalate the movement until events overtook it. Li Lisan reported to a CCP Shanghai Local Committee meeting of May 22 that more than ten thousand people had attended a memorial meeting for Gu Zhenghong.[22] The meeting decided that this support was not sufficient to risk escalating the conflict. "The results that have been achieved so far have not yet caused the petite bourgeoisie to become sympathetic to us in spirit and to assist us," the minutes noted, adding that therefore "large-scale actions clearly identifiable as just of the proletariat, if they go too far, can only invite political suppression." The meeting "withdrew the previous resolution to hold a large protest demonstration."[23]

On the evening of May 30, one CCP member reported to a meeting of the Shanghai Local Committee what the student demonstration, the one organized by Yun Daiying, had led to: "On the thirtieth, students from all schools went out to lecture, and at some point after four o'clock in the afternoon more than two thousand people gathered on the big avenue. The English police then opened fire, killing eight or nine people and injuring many."[24] "Big avenue" was a reference to Nanking Road, the main thoroughfare in the center of Shanghai.

CCP leaders in Shanghai now ordered CCP members to gather the next morning to protest the shootings. They were to obstruct all major tramlines and call for a citywide strike. The committee also told party members to contact student organizations and have them send telegrams to warlords and government officials throughout the country as well as student organizations in their home areas. The committee also issued a request to the Chamber of Commerce and other civic bodies in Shanghai to meet with the CCP the next day to consider a joint response.[25] This was how the May Thirtieth movement was born.

The CCP Overwhelmed CCP members in Shanghai played an important role in sparking the May Thirtieth movement. However, they were operating in a society in which they had many competitors like the Green Gang, but also Japanese, British, and Chinese businessmen, all of whom were eager to establish and maintain their control over employment and recruitment of workers. The CCP continued to have few means to take on these opponents, most of whom had strong organizations and an essential thing to offer workers—income. When the May Thirtieth movement became serious and this led to struggle for influence among workers, the ground under CCP members quickly disintegrated.

While on the surface all Chinese organizations in Shanghai declared that they were fighting a joint battle against imperialism, in reality each group sought to profit from the movement. It was the Shanghai Chamber of Commerce that captured its public leadership. Immediately after the movement erupted, the chamber declared that it would assume the cost of providing burials for the victims of the British shootings and that its long-term goal was the abolition of the "Unequal Treaties." These were important symbolic acts. It also became the agent that received and distributed the money that poured into Shanghai in support of the victims and strikers. It demanded that the responsible Westerners should be brought to justice, that an indemnity be paid, and that Chinese be accorded equal rights by the foreign police. The chamber was responsible for focusing the movement away from the Japanese and on the British, and eventually it negotiated an end to the movement in Shanghai.[26]

Rather than contesting the Chamber of Commerce's public leadership of the movement in Shanghai, the CCP sought to capitalize on it by expanding its institutional influence among workers. It did so by launching a recruitment drive. The Shanghai General Labor Union (GLU) was at the core of this effort. The CCP had run this union covertly for some time, using it in an attempt to tie existing organizations of workers to the CCP. Having arrived in Shanghai shortly before the outbreak of the movement, Zhang Guotao opened a public office of the union to recruit workers on May 31. Li Lisan was the chair of the union, which soon possessed five branch offices in Shanghai's workers' sections.[27] The Shanghai GLU, then, was a CCP effort to establish an umbrella organization for Shanghai workers' organizations outside the cell or 'club' framework.

Two documents provide insight into the CCP's ability to bring Shanghai workers under its control. The first is a May 1926 CCP review of past experiences in the labor movement. Large parts of it were devoted to the party's performance among Shanghai workers after the outbreak of the movement. The second is the recollections of Zhang Weizhen. Zhang was a CCP union organizer in Shanghai during the movement who recently retold his experiences to PRC historians.

The Shanghai GLU was designed to establish a bond between the CCP and existing Shanghai workers' organizations. Li Lisan adopted the same tactic he had used in Anyuan. In public he treated the head of a public bathhouse as his "patriarch" (*lao touzi*). Bathhouse owners in Shanghai often were connected to the underworld, and Li's gesture was designed to fit CCP unions into its culture.[28]

The CCP adopted this strategy despite negative experiences with it previously. Swept up in the maelstrom of the May Thirtieth movement, they probably felt confident that Shanghai workers would abandon their original associations and commit themselves wholeheartedly to the CCP. This was not the case. The 1926 labor review makes clear that the aloof attitudes of CCP members antagonized many workers. Zhang Weizhen's recollections confirm this.[29]

Another recruitment problem was that the CCP did not exclude vagrants (*liumeng*). In the 1920s, many people were lured to Shanghai in search of jobs, others were sent by their family to augment the family's income, and others were brought by foremen. The result was a large unemployed vagrant population, many of whom had a Green Gang connection. The CCP offered strike payments and did so even to vagrants who registered with the Shanghai GLU. Foremen and gang bosses naturally had vagrants in their control sign up with CCP unions to skim off these payments. The dangers of this showed themselves immediately. The vagrants with whom Zhang Weizhen had dealings, he stated, caused endless trouble within CCP unions until Zhang and other CCP members treated their leaders like gang heads.[30]

The result of the CCP's recruitment policy was that as the Shanghai GLU expanded, the CCP's control weakened. It made the CCP dependent exactly on the people and institutions, such as foremen and the Green Gang, it sought to fight. A sign of the CCP's discipline problems was that it was forced to resort to crude intimidation tactics in an attempt to continue a labor strike at the center of the May Thirtieth movement and that even so, it failed. Gu Zhenghong had come as a vagrant to Shanghai, where he linked up with a "big vagrant" (*da liumeng*), a man in charge of several vagrants. Zhang Weizhen recounted how in trying to break the strikes, Japanese factory managers offered Gu Zhenghong's boss a large sum of money. CCP members picked him up and gave him a thorough beating in one of the branches of the Shanghai GLU. In the end, the Japanese did make the payment, and the workers belonging to this big vagrant's ring returned to work.[31]

The CCP labor review suggested not only that the Shanghai GLU suffered from attacks by the Green Gang and its constituent organizations but that the Japanese made payments to and organized unemployed workers, who proceeded to unravel a strike against one Japanese cotton mill. Chinese compradors also controlled workers' organizations, and these too attacked the union.[32] According to the review, it was a mob in the pay of the Chamber of Commerce that destroyed the Shanghai GLU: "The Shanghai General Labor Union used dock workers to smash up the Shanghai Chamber of Commerce; the Chamber then used them to destroy the General Union."[33]

The Canton–Hong Kong Strike

At the same time that the CCP lost its footing in Shanghai, in Canton it succeeded in developing an important role for the CCP in Guangdong. This was true in the city of Canton as well as in the Guangdong countryside. Here I concentrate on the CCP's involvement in the Canton–Hong Kong strike, that is, on the CCP's position in Canton. The Guangdong peasant movement is discussed in a separate section.

The CCP never possessed sole control over the strike, which at its height involved more than 100,000 workers: The strike was a joint CCP and KMT product. There were good reasons for the CCP and the KMT to cooperate at this stage in Canton. For the KMT, the advantage of welcoming communists was that they brought Russian aid as well as a pool of young and energetic cadres on which to draw. The KMT's position in Canton and in Guangdong Province was precarious. In what was not his first attempt to seize control in the province, Sun Yatsen drove Chen Jiongming from Canton in 1923 and set up a government there. To achieve this, Sun had to make complex deals with warlords from outside the province and with Guangdong power holders. None of these pacts was stable.

The situation of the Canton-Sanshui railroad exemplified the entangled circumstances. After seizing Canton, Sun placed a loyal general from his forces in charge of this important railroad in Guangdong. The man appointed people from his home area as railroad workers. Even if they did not do much, the appointments created a basis of support for him within the railroad organization. He also made them KMT members and set up the Overseas Comrades Society as a labor union under his control. In addition to this general, a warlord supporter from outside the province set up camp along the railroad.

This was not all. In Canton, workers of all sorts, from railroad workers to coolies, were organized in some 160 native labor unions, connected with each other in various larger combines. One of the strongest, the one with which the CCP was to clash most sharply, was the Guangdong Machine Workers Union (Guangdong Jiqi Gonghui). This union, or racket, trained some of its members in martial arts, in part to create an instrument to enforce internal discipline. The Machine Workers Union possessed a strong presence among Canton-Sanshui Railroad workers. Finally, the Assembly of Canton Workers Representatives, a union established in May 1924 under direct KMT auspices, was also represented among workers of the Canton-Sanshui Railroad.[34]

From now on, I refer to organizations like the Machine Workers Union in Canton as native labor unions, for want of a better term. While much research still remains to be done on organizations such as the Machine Workers Union, it is probably not appropriate to term these organizations, or those in Shanghai, traditional. They may have employed traditional social relations and authority patterns, but at the same time they were active in sectors of the economy that had emerged only recently, including those of modern industry. In social composition they were probably heterogeneous, involving Canton businessmen, civil and military leaders, vagrant peasants, and so on. Native labor unions had grown up along the interstices of Chinese society in response to the economic changes and political turmoil of the time.

It was in this complex and volatile situation that Sun Yatsen sought to establish a government in Canton. In 1923, he accepted a Russian offer of aid, in exchange for his agreement to the bloc-within policy and the stationing of Russian advisers in Canton. In October 1923, the first Russian agent, Borodin, arrived in Canton, where he quickly secured the trust of Sun Yatsen. He helped with the reorganization of the KMT along Leninist lines, which led to the strengthening of Sun's position in the KMT. Borodin assisted with the establishment of the Whampoa Military Academy, set up to produce an army strictly loyal to the KMT. He also handled the distribution of Russian aid to the KMT.

The first batch of Russian military equipment to arrive in Canton immediately proved its value to Sun Yatsen. In the fall of 1924, the Canton Merchant Corps rebelled against him. The corps was Canton's equivalent of the Shanghai Chamber of Commerce. It had amassed a large mercenary force and attempted to drive Sun from Canton, objecting to the KMT's heavy taxation. It was by using the Soviet Union's first arms shipment that Chiang Kai-shek was able to put down the rebellion.[35]

The importance of the CCP and the Russians to the KMT manifested itself once more in the first months of 1925. KMT forces had set out on an expedition to dislodge Chen Jiongming from his base in the East River area, in the northeast of the province.[36] Warlords from Yunnan and Guizhou used the opportunity to rebel. Russian advisers and cadets from the Whampoa Military Academy played an important role in planning and executing the recapture of the city on June 12.

For the CCP, cooperation with the KMT in Canton was advantageous. Even if the KMT did not possess unchallenged control in Guangdong, it did have a substantial base in the province. Upon his arrival in Canton, Borodin was able to see CCP members appointed to influential positions in the KMT.[37] CCP members headed two important KMT departments, the Organization Department and the Peasant Department, and served as number two in several more, including the Workers Department and the Youth Department.[38] Their positions in the KMT provided considerable leverage to the eighty or so CCP members operating in Canton in early 1925.[39]

The Canton–Hong Kong strike began on June 21, 1925, in Hong Kong. The strike involved large numbers of people and seriously inconvenienced Hong Kong, although it is unlikely that the boycott was watertight.[40] According to a 1930 history of the Chinese labor movement written by Deng Zhongxia, who played a leading role in the strike, the CCP obtained the cooperation for a strike from leaders of native labor organizations in Hong Kong beforehand. These leaders believed that a strike against the British would improve their reputation and would also be financially profitable because of the strike payments to workers in their control.[41] They were also co-opted into leading positions of strike institutions.[42]

This was the time of the May Thirtieth movement. Anti-British passions ran high. In Canton, the situation exploded when on June 23, two days after the beginning of the strike, gunfire exchanged between Chinese protesters showing their support for the strike and British ensconced on Shameen Island led to the death of at least fifty Chinese. Shameen Island is a small island in the Pearl River separated by a narrow canal from the main city of Canton. In the 1920s, free access to the island was restricted to foreigners. After the Shameen incident, the strike caught on immediately, and in the following days, an exodus of workers began from Hong Kong. Many congregated in Canton.

Coming on the heels of a rebellion against the KMT government in Canton, the strike was an opportunity for the KMT, and the CCP, to capture the public leadership of a popular mass movement. At the same time, it required them to establish control over a potentially unruly segment of Canton society. As such, it also formed an opportunity to attack native labor organizations and warlords.

The CCP and the KMT began by forming a Strike Committee. Su Zhaozheng, the leader of the Chinese Seamen's Union and a CCP member who had headed the seamen's strike of 1922, became the chairman of the committee. The committee acted with full authority over the strikers. Meeting every day or two, it became something like a second municipal administration.

The committee was subdivided into a Finance Committee, an Investigation Bureau, and an Executive Office. The Executive Office, in turn, consisted of six departments that provided essential services to maintain the strike. The Strike Committee arranged lodgings for strikers, maintained a communications network, provided entertainment, distributed food, and so on. In other words, the Strike Committee produced a quickly growing bureaucracy.[43]

The committee attempted in several ways to impose its discipline on the strikers, most of whom were attached to native labor organizations. Even in Canton the KMT and the CCP succeeded only partially in breaking the bonds between workers and their native labor organizations. One way they tried to do so was by creating groups of fifty workers and having each elect one representative to a Workers Congress. This congress supposedly elected the Strike Committee and ratified its decisions.

Well aware of the erosion of their power base, Hong Kong native labor leaders resisted the convocation of workers' congresses. Factors against them were that in Canton they did not control the supply of labor and that the CCP and the KMT provided important services to the workers. Despite their objection, workers' congresses did convene, and the Strike Committee was ratified.[44]

Native labor leaders did not give up immediately, however. No doubt, in many cases they were able to see their favored candidates, or themselves, elected as workers' representatives. At an August 11 congress of workers' delegates, people from the floor accused Strike Committee officials of skimming off committee funds and receiving bribes in return for issuing permits for ships to trade with Hong Kong. This created considerable panic in the Strike Committee,[45] and from that day on, it conducted a campaign against "internal traitors."[46] An important instrument of power in the hands of the Strike Committee in conducting this campaign was its "special courts of law" (*tebie fating*). These it turned against strikebreakers who smuggled goods to Hong Kong but also against native labor leaders, executing some of them.[47] The Strike Committee also soon formed armed pickets two thousand men strong to enforce its discipline.[48]

The members of the Strike Committee did not rely only on force and the provision of material resources to decouple workers from native labor organizations. Workers were subjected to a steady barrage of periodicals; they listened to propaganda lectures by Canton students and attended workers' schools established by the committee.[49] In addition, the Strike Committee sought to provide alternative sources of employment. Striking workers were put to work in the construction of a road from Canton to the Whampoa Military Academy, located on the Huangpu River slightly to the east of Canton. Workers were also employed in KMT armies as carriers. There was even an ambitious plan to use striking workers to construct a harbor at Whampoa near Canton to compete directly with Hong Kong.[50]

An internal CCP report, probably from the fall of 1925, makes clear that despite their access to considerable sources of power, the CCP and the KMT did not squeeze out all native labor organizations. It discussed clashes between the Machine Workers Union and the CCP and mentioned that the CCP had abandoned attempts to establish a CCP presence among workers employed in Canton's arsenal and the electricity industry. This was the turf of the Machine Workers Union.[51]

A comparison of the CCP in Canton and Shanghai makes it obvious why the CCP did not suffer the same fate in Canton as in Shanghai. In Canton CCP members were crucial to the KMT at a time when the KMT was in the process of consolidating its rule. It was because of KMT backing that CCP members had access to powerful resources they could use to create a niche for themselves in Canton society.

The October 1925 Enlarged CEC Meeting

With the roar of the May Thirtieth movement still loudly ringing in their ears, CEC members convened in October 1925 in Peking. All agreed that the movement had opened up "a period never seen before,"[52] and no one denied that the CCP should seek to tap the forces thus released.[53] However, the documents of the meeting suggest that the momentous events of the preceding months had been interpreted in widely different ways and that sharp differences of opinion existed about what policies were to be followed to make use of the opportunities created by the May Thirtieth movement.

CCP members could not look back on the CCP's fortunes in Shanghai with much satisfaction. With the exception of Canton, the CCP had not been able to erect and control mass institutions in other places, as reports to the meeting made clear.[54] However, there were also those who voiced criticism of the results achieved in Canton. A resolution on CCP activities there stated that the efforts of the party's members, although impressive in themselves, were not meaningful for creating an independent mass base for the CCP:

> The comrades in the Guangdong region who have engaged in real work did exert a great deal of effort. But only a few individual party members did so. . . . At the level of the regional committee and branches, the organization exists merely nominally. . . . It is not party members but a few individual party members who direct work. The comrades in charge also have not paid sufficient attention to quickly expanding the party organization, so that the party has no concrete manifestation among the masses. In the eyes of the masses, the CCP is no more than an apparition carrying a KMT mask.[55]

A background factor that motivated this negative appraisal of the successes Canton CCP members had achieved by collaborating with the KMT was that in Shanghai CCP-KMT relations had deteriorated rapidly once the May Thirtieth movement began. After Sun Yatsen's death on March 12, 1925, Dai Jitao, a man who had joined in discussions with early Shanghai communists at the time of the Shanghai cell, became the leading figure in the Shanghai Executive Branch of the KMT. He immediately galvanized anti-CCP forces with the publication of two tracts that argued that CCP members should be expelled from the KMT. His arguments were that the KMT should be the party of those who believed in Sun's Three Principles, and only those.[56] Dai's treatises called forth sharp, almost panicky rebuttals by major CCP figures, including Chen Duxiu and Qu Qiubai.[57] CCP members who had to cooperate with KMT members in Shanghai were alert to the dangers of staking the CCP's future on collaboration with the KMT.

Resolutions of the October 1925 CEC meeting also pointed out that in Shanghai CCP membership had nearly quadrupled between May and September 1925, reaching 1,100 members, 80 percent workers.[58] The quote above makes it clear that such gains had not been achieved in Canton.

A majority of those who attended the October 1925 CEC meeting were uneasy about making the CCP dependent on the KMT. The meeting's "Resolution on Organizational Issues" stated that "the most important question in organization now is the solidification of the party's position among the masses."[59] "Only if we transform our party into a real mass party [*qunzhong de dang*]," as the resolution on propaganda put it, "can we consolidate our position as the leadership of the proletariat."[60] The phrase "make a mass party out of the CCP" (*dang de qunzhonghua*) summarized what became official CCP policy.[61] Its proponents took the position that at present the CCP's task was to recruit heavily and then to build up a solid organization based on the principles adopted following the Third Congress:

> We cannot have any illusions about the idea that we can locate many ready-made party members in Chinese society. . . . At this point, the great majority of local party functionaries are the victims of an erroneous concept. They believe that each party member must understand Marxism, that he must have a high level of capability, and that not developing the quality of the membership but developing only its numbers is not only without benefit but also causes the party organization to become even more loose. . . . This erroneous concept is a hindrance to the transformation of the party into a mass party.[62]

The participants in the October 1925 CEC meeting were aware that recruitment was one thing but that building up dependable institutions was another; recent experience had made this abundantly clear. They adopted resolutions that repeated organizational principles contained in the documents of the May 1924 CEC meeting and the Fourth Congress.[63] In this way, new members, who did not necessarily have access to old CCP resolutions, would be informed of them.

If policies in Canton had made the CCP dangerously dependent on the KMT, the strategy of creating a mass party wagered the CCP's future on the ability of communists to establish a firm following in Chinese society. At the congress there were those, no doubt CCP members active in Canton, who refused to abandon the "Canton approach," that is, using the KMT to establish a base in society and attempting to capture as much influence in it as possible. Given that their policy did not become formal CCP policy, it is likely that they were in the minority. However, they were able to achieve a relative endorsement for their strategy.

The evidence for this case is as follows: On April 29, 1927, Chen Duxiu stated in his report to the Fifth Congress that his purpose at the October meeting had been to end the bloc-within policy and to change CCP-KMT collaboration into an alliance format.[64] Chen's proposal would have precluded the Canton approach. However, the October 1925 CEC meeting's "Resolution on the Tasks of the CCP" stated that "in the middle and northern parts of the country, a degree of reaction has set in among representatives of capitalists in the KMT."[65] This was no doubt a reference to Dai Jitao, and the formulation supported a weakening of CCP ties with the KMT. The resolution continued, stating that "it would nonetheless be a big mistake to believe that this phenomenon indicates that the time has arrived for the Chinese Communist Party and the bourgeois-democratic KMT to separate."[66] This formulation may well have been adopted in rebuttal of Chen Duxiu's proposal. While the meeting decided against ending the bloc-within policy entirely, probably in part under Soviet pressure as the Russians must have been reluctant to abandon their base in Canton, it made a careful distinction between "reactionary capitalist" elements of the KMT in central and northern China and a bourgeois-democratic KMT, clearly referring to the KMT in Canton. In essence, the meeting adopted a strategy whereby CCP members in central and northern China, including Shanghai, distanced themselves from the KMT while those in Canton continued to pursue the advantages of the bloc-within strategy.

CCP experiences during the May Thirtieth movement were interpreted in two ways. One group of those present at the October meeting believed that the CCP should continue to fashion a party with an independent base in Chinese society and do so without making itself reliant on the goodwill of the KMT. This had been the general trend of policies adopted after the Third Congress, and besides Chen Duxiu may have been supported by Cai Hesen and Zhang Guotao. Another group was made up of those who believed that the Canton strategy offered more promise. While the first group possessed a majority, it is clear that the second group was not insignificant, as they were able to secure limited approval for their strategy.

The number of members in the CCP for the period from January 1925 to April/May 1927 was as follows:[67]

January 1925	994
October 1925	3,000 +
January 1926	10,000
May 1926	11,000
September 1926	15,000
November 1926	18,500
April 1927	57,967

These figures, which the PRC historian Zhao Bu recently pulled together from CCP statistics of the 1920s, suggest that the policy of making the CCP a mass party was successful, at least in terms of numbers.

THE GUANGDONG PEASANT MOVEMENT

The October 1925 CEC meeting approved two strategies for the CCP to implant itself in Chinese society. The meeting endorsed a situation in which in central and northern China, CCP organizations were to be strengthened in relative independence of the KMT and in Guangdong the opportunities offered by the bloc-within policy were to be exploited, as Maring had originally envisioned. In Guangdong, the bloc-within policy immediately proved highly beneficial in bringing about a peasant movement that swept the province in 1925 and 1926. At its heyday, the movement involved perhaps 600,000 peasants.[68] This was the first large-scale peasant movement in which CCP members played an important role.

The Guangdong peasant movement had a double origin. We have already seen that first Shen Xuanlu, in Zhejiang, and then Peng Pai, in Guangdong, aspired to establish peasant associations in the hope of reconstructing rural relations and ending what they saw as the abusiveness of local elites. A peasant movement also was an important part of Borodin's strategy for the CCP and the KMT in Guangdong. In 1923, he advised Sun Yatsen that a peasant movement was essential for the extension of KMT authority in Guangdong, and he urged Sun to issue a decree promising land redistribution and rent reductions.[69] According to Borodin, for the CCP itself, a peasant movement offered the opportunity to gain influence in the countryside.

In November 1924, Borodin traveled to Peking to attend a CCP meeting at the Russian Embassy at which Li Dazhao, Qu Qiubai, Zhang Guotao, and several others were present. According to the recollections of one participant, Borodin stated at this meeting that CCP members should support Sun Yatsen in his desire to conduct a military campaign aimed at unifying the country militarily. According to the recollection, at this time Borodin opposed forming an independent armed CCP force or assisting the Red Spears or any other heterodox organizations. He advocated the strategy that the CCP build up KMT forces in Guangdong and place CCP members in important positions.[70] A CEC announcement of February 1926 makes it clear that an important aspect of Borodin's strategy was for CCP members to attempt to seize control of KMT institutions set up in the wake of Northern Expedition advances.[71] According to Borodin, the peasant movement was an essential element of the national revolution. While the CCP was to organize mass movements in areas through which the Northern Expedition forces were to pass, such as Hunan, Hubei, and Zhili, he also made it clear that in his opinion substantial peasant movements could be generated only in places where a KMT regime already existed.[72] In short, Borodin's plan was to have CCP members make use of their positions in KMT institutions to foment peasant movements once the Northern Expedition had made it possible for these to be established and to expand the CCP's power on the basis of these peasant associations.

Documents of a CEC meeting of February 1926 confirm that this was the strategic thinking behind the support of Borodin and Guangdong Regional Executive Committee members for a peasant movement. This meeting convened after the Guangdong peasant movement had begun. The CCP had not achieved successes elsewhere, and therefore, to many CCP members at the time, events appeared to bear out the wisdom of the Canton approach. The meeting repudiated the decisions of the October 1925 CEC meeting on the grounds that the urban proletariat had fallen into an isolated position and therefore the Chinese revolution could not depend on it.[73] It decided that the peasant movement should be made the cornerstone of CCP policy throughout China and that the CCP was to pursue this by assisting the KMT in building up a strong army and launching it from Canton on the Northern Expedition, as Sun's campaign to unify the country militarily was called.[74]

The victory of the Canton strategy, however, did not prove lasting. In Guangdong, the movement disintegrated in the summer of 1926 after forces opposed to it in the Guangdong countryside mobilized the KMT on their behalf, culminating in Chiang Kai-shek's March 20, 1926, coup. Nonetheless, the Guangdong peasant movement had important long-term results, in part because it propelled the CCP toward the pursuit of a mass-based rural revolution but also because it generated intense factional conflict in the CCP, deeply affecting its internal organization and culture.

Past scholars studying the Guangdong peasant movement focused mostly on Haifeng and Lufeng counties, where Peng Pai in November 1927 established China's first soviet. These studies examined peasant motivations for joining in a CCP-led revolution and CCP mobilization techniques. Roy Hofheinz argued that the CCP's success at arousing the movement depended on its organizational energy and the vitality of peasant-association organizers. In his study of the peasant movement in Haifeng and Lufeng counties, Robert Marks placed the peasant movement in the context of long-term historical trends, arguing that it derived its impetus from the breakdown of the moral economy due to imperialism. In his biography of Peng Pai, Fernando Galbiati pictured Peng as a catalyst for peasant political consciousness and suggested that Peng gradually developed insight into the peasant world and became the movement's leader largely because of his personal qualities.[75] I differ from these studies by placing the movement in the context of Guangdong power relations and focusing on the effects of the movement's defeat in 1926 on the CCP's strategy of creating a mass party.

The Communists' Aim in the Guangdong Countryside

An extraordinary report of nearly one hundred pages produced by the Guangdong Regional Executive Committee for a meeting in May 1926 of representatives of peasant associations in Guangdong analyzed the history of the Guangdong peasant movement until that time.[76] It was written after March 20, 1926—that is, after Chiang Kai-shek had turned against the CCP and after the peasant movement had already begun to falter. The report nonetheless gives us insight into how CCP members in Guangdong looked at the peasant movement and at Guangdong society in general, as it devoted large sections to these issues. (See map 2.)

The report makes it clear that Chinese communists viewed Guangdong society as one of complete chaos. The report mentioned that there were few large landowners in the province because of the strength of lineages and the lack of primogeniture. However, there was what it called a "gentry" (*shenshi*) dependent on management control of collective-ownership institutions. Lineages, temples, and schools were endowed with land, the report explained, and it was the ability to dominate the management of these that formed the basis for the power of "local bullies and evil gentry" (*tuhao lieshen*), as the report denounced these managers.[77]

According to the report, those in control of collective-ownership institutions wielded great power in local society. They controlled local financing and education, possessed military power in the form of militia forces, and charged extra levies for all kinds of items to squeeze the population.[78] The report did not discuss in detail the link of the rural elites with the government. However, in its depiction of ownership and employment practices, it did note that in areas of reclaimed land, agricultural estates were run by a manager who was elected by the local elites and whose appointment was then approved by either the district magistrate or the provincial governor.[79] Militia bureaus and chambers of commerce also forged links between rural elites and the government, the initiative perhaps coming not only from the state but also from the elites themselves.

The report described a society under intense economic pressures. It blamed this partly on imperialism. As one would expect in a document written by Marxists, it argued that imperialism, to which Guangdong was

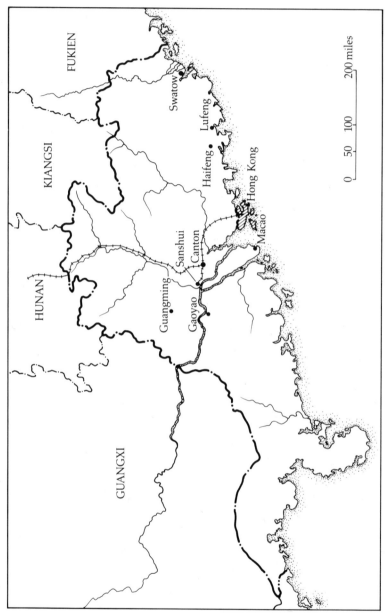

Map 2. Guangdong Province.

exposed more than any other Chinese province, had destroyed the native handicrafts industry. Further causes of the bad state of the Guangdong economy listed in the report included frequent political upheaval, natural disasters, commodity speculation by compradors, and the actions of militias and bandits (see figure 8). The report also mentioned that peasant livelihoods were pressured by comparative deflation as rises in consumer prices outdistanced those of agricultural products.[80]

Secret societies, religious sects, bandit groups, and so on received much attention in the report. It listed a total of seventeen such organizations in the province, attempting to link each with a different area of Guangdong, focusing on the type of land that could be found there. For instance, Triads, according to the report, were especially prevalent in areas of reclaimed land.[81] The lack of a government presence, the distance to marketing centers, and the lack of strong lineage traditions may indeed have provided a fertile ground for the development of Triads in these areas. The report also stated that religious sects dominated in river valleys. The Small Sword Society was relatively insignificant, according to the report, but the Big Sword Society dominated along the North and West rivers. It mentioned that bandit lodges could be found anywhere in the province.[82]

A June 1924 resolution of the Guangdong Regional Executive Committee of the Socialist Youth League provided a concise definition of a peasant association.[83] At that time, the league membership and CCP membership largely overlapped, with the league prevalent in the countryside.[84] Other CCP documents of the 1920s talked about the associations in the same vein.[85] These documents make it clear that CCP members aimed at nothing else than forging an entirely new rural order based on the associations.

The first task of peasant associations, the Youth League resolution wrote, was "secretly to form the future state of the proletariat—a government."[86] Peasant associations were to assume traditional functions of the elite, including management of irrigation systems, running schools, and settlement of local disputes, according to the resolution. It stated that they had to do so by fighting "the gentry class . . . because if we use gentry to arouse the peasants, in the end they will be destroyed by them."[87] The resolution limited peasant-association membership on the basis of property, aiming to annihilate the importance of land ownership. Each member was obliged to obtain peasant-association approval for rent increases, in this way giving the association control over rents. The resolution also said that peasant associations should prohibit peasants from returning land to the owner without association permission. According to the resolution, associations also were to exterminate traditional forms of association.

Within the association, it wrote, "it is absolutely prohibited to refer to such ties as local lineage or kinship."[88]

The May 1926 report by the Guangdong Regional Executive Committee to the congress of peasant-association representatives, in accordance with the basic aim of peasant associations, divided rural institutions in Guangdong on the basis of whether they supported or collaborated with peasant associations. Naturally the gentry opposed them universally. Most Triad lodges, according to the report, joined associations in toto, although some opposed them. It stated that the problem with the Big Sword Society was that while it was a response to gentry exploitation and was large, well organized, and disciplined, its aim was to restore the traditional rural harmony and that therefore it was easily "exploited" by gentry. In one county, it wrote, the Big Sword Society had shown itself a determined foe of peasant associations. The Small Sword Society, according to the report, adopted a neutral stance toward peasant associations, while bandit lodges decided on the basis of immediate material considerations whether they supported peasant associations operating in their area. The report warned of the potentially subversive influence of lineage alliances on peasant associations. "As to the relation between lineage alliances and peasant associations," it wrote, "their entrance into peasant associations amounts [for their members] to being members of two parties."[89]

The attitude of peasant-movement organizers toward the peasantry was one of determination to transform Guangdong rural society, combined with a benign aloofness toward the "backwardness" of peasants themselves. "We should be understanding of whatever mistakes peasants might make," one Youth League document stated, "but we should punish rigorously any violations of association discipline."[90] Once, in the midst of a clash between a peasant self-defense corps and a gentry militia, CCP members staged the charade of having peasant elders, women, and children go to a magistrate yamen to apply for military assistance from Canton. They knew that KMT troops were already on the way, but having peasants believe that they had called forth military support from Canton, they argued, would bolster their self-confidence.[91]

CCP members envisioned themselves as operating in a society that had lost its cohesion and in which peasant associations would form the basis of a new social order of which they were the carriers. This order would be free from what they pictured as the backward and traditional constraints of the past. Their conceptualization of the peasant movement combined cultural, social, and political goals. Their actions were not simply directed against rural landholders.

The Guangdong Peasant Movement Grows

All documents agree that the Guangdong peasant movement exploded in 1925 when peasant-association organizers obtained access to the superior military power of the KMT. The Guangning case formed an early illustration of this. The county is located to the northwest of Canton. It is discussed in detail in the Guangdong Regional Executive Committee report to the congress of peasant-association representatives of May 1926.

Guangning gentry resisted the KMT strenuously. The first attempt at setting up a peasant association ended in March 1924 with landlords smashing it. Two months later, peasant-movement activists returned, calling for the restoration of the association and rent reductions. Guangning gentry exploited the opportunity provided by the Merchant Corps uprising of September–October 1924 to raise the local militia, and in November they combined in a "Conference for the Protection of Property" (Baochan Dahui). Faced with this challenge, Sun Yatsen dispatched armored forces from Canton. Arriving on December 12, these troops defeated the Guangning militia. They encountered stiff opposition, and mopping-up operations continued for several months. In early February, for instance, it took KMT troops two weeks to subdue the heavily armed stronghold of one lineage. After this victory, according to the May 1926 report, peasants flocked to the peasant association.[92] It acknowledged the importance of KMT military support, remarking that throughout the struggle in Guangning, "peasants asked us whether Canton would send troops."[93]

Even if the particulars were different, the struggle to form a peasant association in Gaoyao County, to the west of Canton, illustrated the same point. In Gaoyao, peasant-association organizers at first encountered difficulty in convincing peasants that rents in the county were unfair. They made their case by referring to traditional rural notions of justness. The district was located in an area of reclaimed land, and according to customs that had no doubt long been abandoned if they ever had existed, rents were due to the government rather than to the gentry. When peasant-association organizers moved into the county, they argued that it was only fair that at least part of local rents should be earmarked for such a public good as a peasant school, to be run by the peasant association.

With the approval of the local magistrate, in September 1925, the Gaoyao gentry mobilized the militia. Upon this, according to the May 1926 report, peasant-association members sent their wives and children into the hills. Led to believe that help from Canton was on the way, the peasant self-defense corps remained in the villages, supported by several bandit lodges. However, as militia pressure mounted, peasant-association forces dwindled, and even peasant-association activists feared that a collapse was imminent. Defeat was turned into huge victory when at the last minute some three hundred modern troops arrived and made short shrift of the much larger militia force.[94] As in Guangning, this success was followed by the immediate expansion of the association.[95]

For the peasant movement in the counties of Haifeng and Lufeng, KMT military support proved as essential as in the above cases. CCP members, including Peng Pai and Zhou Enlai, traveled with Chiang Kai-shek's forces during the First Eastern Expedition against Chen Jiongming. Zhou Enlai was in charge of political work among the troops;[96] as such, he and other CCP political workers assisted with or took charge of local administration behind the front (see figure 9).

Peng Pai was given responsibility for Haifeng, a natural choice because of his record of opposition to Haifeng elites. In Lufeng, elites resisted the authority of the peasant association, and the local magistrate turned against it. When Peng heard of this, he dispatched a "propaganda team" and soon followed as "director of the Peasant Department of the KMT Central Executive Council."[97] Peng removed the magistrate, fired all non-KMT officials from the local government, set up a relief organization, and endowed the peasant association with five thousand *yuan*. Additionally, he arrested "evil gentry," proscribed tax farming, and forbade illegal payments to officials.[98]

A rebellion of warlords in Canton forced KMT forces to break off the First Eastern Campaign to recapture the city. Chen Jiongming retook the East River area in the fall of 1925.[99] Chiang Kai-shek once more attacked him, and in November defeated him decisively. As in the first campaign, CCP members joined his force, now as officers in formally constituted political departments in Chiang's army, and took charge of civil administration. In this way, Zhou Enlai became the head of local government in areas controlled by Chiang's expeditionary forces.[100]

The Guangdong peasant movement came down to an attempt at the imposition from above of a radically new form of government. It was revolutionary in its design but also fitted the KMT's power political goal of extending the authority of the Canton Government, a goal that the CCP supported and sought to exploit to its own advantage. The movement succeeded in removing the main challenger to the KMT's control in Guangdong, Chen Jiongming. For a moment, the interests of revolution and KMT power considerations overlapped perfectly.

The Fall of the Guangdong Peasant Movement

In the fall of 1925 and the spring of 1926, CCP members in Canton may well have believed that they had discovered the way to exploit the great forces stored in the Chinese population. They were participating in a quickly expanding peasant movement that seemed to transform Guangdong society before their eyes. It was no doubt this belief that led them to support Borodin at the February 1926 CEC meeting, which made the strategies pursued until then only in Guangdong general CCP policy.

However, on July 22, 1926, one peasant-movement leader, Lo Qiyuan, reported to the Guangdong Regional Executive Committee that "the crises confronting the peasant movement not only have not decreased, they have become increasingly severe."[101] The report mentioned that magistrates opposed peasant associations and that KMT troops attacked them, sometimes in cooperation with bandit gangs and militia.[102] What had happened?

Even if the Guangdong peasant movement succeeded in destroying Chen Jiongming's base in the province, it was not able to eradicate the rural elite or the social institutions on which its rule depended. Faced with the threat of the peasant associations and with their former warlord backer driven out or subdued, the members of the elite successfully mobilized the new institution controlling political power in their spheres of action, the KMT. Peasant associations were never really able to transplant Triads, sects, or lineages. They could not depend on the support of large parts of the peasant population, and they could not fulfill their role as an extension of the Canton government. When the reaction set in, the Guangdong peasant movement crumbled.

The Sun Yatsen-ism Study Society (Sun Wen-zhuyi Xuehui) was the vehicle used by Guangdong gentry to mobilize opposition forces against the CCP within the KMT. One Youth League report asserted that the origins of the society reached back to before the death of Liao Zhongkai in August 1925. However, its formal inauguration took place only in December 1925, and it was at this point that the society's political significance rapidly increased. The society mustered a following in Guangdong for the first time after the First Eastern Expedition. According to Youth League reports of January 1926, its ranks swelled rapidly after the Second Eastern Expedition got underway in October 1925. By December, its membership reached more than two thousand—exceeding the number of CCP members in the province.[103]

The Sun Yatsen-ism Study Society membership was largest in areas where the peasant movement and the CCP were most active. Its following was strong especially in the East River area, the locale of the two expeditions against Chen Jiongming. Here too, KMT forces and CCP peasant organizers like Peng Pai had made the greatest impact. Conflicts arose between the CCP and the Sun Yatsen-ism Study Society in the important harbor town of Swatow after Zhou Enlai overhauled the staffing of the government in and around the city.[104]

The KMT military was also a fertile recruitment ground for the Sun Yatsen-ism Study Society, according to a Soviet report written after Chiang Kai-shek seized control in Canton. It stated that CCP dominance in KMT armies had generated resentment among KMT and regular military officers:

> With their progressive political ideas, the majority of the active members of the Sun Yatsenist [sic] Society could have been affiliated with the Left Wing. Having been squeezed out, however, they turned around and opposed the CCP. In view of their own rank, the military officers feel they should be the directing organs of the army. . . . They also oppose the CCP because they are dissatisfied with the commissar system.[105]

According to a May 1926 Youth League report, the Sun Yatsen-ism Society also possessed a following among Guangdong students. Some of these, it suggested, were resentful of Haifeng people dominating the Canton Government. It wrote that these students "are children from gentry and are extremely opposed to Haifeng men occupying positions."[106] It is unclear whether the CCP and the KMT indeed disproportionally favored Haifengites. Several reasons may have gone into a decision to adopt a recruitment policy weighted toward Haifeng. It would be one way to offset resentment created by the KMT's ouster of Chen Jiongming in Haifeng; it also would have drawn people opposed to KMT rule away from the area.

The platform of the Sun Yatsen-ism Study Society was as follows:

1. No KMT member is allowed to join another political party.
2. Party members who have dual party membership should not enjoy the right to stand for office.
3. No KMT members must be allowed to make propaganda for other isms or parties.[107]

Members of the society did not call for a halt to the peasant movement directly. However, the movement was closely associated with the CCP. It controlled the KMT's Peasant Department and headed the Peasant Movement Cadre Training Institute in Canton, which produced the cadres for peasant associations.[108] They were therefore in a position to determine the staffing of the peasant movement. Thus, the above platform, playing on anti-CCP emotions in the KMT, formed a way of attacking the Guangdong peasant movement.

According to Youth League reports of January 1926, Chiang Kai-shek was heavily involved in the founding of the society, although in late 1926 he appears to have attempted to rein it in, perhaps not to alienate CCP support at the approaching KMT congress in Canton.[109] These reports already warned of the danger the Sun Yatsen-ism Study Society posed to the CCP in Guangdong. They also mentioned that the society began to assert itself firmly in Canton politics in the weeks before the Second KMT Congress in January 1926. Before the opening of the congress, Sun Yatsen-ism Study Society members held demonstrations and created clashes with CCP members at the Whampoa Academy, threatening that if the congress did not adopt their platform, they would take matters into their own hands.[110]

When Chiang Kai-shek staged the March 20 incident of 1926, he could be confident that his move against the CCP and the Soviets would be supported in the KMT's military and in important parts of the Guangdong countryside. Chiang's move, then, was not a sudden and deft military coup, as has been argued in the past.[111] Chiang's action reflected important changes in Guangdong society generated by CCP attempts to impose peasant associations.

If peasant associations truly had become an extension of the KMT's government, Chiang would have had little incentive to switch his support away from peasant associations and toward the Sun Yatsen-ism Study Society. The report of the Guangdong Regional Executive Committee of May 1926 to a congress of peasant representatives noted that peasant associations had rarely been able to establish control over their areas of jurisdiction. In other places, gentry had hired bandit gangs to destroy peasant associations, and elsewhere they had been able to arrange pacts with peasant-association leaders.[112]

In July 1926, a CEC resolution, in a very hardheaded examination of the peasant movement, stated that peasant associations were often not set up according to guidelines, or existed only on paper. Some CCP members, it declared, had run their peasant association as a private kingdom without involving peasants in the association's management. It concluded that peasant-association activists

> were unable to become close to the masses and could not lead them. . . .
> We did not do enough research. We were completely in the dark about the peasant living conditions as well as the situation of merchants, students, handicraft workers, industrial laborers, and the general masses connected with the peasantry. We also lacked an understanding of the relationship between the peasantry and local garrisons, government officials, gentry, landlords, and militias. . . .

Our comrades' approach to associations also was unimaginative. They were capable only of rigidly setting up a district- or ward-level peasant association according to the statutory number of people. At the establishment of an association, all they did was to go through the requisite rituals of giving an admonitory speech and a lecture, as well as presenting a flag and a seal. . . . Often the next day internal wrangling broke out. Or because the membership was smaller than small, the association was suppressed from the outside.[113]

Coming after the disintegration of the Guangdong peasant movement, this criticism was probably deliberately harsh. On the one hand, CCP members were trying to find ways to improve their party's interaction with society and so strengthen its mass base, as I will discuss in the next section. At the same time, these comments may well have been so severe because those in the CCP who had come under fire at the February 1926 CEC meeting used this opportunity to vent their spleen. Nonetheless, though in a more subdued manner, the Guangdong Regional Committee's May 1926 report made the same points.

Chiang Kai-shek turned against the CCP not only because of events in Guangdong. In late 1925 and early 1926, important segments in the KMT called for the ouster of CCP members from KMT ranks. In November 1925, a group of veteran KMT members convened a KMT meeting in the Western Hills near Peking. They presented this as a KMT Central Executive Committee meeting in an attempt to wrest control of the Canton Government from the left-wing members who dominated in Guangdong. They adopted a platform essentially the same as that of the Sun Yatsenism Study Society.[114] It is not clear whether and in what way the two were linked.

While Chiang could draw support from the Western Hills faction and people like Dai Jitao in Shanghai, after he staged his coup he was identified as a member of the KMT left wing until the March 20 incident. It is probably for this reason that he waited until after the KMT left wing had held its congress in January 1926 in Canton to stave off the Western Hills faction's attempt to seize control. The KMT congress organized by the left wing, unsurprisingly, ratified the dominant position of left wing leaders. When Chiang struck, in short, his position in Guangdong had just been reaffirmed; he had ousted Chen Jiongming, the major military threat against him in Guangdong, and he knew that many people in and outside Guangdong would support his action. He made his move when Borodin and other leading Russians were not in the city and did so in a resolute fashion. He did not give either the CCP or its left-wing supporters in the KMT a chance to strike back.[115]

The March 20 incident meant the end of the peasant movement since CCP members no longer could rely on KMT military support in fighting the militia of Guangdong's gentry. The Regional Executive Committee report of May 1926 already mentioned that times had changed: "The KMT left wing first used peasant power to protect itself," it wrote, but "now that they have succeeded, they of course neglect the peasant movement.[116] In September 1926, an internal CCP report stated that Canton had refused to dispatch military support when a militia attacked peasant associations and that the provincial and local government officials had also turned against the associations.[117] In November, a Guangdong Regional Executive Committee report wrote the obituary for the Guangdong peasant movement:

> What we previously called the left wing has also gone over to Li Jishen. . . . Now Guangdong is set to experience a period of rule by new warlords. They will be even harsher than the old ones and may suppress all mass movements. . . . The trend of this new period is toward opposition between the masses and the government. . . .
>
> It is very difficult to deal with the peasant movement because in villages we cannot raise any demand. Just the establishment of a peasant association will lead to clashes. In this current political situation, in which we lack power, we should of course be extremely cautious in arousing conflicts.[118]

Li Jishen was an anti-CCP commander of the Fourth Army of the Canton Government's National Revolutionary Army. After the March 20 incident he became governor of Guangdong.[119]

The March 20 incident did not lead to an end in Soviet assistance for the Canton Government, nor did it produce an end to the CCP-KMT United Front. After the incident, Chiang was careful to declare immediately that he wished to continue the Canton Government's cooperation with the Soviet Union and the CCP. He even disclaimed the March 20 incident as the result of an unfortunate series of mistakes.[120] In the negotiations that followed between Chiang and Borodin, who returned to Canton on April 29, Borodin accepted a reduction of CCP representation on KMT bodies to one-third of the available seats, the exclusion of communists from directorships of central KMT departments, and the withdrawal of all CCP members from the First Army of the National Revolutionary Army. The First Army was under Chiang Kai-shek's direct control. It was the best equipped, with the best officers and soldiers. In return, Chiang agreed to expel a number of right-wing figures.[121]

Soviet documents suggest that the Russians continued the aid program because they thought that Chiang was truly committed to a national revolution and that in the end they would be able to tie him to themselves by playing on his dreams of being China's savior and surrounding him with the KMT left wing and CCP members. They also blamed themselves for having acted too high-handedly, arguing that by withdrawing to the background, they would be able to overcome internal KMT resentment of CCP and Russian domination of important positions in Canton.[122] Of course, although the report did not mention it, they simply might not have been willing to cut themselves off completely from a political party that was likely to play an important role at least in China's near future.

The March 20 incident also affected the Guangdong labor movement. After drawn-out negotiations with the British, the Canton–Hong Kong strike was brought to a conclusion on October 10, 1926—an anniversary of the 1911 Revolution.[123] After the incident, and especially after the beginning of the Northern Expedition according to one memoir, the Machine Workers Union, the Canton police force, and the Canton garrison reasserted themselves.[124] Armed clashes between the Machine Workers Union and CCP-controlled pickets flared up repeatedly. In November, for instance, some sixty armed men surrounded one union office. Communist pickets sent from Canton and a nearby peasant self-defense corps did succeed in breaking the siege;[125] however, a few months later, a CCP union of Canton-Hankow railroad workers was defeated and forced underground. "Arrests" followed throughout Canton.[126]

RECTIFICATION

Following the March 20 incident, CCP members confronted the fact that despite the May Thirtieth movement and the Guangdong peasant movement, they had not been able to construct a mass party. Faced by this crisis, CCP leaders subjected both the labor movement and the peasant movement to a rigorous examination, and CCP documents scrutinized how CCP members had contributed to the defeat. Until the March 20 incident, CCP strategies in setting up a mass base had consisted of applying models of mass organizations derived from Marxism-Leninism. Now the CCP confronted for the first time the issue of how to adapt Leninist techniques to the Chinese situation, or at least how to graft their organizations and programs on the situation as they found it rather than imposing them from above.

No document in the spring and summer of 1926 called this a rectification campaign. As in future rectification campaigns, though, the CCP's aim in this period was to foster new styles of behavior, to reunify the CCP after a period of heavy recruitment, and to see members recommit themselves to their ideals. In this way, the drive foreshadowed later rectification campaigns.

The campaign did not take place in a political vacuum within the CCP. Chapter 5 will describe the intense dispute that roared in the CCP about the peasant movement. In the same way that despite its defeat, Zhang Guotao and Cai Hesen saw the Peking-Hankow railroad strike as a sign that China would soon be submerged in a proletarian revolution, even after the March 20 coup a number of CCP members in Canton continued to believe that China's peasantry was ready to rebel and carry the CCP to victory. While both advocates and detractors of the peasant movement could probably agree that changes in CCP organizational strategies were necessary and that new members had to be introduced to CCP styles of operation, it is also clear that this campaign was part of Chen Duxiu's effort to reassert his authority and to diminish the influence of the Canton group.[127]

Shortly after the March 20 incident, a CEC announcement attributed the CCP's problems to the fact that CCP members had been too eager in arousing rebellions—it called this "immature leftism"—and that they were still possessed by traditional political attitudes: "In the past, we not only were immaturely leftist in carrying out our activities, but we also did not shed our old research-society habits. We do not really deserve the title 'political party.' We really were no more than a study society."[128] This statement is interesting in that by this time, "political party" had acquired a clearly positive ring in CCP ears.

More significantly, it was the idea that CCP setbacks were at least in part the result of old-style elitist attitudes of CCP members and revolutionary overzealousness that led CCP leaders to initiate the rectification campaign. Other considerations were the fact that CCP membership had risen to ten thousand from one thousand a year before, a development that had introduced into the CCP many who had little knowledge of the party's ideals, policies, or organization. One result was a dearth of cadre talent in the CCP. According to a July 1926 CCP document, the CCP required 35 cadres at the regional level, 160 at the local level, and an equal number for special branches (set up in places with few members and reporting directly to the Central Bureau). Only 120 or so of these slots were filled.[129] Additionally, because of past setbacks, there also was a need to revive the spirit of CCP members.

In April 1926, the Central Bureau issued *How Should We Work from Now On?* (Women Jinhou Yingdang Zemmayang Gongzuo).[130] The Central Bureau instructed committees and branches to distribute a copy to all CCP members, organize study sessions, and then report back to the Central Bureau.[131] The pamphlet argued that the conduct of CCP members had made the entrenchment of the CCP in society impossible. "We not only failed to penetrate the masses," the pamphlet declared, "but sometimes we actually divorced ourselves from them on purpose." It criticized CCP attitudes on two grounds:

> There are two mistakes in attitude. One is to display in an excessive way one's communism among the masses. Some comrades must always make sure that everybody knows that they are party members. . . . CCP membership is not at all a matter of hanging out the CCP sign in public or just announcing it; it must show in actual conduct. It is a matter of being able to formulate with ease what the masses want to say and to advocate always the concrete demands of the masses. In short, it is the ability to make oneself into a member of the masses [*zishen qunzhonghua*]. . . . The second attitude problem is that of being too severe with people in general—that is, being rude. Because of this, some people in society who might be sympathetic also have doubts about our attitude. . . . If we are too strict, we cannot become close to them; if we act arbitrarily, they will not understand; if we set ourselves apart, they will think that we are different; if we are too aggressive, we will frighten them.[132]

The point of *How Should We Work?* was to emphasize the importance of close personal contact between CCP members and the Chinese population. It envisioned the relationship as one in which CCP members assumed a position of authority, but very much in a new way, given the Chinese context. According to the pamphlet, the task of CCP members was to arouse popular participation in CCP mass organizations by means of persuasion;[133] at the same time, the conduct of CCP members should be such that they acquired the trust of workers or peasants on the basis of a demonstration in practice of leadership competence, an intimate knowledge of the local situation, and personal integrity.[134]

The pamphlet emphasized that CCP propaganda should foster this type of relationship. It warned CCP members not to scorn local or even trivial issues in propaganda, instructing CCP members in Shanghai to make propaganda against taxes on tobacco and rises in the price of rice, and to expose cases of political bribery in Zhabei.[135] Such propaganda was designed, it seems, to show the CCP's concern with issues of just and competent government, and thus it appealed to popular and traditional expectations of those wielding political power.

This conception of CCP-society relations made the CCP member the point of intersection between party and society. It emphasized personal relations over the imposition on society of bureaucratic institutions and insisted that CCP members act in ways the population could comprehend. A review of the CCP labor movement and a CEC document of July 1926 reiterated these ideas.

In May 1926, the members of the Central Labor Movement Committee gathered to assess past CCP experiences in the labor movement. The resolution that came out of the meeting argued that contact between CCP union organizers and workers in the past had been minimal:

> In many unions, the resolution of the Fourth Congress on union cells has still not been implemented. Union affairs are the burden of a few managers assuming responsibility. Below them there are basic-level leaders . . . but these only function as middlemen between the union and the members. Besides collecting union dues and transmitting orders, they do not pay sufficient attention to the real issues that affect workers directly, and neither do they engage in the training and education of workers. In this way, the relation between a worker and his union is distant, and the purpose of the union gradually disappears. In the end, it is no more than an empty shell. [136]

It also stated that aloof CCP attitudes had alienated many workers and that they had been ignorant of what happened at the basic level of unions. Hence, it stated, CCP members had been unaware of the dangers gang and *bang* organizations posed. [137]

A concrete result of the meeting was the formation of armed pickets. These had been used in the case of the Canton–Hong Kong Strike Committee, but not in Shanghai. According to the meeting's resolution, these labor-union militia were to be the union's principal instrument in the fight against "scabs" (*gongzei*), workers bound to native labor organizations like the gangs or workers in the pay of warlords. CCP members were also instructed to infiltrate native labor organizations and conduct propaganda against them among workers. [138] The CCP's indiscriminate recruitment policy was abandoned as a result of the growing understanding of local society.

An enlarged meeting of the CEC gathered in July 1926 in Shanghai. [139] At least sixteen people attended, including Chen Duxiu, Li Dazhao, Zhang Guotao, Tan Pingshan, Zhang Tailei, and Chen Yannian. [140] It was this meeting that adopted a critical resolution on the Guangdong peasant movement (quoted in the previous section) that blamed CCP organizers of peasant unions as at least partly responsible for the movement's defeat. The point of the critique was the same as those of the pamphlet and the Labor Movement Committee review. It emphasized that peasant-association organizers should have the trust of peasants, involve them actively in the running of the association, conduct propaganda, and display leadership competence and concern for issues of significance to peasants locally.[141]

The meeting's resolution on the peasant movement made the point that "we should not be too rigid in forming peasant organizations or inflexibly cling to the form of peasant associations."[142] It argued that peasant-movement organizers should forge alliances of any existing organizations in the village that represented peasant interests and that they should not immediately declare war on traditional peasant ways.[143]

In his "Political Report," Chen Duxiu attacked membership attitudes in a very harsh and outspoken manner. He stated that CCP members had become greedy for official positions and that they had abused those positions for corrupt purposes. The report deplored the fact that some CCP members treated their assignment as a mere job and lamented that they "lacked our earlier spirit of sacrifice and struggle, as well as a spontaneous revolutionary spirit."[144] In stressing the duty of CCP members to serve their constituency altruistically and with complete commitment and sacrifice, Chen Duxiu restated an important aspiration that had propelled him to found the CCP in the first place.

The new conception of the relationship combined traditional ideals—sacrifice, competence, trust, and care for local society—with modern egalitarian ones. CCP efforts at establishing a mass base following the outbreak of the May Thirtieth movement consisted of imposing its own mass organizations. The failure of this forced CCP members to modify their strategy so that it would conform to popular expectations.

This does not mean that CCP members ceased to aspire to a new social and political order. Even though the time scale for achieving this goal was stretched and CCP members abandoned the belief that a new rural order was about to congeal, the end goal remained the same. A further shift was that the rural population was no longer depicted as consisting of entirely backward people who would be transformed as they accepted the leadership of the carriers of the new age. CCP members were now instructed not to let go of the aspiration of creating a new order but to adjust themselves to rural ways in their behavior.

Andrew Walder has recently made the argument that communism in China created a new type of society, resulting from the CCP's imposition of social and economic institutions from above.[145] At least in the case of the Guangdong peasant movement, communists found it impossible to impose institutions at their will. Rather than their forcing a certain model upon Chinese society, the reverse—traditional social forms replicating themselves in the CCP—appears to have been a not uncommon occurrence. Walder's case was made especially with reference to post-1949 China, when the CCP controlled political power, and hence arguments based on earlier periods of the CCP do not invalidate it. However, one must question whether CCP power was ever so total as to make its institutions impervious to outside forces and processes such as those at work before 1949. The CCP's problem, at least in the 1925–1927 period, was that its membership expanded quickly and that it was unable to transform new recruits into party "cadres" following party procedures scrupulously and loyal to its ideals. There was ample room for the emergence of local despots using the CCP for their own ends or of altruistic local elites trying to use the CCP to make the best of a difficult situation.

THE CCP DURING THE NORTHERN EXPEDITION

The Northern Expedition began on July 9, formally as a joint CCP-KMT military campaign to unify the country militarily.[146] Chen Duxiu was ambivalent about the campaign, stating in public that it could not be regarded as a national revolution and that it should be thought of, and portrayed as, a restricted military action designed to defend the Canton Government from warlord forces approaching from the north.[147] For other CCP members, especially those who had congregated around Borodin, the Northern Expedition offered a new opportunity to create revolution. Many CCP members in 1926 and the first months of 1927 believed that they were on the brink of capturing power.

For Chiang Kai-shek, the Northern Expedition proved an opportunity to establish his power in the KMT and in China. Midway during the Northern Expedition, on April 12, 1927, Chiang Kai-shek suppressed the CCP in Shanghai with the help of the Green Gang. A bloody purge followed in the rest of China; several thousand CCP members and tens of thousands of its mass-organization followers perished.[148] Following the 1945 CCP resolution on its own history, PRC historians have attributed the disaster to the "rightist opportunist" and "surrenderist" leadership of Chen Duxiu.[149] In their stated view, Chen underestimated the strength of the CCP and the revolutionary ardor of its supporters, abandoning leadership of the "Great Revolution" (Dageming) to the KMT.[150] Conrad Brandt has argued that the responsibility lay not with the CCP but with Stalin, who, he believed, refused to endorse the CCP's withdrawal from the KMT and the building of an independent CCP military force, since this was what Trotsky defended, and he and Trotsky were locked in a factional struggle for the leadership of the Communist Party of the Soviet Union.[151] Along the same lines, Maurice Meisner recently argued that in 1927 a "revolution based upon a worker-peasant alliance was not beyond the realm of possibility," but that "critical decisions and policies . . . formulated in Moscow" led to the CCP's defeat. [152]

Neither Chen Duxiu's leadership nor Stalin's stubborn insistence on maintaining the United Front were fundamental, in my view, to the debacle for the CCP. What happened in the countryside during the Northern Expedition was similar to the events in Guangdong that produced the March 20 incident. Behind Northern Expedition forces, CCP peasant organizers set off turbulent peasant movements. As in Guangdong, the response of those affected was to mobilize the KMT to suppress peasant associations. In Shanghai itself, CCP members made a last-ditch attempt to stay Chiang's hand by having the armed pickets of the revived Shanghai General Labor Union take the city. But the same processes that led to that union's destruction in September 1925 also caused the end of this uprising.

The essential assumption of Brandt and Meisner, as well as those made by PRC historians, is that the CCP could have succeeded in defeating Chiang Kai-shek. A crucial element of the case is that Stalin prevented the CCP from building an independent military force. One problem with this argument is that Chinese communists did not raise the idea of setting up an army until 1927, when it was much too late. It was not that CCP members opposed the use of force; many served in the National Revolutionary Army as soldiers or political commissars, and they organized armed pickets and peasant self-defense corps. However, its members did not conceive of the CCP as an organization that should have its own military apparatus.

CCP strategy was to gain leverage in society and in armies by forming cells of soldiers in existing armies, establishing mass organizations, and conducting propaganda. To an extent, antiwarlord attitudes and fears that the CCP would become a "regular" party may have played a role in the CCP's initial oblivion to the need to possess its own armies. Also, when they looked toward the October Revolution, Chinese communists did not see an event in which a large army dominated. It was presented as an uprising of urban workers that swept a vanguard party to power. The Comintern blueprint did not depict communist parties as directing large standing forces; it portrayed them as rising to power on the basis of mass movements. The CCP tried to follow the same strategy. One of the important lessons of the Northern Expedition, and of the whole 1925–1927 period, was the crucial importance of military force in a country like China. However, this lesson was learned only in the course of the 1925–1927 period; CCP members paid little or no attention to building independent military institutions earlier.

It is also not clear that the CCP would have been capable of staffing and controlling its own armed forces as early as 1925 or 1926. It was unable to maintain control over its mass organizations, and, as we shall see, it was not able even to maintain authority over armed pickets. With a booming membership and facing a host of organizational problems, the CCP would have been hard-pressed to field an army of several hundred thousand well-equipped and well-disciplined soldiers, the kind of army it would have needed to be victorious on the battlefield. The Great Revolution was simply not the CCP's to lose.

What happened during the Northern Expedition was that those whose positions were threatened by the CCP's peasant associations swelled the ranks of the KMT. As the expedition progressed, this process eroded whatever natural base the CCP-KMT United Front possessed, and the reasons for the two to oppose each other multiplied. Given the fact that military power was in the hands of the KMT and that CCP members had not been able to root their party deeply into society, the CCP was in a situation in which it could not win, no matter what policies it adopted.

The Northern Expedition in Hunan

The occupation of Hunan Province was the opening chapter of the Northern Expedition (see map 3). Threatened by an opposing warlord in northern Hunan, on June 2, 1926, the Hunanese warlord Tang Shengzhi incorporated himself into the National Revolutionary Army as commander of its Eighth Corps. Two forces were sent to support Tang, and on July 12 the combined armies succeeded in taking Changsha and securing the Xiang River valley, the province's heartland. Leading segments of the troops that took Hunan were sympathetic to the CCP. General Ye Ting, for instance, had studied in Moscow, and he recruited many cadets with a CCP affiliation into his army.[153]

The CCP was quick to capitalize on this beginning of the Northern Expedition. Hunanese students of the Peasant Movement Training Institute in Canton immediately traveled home to set up peasant associations,[154] concentrating on the Xiang River valley,[155] the area under the control of Northern Expedition forces. One issue important to peasants was speculation in rice. Peasant associations in Hunan prohibited rice export out of the county in which it was grown, and they set up patrols to enforce this measure. They also redistributed the contents of local granaries.[156] By October 1926, according to a CCP report from Hunan, sixty-five counties had formed peasant associations with a total membership of 340,000, and CCP members controlled forty-five of the sixty-five county-level peasant associations.[157]

As in Guangdong, the KMT became the vehicle for the opposition to

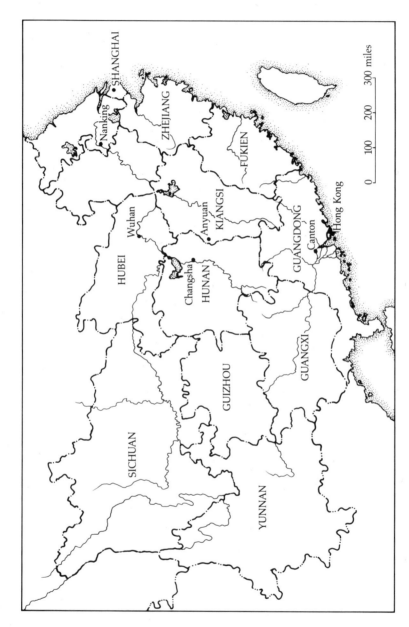

Map 3. Southern China.

CCP peasant associations. At first, the influence of CCP members in the Hunan branch of the KMT was even larger than it had been in Guangdong, and this contributed to the rapid spread of the peasant movement in the province. It was CCP members who had built up the Hunan KMT branch as part of the United Front policy, and initially, until the collapse of the warlord government in the province in March 1926, as a Hunan CCP resolution of October of that year stated, "in a situation of severe repression, the CP assumed control over the KMT branch; otherwise, nobody would have done anything."[158] After March 1926, CCP policy in Hunan had become that of "assisting the left wing politically and organizationally, so that they can come to stand on their own feet."[159]

In an October 22, 1926, report, the secretary of the Hunan Regional Executive Committee foresaw quick victories for the Hunan peasant movement and indicated the extent of support it received from the new KMT government institutions:

> In the Hunan area, the peasant movement has already reached the stage of struggle. The rent-reduction campaign in Hengyang was quite successful, and we managed to prevail everywhere in conflicts with evil gentry and local bullies. . . . The Provincial Peasant Department approved more than 4,000 *yuan* for peasant-movement expenditures, and the Provincial Bureau of Reconstruction allocated 3,000 *yuan* for the Provincial Peasant Association. County governments each allocated separately between 100 and 300 *yuan*. The Provincial Bureau of Reconstruction in addition approved . . . 20,000 *yuan*, which over a ten-month period will be released to assist the Education Association (it was decided to use these funds to run peasant training classes in all counties).[160]

Hengyang is a large city in southern Hunan.

The expansion of the CCP in the province led to a shortage of capable cadres, especially in relation to the vastly expanded scope of activities resulting from the burgeoning peasant movement.[161] As in other places, then, the very expansion of a CCP campaign contributed to its disintegration. Also, rural elites responded quickly to the intrusion of peasant-association cadres. By the middle of November, according to the Hunan Regional Executive Committee of the CCP, the burgeoning peasant movement was beginning to stimulate a sharp reaction:

> Recently reactionary forces grew up everywhere in response to the development of the peasant movement. Their makeup consists of elements of the Western Hills Conference, Zhao Hengti, . . . greedy officials and corrupt clerks, local bullies and evil gentry, as well as evil local militia bureaus. They attack relentlessly. . . .

They also craftily employ destructive and agitational devices such as infiltrating peasant associations and creating false ones. In the name of peasant associations, they create disturbances with the [new] government and destroy tax-collection institutions.[162]

Zhao Hengti, it will be remembered, was the Hunan warlord who with Tan Yankai established an independent Hunan.

One result of this reaction was the loss of CCP control over KMT organizations in Hunan. In November 1926, CCP members controlled only a third of the seats of the provincial KMT branch's executive committee. Late 1926 CCP reports from Hunan stated that Hunan's elites—provincial assemblymen, warlord factions, and prominent local graduates of universities, including Peking University—had joined the KMT.[163] The effect on local government was immediate: On November 14, a Hunan Regional Executive Committee report stated, "The county government consists mostly of rotten eggs; everywhere it incites counterattacks by KMT party branches and civic bodies."[164]

The Hunan peasant movement nonetheless continued, at least through the first months of 1927. This is clear from a short memoir by a man named Wu Jianren, who was involved in the movement in early 1927, and from Mao Zedong's famous "Report on an Investigation of the Peasant Movement in Hunan." After spending one month in a peasant-movement training institute, where he studied CCP and peasant-association resolutions, Wu Jianren was dispatched to the countryside with the assignment to organize a county-level peasant association with a few other CCP members. Wu did so by visiting the county's government offices, including the Education Promotion Agency and local military leaders. He then invited local officials to a congress of peasant representatives to establish the county peasant association.

The local CCP branch, with perhaps ten recently recruited members, compiled a slate to be approved by the congress. Several of those with local power, including representatives of the local militia, were included to make sure that the association had local backing. After the congress, it announced a rent-reduction campaign, began the confiscation of temple land, and fought against opium smoking and gambling. Wu claimed that some local gentry were rounded up and paraded through the streets.

Even if a revolution appeared to rage at the county level, the situation in the villages was different. After the formal establishment of the peasant association, Wu traveled to villages in the north of the county, and to his surprise, he found that no peasant was willing to talk to him. In another area of the county, Wu succeeded in forming a village peasant association, but only after the outbreak of a clan feud gave him the opportunity to adopt the grand style of a county official. Surrounded by horses and soldiers, he had arrived to establish peace.[165]

Mao Zedong's report has become famous for its depiction of the poor peasantry as possessing the potential of contributing to the revolution and even being a revolutionary force in its own right.[166] Written in February 1927 when Wu Jianren's peasant movement was in full swing, it is obvious on which type of events Mao based his observations. The report completed an important shift in Mao Zedong's thinking. At the August 7 emergency conference later in 1927, Mao claimed that it was his personal investigation of peasant turbulence in Hunan that caused him to abandon his doubts about peasant violence and see the revolutionary nature of the peasant movement. "Before I went to Changsha," he stated, "I had no reason to oppose the party's resolutions that favored the landlords. . . . I changed my mind only after I had lived in Hunan for some thirty-plus days."[167]

Mao Zedong's claim is credible. A year earlier, in a March 1926 article, Mao had argued that while he realized the importance of peasants for the revolution, he thought of this as something for the future. He had written that peasants "are destructive now, but if we can establish leadership over them and if we can provide a proper organization, then they have the potential of becoming a revolutionary force."[168] What struck Mao during his period of wandering around the Hunan countryside was that peasants were already carrying out a revolution. In the Hunan report, he described "poor peasants" as

> our main force in the bitter fight in the countryside. They have
> fought militantly through the two periods of underground work
> and open activity. They are the most responsive to communist
> leadership. . . . This great mass of poor peasants . . . are the
> mainstay of the peasant associations, the vanguard in the over-
> throw of the feudal forces, and the heroes who have performed the
> great revolutionary task which for long years was left undone.
> Without the poor peasant class . . . it would have been impossible
> to bring about the present revolutionary situation . . . and
> complete the bourgeois democratic revolution.[169]

Mao Zedong was impressed not only with the peasants' engagement in revolution but also with their willingness to follow CCP leadership. The report was an expression of Mao Zedong's reborn faith in the Chinese capacity to create a revolution, a faith that had been consistently weak throughout the early years of the CCP.

Mao Zedong's report is also an indication that CCP organization in the countryside was in fact not strong. The report, addressed to the Central

Bureau in the first instance,[170] was his appeal to the Central Bureau to change this. Mao Zedong's argument was that if the CCP would throw itself behind the revolution the peasants were setting off in the countryside, it would obtain victory. While he kept his faith in a revolution based in the countryside, Mao quickly abandoned the apocalyptic vision of the report. At the August 7 emergency conference, he no longer argued that poor peasants were producing a revolution almost independently, and he reaffirmed the importance of leadership and especially military power. He now blamed the CCP for ignoring the importance of the military and having a simplistic faith in mass movements:

> Previously we scolded Sun Yatsen for conducting only military campaigns. We, however, did exactly the opposite; we refused to develop a military campaign and engaged only in mass movements. Chiang Kai-shek and Tang Shengzhi established themselves by means of the gun. Only we did not bother about it. Now we have begun to pay attention to this, but we still lack firm concepts. . . . One can say that our defeat in Hunan was entirely the result of our intellectualist outlook. From now on, we must very much emphasize military affairs; after all, political power comes out of the barrel of a gun.[171]

The Hunan peasant movement did not come to a halt until Chiang Kai-shek cracked down on the CCP in April 1927. In May, the commander of Tang Shengzhi's troops in Changsha took action against the CCP as well as peasant associations and labor unions in the area in an extremely tense situation when it appeared that the CCP was about to stage a rebellion.[172] Wu Jianren's memoirs state that he and other CCP members attempted a revolt but were unable to muster any sort of following, the attempt ending even before it had begun.[173]

The Northern Expedition in Hubei and Kiangsi

National Revolutionary Army troops fought their first serious battles as they edged their way toward Wuhan in late August 1926, and it took more than a month of heavy fighting before the last resistance in the city had been defeated.[174] The peasant movement in Hubei was of special importance to the CCP, since the provincial capital Wuhan was the home of the KMT left-wing government, in which Russians and CCP members played an important role. Established in December 1926, the Wuhan Government was set up in order to hem in Chiang Kai-shek, whose powers grew as the National Revolutionary Army advanced. The heavy concentration of CCP personnel in the province reflected the importance CCP members attached to the Wuhan Government. While in July 1926 there were perhaps 280

CCP members in Hubei, by March 1927, more than 2,000 worked in peasant associations alone, and three months later, that figure had nearly tripled.[175]

CCP and Russian influence in the Wuhan Government showed in its laws. In March 1927, the KMT Hubei Provincial Branch passed "Draft Provisional Regulations for the Punishment of Local Bullies and Evil Gentry," which made peasant associations the official rural government in the province.[176] In Hubei, it was law for peasant associations to take charge of local militia, justice, education, and administration, and to implement a rent-reduction campaign.

Despite the high-level backing and the concentration of CCP resources in the province, peasant associations failed to alter local social relations. One problem, a Chinese scholar recently pointed out, was that even at the high point of the peasant movement in Hubei, 40 percent of county peasant associations lacked CCP members. Growth in CCP membership was only partly due to the transfer of experienced CCP members into the province; most were recent and inexperienced local recruits.[177] A May 1927 survey by a provincial-level peasant-association functionary made clear that problems of leadership at the local level were serious and that CCP members clashed sometimes with peasant-association members:

> Lower-level party branches that can exert leadership in the villages are urgently needed. Many county branches lack people with a rural background. This is the most important reason for the fact that peasant associations and party branches attack each other and view each other with hostility. . . . In the past, when peasants struggled with local bullies and evil gentry, peasant-association functionaries relied completely on slogans to direct peasants. . . . Now that we want to set up self-government institutions in villages to deal with questions of land and capital, slogans will not do.[178]

As elsewhere, the peasant association's failure to penetrate local society made it easy for local elites to reassert themselves. In Hubei, the counteroffensive by the elites was "even swifter than the rise of the peasant movement," according to one contemporary account:[179]

> The accuracy of local bullies and evil gentry in carrying out their reaction and counterattacks has advanced much faster than those of the peasant movement. Before the arrival of the National Revolutionary Army, they used political power to oppress peasants. Afterward, when power fell into the hands of the revolutionary government protecting the interests of the peasantry, they changed their methods: (1) They created rumors such as that

if one joined a peasant association, one then must provide manpower for military service and share one's products and one's wife. (2) They organized bogus peasant associations. (3) They formed their own party branches and suppressed real peasant associations in name of the party. (4) They organized secret clubs to create turmoil, such as assassination leagues, the Big Fists Society, the Big Sword Society. (5) And recently, they linked up with military forces.[180]

Little information is available for the peasant movement in Kiangsi. In October 1926, there were no more than around six thousand peasant-association members in the province, which then supposedly expanded in the months afterward to several hundred thousand. Even though this was a monumental increase, the figure remained substantially below those for Hunan and Hubei.[181] The Northern Expedition advance in the fall of 1926 through Kiangsi toward Shanghai was a difficult one, the outcome hanging in the balance for nearly two months during battles for Nanchang, the provincial capital.[182] Chiang was victorious and set up his alternative to the Wuhan Government in Nanchang. The peasant movement in Kiangsi therefore took place in much less favorable conditions than in Hunan and Hubei.

The CCP did not have the organization, the size, the mass following, or the strategy that could have resulted in the capture of power. An essential problem of the CCP's strategy was that its mass organizations evoked a reaction among elites that it was unable to control and was directed against peasant associations. The opening statement of a December 1926 resolution by a special CEC meeting on the CCP's rural strategy expressed the conundrum as follows:

> The problem of political power in the villages involves the substitution of peasant power for the feudal one of local bullies and evil gentry. In this political movement, we must overthrow the reality of the political power of local bullies and evil gentry; to avoid panic among petit bourgeois elements, we do not have to scream slogans about peasant power.[183]

One cannot hope that the enemy one is trying to kill will somehow not notice this.

Urban Failure: The Shanghai Uprising

The CCP-instigated Shanghai uprising began on March 21, 1927, one year and a day after Chiang's coup in Canton. It was an ill-coordinated act of desperation. Before the uprising, Chiang Kai-shek's forces had defeated

Sun Chuangfang, a warlord who had originally blocked Chiang's approach to Shanghai. Now Chiang's road toward the thriving city and the productive coastal areas of Zhejiang and Jiangsu was clear.[184] The Shanghai uprising was the CCP's last-ditch effort to prevent Chiang from occupying this important area, which would make him the most powerful man in China.

The uprising aimed at recreating the May Thirtieth movement. There was some suggestion in preceding events that it would again be possible to mobilize the city's population in large-scale nationalist demonstrations. In January 1927, in urban centers such as Wuhan and Kiukiang along the Yangtze River, such demonstrations had resulted in crowds entering and repossessing foreign concessions.[185] An important difference between Shanghai and the other two cities was that Shanghai was not under the control of the left-wing KMT government.

On February 23, a joint session of the Central Bureau and the Shanghai Local Committee established a special committee to prepare for the uprising.[186] It included Chen Duxiu, Zhou Enlai, Deng Zhongxia, and Zhao Shiyan. The CCP had sought to exploit a power vacuum in the city resulting from warlord withdrawals on two previous occasions. The first took place in October 1926, but collapsed, a CCP document stated, because the uprising was ill-timed, because the CCP attempted to cooperate with a KMT left wing that was feeble, and because of a lack of preparation.[187] The second was halted after two days on February 23, the same day that the special committee was formed, because of military opposition.[188]

A December 1926 Central Bureau document had already noted that in Shanghai "our own organization and ability to struggle is not very strong." It argued that the CCP's weaknesses made it imperative that CCP members lead "a Shanghai self-government movement" involving the "Shanghai bourgeoisie, the workers, and the KMT left wing,"[189] the same reasoning that had led CCP members to adopt a "United Front" strategy in the days leading up to the May Thirtieth movement. One of the things the special committee did was to conduct negotiations with KMT members in the city to obtain their support for an uprising.

The CCP proposed that after the uprising, a Shanghai government be ratified by a "citizens' assembly" of representatives from all civic bodies, including industrial organizations, professional bodies, and associations based on regional origin—a formulation that provided space even for traditional labor organizations. The CCP's proposal to the KMT was for both parties to create a slate for this government prior to the uprising.[190] According to minutes of the March 5 meeting of the special committee, Wu Zhihui and other KMT leaders supported the idea of a United Front government but objected to the uprising itself. They feared that Shanghai's large vagrant population would run amok. The compromise the two sides reached was to organize a general strike. CCP negotiators presented this as "a way to prevent rioting" when Sun Chuanfang's forces were withdrawing from the city and Chiang's forces had not yet arrived.[191]

The February 23 joint Central Bureau and Shanghai Local Committee meeting also instructed CCP members in the city to put their own house in order by "rectifying and developing . . . party blocs and unions."[192] The fact that basic CCP organizations needed improvement underscores the impromptu nature of the uprising. That pickets organized formally under the auspices of the Shanghai GLU, which had continued in an underground form after its suppression in Shanghai in September 1925, was more of a worry to CCP leaders in the city than a source of strength. They lacked weapons,[193] and as Luo Yinong stated at a meeting of the special committee two days into the uprising, "the pickets have a very mixed population; we must rigorously correct this."[194] Chen Duxiu made the suggestion to organize CCP cells within pickets and to eliminate unreliable elements. Zhao Shiyan pointed out that this might backfire and proposed to incorporate pickets of doubtful loyalty to the CCP into the forces of Xue Yue, a general in Chiang's armies whom the CCP believed loyal to the cause of the KMT left wing.

Chiang Kai-shek began the suppression of the Shanghai uprising on April 12. Martin Wilbur has described Chiang's careful preparations for the crushing of the Shanghai GLU and the suppression of the CCP in Shanghai. They were preceded by bloody repressions of CCP unions in Hangzhou and Chungking on March 30 and 31, and were followed by a rash of such actions throughout southern China.[195]

Chiang's main source of power was the military forces now massed around Shanghai. In the city he also had the support of the Green Gang. The suppression of the CCP and the Shanghai GLU began when Du Yuesheng, the leader of the Green Gang, invited his fellow gang member Wang Shouhua to dinner on April 11 and had him killed. Wang was also an important CCP member and the head of the Shanghai GLU.[196] In addition, Du unleashed gang members on the pickets of the GLU. Du Yuesheng probably feared the erosion of his influence among Shanghai workers that the GLU might cause, and he may have received large sums of money from Chiang. Minutes of a March 5 special committee meeting stated that Du had sent a note urging the CCP not to allow the Shanghai GLU to introduce bombs into workers' districts;[197] Du may have also feared that the uprising would lead to uncontrollable violence in the city, something that would not have been in his interest.

A further reason for the failure of the Shanghai uprising is that unlike the May Thirtieth movement, the uprising was not widely supported or even understood by Shanghai's population. Speaking on April 18, 1927, during a meeting in Shanghai that evaluated the causes for the uprising's failure, Zhou Enlai made the point that the CCP had not been able to communicate to Shanghai's population why the CCP wanted to stage this uprising and seize power, leaving it confused. The CCP had been unable to "win over the petite bourgeoisie," as he stated it.[198]

According to figures collected by Zhao Bu, some 3,000 to 4,000 CCP members died during Chiang Kai-shek's White Terror.[199] Not only CCP members were the target of the repression. Between March and August 1927, Zhao Bu claims, nearly 30,000 people died, 40,000 were injured, 25,000 people were arrested, and more than 30,000 became refugees.[200] After disposing of his enemies in this way, Chiang continued the Northern Expedition. He brought Peking under KMT control in the summer of 1928, and on October 10, 1928—an anniversary of the outbreak of the 1911 Revolution in Wuhan—a new KMT government was inaugurated in Nanking, thus bringing the warlord era to a formal close.

The KMT was not solely responsible for the White Terror. In Shanghai, it was the Green Gang that put the pickets of the Shanghai GLU to the sword, and the staggering cruelty of some acts suggests local vengeance, sanctioned in the name of the KMT's purge of "communist bandits." One account, a CCP one, has it that some peasant-association members were drenched in petrol and set ablaze; others were scorched to death with hot irons; some victims were tied to a tree, cut up, and then had small pebbles rubbed into their wounds; and one woman was dragged through the streets naked by a wire pulled through her breasts.[201]

ACHIEVEMENTS, 1925–1927

The CCP's achievements in establishing a mass party in the 1925–1927 period should not be judged by the standard of whether it was able to defeat the KMT but should be examined in light of changes in its position in Chinese society since 1925. In 1925, CCP members were active in a few urban centers. In 1927, they could be found in many parts of southern and central China. Table 1 breaks down the growth of CCP membership by region. It is based on data culled from the CCP Central Committee Archives by Zhao Bu. While the reliability of these statistics is limited, the table does suggest that in the 1925–1927 period, the CCP grew rapidly, first in Guangdong and in the Shanghai area (listed in the table as Jiangsu-Zhejiang), and that during the Northern Expedition, it gained a dramatic

Table 1. Growth of CCP Membership by Region,
October 1925–April 1927

	Oct. 1925	Apr. 1925	July 1926	Sept. 1926	Dec. 1926	Apr. 1927
Guangdong-Guangxi	928	3,700	4,558	5,039		9,027
Jiangsu-Zhejiang	1,080	2,500		2,223	2,688	13,000
The North	253	1,500	2,069			3,109
Henan-Shaanxi	169	700	305	350		1,300
Hubei	88	400		1,000	3,500	13,000
Hunan	702	1,420		2,699	4,714	13,000
Shandong	192	420	515			1,025
Kiangsi		65			500	3,000
Chungking		19	42	120	168	200
Anhui		27	33			233
Shaanxi-Gansu						388
Manchuria						380
Moscow	13	200				

Sources: Zhao Bu, "Organizational History (Five)," 98–99; Chen Duxiu, "Report at the Fifth Congress," 40.

Note: Blank slots indicate that figures are not available, and places with less than 200 members in April 1927 have been omitted. For geographical definitions used in the above table, see Zhao Bu, "Organizational History (Five)," 90–97. They did not remain the same. "The North" refers to Peking, with the Regional Executive Committee based there overseeing all CCP activity in north China and parts of Manchuria.

rise in membership in Hunan and Hubei. It also makes clear that in many other places besides these four areas, the CCP had established a base.

This development should not be visualized as CCP members fanning out from Shanghai and Canton into unknown and alien territory. Earlier chapters have made it clear that the CCP had strong roots in China's hinterland. The establishment of CCP organizations in Hunan and Hubei, in fact, saw them returning to their places of origin, where they had first become active in the CCP. Mao was one example of this. CCP members had congregated in Shanghai and Canton in the context of the United Front to pursue the strategy of bringing about a national revolution. Now they traveled home.

CCP membership had also become more representative of China's population. Chen Duxiu reported at the Fifth Congress of April–May 1927 that 53 percent of the membership consisted of workers and that 19 percent were intellectuals, 18 percent peasants, 3 percent soldiers, and 0.5 percent middle and small businessmen (these figures do not total 100 percent).[202] It is not clear how these categories were defined or whether Chen Duxiu represented them accurately; he probably underestimated the number of peasants and overestimated that of workers to support his own urban-worker-oriented policies. However, there seems little reason to doubt that in comparison to 1925, the CCP's membership had become vastly more representative of the makeup of Chinese society.

The KMT's suppression disrupted the CCP's organization but was unable to eradicate it. Besides the CCP members who died during Chiang's crackdown, no doubt many gave up their membership or ceased to be active. Nonetheless, November 1927 data suggest that CCP membership was still in the 15,000 to 20,000 range.[203] Compared to 1925, this formed a remarkable increase. In numbers, the CCP lost only the gains that CCP statistics claimed had been achieved between November 1926, when there were 18,000 members, and April 1927.[204]

The 1925–1927 period also produced important changes in the CCP's approach toward forming a mass-based party. As they gained experience in constructing mass organizations, CCP members came to recognize the difficulties involved in detaching Chinese from their traditional bonds and linking them to CCP institutions. Because of negative experiences in the labor and peasant movements, the CCP abandoned the strategy of imposing a new order from above and recognized that China's population would not simply flock to CCP institutions. This translated to more realistic recruitment policies for CCP mass organizations. Also, CCP policy emphasized the fostering of a personal sense of loyalty between the Chinese population and the CCP, and its members became responsive to popular expectations of people and institutions asserting a political role.

Another important change was the realization that the CCP needed to control its own military organization. The May 1926 Guangdong Regional Executive Committee report about the Guangdong peasant movement repeatedly stressed the importance of military power for the construction of peasant associations in Guangdong. However, it did not state that the CCP was to control it. It was Chiang Kai-shek's crackdown that led Mao Zedong to state the idea forcefully at the August 7 emergency conference in 1927. A week before the conference, during the Nanchang uprising of August 1, 1927, the CCP for the first time attempted to mobilize a military force of its own. Before the Nanchang uprising, Zhou Enlai and others enticed several units of the National Revolutionary Army to sever themselves from the KMT and accept the command of the CCP.[205] Even before this, in March and April 1927 during the Shanghai uprising, Zhou had already attempted to organize an armed force separate from the KMT. The pickets that took over the city during the Shanghai uprising could not be called an army, and many elements appear to have been linked more to the Green Gang than to the CCP. Nonetheless, this suggests that Mao Zedong, Zhou Enlai, and probably others who had belonged to the Guangdong Regional Executive Committee or been aligned with it had realized the importance to the CCP of developing an independent military capability.

The importance of military power illustrates one of the differences between the situation faced by the Bolshevik Party in Russia and the CCP in China. Operating in a country where the political order had disintegrated and the state was weak, the CCP needed to set up its own institutions, and for this, military force was essential. Until 1927, Chinese communists attempted to set up labor unions and peasant associations merely by persuasion or by "borrowing" armed might from the KMT. An independent military apparatus was important for the CCP in another way. During the Guangdong peasant movement, peasants were keenly aware of who could and who could not mobilize superior military force. Hence, simply the suggestion that the CCP could call forth military force was a powerful mobilization device.

Much has been written about the CCP's "mass line."[206] In the early 1940s, in Yan'an, Mao Zedong articulated the mass line in ideological terms, claiming it as a special characteristic of China's revolution. As Stuart Schram pointed out, the mass line was long in the making.[207] Some of its elements can be traced back to CCP experiences during the 1925–1927 period, including the emphasis on a personal relationship between CCP members and the Chinese population. The most significant way in which the 1925–1927 period contributed to the eventual gestation of the mass line was forcing CCP members to abandon the approach of the wholesale imposition of new institutions and to develop policies and mobilizational strategies that took the Chinese situation into account.

The mass line did not emerge in a linear way. There were periods about which it can be said, with hindsight, that the CCP appeared to veer away from the path leading toward it. After the outbreak of the May Thirtieth movement, the CCP abandoned mobilization techniques formulated between the Third and Fourth congresses that possessed important mass-line features. This occurred in a time of heightened expectations of a coming revolutionary wave and led CCP members to abandon the precautions in establishing mass organizations that had been instituted after earlier disappointments. Chinese communists learned from the past, but they sometimes also forgot, especially when they convinced themselves that a new situation rendered the lessons invalid. Hence, the idea that the mass line was the result of a gradual and steady accumulation of revolutionary experience in Chinese conditions, as CCP writers tend to suggest, is not an accurate depiction of reality.

The conduct of CCP members during the 1925–1927 period suggests that many CCP members had only a limited faith in the revolutionary potential of China's urban proletariat. In Shanghai, CCP members were unwilling to rely solely on urban workers, and they sought to expand the popular base for the revolution, hesitating to take action before such a fundament had been laid. In contrast, CCP activities in the countryside were undertaken with much greater confidence. The issue of whether the CCP's base was to be in the countryside or in the cities was to give rise to a great deal of debate, Mao Zedong in 1927 becoming the first to articulate clearly a conception of the peasantry as possessing a revolutionary force in its own right. The origins of this issue in the practical experiences of CCP members during the 1925–1927 period is clear.

From the wider perspective of China's modern political history, the 1925–1927 period is important, as it signaled the arrival of mass political parties. Mass demonstrations and protest movements attained an enormous symbolic significance. It became politically unwise to denigrate them as mere riots, and they were now presented and seen as true expressions of the people's will. Political parties vied to become associated with a mass demonstration, or better yet, to be seen in the public eye as its leader. Increasing energies were expended on producing propaganda aimed at capturing the rhetorical initiative in the press to convince the population that one's party represented its ideals and its interests, and possessed vision and courage.

Mass politics affected political parties themselves profoundly. Until the May Thirtieth movement, political parties were small, and their sphere of action was limited. With the May Thirtieth movement, both the KMT and the CCP strove to build up a mass base and to attach other social and political organizations to themselves. CCP and KMT propaganda emphasized the idea that they dictated the historical agenda. While the control of military power was to mean that political parties in China had the means to force change, they were not invulnerable to desires of their constituents, as the KMT's experiences in Guangdong in the 1925–1927 period illustrate. Local groupings used the rhetoric as well as the resources of a political party as vehicles for the promotion of their own ends.

China's mass parties took shape in a specific environment. Prasenjit Duara has recently argued that the republican period was characterized by state involution. While bureaucracies at higher levels expanded constantly, according to Duara, they were increasingly less able to exercise authority at the local level. In Duara's view, political relationships frayed at the village level in a process in which ever-higher financial demands were imposed on the community as a whole. This made those responsible for revenue collection more powerful. However, at the same time, campaigns to bring to bring "modernity" to the village—by the establishment of modern schools, the destruction of temples, the construction of a modern bureaucratic system—eroded the traditional norms and values that had legitimized the traditional social order. The result was that traditional village leaders were constantly pressured to deliver greater sums of money while their standing in the local community was undermined. Many left the village world, and local politics became the arena of generally despised but ever more powerful "local bullies and evil gentry."[208]

This situation had a number of consequences for both the CCP and the KMT. The main differences—in social base, ideology, styles of organization, and norms—in the CCP and KMT responses to the disorder of the Republic have been pointed out at length in the past. The similarities have received less attention. Both the KMT and the CCP were forced to take on tasks normally conducted by government bureaucracies. The lack of a coherent national political system made it impossible for the emergence of mass politics to take the shape of increasing popular involvement in a cohesive political system centered around a state bureaucracy, as has happened in the West. The integration of the local and the central was a constant concern for both parties. Finally, a "civilian" political culture was difficult to achieve in this situation, and it is remarkable that the CCP and the KMT in the 1930s both became increasingly militarized—they not only controlled or sought to control vast military forces but the CCP and KMT also turned increasingly toward the military as a source of new norms and values.

5/The Party Arises

In the Introduction, I stressed that Marxism-Leninism is not just a worldview and a strategy to seize power. In the CCP, it also became the basis of a new mode of communication, with its own norms and values, and assumed important institutional functions, including in the area of legitimation. Before the May Thirtieth movement, Chinese communists had already begun to use Marxism-Leninism in some of these ways to develop their own culture, even if it did not yet penetrate deeply and was to prove fragile. It was as the result of several processes and events after the outbreak of the May Thirtieth movement that new styles of operation and norms of behavior based on Marxism-Leninism became firmly entrenched in the CCP.

While the behavior of CCP members had changed in several ways by the time of the Fourth Congress of January 1925, socially and culturally they continued to be a small, uniform group. Because of the influx of new members after the May Thirtieth movement, the CCP was required to adopt patterns of operation and norms its entire membership could share. At the same time, the CCP's base in society, its audience, expanded vastly. The continued adoption of modes of behavior associated with traditional elites was a barrier to the entrenchment of the CCP in local society. This too built pressure to develop new modes of operation.

The CCP lacked effective means to solve internal disagreements. In the early CCP, legitimation—understood here as the act of demonstrating that a decision is made and implemented with proper authority—was highly problematic, as the difficulties Chen Duxiu experienced in integrating the CCP made clear. Following the May Thirtieth movement, the "collective-leadership" style of operation as it had emerged after the Third Congress in central executive committees quickly collapsed under the strains imposed by the CCP's failure to capitalize on the movement, a sign that whatever new procedures had been announced were not dependable. The growing size of the CCP and the increasing complexity of its bureaucracy also strengthened the need for firm processes of legitimation.

It was in the clash between Chen Duxiu and the members of the Guangdong Regional Executive Committee, which is discussed extensively in this chapter, that CCP members brought Marxism-Leninism as a mode of communication into full play. They articulated their grievances in Marxist-Leninist terms and presented their preferred policies as derived from Marxism-Leninism. Both sides also began to treat such concepts as party discipline or central leadership not just as organizational principles but as sacrosanct norms, adherence to which, they asserted, distinguished the very being of a CCP member.

The CCP's defeat by the KMT produced a situation in which the CCP's legitimation crisis came to a head. In the spring of 1927, the CCP's leadership had disintegrated, and Chen Duxiu's period of reign came to an end. As a result of Chiang's action, many CCP members lost faith in their party. Some explanation had to be advanced to account for what had happened, and the case had to be made that the CCP continued to be a worthwhile investment for its members, especially now that the White Terror had raised the risks of participating in it dramatically. While new policies were announced, they were not accompanied by any sort of justification. A credibility crisis loomed.

As in other Leninist parties, legitimation in the CCP came to center around the demonstration that decisions were based on the correct party line. The correct line, as Kenneth Jowitt has written, can be thought of as a set of statements presented as derived from the correct application of Marxism-Leninism to a historical context and the set of policies that are argued to be based on this analysis.[1] In *What Is to Be Done?* Lenin had portrayed the party—not a particular person or text—as the source of all authority. For Lenin, it was the Party—with a capital P—to which communists owed obedience, and it was in the name of the Party that orders were issued. Even if Lenin was confident that he grasped the correct party line, he nonetheless did not claim that he possessed it by virtue of his special genius; he argued and expected argument.[2] In Jowitt's words, "For Lenin the Party is Hero."[3] Leadership, in Lenin's view, was not a matter of individual courage, moral fortitude, or saintly wisdom but the formulation of the correct Party line. The Leninist conception of leadership incorporates the possibility that individual leaders and even whole party organizations lose their hold on the correct party line and so lead the party astray.

It was at their August 7 emergency conference of 1927 that CCP members firmly asserted the above conceptions as valid for the CCP, and exploited them to justify leadership and policy changes. The "Letter of Warning to All Party Members" produced by the conference portrayed Chen Duxiu's failure to grasp the correct party line as the cause for the CCP's defeat by the KMT and asserted that "the opportunist errors of the party leadership had their base in the failure to understand the nature of the Chinese revolution, the function of various social classes in different revolutionary stages, and the communist party. More precisely, it did not possess a Bolshevik and Marxist understanding of these issues."[4] The letter argued that the CCP's defeat was the result not of Chiang Kai-shek's military force or CCP membership problems but Chen Duxiu's ideological mistakes, caused by his erroneous understanding of the historical situation and easily corrected by his removal.[5] All that needed to be done for the CCP to regain its preordained historical role, the letter asserted, was to put into place a leadership that based itself upon the correct line. The concept of the party line made it possible for CCP members to suggest an accounting for the disasters of the past and to assert that party membership remained a worthwhile commitment.

I have adopted the August 7 emergency conference as an appropriate hallmark to signal the end to the founding period of the CCP because it was at the conference that Chinese communists used Marxism-Leninism as a legitimation device and exploited it to account for the recent disasters they had suffered. The argument here is not that after the conference regionalist ties were no longer important in the CCP, that kinship had lost its meaning for CCP members, and that they truly accepted the authority of the CCP leadership in all areas of life. Traditional norms, elite as well as nonelite, did not lose their importance entirely, and some remained very important. Even if any CCP leader now had to demonstrate that he was the formulator of the correct party line, this was not the only quality on which his leadership depended. The creation of new forms of political organization or the articulation of new norms did not stop with the emergency conference. In addition, Marxism-Leninism could serve merely as device by which to represent a particular interest within the CCP. However, CCP members now asserted that the party was the Party, and new rules of the game had emerged.

THE RISE OF FACTIONALIST CONFLICT

In this section, I discuss the conflict between the Guangdong Regional Executive Committee and Chen Duxiu to describe how conflict articulation in the CCP changed after the May Thirtieth movement. Both sides increasingly asserted the importance of party discipline, obedience to central leadership, and the derivation of policy from Marxism-Leninism. At the same time that these ideas were organizational concepts important to CCP members, they were increasingly used by them as a medium of communication. They expressed themselves using concepts, dogmas, norms, and anecdotes derived from Marxism-Leninism, which at one level were the basis of strongly held beliefs but were also mobilized as political assets in the fight against opponents.

My interest is not the nature of factions. I do not intend to analyze how factions were bound together, a question that past scholars have discussed extensively.[6] The focus is on the way Chinese communists substituted for previous ways of conducting conflicts one that depended on Marxism-Leninism.

Origins of the Rift

In pursuing the peasant movement and the bloc-within strategy, the members of the Guangdong Regional Executive Committee became a special group in the CCP. The committee was dominated by returned students, most of whom had spent time in western Europe and Moscow, only one member never having been abroad for an extended period, most having been born outside Guangdong.[7] It included Peng Pai, Zhou Enlai, Chen Yannian, and Huang Ping. CCP members of the Canton–Hong Kong Strike Committee like Deng Zhongxia and Borodin's translator, Zhang Tailei, often met with members of the committee in Borodin's home.[8] Before the March 20 incident, they seemed singularly successful: Young, versed in Marxism-Leninism, trusted by Borodin, with high positions in the KMT and in the Canton Government, they were leading, they could claim with some accuracy, the Canton–Hong Kong strike and the Guangdong peasant movement.

The ostensible point of conflict between Chen Duxiu and the Guangdong Regional Executive Committee was the CCP's relationship with the KMT. This relationship had created contention in the CCP from the time that Maring first suggested the bloc-within policy. The Fourth Congress led some CCP members to believe that they had put the issue behind them, but as soon as the May Thirtieth movement broke out, it returned.

Until Chiang Kai-shek's seizure of power in Canton, events in Guangdong suggested, at least to Borodin and the members of the Guangdong Regional Executive Committee, that their strategy toward bringing about the mass party was highly promising. While the October 1925 Central Executive Committee had left room for both the Canton and Shanghai strategies, the resolutions of the February 1926 special CEC meeting ordered the bloc-within policies pursued in Guangdong to be applied throughout China. The fact that members of the Guangdong Regional Executive Committee, prompted by Borodin, sought to capture control of the CEC and were not content to pursue their preferred policies only in Guangdong is an indication of the changes that were taking place in the CCP. Regionalism was no longer able to diffuse conflicts about policy. It also suggests that the conflict between members of the Guangdong Regional Executive Committee and Chen Duxiu concerned not just CCP policy toward the KMT but also how the CCP was to operate.

The meeting's resolutions argued that the urban proletariat in the cities had become isolated and had lost the support of the petite bourgeoisie and students. Urban nationalistic mass movements like the May Thirtieth movement, they argued, were a thing of the past. The resolutions asserted that instead the peasant movement should become central in the CCP's policies and that the CCP was to support the KMT in the Northern Expedition to be able to create a peasant movement.[9]

Chen Duxiu was not present at the meeting. According to a CEC announcement that conveyed the decisions of the February 1926 special CEC meeting to the membership, Chen was ill and for more than a month had been unable to discharge his duties as CCP leader.[10] It is not impossible that Chen Duxiu was indeed in bad health; later in 1926, when Chen Duxiu had managed to recapture control over the CEC, he directed CCP affairs from a hospital bed, according to a Central Bureau document.[11] It is also possible that the meeting's documents quoted Chen Duxiu's health problems as a face-saving gesture for Chen and to "excuse" itself for taking control of party policy.

Chiang Kai-shek put an end to whatever victory celebrations Borodin and his CCP supporters held when Chiang took power in Guangdong on March 20, 1926, only weeks after the February 1926 CEC meeting. Following the March 20 incident, Chen Duxiu sought to reassert himself in the CCP. It was the policy he then articulated that became the ostensible source of conflict between him and members of the Guangdong Regional Executive Committee. The latter, as I will detail shortly, called for an immediate counterattack against Chiang Kai-shek and strove to seize power by usurping the KMT from within.

What was the position Chen came to represent and to push within the CCP? To speak of one policy is a simplification. From the summer of 1926 on, as the Northern Expedition advanced, CCP policies changed rapidly, as did opinions in the CCP. Its members faced a rapidly changing situation in which they were heavily involved but did not control the course of events. CCP policies in this period did not derive from a carefully considered strategy but were often impromptu responses to a rapidly changing situation. At the same time, large urban demonstrations and peasant movements in Hunan and Hubei stimulated quite a few CCP members to believe that they would yet be able to capture the initiative and turn the situation to their advantage. The sense of both vast opportunity and imminent calamity fueled conflicts in the CCP.

As the situation was so fluid and complex, I first sketch the position with which Chen Duxiu became identified as if it were constant. I then describe the conflict between Chen Duxiu and members of the Guangdong Regional Executive Committee and Borodin. In doing so, I also indicate how the positions changed.

As mentioned, Chen did not see the Northern Expedition as coterminous with the national revolution. In a June 1926 article, he expressed disagreement with such an interpretation of the Northern Expedition, stating that it should be seen as a defensive action to protect the KMT Canton Government from advances made by northern warlords.[12]

Second, Chen Duxiu appears to have supported a dissolution of the United Front, or at least a drastic loosening of the coalition between the CCP and the KMT. In two letters, one addressed to Chiang Kai-shek and one to the KMT as a whole, Chen Duxiu hinted at this. He stated that he thought of the bloc-within strategy instrumentally, as one way two parties committed to carrying out a revolution could cement their cooperation. He denied that CCP members were out to use this form to take control of the KMT, as KMT members thought. The task at hand, Chen argued, was to struggle for the national revolution, and the differences among those in favor of this goal were not to be allowed to become obstacles preventing its attainment.[13]

The issue of the United Front was one of extraordinary complexity for CCP members. They had been continuously suspicious of KMT intentions, and Chiang Kai-shek's crackdown on the CCP in Canton had added real worries to that. But within the CCP ranks there were those who continued to believe that it would be possible to use the KMT instrumentally and therefore opposed a relaxation of the ties between the two parties. The relationship was also problematic for CCP propaganda writers. It would be difficult for the CCP to make its nationalistic propaganda believable when at the same time it severed its ties with the KMT. Chen Duxiu, the two documents referred to above indicate, aimed to place the onus of a breakup of the United Front on the KMT.

The most controversial part of Chen Duxiu's policy, which was related to his view of the bloc-within policy, was to abandon attempts to augment CCP power within the KMT, even in Guangdong. This position collided head-on with the Canton strategy. In letters in the fall of 1926 to the Guangdong Regional Executive Committee, Chen explained that his aim was to build up the strength of the KMT left wing in Guangdong under Wang Jingwei's leadership in the hope of using Wang as a counterweight to Chiang Kai-shek.[14] Following Sun Yatsen's death, Wang and Chiang had emerged as the two most powerful KMT figures in Canton. Wang, an eloquent speaker and the political leader of the KMT left wing, had left Canton to go into voluntary exile shortly after the March 20 incident. What Chen seems to have been after, in short, was a United Front of a strong and independent CCP with a KMT dominated by the left wing.

Many elements of Chen Duxiu's position became CCP policy at the July 1926 CEC meeting. The political report at the July 1926 meeting, delivered by Chen Duxiu, and the meeting's resolutions exposed problems in the peasant movement, as mentioned in chapter 4; they reasserted the importance of creating an independent base for the CCP, especially among urban workers, and restated the centrality of Shanghai in the revolution. The report blamed the March 20 incident on CCP members having created a backlash in the KMT by dominating KMT offices, crowding out even left-wing KMT members—a clear gibe at the Guangdong Regional Executive Committee.[15] The July 1926 CEC resolutions constituted a repudiation of the policies installed at the February 1926 CEC meeting at which Borodin and representatives from Guangdong had dominated.

Only documents from the Comintern Archives in Moscow, which are not accessible, can settle whether the policy sketched above was Chen Duxiu's creation or derived from Soviet advisers. The policy was consistent with views Chen Duxiu had articulated all along. He had supported the bloc-within policy at the Third Congress, but not very enthusiastically and only because he was pessimistic about the CCP's revolutionary potential. At all other times, he favored the construction of an independent CCP base of power and a strong party organization, aims to which the above policy contributed. Chen had been consistently suspicious of the KMT. For him, the policy was also a good opportunity to reassert his authority in the CCP. He had many reasons to support it.

Even if large parts of the policy were consistent with Chen's views, it is unlikely that he would have decided on a course that departed so radically from that set out by Borodin in February 1926 on his own initiative. In a letter dated September 17, Chen stated that his proposals of that time reflected a meeting in which he and representatives of the Far Eastern Bureau of the Comintern had participated.[16] Comintern agents in China, including Voitinsky; several Russian advisers in Canton; and a delegation from Moscow that was traveling through China at the time of the March

1926 incident on an investigation tour in all likelihood played a central role in making the policy.[17]

It was a report of a Russian adviser in Canton that argued that CCP members and the Russians themselves had been too eager in taking control of KMT institutions, thus provoking resentment.[18] According to a recent chronological biography of Voitinsky published in China by prominent Chinese historians, in late 1925 or early 1926, at the time of the Western Hills Conference and the Second KMT Congress, when the KMT left wing was under great pressure, Voitinsky arranged a meeting at the Shanghai Consulate of the Soviet Union at which were present Chen Duxiu, Zhang Guotao, and prominent KMT left-wing leaders. The meeting, according to this biography, produced a seven-point agreement that included the idea of limiting CCP activity in the KMT to create a greater role for the KMT left wing.[19] Even Borodin may have played a role in the formulation of the policy, though he later came to oppose it. He was the Soviet negotiator who concluded the agreement with Chiang Kai-shek to reduce the presence of CCP members and Russians in the KMT and the Canton Government.

The extent of involvement of Comintern and Soviet leaders in Moscow is difficult to gauge. Conrad Brandt has argued that Stalin's involvement in Chinese affairs began only with the Comintern Central Executive Committee's Seventh Plenum of December 1926, and Trotsky did so only afterward.[20] When at that point Stalin did formulate a detailed policy for the CCP, the CCP response was surprise at the unprecedented direct intervention from Moscow.[21] Yet even without direct involvement, certainly Comintern agents in China acted with at least one eye on Moscow. The dispatch of delegations also suggests that at least within the Comintern bureaucracy, there was real interest and involvement in affairs in China.

Chen Duxiu was perhaps not alone responsible for the creation of the policy for which later Chinese communist historiographers have vilified him. The section below, however, will suggest that he became its principal defender. He staked his authority on it. This itself was a departure from his behavior in the past, indicating the changes taking place in CCP modes of operation. Before the May Thirtieth movement, Chen was not firmly wedded to a well-articulated policy, and setbacks did not immediately create a leadership challenge. At the time of the Fourth Congress, CCP documents had asserted that CCP problems resulted not from erroneous ideological views of the leadership but from "backward" attitudes of rank-and-file members.

The Guangdong Committee and Chen Duxiu

Reservations among communists in Guangdong about formal CCP policy were expressed with growing forcefulness following the March 20 incident. According to Voitinsky's biography, Chen Yannian and other members of the Guangdong Regional Executive Committee voiced their opposition to compromise with the KMT at a meeting of Soviet advisers in Canton and Chinese communists several days after the incident.[22] Recollections of Lai Xiansheng, a Guangdong CCP member involved in the events, confirm this. After the incident, according to Lai, Chen Yannian—a son of Duxiu—spoke out forcefully against any suggestion that the CCP reduce its revolutionary efforts in Canton.[23] Lai also states that by the end of May, after the KMT had passed the resolution restricting CCP influence, Chen Yannian and other members took to speaking of Chen Duxiu with contempt.[24]

Differences of opinion between CCP members and Canton (and Soviet advisers there) can be traced back to the October 1925 CEC meeting, as I have suggested. The resolutions of the February 1926 meeting suggest that by that time, the disagreements were already very serious and could no longer be settled by the kind of compromise the October 1925 CEC meeting had produced. The March 20 incident may have led to a temporary cessation of hostilities. The resolutions of the July 1926 CEC meeting suggest that at that time Chen Duxiu was able to muster a majority of representatives and see his ideas installed as official CCP policy. In the fall of 1926, however, the struggle between Chen and CCP members in Canton reached a new stage.

Chen Duxiu had few hard instruments, such as an internal CCP police, to secure the compliance of CCP members with his policies. That does not mean, though, that he was entirely powerless. He dispatched representatives, including Zhang Guotao and Peng Shuzhi, at this point the head of the Propaganda Department,[25] to Guangdong to persuade the Guangdong Regional Executive Committee of the wisdom of his policies. Most important, in letters and instructions he mobilized the normative weight contained in Marxism-Leninism to put the committee under pressure. A September 22 letter by Chen Duxiu, for instance, called into question the respect for party discipline of the Guangdong committee. "As to the issue of Wang [Jingwei] and Chiang [Kai-shek]," he wrote, "we have already analyzed it in detail in a letter of September 17, and we have also already pointed out which policy the Central Bureau has adopted."[26]

While resistance to Chen Duxiu in Guangdong probably began earlier, there is positive evidence that by September 1926, members of the Guangdong committee had determined their own set of policies, had begun to pursue them in Guangdong in defiance of Chen Duxiu, and had begun to seek their installation as party policy. Their views were summarized by Qu Qiubai in September 1926. Qu explained that Borodin believed the object of CCP policy should be the restoration of the peasant movement and the establishment of a left-wing regime in which CCP members were dominant. To defuse the problem of KMT left-wing resentment, an agreement had been signed committing the CCP to accept the restrictions on CCP influence in the KMT, on the conditions that the new regime would restore the peasant policy followed before the March 20 incident and that a national congress would be convened after the fall of Wuhan. According to Qu, Voitinsky, who also had traveled to Guangdong, and Borodin had argued at length about CCP policy. Qu reported that when Voitinsky suggested that Borodin's proposal might entail ousting Chiang, Borodin answered that if Chiang Kai-shek could not agree to his policies and was not attacked, power in Guangdong would fall into the hands of local bullies and that the CCP then might as well abandon the province. A further point of contention between Borodin and Voitinsky was the CCP's attempt to strengthen the cooperation between Wang Jingwei and Chiang Kai-shek. Borodin objected to this because this would mean that the CCP would have to withdraw from the KMT, to which he was opposed. He also did not favor an immediate return of Wang Jingwei.[27]

Borodin's ideas, Qu's report noted, were widely supported among CCP leaders in Guangdong, and "after Voitinsky arrived in Guangdong, he spent some time listening to reports of the Guangdong region. However, because he had no concrete experience with the situation, his criticism could not persuade the regional committee."[28] This formed a clear rejection of central policies. No doubt to Chen's great frustration, Qu wrote in the report that he was in agreement with the ideas of Borodin and Guangdong committee members and that he believed no fundamental mistakes had been made in Canton. The copy we have of the report includes, in parentheses, fuming comments by Chen at Qu's remarks:

> In my view, during Wang Jingwei's period (before March 20) our policy in Guangdong really on the whole was correct. (Chen Duxiu: Actually, there was no policy.). . . . However, it is true that there have been a few little glitches in implementation. For instance, it really was not wrong to dominate and control [*baoban*] the KMT; we did not do anything with our control [*bao er buban*]. (Chen Duxiu: On the one hand, they occupied the KMT, and on the other, the CCP disappeared.)[29]

(Parentheses and the ellipsis are as in the original.)

Between September 17 and December 4, at least eight letters went back and forth between Shanghai and Canton.[30] On September 17, a letter from Shanghai clarified and defended Chen's position, stating that with Chiang Kai-shek in power, a peasant movement had become impossible. To try to overthrow Chiang during the Northern Expedition was very dangerous, it went on, and hence the CCP should press Chiang to accept Wang Jingwei's return.[31] Only with the left wing in power, it argued, could the peasant movement be reignited. "If the Canton members believe that there is no left wing," it concluded pointedly, "you should in this instance begin with creating one."[32] Chen noted that the CCP's aim remained to establish cooperation between Chiang and Wang but that if it became apparent that this would drive Chiang to take action against the KMT left wing or seek cooperation with warlords, it would then be wise to reduce pressure on Chiang. The demand for Wang Jingwei's return should in that case be postponed, but propaganda in favor of the left wing was to be maintained to entice Chiang to remain close to the left wing.[33]

On October 4, Chen Duxiu issued a letter in the name of the CCP Central Committee that used very sharp language.[34] A letter of the previous day had been conciliatory and had concluded with the suggestion that eventually it would be possible to oust Chiang, a statement that must have been welcomed by Canton CCP members.[35] The reason for the sudden outburst of Chen Duxiu, it appears, was that he had come to fear that a secret opposition group had risen once more in the CCP.

In the October 4 letter he stated, "Today two comrades . . . returned from Guangdong, and from my discussions with them, there are three issues to which I must instruct the Guangdong region to pay very careful attention."[36] Chen had learned from these discussions, the letter suggests, that CCP members in Canton continued to refuse to follow his policy of support for the KMT left wing and continued to denounce it. He wrote that he had heard that the members of the Guangdong committee had "selected some party members from those among the troops advancing into Jiangxi to constitute a party bloc. This bloc did not at all deal with military activities but was given responsibility for planning the development of the party in Jiangxi."[37] Chen "reminded" the Guangdong Regional Committee that "whatever ideas you might have for local party departments or activities, they must go through the center; you cannot act on your own. Not only should it be so according to organizational principles, but the Guangdong region also cannot equal the center in its knowledge of the local situation."[38] Furthermore, Chen asked why members of the Guangdong committee acted "mysteriously" (*shenmi*), not informing or involving the rank-and-file CCP membership in the province.[39] While the conflict between Chen and the Guangdong committee began as a dispute about policy, other issues soon became important.

The response by the Guangdong committee, made in a letter dated October 21, can have done little to assuage Chen's fears. It stated that members of the committee had actually worked very hard to help the KMT left wing, although by this it meant, it explained, not a few individual left-wing leaders but "the masses of workers and handicraft workers."[40] This left wing, it pointed out, "is not at all suspicious of us."[41] It denied the charge that CCP members in Canton had attempted to dominate and control (*baoban*) the KMT, explaining that its activities aimed at assisting left-wing masses to establish left-wing KMT branches run by left-wing KMT figures, not CCP members. "If this method is not correct," it chided, "we hope that the center will provide guidance."[42] The authors of the Guangdong letter indulged in a labeling game in an almost childish fashion. The relationship between Shanghai and Guangdong was strained to its breaking point.

Chen made a report on KMT-CCP relations to a leadership meeting on November 4 and 5.[43] Who attended the meeting is not known, but the subject was the divergent views in the CCP about the CCP's KMT policy. The meeting was triggered by a communication from the Guangdong committee. Its opening paragraph stated that the committee's members "together submit the ideas below about the left-wing issue in the hope that the Central Committee will consider them and come to a final decision and that it will issue an announcement to all areas so that they become the standard in our KMT work."[44] It also noted that the members supported Borodin's views. At the leadership meeting, Chen responded to the challenge as follows:

> As to the KMT issue, the first point is whether the Chinese
> national revolution has already happened. There are some foreign
> comrades who have this idea, and among Chinese comrades there
> are also those who think that the national revolution has
> succeeded, or that it soon will do so, and that the revolution of the
> proletariat is about to take place.[45]

The rift between Canton and Shanghai had blossomed into an open struggle, neither side wanting to give way.

Several things should be pointed out. First, the harder Chen Duxiu and members of the Guangdong committee fought, the more they asserted the importance of central leadership and CCP policies being arrived at by proper procedure. The October 21 response of the Guangdong committee to Chen's October 4 letter (asking for clarification about the committee's activities in Kiangsi) asserted that the committee had no intention of transgressing Central Bureau authority. It stated that the committee would file a report immediately, and "if the Central Bureau in its investigation finds that the party bloc in Kiangsi interfered in local party affairs," it went on, "then party discipline has to be promptly enforced, and severe punishments should be meted out."[46] Of course, the Guangdong committee probably did act in contempt of the Central Bureau in Shanghai, but its members described circumvention of the Central Bureau as an "improper act."

Second, both sides cast their arguments in Marxist-Leninist terms and tried to suggest that they acted in accordance with Leninist principles of party organization. They did not yet raise the specter of ideological deviance but sought to demonstrate the validity of their position as derived from a Marxist analysis of the situation they confronted. If the CCP was to take over the KMT from within, as Borodin and his supporters believed, the way to express this in ideological terms was to say that the national revolution had succeeded, and according to Chen Duxiu's quote mentioned above, this is what they did. Chen scoffed at the notion, stating that two-thirds of China remained under outright warlord control and that colonial powers remained firmly in charge.[47]

Personality issues probably entered into the conflict. While it is impossible to reconstruct personal relations among CCP leaders in the fall of 1926 with much certainty, Zhang Guotao's memoirs suggest that personal animosity existed between Peng Shuzhi on the one hand and Qu Qiubai and Cai Hesen on the other. Qu and Cai had initially worked under Peng in the CCP's Propaganda Department.[48] According to Zhang Guotao, an on-the-scene observer, Peng Shuzhi's flamboyance and happy-go-lucky attitude clashed with the serious dispositions of Cai Hesen and Qu Qiubai, especially after Cai's wife, Xiang Jingyu, had an affair with Peng. Cai and Qu, Zhang wrote, both devoted all their time to CCP affairs and in every free minute studied Marxism or wrote articles. They suspected Peng, said Zhang, of flattering Chen Duxiu and trying to build him up as the party's "emperor" as a way of increasing his own influence. As this strategy was reminiscent of Han dynasty Confucians', Peng carried the nickname "Confucius."[49]

Chen Duxiu had now become firmly identified with a policy that probably originated from both him and Comintern agents. For him to abandon it would have come at a great cost to his stature within the CCP. While Qu Qiubai argued that Voitinsky had gone over to Borodin's side, it is not clear whether this was a momentary vacillation or a permanent shift.

Chen Duxiu's Denunciation of the Guangdong Committee

Chen was able to extract from a December 13 special CEC meeting a resolution that endorsed him, even if it did not do so wholeheartedly. Present were Chen Duxiu, Zhang Guotao, Qu Qiubai, Peng Shuzhi, Voitinsky, and Borodin.[50] The meeting's "Resolution on the Political Report" stated:

> The dangerous tendencies facing the national revolutionary United Front pointed out by Comrade Zhongfu [Chen Duxiu] in his political report are all real. . . .
> Comrade Zhongfu suggested in his report several strategies to save the situation. They are in general correct. . . .
> After the conclusion of this meeting of the Central Executive Committee, all party branches must immediately convene meetings of all types to explain the policies the meeting decided upon from the perspective of the concrete situation at the local level and to determine ways to implement them.[51]

At this meeting, Chen Duxiu took the ideological high ground, perhaps again with the assistance of Voitinsky. In a report to the special CEC meeting (*tebie weiyuanhui*) on December 13, Chen Duxiu branded CCP members in Canton as sufferers of infantile leftism, or "the children's disease of leftism" ("*zuo*" *zhibing*), as the text stated literally.[52] Chen then defined the features of infantile leftism.[53] He first stated that "traditional habits of thinking, especially prevalent among Guangdong comrades," had made some CCP members "despise the KMT."[54] He quoted one as having said, " 'With the March 20 incident, the KMT died. After May 15, the corpse began to stink. Now, why do we clench this stinking corpse to our bosom?' "[55] May 15 was the date on which the KMT Central Executive Committee passed resolutions restricting CCP influence in the KMT.[56] Chen noted, apropos of the above quote, that "the influence of the military victory of the Northern Expedition on the warlords in the north and on the rapid takeoff of the mass movement demonstrates that the KMT is not yet a dead corpse."[57]

A second feature of infantile leftism, Chen stated, was the habit of CCP members to attempt to dominate the KMT. He argued that it had been this attitude and not CCP policies that had caused left-wing KMT members to oppose communists. The same attitude also manifested itself, he argued, in CCP members' seeking sole control of mass movements, leading some CCP members to deny the existence of a KMT left wing. This, he wrote,

Guangdong CCP members had been prone to do. Finally, infantile leftism had led people to refuse to cooperate with left-wing KMT members in running mass organizations, a problem that existed not only in Guangdong but also in Hubei and Peking, Chen declared.[58]

Chen Duxiu was aware of the struggle between Trotsky and Stalin that then raged in Moscow. On December 4, a letter from the Central Bureau to the Guangdong committee attempted to drive a wedge between Guangdong committee members and Borodin: "Borodin did not perceive the real situation at the front or the rear clearly (for instance, his statement that the Guangdong masses were already standing up and that they could be independent. . . . We believe that these notions were Borodin's and not those of you, the Canton Regional Executive Committee)."[59] The same letter stated that "the errors and dangers" of Borodin's views had "origins in the same theory as that of the opposition faction in the Soviet CP . . . Trotskyism."[60] To judge from this letter, Chen appears to have attempted to reunify the CCP by isolating Borodin.

The December 1926 special CEC meeting produced a superficial reunification of the CCP leadership. The meeting issued resolutions in the name of the major figures involved with the CCP. It was at this time that a left-wing KMT government was being set up in Wuhan, and it was expedient for everybody to pay lip service to the idea that there was a strong left wing in China. However, underlying policy and personality tensions remained high, and the institutional problems were not addressed.

The meeting was important for the organizational development of the CCP; Chen Duxiu used the idea of ideological deviance to attack his opponents and to strengthen his position. As the relationship between Shanghai and Canton worsened, Chen appealed increasingly to Marxist-Leninist sensibilities in the Guangdong committee, perhaps in part because they, just returned from Moscow, projected themselves as more thorough Marxist-Leninists than the majority of CCP members. At the same time that Chen increased the normative pressure on his opponents in Canton, he thereby also closed avenues for compromise. At the December meeting he seemed to have achieved victory; at the same time, he was now in a position in which any disagreement with his policies could be seen only as a challenge to his leadership.

It should be noted that Chen Duxiu used Marxist-Leninist arguments clumsily. He depicted "immature leftism" as the result of traditional attitudes, a statement highly reminiscent of the type of arguments he made during the New Culture movement. He did not state that immature leftism was a sign of the lack of a real Marxist-Leninist mind-set.

Disintegration of CCP Leadership and Deepening Factional Strife

It is probable that in December Chen believed that he had the support of Moscow. According to Brandt, Stalin took everybody by surprise at the Comintern meeting of December 1926 by insisting that the Comintern adopt a radically new policy in China, one that contradicted on all important points the resolutions of the December 1926 CCP special CEC meeting for which Chen had fought hard. Pavel Mif, the man responsible for drafting the Comintern's resolution on China, according to Conrad Brandt, still modeled his first draft after Chen Duxiu's views. Only after this, Brandt has argued, did Stalin pronounce his disapproval.[61]

The opening paragraph of the Comintern's final "Resolution on the China Question" of December 1926 stated that "the result of the victory of the National Revolutionary Army in the Northern Expedition is that it effectively wiped out imperialist rule from half of China."[62] This was a radically different depiction of the Northern Expedition than Chen Duxiu's. The Comintern resolution then went on to argue that China was on the brink of a new revolutionary stage in which the proletariat, and therefore the CCP, would capture the initiative.[63] Only if led by the CCP could the national revolution succeed in China.[64] In contrast, Chen had spoken of CCP weaknesses and the need for CCP members not to dominate KMT institutions and mass movements.

The resolution expressed support for a radical land policy, although it softened this position by stating that while the fundamental CCP objective was the nationalization of all land, this policy should be implemented in accordance with local conditions.[65] Defeats suffered by the National Revolutionary Army were not due to the strength of antirevolutionary forces, according to the resolution, but to the CCP's having failed to place the land issue firmly at the center of the national liberation movement.[66] It concluded that the "land issue is . . . now the central question"[67] and formulated a detailed rural policy to arouse and support the peasant movement. It included arming the peasantry, dissolving local militia, and confiscating land belonging to warlords, temples, and gentry who opposed the revolution.[68]

The Comintern also rejected Chen Duxiu's strategy of building up the KMT left wing and transforming the bloc-within into an alliance of two independent parties. "The idea that the CCP leave the KMT is wrong. . . . The whole development of the Chinese revolution, its nature and its future," the Comintern insisted, "demands that the CCP remain in the KMT, and moreover it must increase its activities in it."[69]

In January or February, CCP leaders produced a formal response to the Comintern's resolution. It acknowledged that the CCP had made "a fundamental mistake. . . . That is, we assumed an unbridgeable gap between the national and socialist revolutions."[70] The response also stated that Chinese communists had failed to develop the policy the Comintern now had instructed them to install because they still were in the grip of traditional ways of thinking. This statement must have been painful for Chen Duxiu because he had argued less than two months previously that immature leftism in the Guangdong committee resulted from their traditional ways of thinking.

The Comintern resolution has received wide attention as an instruction that forced the CCP to adopt an "unimplementable" policy with a number of insoluble contradictions, such as the Comintern's call to seize control in the KMT from below, while the KMT was a Leninist organization controlled from above, or its insistence that the CCP mobilize and arm the peasantry but do so within a KMT framework, though many KMT leaders and army officers were natural targets for peasant actions.[71] It has also received wide attention as flowing from the Trotsky-Stalin struggle.[72] Within the CCP, the effect of the resolution was that it reignited factional strife. By December 1926, the Guangdong committee's opposition to Chen's leadership was declining, and Chen Duxiu had been able to convene a leadership meeting that produced a single strategy for the CCP. The Comintern's resolution nullified his efforts and plunged the CCP leadership again into a period of internal struggle.

Qu Qiubai's Challenge

In early 1927, Qu Qiubai staked his claim to CCP leadership. He did so by attacking Chen Duxiu's views and policies as a deviation from a correct line, arguing that they had resulted from Chen's inability to apply Marxism-Leninism creatively to the Chinese situation. Qu's views are interesting because they contained a vision of the CCP and its position in Chinese society that differed from Chen Duxiu's and was to exert considerable influence in the CCP. But most important for the organizational history of the CCP, Qu articulated his views using the Leninist mode of communication, and he did so skillfully. He also articulated a new form of leadership legitimation, one based on the idea of the correct party line.

Several factors were in Qu Qiubai's favor. He had a good knowledge of Marxism-Leninism and possessed a lively pen. Qu knew Russian, which was helpful in obtaining the trust and support of the Comintern and its representatives. Furthermore, the formation of the Wuhan Government in late 1926, the decline of the Guangdong peasant movement, and the extension of CCP activities into Hunan and Hubei was bound to affect factional alignments in the CCP.

In February 1927, Qu Qiubai published two books. One was a collection of his previous essays, the other a volume of new articles entitled *Controversial Issues in the National Revolution*. In the first collection, Qu asserted the importance of theoretical work and claimed a position for himself as a leading theoretician. He also subtly suggested that Chen Duxiu had been a pioneer in the CCP but that it was time for a new generation to take over.

The very opening statement of Qu's collection of earlier essays asserted the importance of Marxism as something that was to ground all CCP policies. Echoing Lenin, he stated that "revolutionary theory must never be divorced from revolutionary practice."[73] Writing about his earlier activities in the CCP, Qu Qiubai wrote that many of "our predecessors" were interested in Marxism but that among these, only Chen Duxiu had attempted to unite Marxism in revolutionary practice with popular mass movements. With theory being so important and Chen Duxiu the guiding light, Qu wrote, he had gladly worked under Chen Duxiu to develop the Marxist understanding of China's reality: "After I returned to China [from Moscow] in 1923 straight until October 1926 when I fell ill, I continuously labored under Comrade Chen Duxiu's guidance, . . . even though I was aware that I was not up to the task. However, the work of applying Marxism to Chinese national conditions could not be relaxed for one day."[74] The essays were grouped according to various topics, creating the suggestion that Qu had shown his mettle as a theoretician in many fields.

It was in *Controversial Issues in the National Revolution* that Qu Qiubai claimed the role of defender of the correct line against a strayed leadership. The main essay, "Internal Problems in the CCP during the Chinese Revolution," explained why Qu Qiubai issued his critique of the CCP leadership. The CCP, Qu argued, was in the control of a faction that did not understand Marxism correctly and hence had brought disaster to the CCP. A commitment to the correct interpretation of Marxism-Leninism, which transcended individual or party loyalties, compelled him to speak out, he argued. The following quote illustrates this and also gives a sense of Qu's provocative and vivid style, a style whose passion was no doubt designed to underscore the sincerity of his commitments:

> When somebody is ill, he will die if he seeks to hide it and fears treatment. If somebody says, "Factions have emerged in the CCP," well, then, "everybody" will certainly say, "According to the stipulations of Leninism, factions should not exist within a communist party. . . . Therefore, since this party in China carries

the name 'Communist Party,' of course it cannot contain factions. You, young fellow, you are just creating rumors and inciting people, and in accordance with item 1001 of Leninist discipline, take him outside the yamen gate and decapitate him. . . ." Of course, decapitation is the Chinese imperial culture of the East. . . .

However, I want to be a Bolshevik and follow real Leninist discipline, and I am not afraid of imperial decapitation. Our party does contain factions. . . .

Our party is ill, and the name of the illness is Peng Shuzhi-ism.[75]

Qu did not mention Chen Duxiu but blamed Peng Shuzhi as the source of current CCP policies. Readers of the essays cannot have been mistaken that Qu Qiubai criticized the policies pursued by Chen Duxiu, as other scholars have argued.[76] Qu's personal vendetta against Peng played a role here, but Qu perhaps adopted this approach also to display a certain circumspection in attacking a revolutionary elder—important in mustering support in the CCP. This strategy was widely imitated later.

Qu's core argument was that theoretical rigidity had been responsible for the disastrous policies the CCP had followed regarding the KMT. According to Qu, it had been the inability to apply creatively to China Marxist axioms such as "the proletariat must have its own independent party" or "a nationalist revolution must be led by a nationalist party" that had produced a policy that desisted from taking over the KMT from within. The central point in the CCP's response to the Comintern resolution also had argued that the lack of ideological creativity had led to erroneous policies in the CCP. It may be that Qu had a strong hand in its composition.

Qu ridiculed ideological inflexibility as the result of traditional bookish (shushengshi) attitudes. Such bookishness, Qu explained, made people conduct revolution according to "dead formulas" such as "first one must make propaganda, then one must organize, and then one must create uprisings." Qu lamented that everything in the CCP was done according to rigid procedures, with CCP leaders acting as old-fashioned schoolteachers. CCP leaders, he wrote, treated Marxism-Leninism as "scientific revolutionary methods."[77]

In a piece of skilled diatribe, he laboriously traced the many twists and turns in CCP policy toward the KMT from the beginning, thus ridiculing them. The style suggested that the CCP leadership was confused in its thinking and thus implied that this leadership lacked a firm ideological grasp of the historical situation:

Initially they wanted to engage in a workers' movement and not in a national revolution; then they did want a national revolution, but they refused to enter the KMT; then they said that they themselves could enter the KMT but that workers could not and that in the south they could join the KMT but not in the north; then they said that industrial workers could not join; then that this was all right but that they did not want to take part in military activities, and they actually tried to educate Sun Yatsen about halting them; then they said that we had to have independent political standpoints, to show people that we were a little better than the KMT.[78]

Bureaucratism was one of Qu's prime targets. The CCP had been rigidly carved up in bureaucratic systems, he complained, with jurisdictions carefully delineated and set procedures squelching all initiative from individual members. He wrote that accusations of violations of party discipline had easily been levied.[79] While orders should indeed be regarded with the utmost seriousness, he wondered "why they are usually not explained and are merely like military commands?"[80] Qu also stated that bureaucratism had brought about the situation that "lower-level party members are not allowed to discuss political issues." The result of this was that "the masses of comrades . . . lack initiative, or even revolutionary will."[81] Propaganda, Qu wrote, had been aimed at making people follow party policy rather than inspiring them.[82]

There is a touch of melancholy in Qu's criticism, hinting at a more pristine time when CCP bureaucracies did not confine the revolutionary drive and creativity of its members. A "mentality of despising and fearing the masses," Qu wrote, "repressed the spontaneous and creative forces in active struggle."[83] Qu may well have thought that the attempt to build an institutional framework to control mass movements had missed the point, namely, releasing the energies of China's population. His writings were anything but dry, making serious theoretical statements while deriding and chastising Chen Duxiu's policies. Passion can be found in each sentence, and he asserted the worth of individual CCP members and lent grandeur and dignity to their activities. This contrasted sharply with the relentless bashing of low-level CCP members that characterized CCP resolutions and announcements coming from Shanghai.

Most of the specific policy criticisms Qu made were derived from Stalin's instructions. However, Qu's remarks about theoretical creativity, his insistence that Marxism-Leninism be made relevant to Chinese conditions, and his attacks on bureaucratic rigidity cannot be traced to Stalin. Qu's call to apply Marxism-Leninism to China rather than to treat it as a series of scientific prescriptions for revolution no doubt expressed the fears of many CCP members who felt their Chinese core quashed by a foreign model. Qu also articulated the strong resentment against Chen Duxiu and expressed the idea, shared by many CCP members, that the CCP should adopt a more aggressive stance.

Qu Qiubai's attack on Chen Duxiu exhibited many features of the Marxist-Leninist mode of communication, and he may have consciously imitated Lenin's rhetorical strategies or even wanted to be China's Lenin. He appealed to such values as party discipline and portrayed the CCP as a larger-than-life institution that was of preeminent importance to him. He employed Marxism-Leninism as a means to articulate his specific concerns and exploited its vocabulary and images skillfully in making Chen Duxiu look foolish and incompetent.

While Qu was a talented pamphleteer and addressed issues close to the hearts of many CCP members, he never succeeded in establishing himself as a solid CCP leader. He was not able to capture the CCP leadership at the Fifth Congress, which did not even elect him to the Politburo. At the August 7 emergency conference, he depended on the Comintern for capturing that position, but he lost it before the year was over because of opposition to him from all sides of the CCP.[84]

Several reasons may account for his lack of general popularity among CCP members. His well-known personal resentment of Chen Duxiu clashed with his holier-than-thou claims of a transcending commitment to the CCP. His docile acceptance of Comintern instructions may also have rankled CCP members, a number of whom, as we shall see, believed that the Comintern was as much to blame for the disasters that befell the CCP as Chen Duxiu. Later, Mao Zedong was careful to maintain a certain distance between himself and Moscow, as Chen Duxiu had done through much of his tenure as CCP leader, and to cultivate a style that combined claims of ideological expertise and orthodoxy with earthiness, a certain solitariness, and at times scholarly and artistic attributes. CCP leadership was never a matter of Marxism-Leninism alone.

THE FIFTH CONGRESS AND THE FORMAL ESTABLISHMENT OF A STRONG CENTER

The Fifth Congress of April–May 1927 led to a restructuring of the CCP. A Politburo replaced the Central Bureau, party discipline was carefully defined, and extensive and powerful supervisory institutions were set up to enforce party discipline and monitor the behavior of cadres. In addition, the leadership was rearranged organizationally to strengthen the bonds between the party center and its different social and factional constituencies.

These steps were a symbol of the fact that all CCP leaders now agreed on the importance of the centralization of authority and the unification of the CCP. They also reflected the party's growing social complexity. In 1925, at the time of the Fourth Congress, CCP members had not yet confronted the problems involved in running a large nationwide organization with a diverse membership. CCP central leadership institutions had continued to be thought of as a clearinghouse or a facilitating agency. The ideological form of legitimation, or the idea of the Party, had still been very much in the background.

Further Factionalism

Convening on April 27 in Wuhan, the Fifth Congress (see figure 10) opened when CCP members were just awakening to the full consequences of Chiang Kai-shek's smashing of the Shanghai uprising. Already, however, the uprising had affected the constellation of factional relations in the CCP. Chen Duxiu had left Shanghai for Wuhan on April 5, a week before the crackdown, after Wang Jingwei had returned from exile to take up the leadership of the KMT left-wing Wuhan Government. Following the uprising, a CCP and Comintern delegation from Wuhan traveled to Shanghai with resolutions blaming the members of the Shanghai special committee, which had led the Shanghai uprising, for the uprising's defeat. On April 18, these members wired a telegram to Wuhan that "the next congress must bring up the errors of Shanghai and Guangdong, and the Central Committee must acknowledge this completely before it can lead the country."[85] The Shanghai special committee included Chen Yannian, Zhou Enlai, and Li Lisan, all of whom had occupied leading positions in the Guangdong Regional Executive Committee. Its telegram demanded that the Fifth Congress discuss Chen Duxiu's errors in his policies in Guangdong and in Shanghai. The members of the Shanghai special committee probably objected to the CCP's staging the Shanghai uprising in conjunction with the KMT; as members of the Guangdong committee, they had also been opposed to this aspect of Chen Duxiu's policies.

What stands out in the style of their protest is that the members of the Shanghai special committee did not picture their struggle with the CCP leadership as a conflict between their correct line and the leadership's deviant one. Their rejection of the Wuhan resolutions derived from their refusal to be made scapegoats for the failure of the Shanghai uprising; they insisted on a "fair" allocation of blame. The only condition they made was that "Peng Shuzhi no longer occupy a seat on the Central Committee; at the least, he cannot again be the editor of the *Guide*."[86] This makes it clear that a Marxism-Leninism–based mode of communication and legitimation had not become entrenched with the December 1926 special CEC meeting.

During a Shanghai special committee meeting of April 18, Zhou Enlai, who was asked to draft the telegram, criticized past CCP leadership not for ideological errors but for cowardice in leadership.[87] Similarly, during a meeting two days earlier, he stated that CCP leaders "were afraid of old Chiang's military strength and thought that they themselves were totally weak" and that therefore they had not taken military action against Chiang.[88] Along similar lines, the minutes of the Shanghai special committee make it clear that its members did not assert their own infallibility and acknowledged their mistakes, which Qu Qiubai had not done. Zhou Enlai mentioned the failure to involve Shanghai's population and that because of this, it had not understood the point of the uprising, seeing the uprising as yet another case of infighting among politicians. Other Shanghai mistakes the telegram mentioned were a lack of preparation in the areas of propaganda, unions, and the military.[89]

The members of the Shanghai special committee were not in league with Qu Qiubai. According to a summary explanation by Voitinsky at the April 18 meeting of the Shanghai special committee, it was Borodin and Qu Qiubai who had made the criticism of Shanghai. At the same time, they did not support Chen Duxiu. Minutes of the April 18 meeting of the Shanghai special committee make it clear that the earlier struggle between them and Chen Duxiu had left deep scars, with many voices arguing that the revolution in Guangdong had collapsed because of leadership vacillation.[90] Many of the leaders of the Shanghai uprising—including Zhou Enlai, Chen Yannian, Zhao Shiyan, and even Li Lisan—stated at the time of the uprising that they were convinced that the CCP could have succeeded in overcoming Chiang Kai-shek in Guangdong in 1927 and then in Shanghai, had it not been for the irresolute policies of the formal CCP leadership. They also made plans for the immediate future as if a counterattack before Chiang Kai-shek had consolidated his position could still succeed.[91]

Mao Zedong joined the factional fray at about the same time as the Shanghai special committee. This is clear from the fact that at the August 7 emergency conference, he asserted that he began to oppose Chen Duxiu only after he finished his tour of Hunan,[92] which he did on February 5, 1927.[93] Mao joined the factional fighting, he stated, to be able to air his views about the importance of the peasant movement. Whereas the *Guide* had halted the publication of the report after a first installment, Qu Qiubai arranged for its publication by a publisher in Wuhan in April 1927 and wrote a foreword for it.[94] The foreword was dated April 11.

However, for Mao, Qu's publication of his report on the peasant movement in Hunan was a way of announcing his opposition to Chen Duxiu and thus returning to the center of activity in the CCP. It may be that he found himself in the Hunan countryside in January 1927 because until then, he had supported Chen Duxiu, something that was probably not appreciated by communist leaders in Wuhan, preeminently Qu Qiubai and Borodin.

For Qu Qiubai, Mao's description of the peasant movement in Hunan provided proof of his charge that the CCP was choking off mass movements. Mao's report also buttressed the theory of Qu and Borodin that the peasant revolution was central to China's revolution. Of course, as Benjamin Schwartz has pointed out, Mao Zedong's Hunan report was a radical ideological departure from the way Borodin and Qu described the peasantry. Mao depicted the Chinese revolution as a peasant revolution, taking place in the countryside and led by the class of poor peasants.[95]

Qu and Borodin, in contrast, and in accordance with Leninist orthodoxy, continued to assert one of the fundamentals of Marxism-Leninism—the leadership in the revolution of the urban proletariat. According to them, and according to Marxist-Leninist orthodoxy, only the urban proletariat can be the force creating the revolution. Qu was careful to make the point in his foreword that the peasantry was important as an auxiliary army of the revolution but that it acted under the leadership of the proletariat in the cities.[96] It may be that in this respect Qu's foreword was "touched up" by editors desiring to make the difference between Qu and Mao Zedong clear, but without access to the original, we may not assume this.

At the same time, Mao Zedong's assertion that the peasantry was a revolutionary force and that it was so instinctively did not really come as a bolt from the blue, even if he expressed himself in more radical and innovative terms than most other Chinese communists. Numerous CCP members had shown support for it, and CCP documents had already argued that in China the proletariat would not be able to form the foundation on which to base the revolution.

Even if Mao formulated a "marginal" ideological position, as Schwartz wrote,[97] in other ways he was very much in the midst of developments in the CCP. He demonstrated the importance of the peasantry by using Marxist-Leninist terminology and demonstrating its importance for revolutionary strategy, thus doing what Qu exhorted CCP members to do—apply Marxism-Leninism creatively to the Chinese situation. And Mao's position was not that far removed from the resolutions of the February 1926 special CEC meeting, which had declared that the urban proletariat had fallen into an isolated position. Like Qu Qiubai, Mao expressed in the Hunan report a concept of a transcending party line and a leadership that followed a correct line or deviated from it. Mao Zedong, then, was acutely aware of the issues in the CCP leadership, and he showed himself adept at using the new rules of the game and turning a difficult political situation to his advantage.

It should also not be forgotten that this was a period of great confusion in the CCP and enormous upheaval in the larger political arena. Internal infighting in the CCP and growing doctrinal polemics created an environment in which new ideas could emerge and be expressed. The peasant movements, the mass demonstrations, the hope that a new political order was taking shape, and the signs that the forces against it might yet prevail produced an atmosphere calling for the formulation of new perspectives providing some grip on the complex changes that manifestly were under way.

Strengthening the Center

It was in this difficult factional situation that the Fifth Congress took place. The congress did not end the conflicts that tore the CCP leadership apart. However, the organizational changes the congress produced in the CCP's leadership structure would not have been possible if despite all their differences, leading CCP members did not all assert a commitment to the concept of the CCP as a unified body under strict central leadership.

The congress's "Resolution on Organizational Questions" acknowledged the CCP's problems of integration and its lack of effective central leadership institutions. It stated that although "our party really has become a true mass party, . . . it must be not only a mass party but a Bolshevik party."[98] The rapid development of the CCP and the shortage and youth of the CCP's "cadre talent" (*ganbu rencai*) had blocked, the resolution explained, "the completion of the organization of the party and its consolidation."[99]

Strengthening central leadership was an important concern of the meeting. The resolution urged the Central Committee to enforce "party discipline" and "political discipline." The first referred to CCP members following instructions from higher-level CCP organizations; the second meant that CCP members had to express in public only those views that had the endorsement of the leadership.[100] The new constitution, endorsed shortly after the congress by the new Politburo, defined party discipline. "In the period of protest before a decision has been reached," the constitution warned, "one must still implement all orders from above."[101] An important qualification to the right of appeal was that a member could mount a challenge to an order only if he was supported by a majority of the party institution directly responsible for him. The resolution limited the democratic aspect of "democratic centralism" to a far greater degree than the Comintern blueprint had done.

Violations of party discipline were to be dealt with in several ways. If the punishment fell upon an individual, he could receive a warning made public within the party, be relieved of his functions, or be expelled. A warning could be issued to the unit to which the violator belonged, with demands for the reelection of its leadership. The unit could also be disbanded and its members forced to reapply for membership.[102] The fear of local cliques bound by personal connections apparently ran deep.

The congress also overhauled the leadership structure of the CCP. As before, ultimate authority was declared to reside with the party congress. When the congress was not in session, the Central Committee—no longer called the Central Executive Committee—elected by the congress was to exercise its authority. The Central Committee in turn elected a Politburo (Zhengzhiju), not a Central Bureau. Whereas the latter was thought of as a facilitating and liaison body, the constitution stipulated that the Central Committee "elects the party's secretary-general as well as several others to form the Central Politburo in order to lead all political work throughout the country."[103] The Politburo was to be an active leadership body. In turn, it elected a Standing Committee, which the constitution itself translated into English as "Secretariat."[104] Significantly, it was not the congress but the new Politburo that issued the new constitution.

This structure made it possible for various elements of the CCP membership to be represented at its organizational center. A mere twenty party members had attended the Fourth Congress of January 1925,[105] and it had elected only a nine-member Central Executive Committee and a five-member Central Bureau.[106] Eighty delegates with voting rights were present at the Fifth Congress, which produced a Central Committee made up of twenty-nine regular and ten alternate members.[107] The congress delegates represented the important regions of party activity. Those of Guangdong, Hunan, Hubei, Shanghai, and northern China dominated, but places of lesser importance were certainly not excluded. They also reflected the party's types of activity.[108] There were quite a few obscure names, suggesting that new constituencies were also represented.

In contrast, the Central Committee consisted entirely of well-known CCP members whose names had dominated in CCP documents.[109] Yet here too different regional backgrounds and party activities, it appears, were fairly evenly represented. The most striking feature of the makeup of the new Central Committee was that it drew from the membership of all factions. Qu Qiubai, Cai Hesen, Zhou Enlai, Chen Duxiu, Peng Pai, Yun Daiying, Zhang Guotao, Chen Yannian, and so on were all members of the Central Committee.[110]

Presumably to promote decisive leadership, the Central Committee of the Fifth Congress elected seven members to the Politburo, and these in turn voted for a Standing Committee that initially had three members but subsequently was enlarged by two. Chen Duxiu, Zhang Guotao, and Cai Hesen constituted the first Standing Committee. Qu Qiubai and Li Weihan were added later.[111] It is unclear how and when that happened.

It was the Central and Provincial Investigation Committees (Jiancha Weiyuanhui) that became the institutions responsible for the enforcement of party discipline. They were intended not as internal propaganda institutions but as watchdog agencies supervising party cadres with executive powers. Elected by the national and provincial congresses, Central or Provincial Committee members could not serve simultaneously on an investigation committee. Investigation Committee members were to attend Central Committee or Provincial Committee meetings, where they had the right to speak but not to vote. Executive powers remained clearly in the hands of the two latter committees; their approval was required before resolutions of investigation committees became effective.[112]

The new constitution also changed the local CCP hierarchy, eradicating the bureaucratic vestiges of regionalism. The regional committees, which had grown nearly spontaneously out of the regional study societies, disappeared. Below the Central Committee was now a hierarchy of provincial committees, city or county committees, and below them regional committees and finally branches.[113]

Even if the Fifth Congress led to the centralization of power and the tightening of internal party discipline, the constitution stipulated that if one-third of the membership or provincial party committees so desired, a party congress was to be convened.[114] In an organization as large as the CCP had become at the time, this stipulation was far less threatening to a leadership than it had been in the early days of the CCP when everybody knew each other and it was easy to mobilize a third of regional committees. However, the stipulation was nonetheless one check on the central leadership, no doubt of importance to those who disagreed with Chen Duxiu's policies.

The Fifth Congress brought important changes in CCP organization and leadership organization. What it did not bring, however, was a change of leadership. The Central Committee's vote for the post of party secretary-general led to the election of Chen Duxiu. Without access to the voting record or to minutes of deliberations on the vote (if a discussion took place), we cannot know for what reason those who opposed Chen Duxiu were unwilling or unable to elect a different leader. One factor was probably that the opposition to Chen Duxiu was split and Li Dazhao, probably the only alternative who might have been acceptable to a majority of the congress, had just been executed.[115]

The CCP's leadership struggles took place at a moment of grave crisis. It was not so much that the CCP's central institutions broke down under the pressures generated by the difficult position in which the CCP found itself. Except for a short interlude at the time of the Fourth Congress, the CCP's leadership had never been unified, and the powers of central leadership institutions had been severely circumscribed. In fact, these pressures had the opposite effect. By December 1926, the CCP had gone far along the road of constructing on its own accord a strong central leadership. It was the Comintern's resolution that pushed the CCP back into a period of internal leadership strife. Even then, as the Fifth Congress showed, the idea that there should be a centralized party had become entrenched.

An interesting question is to what extent Chiang Kai-shek and the leader of the Green Gang, Du Yuesheng, were aware of the splits in the CCP leadership and to what extent they were influenced by their existence. We cannot know the answer at this point, but it seems unlikely that the internecine struggle in the CCP escaped their notice or that it enhanced their regard for the CCP.

THE FALL OF CHEN DUXIU AND THE AUGUST 7 EMERGENCY CONFERENCE

It is perhaps anticlimactic to admit that it is unclear exactly how Chen Duxiu's fall from power in the CCP came about. According to the recollections of Li Weihan, a man who was present at the August 7 emergency conference, a Central Committee meeting held at some point between July 4 and July 12 elected a new Politburo, as it was entitled to by the constitution. Li wrote that the meeting decided that Chen Duxiu was to go to Moscow "to discuss the problem of the Chinese revolution."[116] The new Politburo was staffed by Zhang Guotao, Zhou Enlai, Li Lisan, Zhang Tailei, and Li Weihan.[117] A recent study issued in the name of the CCP confirms Li Weihan in this assertion.[118] Qu Qiubai was added to the Politburo after it began to exercise power, no doubt partly because of Comintern pressure but perhaps also, as Li Weihan suggested, in recognition of his contributions in leading the opposition to Chen Duxiu in the ideological realm.[119] As of the middle of July at the latest, Chen Duxiu no longer exercised formal authority in the CCP.

According to Zhang Guotao, Chen resigned in protest of Comintern instructions of May 1927. These ordered him to organize an independent CCP army by arming twenty thousand CCP members and adding fifty thousand peasants and workers to KMT armies, from which the CCP was to eliminate all "reactionary" elements. At the same time, the CCP was to begin a radical land revolution by confiscating all land and property of the gentry. It was to take over the Wuhan Government and the KMT left wing by filling important posts with workers and peasants. Martial law courts were to eradicate all army officers from armies allied with Wuhan who resisted the CCP.[120] On June 15, Chen Duxiu sent a telegram in the name of the Politburo to the Comintern that stated, "Your instructions are correct and important, and we express our complete approval" but also explained why "they cannot be implemented for the moment."[121]

It may be that the new Politburo took over, as Zhang Guotao suggested, after a resignation by Chen Duxiu. It is also possible that Moscow had sent an instruction relieving Chen Duxiu from his functions or that the CCP Central Committee acted on its own initiative, as it could have done by the stipulations of the constitution.[122] Also, if Chen resigned, he may have done so not because he disagreed with Comintern instructions but because he was fed up with the CCP. Zhang's account is subject to doubt because as the man in charge of the new Politburo, he profited directly from Chen's departure, and a resignation out of anger with the Comintern makes Zhang appear as the man who rushed to the CCP's rescue in its darkest hour. It is unlikely that in his memoirs he would have admitted to a CCP ouster of Chen under his initiative. Given the powerful resentments that had accumulated against Chen Duxiu within the CCP, it is certainly possible that Chen was removed by CCP members themselves.

Chen's departure brought his reign over the CCP to a close. His authority in the CCP had been severely undermined since the arrival of the December 1926 resolutions of the Comintern. His formal departure made it possible for the new Politburo to assert itself as the CCP's leadership organization. This, as well as Chen's disappearance from the scene, rendered acute the issue of how all the changes in the CCP were to be legitimated.

The Politburo Takes Command

The first task the new Politburo tackled was to organize the departure of CCP members from Wuhan. In early July, Wang Jingwei and the Wuhan Government ended their opposition to Chiang Kai-shek. Subsequently the KMT hunt for CCP members spread to this city, where many CCP members had congregated during the Northern Expedition.[123] CCP members were ordered back to their home areas, put to work somewhere else, or sent to Moscow.[124]

The new Politburo also organized the Nanchang uprising, which began on August 1, 1927. This was an urban uprising aimed at precipitating the defection of Northern Expedition units sympathetic to the CCP and establishing once more a United Front government with the KMT left wing. Its overall strategy echoed the Shanghai uprising, with the difference that the insurgents formed their own army to attack Chiang Kai-shek's forces, something that fitted the critique they had made of the CCP's approach to the Shanghai uprising. Not surprisingly, Zhou Enlai, Li Lisan, and Peng Pai were among the top leaders of the insurrection. The attempt to achieve a restoration of the United Front with the left wing came to nothing as no KMT members accepted the invitation to join the new government. The uprising collapsed quickly as CCP forces dwindled through defeats and desertions.[125]

The new Politburo also laid the foundation for the Autumn Harvest uprising. The idea was to arouse peasant uprisings in the countryside of Guangdong, Hunan, Hubei, and Kiangsi. Once the uprisings were under way, according to CCP plans, CCP members in urban centers would stage revolts in the cities. The CCP hoped to capture power this way. In this case too, CCP plans called for a United Front with the left-wing KMT. Like the Nanchang uprising, the Autumn Harvest uprising that began in September quickly petered out.[126]

The new Politburo finally issued statements about the CCP-KMT relationship. Any CCP propaganda author could have turned loose all manner of communist invective were it not for the Comintern's insistence that the fiction of the bloc-within be upheld. Resolutions of the Eighth Comintern Plenum of May 1927 confirmed to CCP members that Stalin's line was still operative.[127] On July 13, the Politburo issued a statement that castigated the KMT, denounced its actions, withdrew all CCP members from the Wuhan Government,[128] but stated that "in all its revolutionary activities, the Chinese Communist Party wishes to cooperate with all the truly revolutionary elements among the masses of KMT members—therefore, Communist Party members have absolutely no reason to withdraw from the KMT."[129] A platform to constitute the basis of that cooperation was outlined shortly thereafter.[130]

These statements on KMT-CCP relations must have puzzled many CCP members. After all, the KMT had delivered a serious blow to the CCP, and thus it was strange for the CCP to call not only for a continuation of the United Front but even for membership of CCP members in that party. It made the CCP look naive and foolish, and unable to take tough and decisive decisions. It did nothing to bolster the tattered confidence of its membership in their organization.

When the emergency conference convened, Chen Duxiu's leadership had ended, and a beginning had been made with the formulation and implementation of new policies. However, the Politburo had not given an explanation or a justification for either Chen's departure or the new policies. In addition, the Politburo had failed to account for the setbacks the CCP had suffered, and it had not done anything to pull CCP members together and stiffen their resolve. A grave crisis loomed.

The Emergency Conference

It was the Executive Committee of the Comintern that ordered CCP members to hold an emergency conference. On July 14 it adopted an instruction to the CCP commanding its members to convene a meeting for the specific purpose of criticizing the CCP's past leadership for ideological errors. The Comintern, it wrote, "calls on all members of the CCP to fight resolutely against the opportunist deviations of the party's leadership. . . . The ECCI is confident that the CCP will find within itself adequate forces to change its own leadership and to disavow the leaders who have violated international Comintern discipline."[131] (ECCI stands for Executive Committee of the Comintern.)

To comply with the Comintern's instruction by heaping blame on Chen Duxiu—the instruction had not said which "leadership" was to be accused of opportunism—was convenient since his rule in the CCP had ended. However, speeches made at the meeting make it clear that much more was involved. They, and later recollections, illustrate that a number of participants found the meeting a highly traumatic affair. The meeting was much more than a ritual denunciation of an already fallen leader.

One issue was the Comintern's insistence that the CCP take all the blame. Luo Yinong, for instance, stated:

> I must publicly criticize the Comintern. Its political leadership was fine, there is no problem here, but in providing expertise it has been very bad. While acknowledging that the Chinese revolution was important, it sent Voitinsky and Roy to provide leadership. Neither participated in the October Revolution. Voitinsky . . . opposed us when we wanted to stage an uprising in Shanghai and refused to provide assistance. As for Roy, everybody knows that he suffers from immature leftism. How can such people lead the Chinese revolution? The Comintern's resolutions are good, but its representatives are lousy.[132]

CCP members believed, the above quote suggests, that Russian communists did not take them seriously. Lominadze eventually acknowledged that Borodin and Voitinsky had committed errors, but, he declared, "no matter what Borodin's and Voitinsky's lines were, they were on the whole still better than our [the CCP's] Central Committee, which made mistakes but refused to change. Whether or not Comintern representatives made errors, the main problem was still the strength of the central institutions of the Chinese Communist Party."[133] This statement cannot have assuaged Chinese sensitivities.

The most important issue, however, was the repudiation of Chen Duxiu. Even if he evoked resentment and loathing among CCP members, it nonetheless seems to have been difficult for CCP members not to find a new leader but to denounce and criticize an already fallen leader at a public meeting. Zhang Guotao in his memoirs claimed that he found this distasteful and that he accepted it only gradually as in the best interest of the CCP.[134] Others thought it inappropriate that Chen was not given a chance to speak for himself.[135] Li Weihan wrote that he and Qu visited Chen Duxiu after the meeting to inform him of its decisions and that the CCP assisted Chen in moving back to Shanghai in the fall of 1927. He also stated that until Chen Duxiu organized an internal CCP opposition in 1929, the CCP did not impose punishments on him and that its members treated him with considerable deference.[136]

When push came to shove, however, CCP members at the August 7 emergency conference were not interested in contemplating the nature of Chen Duxiu's leadership and rendering a fair judgment on him. They also were not primarily concerned with engaging in a judicious examination of the causes of the CCP's recent defeats. All asserted that the importance of the party was paramount and stated that the interest of the party outweighed everything, assigning it an importance that transcended whatever qualms they may have had about denouncing Chen Duxiu. This was an important moment in the history of the CCP. The days when Chen Gongbo had declared that CCP members should all be friends had receded into the distant past.

Statements by CCP members at the conference make it clear that some truly believed that Chen was responsible for the party's setbacks because he was not a good Marxist. Cai Hesen, for one, put forth this line of argument. In addressing an issue that some had apparently raised, whether this was the time to make changes in the CCP's leadership, he argued:

> Some sort of panic has gripped the higher levels of the CCP. They think that if these old CCP leaders are all removed, organizational chaos must follow. This is not at all something the masses are

worried about; it is a worry of the higher-ups. . . . We must have faith in the power of the masses. . . . Once the political party of the proletariat has the right political line, organization will not be an issue.[137]

For Cai, then, CCP leadership was to be based on a correct party line. Chen Duxiu's leadership had failed, he stated, because it "did not stand on the side of the masses, so that the Central Committee became nothing but a regular political body and not the leadership of one class. Once this had happened, the leadership of the Politburo simply became identical to that of the KMT."[138] Cai mentioned that Chen Duxiu's ideological errors had led him to become obsessed with maintaining relations with the left-wing KMT. Cai objected to holding the Comintern responsible because this amounted to blindness to the CCP leadership's mistakes.[139]

Others at the conference couched their support for leadership changes and new policies in similar language. Deng Zhongxia did so in the most extreme way, repudiating the entire history of the CCP:

In the whole period from the formation of the party right up until now, one can say, our party consisted of just some petit bourgeois, with some feudal relations and concepts belonging to professional politicians mixed in. With every issue that came up, they loved to use their elbows, and they employed this one to attack that one, but never did they use a class standpoint to decide questions. At the same time, the scholastic odor [*shusheng qigai*] of our party was also pronounced. It was inevitable therefore that the Central Committee vacillated constantly.[140]

For Deng, then, Chen Duxiu's failure to base himself on a "class standpoint," on ideology, had led him astray.

Some might argue that Cai Hesen and Deng Zhongxia were disingenuous in repeating the Comintern's charge of opportunism in their criticism of Chen Duxiu. However, their statements indicate that they truly thought that leadership was a matter of deriving the right policy from the right Marxist-Leninist analysis of society, and in this they showed themselves real Marxist-Leninists. In addition, what is important is that they used Marxism-Leninism as a way to communicate and justify their support for Chen Duxiu's dismissal.

This is not to say that personal antagonism to Chen Duxiu did not play a role. By the time of the emergency conference, Chen Duxiu had become an intensely disliked man. Cai Hesen concluded his statement at the conference with the declaration that "the past patriarchal system [*jiazhang-zhi*] is now no longer fitting; it must be torn down."[141] The reference to

Chen Duxiu as a "patriarch" was a provocative way of saying that he was an old-fashioned man who had run the CCP like an old bully. The charge may have had added poignancy because Chen Duxiu had stationed two of his sons in important positions, with Chen Yannian in charge of the Guangdong Regional Executive Committee and another son heading the Organization Department of the Peking Regional Executive Committee.[142] While Chen may have hoped to consolidate his influence in the CCP by using family relations, in the case of Chen Yannian this did not work out; the rivalry between him and his father is well known. In fact, it may be that Chen Yannian was the first to describe Chen Duxiu as a "patriarch," something, according to a recent biography, he did shortly after the March 20 incident.[143] Ren Bishi, one of the few ranking CCP members able to weather all factional struggles through the 1930s and 1940s, echoed Cai Hesen and Chen Yannian when he stated that "the old man should go to Moscow."[144] Ren used the more colloquial term *lao touzi*.

Chen had constantly upbraided the general membership for being backward and had argued that the CCP was not yet ready to play a major role in the revolution. Attaching the label of opportunism to Chen Duxiu was a way of stating that Chen lacked faith in the CCP. In the fall of 1926, the Guangdong committee had wanted to see the CCP adopt an aggressive policy toward the KMT. Qu Qiubai and Mao Zedong took up this theme in early 1927. Many of the speeches at the conference echoed this concern. Typically, Mao Zedong did this most pithily. In a statement that echoed the tone and argument of Qu Qiubai's attack on Chen, he likened the attitude of the previous CCP leadership to that of a demure bride:

> The issue of the KMT is one with a long history in our party and today has not yet been solved. First the issue was whether or not to enter, then about who would enter. . . . Everybody at the time had the basic idea that the KMT was somebody else's home; they did not realize that it was an empty building waiting for somebody to occupy it. Later, they behaved like a new bride, forced in a sedan chair to enter this empty home but never with enough confidence to act as master of the household.[145]

It was the same frustration with a lack of party pride, so to speak, that led Luo Yinong, also a CCP member with origins in the New Citizen Study Society, to say, "I think that the Chinese Communist Party acted as a guest at a revolution, not as the host."[146] Chen's detached attitude toward the CCP, which made the organization subordinate to other goals and norms, had been widely shared in the early years of its history. As statements by Luo and Mao suggest, by the time of the emergency conference, the commitment to the CCP had intensified greatly.

The ideological ailing the emergency conference diagnosed Chen Duxiu to have suffered was opportunism (*jihuizhuyi*). The meeting's most important document was the "Letter of Warning to All Members of the Party." "The basis of the errors of opportunism of the party leadership," it explained, "lay in not understanding the nature of the Chinese revolution, the function of each class in the various stages of the revolution, or the function of the CCP; more precisely, it did not have a Bolshevist and Marxist understanding of these issues."[147] Its concrete manifestation was the belief that class struggle and the national revolution were contradictory. This belief had led Chen Duxiu, the letter argued, to "forsake the proletarian leadership of the bourgeois-democratic revolution . . . so that the proletariat became the appendage of the democratic camp."[148] The letter quoted as one piece of evidence for opportunism a letter from the Central Committee sent to Shanghai in June 1927 defending the reining in of the peasant and labor movements on the grounds that

> on the one hand, the anti-imperialist movement has become depressed, and on the other hand, the worker and peasant movements have developed to the highest levels. At least this is how the petite bourgeoisie sees it. To do nothing but arm workers and peasants to confiscate land and shout slogans about the noncapitalist future and so on will cause the petite bourgeoisie to wonder whether the CCP wants to overthrow the KMT and carry out class warfare.[149]

The advantage of the line of argument of the "Letter of Warning" was that it was feasible to paint CCP uprisings and the majority of its members in a heroic light. The letter to the membership made the most of this opportunity. It praised the "heroic struggles" of the "normal masses of party members" that had resulted in great achievement under "excellent leaders such as Chen Yannian and Zhao Shiyan" in Shanghai, Guangdong, and Hunan.[150] This line of argument also preserved the idea that the CCP controlled its own fate as well as that of China. The CCP had lost, it implied, not because it could not have been victorious but because of bad leadership. In this way, the myth of the CCP as the organization that would lead China to its future was preserved. According to the letter, leadership had brought calamity, but "the masses of the party are the source of our strength, and with their assistance, the errors of CCP leadership institutions are easily corrected, no matter how large."[151] This careful formulation, it should be noted, left policy initiative with the CCP leadership. It further emphasized the point when immediately following the above statement, it added "provided that from now on, we have a correct revolutionary Bolshevik leadership."[152] This formulation also carefully established the importance of the "party line."

At the emergency conference, CCP members exploited the rhetorical possibilities of Marxism-Leninism. They used them in the attempt to strengthen the faith of CCP members in the future of their party and to provide an accounting for the recent calamities that had befallen it. They also employed Marxism-Leninism to explain and justify Chen Duxiu's departure from the CCP leadership and to sanction new policies.

The assertion of the primacy of the CCP might appear as a classic case of goal displacement. When Chinese communists began to create the CCP in 1920 and 1921, they justified the creation of the CCP not as a good in itself but as the best possible means they could think of to create a new order in Chinese society. They now presented the CCP as the institution to which CCP members should devote all their energy and for which they should sacrifice themselves. To an extent, such goal displacement was probably a reality. However, while Qu Qiubai was the first man to oversee a CCP purge in the name of weeding out "opportunism," he also reminded Chinese communists of an earlier time when the CCP bureaucracy was less oppressive and the emphasis was on individual creativity.

In addition, as their commitment to the party and their dependence on it grew, CCP members seem to have developed a dual image of the CCP. On the one hand, there was the idealized party, the hero that would lead China toward a new future and to which service was a privilege. On the other hand, there was the party as it existed day to day, striving to come close to the ideal but held back by ideological shortcomings, individual pettiness, and faulty leadership. This double vision was probably essential to sustain the commitment of CCP members, faced as they were with attacks from the outside and vicious internal strife.

Resolutions of the Emergency Conference

The emergency conference passed resolutions on the peasant movement, the labor movement, and party organization. Like the conference's letter to the membership, these resolutions were intended to demonstrate that the ideological mistakes that had led the previous leadership astray and the installation of new leaders resulted from the reassertion of the correct party line in the CCP. The "Resolution on the Struggle of the Peasantry" emphasized that attacks on the peasant movement had succeeded because of a lack of determined CCP leadership. It stated that political repression would only intensify class conflict in the villages and that therefore a new revolutionary upsurge would arrive shortly. Even if this policy had its origins in Stalin's directives, the statements made at the emergency conference suggest that many CCP members still thought they could vanquish Chiang Kai-shek by arousing China's masses.

The resolution declared that "to the extent possible, the CCP and the Socialist Youth League must in the shortest possible time assign the most activist and determined comrades with a stable commitment to the revolution and with experience in struggle to the most important provinces to work as organizers of peasant uprisings."[153] The resolutions also listed a number of slogans for these uprisings, such as "Village Power to the Peasant Association" and "Confiscate Land of Large and Middle Landlords and Give It to the Tenants and Landless Peasants."[154]

The resolution on the labor movement acknowledged that "antirevolutionary cliques have occupied or reorganized general labor union institutions in Shanghai, Nanking, Guangdong, Fujian, Zhejiang, Anhui, and other provinces, including Hubei most recently."[155] It reaffirmed the leading position of the urban proletariat. However, it committed few CCP resources to the labor movement.

The "Resolution on Organizational Issues in the Party" first announced what it called the "removal of unreliable elements of the members of all party branches."[156] The Investigation Committee network was to be extended throughout the party, and this was to conduct the party purge. The resolution did not state criteria for unreliable behavior or thought. Not surprisingly, it called for the eradication of "opportunist" thinking from the CCP. This was to be achieved first by having a general discussion within the party of past opportunism, then all party institutions were to be cleared of officers who still displayed opportunist ways of thinking and acting. This drive was to begin at the branch level and work itself up the CCP hierarchy.[157] It is unlikely that the purge was targeted only at CCP members deemed ideologically opportunist. Party membership was no doubt attractive to lineage heads, bandits, tax collectors, and the like at many points during the 1925–1927 period because the CCP seemed to be a major political player and association with it provided political capital that could be used in many ways. An important goal of the purge against opportunists was probably a general cleansing of the ranks.

The legality of the conference, in light of the CCP's constitution, was a nettlesome issue because the conference did not constitute a quorum of the Central Committee. In the Comintern scheme, the allocation of ultimate authority was ambiguous; both the Comintern leadership and party congresses of the member parties were defined as the final authority. Lominadze sought to establish the first principle, stating that the conference's actions would become official after Comintern approval was received.[158] The "Resolution on Organizational Issues" softened the impact of this by stipulating that the new Politburo was a provisional Politburo and ordering it to convene a new CCP congress within the next six months.[159]

The conference was the scene of a testy exchange between Mao and Lominadze about the CCP's peasant policy. Mao challenged the proposed resolution on the peasant movement. He insisted that terms used in it, such as "big landlord" and "middle landlord," should be defined. His suggestion was that the CCP's policy should be the confiscation of all land holdings in excess of fifty *mu*, regardless of the quality of the land. (A *mu* is about one-sixth of an acre.) Mao also advocated a confiscation policy for small landholders. "The difficulty is," he explained, "that if we do not confiscate the land of small landholders, peasant associations have nothing to do in places where there are no landholders."[160] This was the case in Guangdong, as we have seen.

Lominadze refused to accept any of Mao's propositions. Speaking about the peasant resolution, he said, "I think that the text can stand as is. . . . These questions should be determined by the peasant associations."[161] His defense for making this argument was that the answer to Mao's questions depended on local conditions and therefore decisions about them should be made locally. The fact that Mao became only an alternate member of the new Politburo was no doubt a result of his obduracy.[162]

By the time of the emergency conference, Marxism-Leninism had become entrenched as the basis for the CCP's internal culture. At the conference itself, CCP members asserted the myth of the historical necessity and ultimate infallibility of the party and legitimated leadership changes and policies in Marxist-Leninist terms. Norms such as party discipline and obedience to central leadership were asserted to be sacrosanct. CCP members had grown accustomed to articulating their views in terms of Marxism-Leninism, and they used its norms and symbols to make their case.

The new conception of leadership implied a vision of the CCP membership as consisting of a small group of CCP members qualified to exert authority in the CCP because they grasped and embodied the correct party line. The rest of the CCP membership had the obligation of implementing that leadership's orders, even if they did not understand their meaning and purpose. While this conferred enormous status on those in power in the CCP, their position became one of fragility as they now became solely responsible. If they followed the correct line, the CCP achieved what it was supposed to accomplish; however, a leadership could no longer present crises as resulting from objective conditions or the "backwardness" of the general CCP membership. Any setback would easily give rise to the charge that a leadership had strayed from the correct line.

By the emergency conference, Marxism-Leninism had seeped into all areas of life. The pressures and crises produced by the mass party led Chinese communists to exploit Marxism-Leninism to deal with unprecedented problems. They used it to create a new form of communication that made it possible for people from diverse backgrounds to develop a common culture. They also employed it to centralize the CCP and establish a common leadership. The founding history of the CCP illustrated how difficult that was—regionalism, suspicion of central authority, and differences of opinion about policies and the proper character of the CCP keeping it divided for nearly the entire first seven years of its existence.

Of course, CCP members did not all become good communists who followed the dictates of the central leadership obediently. CCP factions in many ways functioned like regionalist factions of China's dynastic past. Factionalist behavior was frowned upon, but in the same way that Feng Guifen employed the Confucian ideology to represent regional interests and to articulate his vision of better local government, members of a faction used Marxism-Leninism to articulate their ideals, mobilize support in the party for their policies, and represent individual, departmental, or regional causes. Factionalism is an integral aspect of communist parties. Feeding off the limited access to power imposed by the centralization of authority and articulated in the language of Marxism-Leninism, it elucidates much about their nature.

Even if Marxism-Leninism became the basis of the CCP's culture, that does not mean that all who used it were Marxist-Leninist. While there might be little reason to doubt the commitment to the CCP of men like Deng Zhongxia and Cai Hesen, others might have entered the CCP out of instrumental considerations. They could use Marxism-Leninism as a mode of communication without a commitment to the CCP.

The following example shows that by the summer of 1927, the new mode of communication had become firmly established. On August 23, 1927, Mao Zedong wrote from Hunan to the Politburo, asking for permission to establish a peasant soviet; to carry out a policy of confiscating all land, including that of small landholders; and to have peasant associations redistribute it. He phrased his request as follows:

> Comrade So-and-so came to Hunan with a new Comintern instruction calling for the immediate establishment in China of soviets of workers, peasants, and soldiers. I jumped up and down

with happiness; objectively, China had reached 1917 some time ago; however, previously we made the big mistake of believing that we were still in 1905. Soviets of workers, peasants, and soldiers are appropriate to the objective conditions. . . . I hope that the Central Committee accepts without reservation the Comintern instruction and implements it in Hunan.[163]

Here we see Mao Zedong attempting to induce the Politburo to sanction policies he hoped to pursue, or was pursuing, in Hunan, arguing that they were correct in Marxist-Leninist terms. He stated that China's conditions were now like those of the Soviet Union at the time of the October Revolution. A mistaken policy would be the result, he suggested, of believing that Chinese conditions were as they had been at the time of the failed attempt to seize power in 1905, when the czarist regime had been able to destroy workers' soviets easily and Russian middle classes had proven unsympathetic to a national revolution.[164] Mao Zedong, then, used famous incidents in Bolshevik history and the Marxist-Leninist conception of historical development to induce CCP Politburo approval for his policy. He also played on the norm that the CCP should implement Comintern policies, a norm that had always been important but had become even more so following Stalin's direct intervention in CCP affairs in December 1926.

He was not successful. The Politburo disagreed with Mao, following a policy of linking several rural uprisings together and coordinating them with urban uprisings.[165] It also stated in its reply to Mao that military preparations for uprisings in Hunan had not been completed and that more propaganda was necessary before the Hunan population could be expected to be sympathetic to an uprising. It deployed the same rhetorical strategies as Mao:

China has still not completed the national revolution. . . . We must support in the name of the KMT the democratic government of peasants and workers, although of course not as before. . . . You are wrong if you believe that . . . the national revolution has reached the third stage [of moving on to establish soviets] and can abandon the KMT's standard to realize a soviet regime or if you believe that objectively China now has reached 1917. The Central Committee has shown in many ways that the Political Resolution is correct . . . and the directive of the Comintern agrees.[166]

Even if CCP members used Marxism-Leninism as a means of communication and a legitimation device, it does not follow that as an ideology it lost all meaning for them. However, it does mean that their statements had become part of a political process and that they were made with political considerations in mind. Therefore, without a very careful consideration of the political context, it is impossible to infer from a statement by a CCP member what his real thoughts might be. This became increasingly true following the May Thirtieth movement as Marxism-Leninism gained ground as a mode of communication within the CCP. It had become a fact for all CCP members with the emergency conference.

6/Conclusion

In 1920, Chinese communism consisted of small groups of idealistic students ready to take on any and all in political power, with full confidence in the rectitude of their own commitments and the readiness of the Chinese people to follow their leadership. By 1927, much had changed. The CCP's social base had been broadened, and its members had lost their naiveté. They asserted the absolute importance of party discipline and justified policies in terms of a party line. While they were still convinced that China's nonelite population would support them once informed of their ideas, they had also developed a hardheaded understanding of the forces against them and of the need for military power.

Membership attitudes toward leadership had also changed. If in 1919 and 1920 Chen Duxiu appeared light-years ahead of his time, by 1927, he was thought to be set in his ways. Moral courage, independence, and intellectual achievement made Chen a much-respected man among Chinese communists in the first years of the CCP, even if they did not believe that they needed to accept his authority in all areas. By 1927, a CCP leader needed to assert that he personified the party line and to convince the CCP membership that he possessed political skill, leadership courage, and belief in the CCP. If Chinese communists in the first years of the CCP despised Sun Yatsen's militarism and frowned upon his involvement with secret societies, CCP members had begun to accept such actions by 1927. In 1927, Mao Zedong already flaunted his earthiness, relished a good political fight, and was deeply involved with bandit gangs. A Mao Zedong could never have been the founder of the CCP; a Chen Duxiu could never have led the CCP to capture power on the basis of a peasant revolution.

This study has identified four stages in the emergence of the CCP. The first involved the decision of Chinese communists to cut all remaining ties with the Republic and to reject study societies with their emphasis on education as a means to achieve change. Chinese communists found in Marxism-Leninism new ways of looking at what they understood as the deepening brutalization of politics and suggestions about how to restructure and validate their political activities. The establishment of communist cells was the result.

The second stage lasted from the First Congress in July 1921, when regional representatives of a number of communist cells came together and established a common organization, the CCP, until the Third Congress of June 1923. In this period central leadership institutions were weak, and a number of organizations remained outside the CCP framework. Conflicts about the distribution of authority and between Chen Duxiu and regional CCP branches were intense. The activities of CCP members among workers and peasants showed a lack of knowledge about the power structure of Chinese society and how to organize a mass movement.

Following the near disintegration of the CCP in the first half of 1923, the period from the Third Congress until the Fourth Congress of January 1925 was one in which CCP members for the first time seriously addressed problems of organization, using Leninist ideas. Central leadership institutions expanded; the inculcation of shared ideas and norms was taken in hand, as was the creation of common modes of operation. Chinese communists also formulated a new way, based on cells, to entrench their organization in society. Several communists who had knowledge of the ways of Russian communists from personal observation stated that the CCP was well on the way toward becoming a real Bolshevik party.

It was in the 1925–1927 period that the CCP finally became a mass political party with an internal culture based on Marxism-Leninism and a centralized organization. The period began with the May Thirtieth movement engulfing the CCP. It retreated from the organizational principles that had emerged after the Third Congress in a number of ways, and the CCP was again divided by internal conflict. Several factors, however, produced a radical transformation. The rapid influx of members from disparate social and regional backgrounds stimulated the emergence of a new mode of communication and fundamentally undermined regionalist ways of operation. The greater complexity of the CCP and its involvement as a major player in the turbulent revolutionary events of the time, requiring the commitment of life, encouraged the centralization of authority in an attempt to make the CCP cohesive and strong and at the same time fostered the growth of a sense of common destiny and fate. Conflict within the CCP came to concern the right to determine CCP policy and organization for the entire party; regional branches no longer formed the CCP's fault lines.

While the limited nature of the evidence discussed here prevents any categorical conclusions, it does indicate that it may be necessary to reconsider the existing understanding of a Leninist party as a bureaucracy controlled from the center and used by its leaders to pursue ideologically determined goals. Here I would like to spell out some of the ways in which this might be done, for the sake of clarity. While Lenin pictured the leadership of the Bolshevik Party as a body of seasoned revolutionaries unattached to parochial interests, reality in the early CCP was different, even after strong central-leadership institutions had emerged. These institutions formed the battleground of divergent groups in the CCP's constituency. This is not to argue that one should think of a communist party in corporatist terms, with central institutions functioning as mechanisms for various interest groups to establish compromises and arrive at a joint policy through negotiation. Even though negotiation occurred, a corporatist interpretation of the CCP would fail to take account of the fact that different groups and individuals within it fought with each other for dominance to dictate what the CCP stood for and what policies were to be followed.

The reason the CCP could function as a political system in which different people and groups pursued their own goals was that Marxism-Leninism offered a mode of communication by which CCP members could articulate and fight for their different views and interests. It also provided ways to legitimate decisions, essential in the maintenance of the organization. CCP members exploited the texts of Marxism-Leninism as a source of symbols and values with which to argue their ideas and their causes. These were, as I have sought to show, influenced not only by Marxism-Leninism but also by traditional norms, partial interests, personal antagonisms, and so on. Norms and values, it should be stressed, came to function in the CCP not only as motivators of behavior but also as political capital, marshaled in the pursuit of goals determined in various, not necessarily ideological, ways.

A further point suggested by this study is that it is not correct to think of the CCP and Chinese society as exclusive categories. The boundaries between the two were porous. Not all CCP members were firmly attached to the CCP organization. While there was a core group of professional CCP members, large parts of the membership had only a limited link with the CCP. In addition, the CCP was not impervious to existing social organizations and conflicts in Chinese society. As one of the centers of power in Chinese society, the CCP itself became subject to infiltration and manipulation by various social groups.

Finally, the material I have discussed has illustrated the changeability of the CCP. In the 1920–1927 period, its members gave it various meanings at different stages and in different contexts. It was a framework in which they were able to develop new political roles and adjust the framework itself. While by 1927 a number of fundamental norms and organizational principles were established, even these proved open to manipulation.

On the basis of the evidence that has recently become available, I have also sought to shed light on a number of more limited issues that have been featured in previous historiographical writings on the CCP. I have underscored Arif Dirlik's point that the October Revolution was not as important an event in the founding of the CCP or the spread of Marxism-Leninism in China as once thought. The CCP's birth, I have argued, was not dependent on the activities of a few Comintern agents and intellectuals in Shanghai but resulted from initiatives of Chinese intellectuals throughout China and in Europe. With regard to the founding of the CCP, I have raised the question of how the various Chinese communist organizations combined into one institution. Some aspects of this process remain unresolved, including the incorporation into the CCP of communist organizations in Sichuan.

I have attempted to show that the relationship between the Comintern and the CCP was not as straightforward as once thought, if only because Comintern documents were never a simple source of information about organization and policy for CCP members. Their consumers and their producers operated in difficult situations. The effects of Voitinsky, Maring, and Borodin on the CCP were not restricted to policy. Maring evoked strong personal resentments, but he was nonetheless instrumental in bringing CCP members together at an important crisis point, and in his own personal conduct he exemplified differences between Chinese and communist ways of operation. Borodin was important in bringing about the Guangdong peasant movement; he was also one of the causes for the emergence of the factional conflict between Chen Duxiu and the Guangdong Regional Executive Committee.

The idea that Stalin's intervention in the Chinese revolution produced the CCP's defeat by the KMT in 1927 seems no longer tenable. It was the result of the CCP's inability to secure a firm base in society and its lack of the required organizational skills. In addition, the CCP's strategies at the time were not of a nature that could have produced victory. The appreciation of the importance of independent control of military power remained limited until it was too late.

Previous scholarship has asserted that it was the genius of Mao that led him to see the possibilities of the peasant movement in China. While some have made the case that Peng Pai was the real originator of the CCP's peasant movement, this too does not seem to take sufficient account of the fact that support for a peasant movement was widespread throughout much of the CCP and existed before the KMT pushed the CCP into the hills. Issues that should receive far more attention than they have in the past are the organization of military violence by Chinese communists and the militarization of the CCP itself.

Until recently, a lack of sources made it virtually impossible to discuss with much confidence, if any, the involvement in the CCP of people like Yun Daiying, Cai Hesen, Qu Qiubai, Zhang Guotao, or Li Lisan. We are still far from being able to produce a prosopography of the early CCP. Nonetheless, the evidence that has become available indicates the diverse backgrounds, views, and aspirations of the people involved in the construction of the CCP. While Chen Duxiu has been the subject of two biographies in the West, both have had to avoid an examination of his leadership of the CCP because of the scarcity of sources. This study, I hope, will have made some progress toward correcting this.

Mao Zedong's involvement in the CCP, especially in its early years, can now be better understood also. He was an important CCP member from the beginning of its history. As far as his early thought is concerned, his statements discussed here suggest that Mao's mind possessed dark corners and at times he was deeply skeptical of China's ability to regenerate itself. He despised China's ruling elites with a blind passion, regarding them as a scourge that could be removed only by the application of harsh violence.

This book began by placing Chinese communism in the context of China's political crisis. It is tempting to see the CCP as the replacement of China's dynastic system, providing the essentials of the country's political framework. The temptation should be resisted. While the CCP has endured, its institutions have proved anything but stable. When Chinese communists set up the CCP, they were more certain of what they rejected than what they believed the future should look like. They set out on a search for a new political order, but they have not asserted that this order is in place. Until now Chinese have remained deeply divided about how to organize the public realm of their society and how extensive that realm should be. The future shape of China's political order will remain uncertain as long as that is the case and as long as Chinese society and culture continue to undergo rapid change.

Nonetheless, the 1920–1927 period and especially the 1925–1927 pe-

riod brought changes in Chinese politics that have had lasting consequences. Mass political parties in several areas began to replace warlord
and reformist political institutions that had resulted from the New Policies.
This is not to say that local representative institutions and other elements
of the New Policies completely lost their appeal; experiments with them
continued in the 1930s and 1940s. Both the KMT and the CCP paid lip
service to them at times and sought to incorporate aspects of them into
their own institutions. However, political parties drawing their membership from different areas and segments of the population became central
to Chinese political life. From 1927 on, it was difficult to be a national
figure without the backing of a mass political party. Politics was no longer
the affair of a narrow, cultured elite.

In the area of the organization and legitimation of violence, the period
also saw the beginnings of important changes. Both the CCP and the
KMT began to develop a military arm, justifying this action in terms of a
revolutionary agenda, the fragmented state of the Chinese polity, the
corrupt nature of much of the political realm, and the brutality of most
existing armed forces in the country. The relationship between political
parties and their armies, including its cultural dimensions, needs further
study; it was not one without contradictions or unresolved issues, as the
careers and writings of Mao Zedong and Chiang Kai-shek show.

Something like a mass revolutionary political culture also began to take
shape. Acting briskly and speaking grandly, CCP members—and KMT
members—enacted revolutionary roles, using revolution as a metaphor
to suggest that they represented the forces of dignity battling on behalf
of the weak and needy masses against immoral brutes controlling political
power. They employed this metaphor to justify their political endeavors.
Mass demonstrations became important, and political actors believed that
it was politically essential to be identified with them. These demonstrations displayed a style that later mass demonstrations have echoed. They
were portrayed by their participants as spontaneous outbursts directed
against self-seeking rulers and foreign aggression. The protesters suggested that they were ready to sacrifice all for their cause, that they represented all Chinese, and that they acted on the basis of a pure commitment.
For the CCP the 1925–1927 period was significant for many reasons;
among others, the beating they suffered enabled them to claim credibly
that their party was indeed made up of heroic revolutionaries battling for
the salvation of the Chinese people.

The founding of the CCP has not meant the end of China's political
troubles. It reflected and produced important changes in Chinese politics
that will continue to cast long shadows over the future, and it consum-

mated a break with the past. While the future remains impossible to discern, it is important to keep in mind that what we are witnessing is the creation of an order to replace one that lasted for many centuries and was deeply involved in many aspects of Chinese society, culture, and values. It is a profoundly serious process.

Abbreviations

CEC   Central Executive Committee.

CHOC   John Fairbank, ed. *Cambridge History of China.* Cambridge: Cambridge University Press, 1978–present.

DSYJ   Zhonggong Zhongyang Dangxiao *Dangshi Yanjiu* Bianjibu (Central Party School, Editorial Board for *Dangshi Yanjiu*), ed. *Dangshi Yanjiu* (Party History Research).

DSYJZL   Zhongguo Geming Bowuguan Dangshi Yanjiushi (Party History Section of the Museum of the Chinese Revolution), ed. *Dangshi Yanjiu Ziliao* (Source Materials for and Research on Party History).

DSZL   *Dangshi Ziliao* Bianjibu (Editorial Board for *Dangshi Ziliao*), ed. *Dangshi Ziliao* (Source Materials for Party History).

EDHSD   Shi Guang, Zhou Cheng'en, et al., eds. *"Erda" he "Sanda": Zhongguo Gongchandang Dier-san Daibiao Dahui Ziliao Xuanbian* (The Second Congress and the Third Congress: An Edited and Selected Compilation of Sources for the Second and Third Congresses of the Chinese Communist Party). Beijing: Chinese Academy of Social Sciences Press, 1985.

FFSL   Qinghua Daxue Zhonggong Dangshi Jiaoyanzu (Teaching and Research Group for CCP History at Qinghua University), ed. *Fu'Fa Qin'gong Jianxue Yundong Shiliao* (Source Materials for the Work-Study Movement to France). Beijing: Beijing Press, 1979.

GDDSZL   Zhonggong Guangdong Shengwei Dangshi Ziliao Zhengji
            Weiyuanhui (Editorial Committee for Source Materials for
            Party History, Guangdong Provincial Committee of the
            CCP), Zhonggong Guangdong Shengwei Dangshi Yanjiu
            Weiyuanhui (Research Committee for Party History,
            Guangdong Provincial Committee of the CCP), eds. *Guang-
            dong Dangshi Ziliao* (Source Materials for Party History in
            Guangdong), 1983.

GLU   General Labor Union.

GQDTYS   Guangdongsheng Dang'anguan (Guangdong Provincial Ar-
            chives) and Guangdong Shengwei Dangshi Yanjiu Wei-
            yuanhui Bangongshi (Office of the Party History Research
            Committee of the Guangdong Provincial Committee), eds.
            Guangdongqu Dang, Tuan Yanjiu Shiliao (1921–1926)
            (Source Materials for Research on the History of the Party
            and the Socialist Youth League in the Guangdong Region
            [1921–1926]). Guangzhou: Guangdong People's Press,
            1983.

KMT   Guomindang (Kuomintang).

LDYL   Zhonggong Zhongyang Shujichu (Secretariat of the CCP
            Central Committee), ed. *Liuda Yilai—Dangnei Mimi Wen-
            jian* (Since the Sixth Congress: Secret Internal Party Docu-
            ments). Beijing: People's Press, 1980.

LDYQ   Zhonggong Zhongyang Shujichu (Secretariat of the CCP
            Central Committee), ed. *Liuda Yiqian—Dangde Lishi Cai-
            liao* (Before the Sixth Congress: Historical Documents for
            the Party's History). Beijing: People's Press, 1980.

WSSQDST   Zhang Yunhou et al., eds. *Wusi Shiqi de Shetuan* (The
            Societies and Leagues of the May Fourth Period). Beijing:
            Three Unity Press, 1979.

YDDAZL   Zhongyang Dang'anguan (Central Committee Archives),
            ed. *Zhongguo Gongchandang Diyici Daibiao Dahui
            Dang'an Ziliao: Zengdingben* (Archival Sources for the
            First Congress of the CCP: Revised and Enlarged Edition).
            Beijing: People's Press, 1984.

YDQH   Zhongguo Shehui Kexueyuan Xiandaishi Yanjiushi/Zhong-
            guo Geming Bowuguan Dangshi Yanjiushi (Contempo-

rary History Section of the Chinese Academy of Social Sciences / Party History Section of the Museum of the Chinese Revolution), eds. *"Yida" Qianhou: Zhongguo Gongchandang Diyici Daibiao Dahui Qianhou Ziliao Xuanbian* (The Period of the Founding of the Party: Selected Source Materials for the Period of the First National Congress of the Chinese Communist Party). Beijing: People's Press, 1980 and 1984.

YDQHGD   Zhonggong Guangdong Shengwei Dangshi Yanjiu Weiyuanhui, Guangdongsheng Dang'anguan (Research Committee for Party History of the Guangdong Provincial Committee of the Chinese Communist Party, Guangdong Provincial Archives), eds. *"Yida" Qianhou Guangdong de Dang Zuzhi* (The Guangdong Party Organization at the Time of the First Congress). N.p., 1981.

ZGDSSJRWL Zhou Qisheng, *Zhonggong Dangshi Shijian Renwulu* (List of Important Events and People in Party History). Shanghai: Shanghai People's Press, 1983.

ZZWX   Zhongyang Dang'anguan (Central Committee Archives), ed. *Zhonggong Zhongyang Wenjian Xuanji* (Selected Documents of the CCP Central Committee). Beijing: Central Party School Press, 1982, 1983, ?.

Notes

In collections of source materials, Chinese editors frequently include the date of a document in the title. In the notes referring to Chinese sources, I have followed their conventions. The dates appear in parentheses in the transliteration and in square brackets in the translation.

INTRODUCTION

   1.   Cohen, *Discovering History in China*, 57–96; Dirlik, ''Culture, Society, and Revolution,'' 30.
   2.   Levenson, *Confucian China*, 1:134–45.
   3.   Schwartz, *Chinese Communism*, 7–27, 73–78, 189–204. In his study of the first Chinese to profess a commitment to Marxism-Leninism, Maurice Meisner followed through on what Schwartz was arguing, emphasizing the nationalist and populist elements of Li's views.
   4.   Addressing the issue of the continuity with China's past, Lin Yu-sheng, in *Crisis of Chinese Consciousness*, advanced the thesis that Marxism-Leninism continued totalistic modes of thought characteristic of neo-Confucianism, while Thomas Metzger argued that it provided escape from paralyzing tensions within it (Metzger, *Escape from Predicament*). Kwok, in *Scientism in Chinese Thought*, argued that Marxism-Leninism attracted Chinese intellectuals because it claimed to do for society what science did for nature, that is, formulate its eternal principles. Kwok's interest, then, was also primarily in intellectual history. Lee Feigon's biography of Chen Duxiu also continues Levenson's problematique.
   Others heeded Schwartz's call to study the nature and the emergence of Chinese forms of communism. Stuart Schram did so in his studies of Mao Zedong. Raymond Wylie and Joshua Fogel both demonstrated that other thinkers than Mao helped shape Maoism, in the process illustrating the diversity of Marxist-Leninist thought in China until at least the Rectification Campaign of 1942 (Wylie, *The Emergence of Maoism*; Fogel, *Ai Ssu-ch'i's Contributions*). In *Revolution and History*, Arif Dirlik discussed the growth of Chinese interpretations of their own history based on Marxism-Leninism.
   A secondary but nonetheless important strain of scholarship in this group dealt

with the CCP's relation with Soviet communists. Books in this genre include Whiting, *Soviet Policies*; Wilbur and How, *Documents on Communism*; Isaacs, *Tragedy of the Chinese Revolution*; Brandt, *Stalin's Failure*; and North and Eudin, *Roy's Mission*.

5. Geertz, "Ideology as a Cultural System," 218–19.

6. Ibid., 218.

7. Kuhn, "Origins of the Taiping Vision," 365–66.

8. For concise statements of the major issues, see Wakeman, "Rebellion and Revolution," *Journal of Asian Studies* 36:2 (1977): 201–37; "Peasant Strategies in Asian Societies," *Journal of Asian Studies* 42:4 (1983): 747–868.

9. Johnson, *Peasant Nationalism*, 1–30. Mark Selden provided the opposing view in *The Yan'an Way*.

10. See Barrington Moore, *Social Origins of Dictatorship and Democracy*, and James Scott, *The Moral Economy and the Peasant: Rebellion and Subsistence in Southeast Asia*.

11. Thaxton, *China Turned Rightside Up*.

12. Robert Marks, describing the Hailufeng peasant movement in the 1920s, for instance, rejected Roy Hofheinz's argument, made in *Broken Wave*, that the CCP's ability to impose a superior organization from the outside was essential in the CCP's mobilization of the Guangdong peasantry in the 1920s. Instead he saw peasant mobilization as a reaction of peasants to the disruption of the moral economy in which communist efforts were only marginally significant (Marks, *Rural Revolution*). In his study of Hailufeng, Fernando Galbiati presented a similar picture of the nature of society but argued that the charismatic qualities of Peng Pai, a peasant movement activist, was crucial in leading peasants to rebel (Galbiati, *P'eng P'ai*).

In an early and intellectually very stimulating account, Edward Friedman, in *Backwards Toward Revolution*, argued that while the CCP and China's peasant rebels possessed mutually exclusive mental worlds, there was a confluence of aims that led to CCP-led peasant rebellions.

13. Ch'en Yung-fa, *Making Revolution*; Averill, "Party, Society, and Local Elite," 279–304.

In an attempt to deal with many of the above issues, Elizabeth Perry, in *Rebels and Revolutionaries*, developed two typologies of collective peasant violence, with peasants deploying a protective or predatory strategy to acquire or defend minimal resources, and then argued that the communist effort at forging systemic social change collided with the parochial and conservative character of both traditional forms of peasant rebellion.

1. CHINESE COMMUNISTS AND CHINA'S POLITICAL CRISIS

1. Schwartz, *Chinese Communism*, 27. See also Maurice Meisner, *Li Ta-chao*, xiv–xv. For a concise restatement and critical analysis, see also Dirlik, *Origins of Chinese Communism*, 1–22.

2. Meisner, *Li Ta-chao*, 60–70, 102–4; Schwartz, *Chinese Communism*, 18–19.

3. He Ganzhi, *Zhongguo Xiandai Gemingshi* (History of the Contemporary Chinese Revolution). A more recent and more detailed treatment of the founding

of the CCP is Li Xin and Chen Tiejian, *Weida de Kaiduan: 1919–1923* (The Great Beginning: 1919–1923). While incorporating much new material, Li Xin and Chen Tiejian remain within the established CCP view of its own history and of course had to do so. For a concise statement, see Xiao Chaoran, *Zhongguo Gongchandang Jianming Cidian* (A Concise Dictionary of the Chinese Communist Party's History), 1:22.

For a different Chinese view, see Cai Hesen, "Zhongguo Gongchandangshi De Fazhan (Tigang): Yijiuerliunian" (The Historical Development of the Chinese Communist Party (Outline): 1926), in *Cai Hesen de Shierbian Wenzhang* (Twelve Essays by Cai Hesen). Cai Hesen wrote this history in 1926 before the CCP's views on its own founding had crystallized. He emphasizes the background of the CCP in study societies, the internal divisions among early Chinese communists, and their ideological and organizational immaturity.

4. Dirlik, *Origins of Chinese Communism*, 53–54, 142–44.

5. Kuhn and Jones, "Dynastic Decline," in CHOC, 10:148–54.

6. Ibid., 108–13.

7. Kuhn, "The Taiping Rebellion," in CHOC, 10:264–310.

8. Mary Rankin, *Elite Activism*, 92–135; James Polachek, "Gentry Hegemony: Soochow in the T'ung-chih Restoration," in Wakeman and Grant, *Conflict and Control*, 211–56.

9. Schwartz, *In Search of Wealth and Power*, 237–47.

10. Chang Hao, "Intellectual Change," 283–91.

11. Chang Hao, *Chinese Intellectuals*, 5–9

12. Rankin, *Elite Activism*, 28–29, 205–26.

13. Kuhn, "Local Self-Government under the Republic," 276–80.

14. Ibid., 272–75.

15. Gasster, "Republican Revolutionary Movement," 465–506.

16. Ernest Young, "Politics in the Aftermath," 208–25.

17. Ibid., 225–36.

18. Ibid., 246–49.

19. Ibid., 249–55.

20. A rich literature exists on the movement. Chow Tse-tsung's *May Fourth Movement* remains a standard account. See also Schwarcz, *Chinese Enlightenment*; Schwartz, ed., *Reflections*; and Lin Yu-sheng, *Crisis of Chinese Consciousness*. The movement will be discussed at length in this chapter.

21. Research on the early life of Chen Duxiu remains scanty. See Feigon, *Chen Duxiu*, 23–95, and Maeder, *Trois Textes*. See also Zhengxie Anhuisheng Weiyuanhui Wenshi Ziliao Gongzuozu (Work Group for Source Materials for Culture and History, Political Consultative Committee of Anhui Province), "Xinhaiqian Anhui Wenjiaojie de Geming Huodong" (Revolutionary Activities in Cultural and Educational Circles before the 1911 Revolution), in Zhongguo Renming Xieshang Huiyi Quanguo Weiyuanhui Wenshi Ziliao Yanjiu Weiyuanhui (Research Committee for Source Materials for Culture and History, National Committee of the Chinese Political Consultative Conference), ed., *Xinhai Geming Huiyilu* (Recollections of the 1911 Revolution), 4:379–84. The writings of Chen predating the 1911 Revolution have been published in DSZL, vol. 4 (1980).

22. Chen Duxiu, "Shuo Guojia" (On the State), in DSZL, 4(1980):104. (According to the editor of DSZL, the essay was published in *The Anhui Colloquial*

(Anhui Suhuabao) on June 14, 1904). Also, "Wangguo Bian" (On National Decline), ibid., 114 (published originally on July 27, 1904, in *The Anhui Colloquial*). See also Feigon, *Chen Duxiu*, 55–95.

23. Feigon, *Chen Duxiu*, 92–95.

24. Chen Duxiu, "Aiguoxin yu Zijuexin (Yijiuyisinian, Shiyiyue Shiri)" (Patriotism and Consciousness [November 10, 1914]), in Chen Duxiu, *Chen Duxiu Wenzhang Xuanbian* (Selected Articles by Chen Duxiu), 1:67, 68. Lin Yu-sheng, *Crisis of Chinese Consciousness*, 59–62.

25. Ibid., 1:67–69.

26. For a summary of the values and ideas Chen Duxiu espoused, see "Jinggao Qingnian (Yijiuyiwunian, Jiuyue Shiwuri)" (Warning the Youth [September 15, 1915]), in Chen Duxiu, *Chen Duxiu Wenzhang Xuanbian* (Selected Articles by Chen Duxiu), 1:73–78.

Some of the more important articles in which Chen discusses his preferred attitudes and values and attacks elements of the old order are, in addition to the above: (1) "Jinri zhi Jiaoyu Fangzhen (Yijiuyiwunian, Shiyue Shiwuri)" (A Guideline for Modern Education [November 15, 1915]), in Chen Duxiu, *Chen Duxiu Wenzhang Xuanbian* (Selected Articles by Chen Duxiu), 1:84–89; (2) "Dong-Xi Minzu Genben Sixiang de Chayi (Yijiuyiwunian, Shieryue Shiwuri)" (Basic Differences in Western and Eastern Thought [December 15, 1915]), ibid., 97–100; (3)"Yijiuyiliunian (Yijiuyiliunian, Yiyue Shiwuri)" (1916 [January 15, 1916]), ibid., 101–5; (4) "Xin Qingnian (Yijiuyiliunian, Jiuyue Yiri)" (The New Youth [September 1, 1916]), ibid., 112–14; (5) "Dangdai Erda Kexuejia zhi Sixiang (Yijiuyiliunian, Shiyue Yiri)" (Two Contemporary Scientists [September 1 and November 1, 1916]), ibid., 115–26; (6) "Xianfa yu Kongjiao (Yijiuyiliunian, Shiyue Yiri)" (The Constitution and Confucianism [November 1, 1916]), ibid., 144–48; (7) "Kongzi zhi Dao yu Xiandai Shenghuo (Yijiuyiliunian, Shieryue Yiri)" (The Way of Confucius and Modern Life [December 1, 1916]), ibid., 151–57; (8) "Po Kang Youwei *Gonghe Pingyi* (Yijiuyibanian, Sanyue Shiwuri)" (A Rebuttal of Kang Youwei's *Critique of the Republic* [March 15, 1918]), ibid., 241–58.

27. Lin Yu-sheng, *Crisis of Chinese Consciousness*, 63–81; Schwartz, *Chinese Communism*, 8–9.

28. Chen Duxiu, "Aiguoxin yu Zijuexin (Yijiuyisinian, Shiyiyue Shiri)" (Patriotism and Consciousness [November 10, 1914]), in *Chen Duxiu Wenzhang Xuanbian* (Selected Articles by Chen Duxiu), 1:78.

29. Benjamin Schwartz, "Themes in Intellectual History," in CHOC, 12:426.

30. Chen Duxiu, "Tan Zhengzhi (Yijiuerlingnian Jiuyue Yiri)" (Talking about Politics [September 1, 1920]), in *Chen Duxiu Wenzhang Xuanbian* (Selected Articles by Chen Duxiu), 2:1–10 (first published in *The New Youth*, 8:1, on the date provided in the title).

31. Ibid., 10.

32. Chen Duxiu, "Chu Sanhai (Yijiuyijiunian, Yiyue Shijiuri)" (The Three Evils to Be Eliminated [January 19, 1919]), in *Chen Duxiu Wenzhang Xuanbian* (Selected Articles by Chen Duxiu), 1:325–26 (first published in *Weekly Critic* [Meizhou Pinglun], vol. 5, on the date mentioned in the title); "Wode Guonei Heping Yijian (Yijiuyijiunian: Eryue Erri)" (My Suggestions for Domestic Peace [February 2, 1919]), ibid., 329–42 (first published serially in *Weekly Critic*, vols.7,

11, 12); "Wei Shemma Yao Nan-Bei Fenli (Yijiuyijiunian: Eryue Ershisanri)" (Why Should North and South Separate [February 20, 1919]), ibid., 367–69 (first published in *Weekly Critic* on the date mentioned in the title).

33. Chen Duxiu, "Women Yinggai Zemmayang? (Yijiuyijiunian, Siyue Shi-wuri)" (What Should We Do? [April 15, 1919]), *Chen Duxiu Wenzhang Xuanbian* (Selected Articles by Chen Duxiu), 1:380 (first published in *The New Youth*, 6:4, on the date mentioned in the title).

34. Chow, *The May Fourth Movement*, 171. Feigon, 131–36.

35. Chen Duxiu, "Women Jiujing Yingdang Buyingdang Aiguo (Yijiuyijiu-nian, Liuyue Bari)" (Should We Be Patriotic [June 8, 1919]), in *Chen Duxiu Wenzhang Xuanbian* (Selected Articles), 1:419–20. Chen Duxiu, "Shandong Wenti yu Guomin Juewu (Yijiuyijiunian, Wuyue Ershiliuri)" (The Shandong Question and the Awakening of the Citizens [May 26, 1919]), ibid., 410–11.

36. Chen Duxiu, "Xueshengjie Yinggai Paichi de Rihuo (Yijiuerlingnian, Yiyue Yiri)" (The Japanese Product Which Chinese Students Should Destroy [Jan-uary 1, 1920]), ibid., 470–71. Chen referred to the blind nationalism of the Japanese.

37. Chen Duxiu, "Zishalun—Sixiang Biandong yu Qingnian Zisha (Yijiuer-lingnian, Yiyue Yiri)" (On Suicide—Revolutions in Thought and Youth Suicide [January 1, 1920]), ibid., 453.

38. Ibid., 465.

39. Chen Duxiu, "Xin Wenhua Yundong Shi Shemma (Yijiuerlingnian: Siyue Yiri)" (What is the New Culture Movement [April 1, 1920]), in *Chen Duxiu Wenzhang Xuanji* (Selected Articles of Chen Duxiu), 1:514 (published in *The New Youth*, 7:5, on the date provided in the title).

40. Li Dazhao, "Tuanti de Xunlian yu Gexin de Shiye" (The Training of Cooperation and the Business of Reform), YDQH, 1:158–59 (first published in *Shuguang* [Dawn], 2:2, in January 1921). An editorial footnote suggests that Li probably wrote the piece sometime in 1920.

41. Cai Hesen, "Cai Linbin Gei Mao Zedong (Yijiuerlingnian, Bayue Shisan-ri)" (Letter from Cai Hesen to Mao Zedong [August 13, 1920]), in Zhongguo Geming Bowuguan (Museum of the Chinese Revolution), *Xinmin Xuehui Ziliao* (Source Materials for the New Citizen Study Society), 130; Yun Daiying, "Zhi Wang Guangqi Xin (Yijiuyijiunian, Jiuyue Jiuri)" (Letter to Wang Guangqi [Sep-tember 9, 1919]), in Yun Daiying, *Yun Daiying Wenji* (Collected Works), 106–9.

42. "Beijing Gongchanzhuyi Zuzhi de Baogao" (Report of the Peking Com-munist Organization), in Zhongyang Dang'anguan (Central Committee Archives), ed., *Zhongguo Gongchandang Diyici Daibiao Dahui Dang'an Ziliao* (Archival Sources for the First Congress of the CCP), 16.

43. Chen Duxiu, "Shixing Minzhu de Jichu (Yijiuyijiunian, Shieryue Yiri)" (The Basis for the Realization of Democracy [December 1, 1919]), in Chen Duxiu, *Chen Duxiu Wenzhang Xuanbian* (Selected Articles), 1:435 (first published in *The New Youth*, 7:1, on the date provided in the title).

44. E-tu Zen-sun, "The Growth of the Academic Community," in CHOC, 13:384.

45. Schwartz, *Chinese Communism*, 19.

46. Chen Duxiu, "Shixing Minzhu de Jichu (Yijiuyijiunian, Shieryue Yiri)" (The Basis for the Realization of Democracy [December 1, 1919]), in Chen Duxiu, *Chen Duxiu Wenzhang Xuanbian* (Selected Articles), 1:431.

47. Chen Duxiu, "Tan Zhengzhi (Yijiuerlingnian, Jiuyue Yiri)" (Talking about Politics [September 1, 1920]), ibid., 2:1–10 (originally published on the date in the title in *The New Youth*).

48. Ibid., 2:4.

49. Ibid., 2:7.

50. Ibid., 2:4.

51. Ibid., 2:8.

52. Ibid., 2:9–10.

53. Kuhn and Mann, "Dynastic Decline," in CHOC, 10:161.

54. Rankin, *Elite Activism*, 15–24.

55. Chen Duxiu, *Chen Duxiu Xiansheng Jiangyanlu* (Speeches by Mr. Chen Duxiu), 10.

56. Mao Zedong, "Minzhong de Dalianhe" (The Great Unity of the People), YDQH, 1:82–95. For a translation into English, see *The China Quarterly* 49 (January 1972): 76–87. Mao's article originally appeared serially in *The Xiang River Review* 2, 3, 4 (July 21, 28, August 4, 1919).

57. For the first, see Womack, *Foundations*, 20; Solomon, *Mao's Revolution*, 184; Schram, "From the 'Great Union,' " 90–91. It was Schram who pointed out similarities between Mao in the summer of 1919 and during the Cultural Revolution (Schram, "From the 'Great Union,' " 99–105).

58. For Mao, see Mao Zedong, "Minzhong de Dalianhe" (The Great Unity of the People), YDQH, 1:82–83. For the intellectual context, see Chang Hao, "Intellectual Change," in CHOC, 11:296–98, 311.

59. Mao Zedong, "Minzhong de Dalianhe" (The Great Unity of the People), YDQH, 1:93.

60. Ibid., 90.

61. Ibid., 93.

62. Ibid., 94.

63. Ibid.

64. Ibid., 95.

65. "Wenhua Shushe Zuzhi Dagang" (Outline of the Organization of the Culture Book Society), WSSQDST, 1:45, dated August 25, 1920. For the founding date, see "Faqi Wenhua Shushe" (Announcing the Culture Book Society), WSSQDST, 1:44–45, dated July 31, 1920. For the founders, see "Wenhua Shushe Diyici Yingye Baogao" (First Report on the Commerce of the Culture Book Society), WSSQDST, 1:53–54, dated November 1920.

66. "Xinmin Xuehui Huiwu Baogao (Diyihao; Guomin Jiuniandong Kan)" (Report on the Affairs of the New Citizen Study Society [Number One; published Winter 1920]), WSSQDST, 1:574.

67. For the journal, see Nathan, *Chinese Democracy*, 55.

68. Zhongguo Geming Bowuguan (Museum of the Chinese Revolution), eds., *Xinmin Xuehui Ziliao* (Source Materials for the New Citizen Study Society), 42–163.

69. McDonald, "Mao Tse-tung," 751–77.

70. Boorman, *Biographical Dictionary*, 3:222–23. Tan became president of the Executive Yuan of the Nanjing Government in the late 1920s.

71. McDonald, "Mao Tse-tung," 752–53. Li Rui, *Mao Zedong de Zaoqi Geming Huodong* (Early Revolutionary Activities of Mao Zedong), 263–79.

72. McDonald, "Mao Tse-tung," 752–55.

73. Translated in McDonald, "Mao Tse-tung," 772–77.

74. Ibid., 764–67.

75. "Mao Zedong Gei Xiang Jingyu: Hunan Wenti" (Letter from Mao Ze-dong to Xiang Jingyu: the Hunan Issue), in Zhongguo Geming Bowuguan (Museum of the Chinese Revolution), *Xinmin Xuehui Ziliao* (Source Materials for the Xinmin Xuehui), 75–76, dated November 25, 1925.

76. "Mao Zedong Gei Xiao Xudong, Cai Linbin, Bing Zai Faguo Zhu Huiyou (Yijiuerlingnian, Shieryue Yiri)" (Letter from Mao Zedong to Xiao Zisheng, Cai Hesen, and All Society Members in France [December 1, 1920]), in *Xinmin Xuehui Ziliao* (Materials Concerning the New Citizen Study Society), 148.

77. Ibid., 147–48.

78. In Li Dazhao, *Li Dazhao Wenji* (Collected Works), 4–7 (published in *Speech and Government* [Yanzhi] on April 1, 1913).

79. Li Dazhao, "Fa-E Geming zhi Bijiaoguan" (A Comparison of the French and Russian Revolutions), ibid., 572–75 (originally published in *Speech and Government* [Yanzhi] on July 1, 1918). Meisner, *Li Ta-chao*, 63.

80. Schwartz, *Chinese Communism*, 12.

81. Meisner, *Li Ta-chao*, 24–25.

82. Ibid., 24.

83. Ibid., 29–30.

84. Ibid., 31. See also Li Dazhao, "Minyi yu Zhengzhi (Yijiuyiliunian, Wuyue Shiwuri)" (The Popular Will and Politics [May 15, 1916]), in *Li Dazhao Wenji* (Collected Works), 153–76.

85. Meisner, *Li Ta-chao*, 21–29.

86. Li Dazhao, "Yanshixin yu Zijuexin," (Pessimism and Self-Awareness), in *Li Dazhao Wenji* (Collected Works), 145–52.

87. Meisner, *Li Ta-chao*, 33.

88. Li Dazhao, "Bolshevism de Shengli (Yijiuyibanian Shieryue)" (The Victory of Bolshevism [December 12, 1918]), in *Li Dazhao Wenji* (Collected Works), 603 (first published in *The New Youth*, 5:5, on the date in the title).

89. "Lianzhizhuyi yu Shijie Zuzhi (Yijiuyijiunian, Eryue Yiri)" (Federalism and the Organization of the World [February 1, 1919]), in *Li Dazhao Wenji* (Collected Works), 622.

90. Ibid., 621–22.

91. Meisner, *Li Ta-chao*, 64.

92. Li Dazhao, "Bolshevism de Shengli" (The Victory of Bolshevism), in *Li Dazhao Wenji* (Collected Works), 598–603.

93. Li Dazhao, "Xinde! Jiude! (Yijiuyibanian, Wuyue Shiwuri)" (The Old! The New! [May 15, 1918]) in *Li Dazhao Wenji* (Collected Works), 537–38 (first published in *The New Youth*, 4:5, on the date mentioned in the title).

94. Li Dazhao, "Xin Jiyuan (Yijiuyijiunian, Yuandan)" (The New Age [New Year's Day, 1919]), ibid., 606.

95. Li Dazhao, "Tuanti zhi Xunlian yu Gaige de Shiye" (The Training in Cooperation and the Business of Reform), YDQH, 1:158 (published originally in *Dawn* [Shuguang], 2:2, in 1921).

96. Ibid., 158.

97. Ibid., 157–59.

98. Ibid., 158–90.

99. See Ren Wuxiong et al., "Yun Daiying," 9–40.

100. Yun Daiying, *Yun Daiying Wenji* (Collected Works of Yun Daiying).

101. Yun Daiying, *Yun Daiying Riji* (Yun Daiying's Diary) and *Lai Hong Qu Yan Lu* (Records of Arriving Geese and Departing Swallows). In classical Chinese, geese and swallows often symbolize news from and to distant friends.

102. Yun set out his ideas in "Weilai zhi Meng (Yijiuerlingnian Shiyue)" (My Dream for the Future [November 1920]), in Yun Daiying, *Yun Daiying Wenji* (Collected Works), 228–45 (originally published in *Mutual Aid* [Huzhu], 1, on the date provided in the title).

103. Yun Daiying, "Zhi Wang Guangqi Xin (Yijiuyijiunian, Jiuyue Jiuri)" (Letter to Wang Guangqi [September 9, 1919]), in Yun Daiying, *Yun Daiying Wenji* (Collected Works), 106–7.

104. Furth, "Intellectual Change: From the Reform Movement to the May Fourth Movement," CHOC, 12:352–53.

105. Yun Daiying, "Shixian Shenghuo (Yijiuyibanian, Liuyue Ershiri)" (Real Life [June 20, 1918]), in Yun Daiying, *Yun Daiying Wenji* (Collected Works), 66.

106. Ibid., 66–67.

107. "Zhi Shen Zeming, Gao Yuhan (Yijiueryinian, Siyue Ershijiuri)" (Letter to Shen Zeming and Gao Yuhan [April 29, 1921]), ibid., 298.

108. "Liqun Shushe" (The Benevolence Book Society), WSSQDST, 1:124–32 (first published in *Mutual Aid* [Huzhu], 1 [November 1920]). Liao Huanxing, "Wuchang Liqun Shushe Shimo" (History of the Benevolence Book Society in Wuchang), in WSSQDST, 1:202–7, dated 1953.

109. Yun Daiying, "Zhi Wang Guangqi (Yijiueryinian, Liuyue Shiwuri)" (Letter to Wang Guangqi [June 15, 1921]), in Yun Daiying, *Yun Daiying Wenji* (Collected Works), 305–12.

110. "Nanjing Dahui Jilüe (Jielu)" (Record of the Nanjing Conference [Excerpts]), WSSQDST, 1:354–65 (published in *Young China* [Shaonian Zhongguo], 3:2 [September 1, 1921]).

111. "Daiying zhi Zhongjian" (A Letter from Yun Daiying to Yang Zhongjian), WSSQDST, 1:392 (published in the first volume of *The Correspondence of Young China Study Society Members*, which covered the August 1921 to March 1922 period).

112. "Wei Shaonian Zhongguo Xuehui Tongren Jin Yijie" (A Further Explanation to the Comrades of the Young China Study Society), WSSQDST, 1:393 (first published in *Young China* [Shaonian Zhongguo] 3:11 [June 1, 1922]).

113. Ibid., 394.

114. Ibid., 394.

115. Ibid., 394–95.

116. Ibid., 397–99.

117. Ibid., 395.

118. Ibid., 393.

119. Li Weihan, "Huiyi Xinmin Xuehui" (Remembering the New Citizen Study Society), in WSSQDST, 1:633, dated December 22, 1978.

120. "Cai Linbin Gei Mao Zedong" (Letter from Cai Hesen to Mao Zedong), in Zhongguo Geming Bowuguan (Museum of the Chinese Revolution) et al., eds.,

Xinmin Xuehui Ziliao (Source Materials for the New Citizen Study Society), 125, dated May 28, 1920.

121. "Cai Linbin Gei Mao Zedong" (Letter from Cai Linbin to Mao Zedong), ibid., 127.

122. For a short biography, see Ren Wuxiong et al., "Yun Daiying," 1–47.

123. "Cai Linbin Gei Xiao Xudong" (Letter from Cai Linbin to Xiao Zisheng), in Zhongguo Geming Bowuguan (Museum of the Chinese Revolution) et al., eds., *Xinmin Xuehui Ziliao* (Source Materials for the New Citizen Study Society), 45, dated July 7, 1919 (published in the first volume of *Xinmin Xuehui Huiyou Tongxinji* [Correspondence of the Members of the New Citizen Study Society]). The preface of the second volume was dated November 30, 1920 (ibid., 74). The first volume probably appeared in the last days of that month, as the last letter in the first volume was November 26, 1920.

124. On Yang, see Boorman, *Biographical Dictionary*, 4:1–3. Cai discussed Yang's exhortation to moral integrity in a letter to Mao Zedong; see "Cai Linbin Gei Mao Zedong" (Letter from Cai Linbin to Mao Zedong), in Zhongguo Geming Bowuguan (Museum of the Chinese Revolution) et al., eds., *Xinmin Xuehui Ziliao* (Sources for the New Citizen Study Society), 43. For a discussion of Yang's thought, see Li Jui, *Mao Zedong de Zaoqi Geming Huodong* (Early Revolutionary Activities of Mao Zedong), 25–35.

125. Li Jui, 43.

126. Cai Hesen, "Cai Linbin Gei Mao Zedong (Yijiuyibanian, Bayue Ershiyiri)" (Letter from Cai Linbin to Mao Zedong [August 21, 1918]), in Zhongguo Geming Bowuguan (Museum of the Chinese Revolution), et al., eds., *Xinmin Xuehui Ziliao* (Sources for the New Citizen Study Society), 57–58.

127. Ibid., 58.

128. Ibid.

129. Ch'eng I-fan, "Kung as Ethos in Late Nineteenth Century China: The Case of Wang Hsien-ch'ien (1842–1918)," in Cohen and Schrecker, *Reform in Nineteenth Century China*, 170–80.

130. "Cai Linbin Gei Mao Zedong (Yijiuerlingnian, Bayue Shisanri)" (Letter from Cai Linbin to Mao Zedong [August 13, 1920]), in Zhongguo Geming Bowuguan (Museum of the Chinese Revolution) et al., eds., *Xinmin Xuehui Ziliao* (Source Materials for the New Citizen Study Society), 128.

131. "Cai Linbin Gei Mao Zedong (Yijiuerlingnian, Bayue Shisanri)" (Letter from Cai Linbin to Mao Zedong [August 13, 1920]), ibid., 51, 130.

132. "Cai Linbin Gei Mao Zedong (Yijiuerlingnian, Jiuyue Shiliuri)" (Letter from Cai Linbin to Mao Zedong [September 16, 1920]), ibid., 154–55.

133. "Mao Zedong Gei Cai Hesen (Yijiueryinian, Yiyue Ershiyiri)" (Lett r from Mao Zedong to Cai Hesen [January 21, 1921]), ibid., 163. For Mao's enthus asm about what he found in Cai's letter, see also "Mao Zedong Gei Xiao Xudong, Cai Linbin, Bing Zai Faguo Zhu Huiyou (Yijiuerlingnian, Shieryue Yiri)" (Letter from Mao Zedong to Xiao Zisheng, Cai Linbin, and All Society Members in France [December 1, 1920]), in Zhongguo Geming Bowuguan (Museum of the Chinese Revolution), *Xinmin Xuehui Ziliao* (Materials Concerning the New Citizen Study Society), 144–45.

134. Nivison, "Ho Shen and His Accusers," 221.

135. Wakeman, *Great Enterprise*, 941.

136. Nivison, "Ho Shen and His Accusers," 225–28.

137. Wakeman, *Great Enterprise*, 1050–52.

138. This paragraph and the following on *What Is to Be Done?* rely heavily on Robert Service, "Foreword," in Lenin, *What Is to Be Done?*, 1–66.

139. Lenin, *What Is to Be Done?*, in *Selected Works*, 1:349.

140. Ibid., 234–63, 287–307.

141. Ibid., 226.

142. For the philosophical argumentation behind this, see Fogel, *Ai Ssu-ch'i*, 37–53.

143. Lenin, *What Is to Be Done?*, in *Selected Works*, 1:222–33.

144. Dirlik, *Origins of Chinese Communism*, 157.

145. Cai Hesen, "Zhongguo Gongchandangshi de Fazhan (Tigang): Zhongguo Gongchandang de Fazhan ji qi Lishi Shiming (Yijiuerliunian)" (The History of the Development of the CCP [Outline]: The Background to the Birth of Our Party and Its Historical Mission [1926]), in Cai Hesen, *Cai Hesen de Shierbian Wenzhang* (Twelve Essays by Cai Hesen), 8.

146. Li Zepeng, "Sanshiwunian Lai zhi Zhongguo Chubanye (Yibajiuqinian–Yijiusanyinian)" (Chinese Publishing in the Last Thirty-five Years [1897–1931]), in Zhang Jinglu, 4:381–94; Ge Gongzhen, "Zhongguo Baozhi Jinhua zhi Gaiguan" (An Overview of the Modernization of Chinese Periodicals), written in 1927, in Zhang Jinglu, 4:11.

147. Chang Hao, "Intellectual Change," in CHOC, 11:293.

148. Thompson, *Visions of the Future*, 114–37.

149. Zhang Yunhou, *Wusi Shiqi de Shetuan* (Societies and Leagues of the May Fourth Period).

150. Schwarcz, *Chinese Enlightenment*, 15–17, 67–72.

151. Leung, *Chinese Work-Study Movement*. See also Bailey, "Chinese Work-Study Movement in France." Original documents concerning the movement can be found in Zhang Yunhou, *Liu'Fa Qin'gong Jianxue Yundong* (Work-Study Movement to France), and FFSL.

152. Zhongguo Geming Bowuguan (Museum of the Chinese Revolution) et al., eds., *Xinmin Xuehui Ziliao* (Source Materials for the New Citizen Study Society).

153. Schwarcz, *Chinese Enlightenment*, 69–71.

154. Ibid., 70.

155. "Xinmin Xuehui Huiwu Baogao (Diyihao; Minguo Jiunian Dongkan)" (Report of the New Citizen Study Society [Number One; published Winter 1920]), WSSQDST, 1:575.

156. Ibid.

157. For an example, see "Shaonian Zhongguo Xuehui Guiyue" (Stipulations of the Young China Study Society), WSSQDST, 1:225–30 (published in *Shaonian Zhongguo Xuehui Zhounian Jiniance* [First Anniversary Booklet of the Young China Study Society] of 1920).

158. "Shaonian Zhongguo Xuehui Guiyue" (Stipulations of the Young China Study Society), WSSQDST, 1:225–26.

159. Ibid., 226.

160. "Xinmin Xuehui Huiwu Baogao (Diyihao; Minguo Jiunian Dongkan)" (Report of the New Citizen Study Society [Number One; published Winter 1920]), WSSQDST, 1:575–76.

161. Ibid., 575.

162. Ibid.

163. "Shaonian Zhongguo Xuehui Guiyue" (Stipulations of the Young China Study Society), WSSQDST, 1:225–28.

164. "Peng Huang Fu Yue Seng de Xin" (Peng Huang's Reply to Yue Seng), in WSSQDST, 2:455–56 (published in June 1920 in *The Lantern* [Xuedeng], a supplement of *The Times* [Shishi Xinbao]).

165. Shi Cuntong, " 'Gongdu Huzhutuan' de Shixian he Jiaoxun" (The "Work-Study Mutual Aid Societies": Realities and Lessons), in WSSQDST, 2:424–25 (published on May 1, 1920, in *Weekly Critic* [Xingqi Pinglun]).

166. "Gongdu Huzhutuan Jianzhang" (Short Constitution of the Work-Study Mutual Aid Society), in Wang Guangqi, "Gongdu Huzhutuan" (Work-Study Mutual Aid Societies) (published in *Young China*, 1:7 [January 15, 1920]), in WSSQDST, 2:373–74.

167. Wang Jianying, ed., *Zhongguo Gongchandang Zuzhishi Ziliao Huibian* (Edited Source Materials for the Organizational History of the Chinese Communist Party), 61.

168. Zheng Chaolin, "Zhongguo Shaonian Gongchandang de Ruokan Shishi" (Some Historical Facts concerning the Communist Party of Chinese Youth), in *Wenshi Ziliao Xuanji* (Compilation of Sources for History and Civilization) (Shanghai), 3(1981):13–26, 19–20.

169. Ibid., 20.

170. "Xinmin Xuehui Huiwu Baogao (Diyihao; Minguo Jiunian Dongkan)" (Report of the New Citizen Study Society [Number One; published Winter 1920]), in WSSQDST, 1:585.

171. Hu Shi, "Gongduzhuyi Shixing de Guancha" (A Survey of the Implementation of Work-Study-ism), in WSSQDST, 2:401–5 (first published in *The New Youth*, 7:5 [March 1920]).

172. [Chen] Duxiu, "Gongdu Huzhutuan Shibai Yuanyin Zai Nali?" (What Is the Cause for the Failure of the Work-Study Mutual-Aid Societies?), in WSSQDST, 2:416 (first published in the *New Youth*, 7:5 [March 1920]).

173. [Dai] Jitao, "Gongdu Huzhutuan yu Zibenjia de Shengchanzhi" (Work-Study Mutual-Aid Societies and the Capitalist Production System), in WSSQDST, 2:405–12 (first published in the *New Youth* 7:5 [March 1920]).

174. Boorman, *Biographical Dictionary*, 3:200–205. See also Shi Cuntong, "Gongdu Huzhutuan de Shijian he Jiaoxun" (The Work-Study Mutual-Aid Societies: Realities and Lessons), in WSSQDST, 2:423–40.

175. Schwartz, "Themes in Intellectual History," in CHOC, 12:433–44.

176. "Xinmin Xuehui Huiwu Baogao (Dierhao)" (Report on New Citizen Study Society Affairs [Number Two]), in WSSQDST, 1:592. Probably written shortly after January 16, 1921; that day, participants in the New Year's Conference met again to discuss business not covered during the conference, and this is the last business covered in the report.

177. Ibid., 592.

178. Ibid.

179. Ibid.

180. Ibid.

181. Ibid., 594.

182. Ibid.

183. Ibid.

184. For Cai Hesen's involvement, see "Cai Linbin Gei Mao Zedong (Yijiuyi-banian, Liuyue Sanshiri)" (Letter from Cai Linbin to Mao Zedong [June 30, 1918]); "Cai Linbin Gei Xiao Xudong (Yijiuyibanian Qiyue)" (Letter from Cai Linbin to Xiao Xudong [July 1918]); "Cai Hesen zhi Chen Shaoxiu, Cai Zizhang, Xiao Zisheng, Mao Zedong" (Yijiuyibanian, Bayua Ershiqiri)" (Letter from Cai Hesen to Chen Shaoxiu, Cai Zizhang, Xiao Zisheng, and Mao Zedong [August 27, 1918]); and "Cai Hesen zhi Zou Yiding (Letter from Cai Hesen to Zou Yiding); all in Zhongguo Geming Bowuguan (Museum of the Chinese Revolution) et al., eds., Xinmin Xuehui Ziliao (Sources for the New Citizen Study Society), 43–59.

185. Xiao Zisheng, "Liu'Fa Qin'gong Jianxue de Qingxing (Er; Jielu)" (The Situation of the Work-Study Movement in France [Two; Excerpts]), in Zhang Yunhou, 230–37, dated 1920; Xiao Zisheng, "Li'ang Zhongguo Daxue Zuijin zhi Jinxing" (Recent Developments with Regard to the Chinese University at Lyon), FFSL, 2b:588–91 (published on June 11 and 12, 1920, in the Morning Post [Chenbao]).

186. Leung, Chinese Work-Study Movement, 31–45. Scalapino and Yu, Modern China, 231–59, 618–26.

187. See Bailey, "Chinese Work-Study Movement in France," 441–61.

188. "Xiao Xudong Gei Mao Zedong" (Letter from Xiao Xudong to Mao Zedong), in Zhongguo Geming Bowuguan (Museum of the Chinese Revolution) et al., eds., Xinmin Xuehui Ziliao (Source Materials for the New Citizen Study Society), 137, dated August 1920.

189. Cai Hesen, "Faguo Zuijin de Laodong Yundong (Yijiuerlingnian, Liuyue Shisanri)" (The Recent Labor Movement in France [June 13, 1920]), in Cai Hesen Wenji (Collected Works), 33–48 (published in The World of Youth [Shaonian Shijie], 1:11).

190. "1919nian 1yue 23ri Shanghai Huiyuan Zai Wusong Tongji Xuexiao Kaihui Jilüe" (Minutes of the January 23, 1919, Meeting of Society Members at the Tongji School in Wusong), in WSSQDST, 1:286 (published on March 1, 1919, in Shaonian Zhongguo Xuehui Huiwu Baogao [Young China Study Society Report], vol. 1).

191. Ibid., 286–87.

192. Ibid., 287.

193. "Shanghai Huiyuan zhi Beijing Huiyuan" (A Letter from Members in Shanghai to Members in Peking), in WSSQDST, 1:318–19 (published July 15, 1919, in Young China); "Beijing Huiyuan Da Shanghai Huiyuan" (Response of Members in Peking), ibid., 319 (published in Young China on July 15, 1919).

194. "Bali Benhui Tongren Zhi Jing, Hu Benhui Tongren" (Letter from Members of the Society in Peking to Members in Peking and Shanghai), in WSSQDST, 1:320, dated September 27, 1919 (published in Young China on January 15, 1920).

195. Ibid., 321–25.

196. Ibid., 352.

197. For the articles, see WSSQDST, 1:336–99.

198. "Nanjing Dahui Jilüe (Jielu)" (Proceedings of the Nanjing Conference [Excerpts]), in WSSQDST, 1:354.

199. Ibid.

200. Ibid., 357.

201. Ibid., 361.

202. Ibid., 560–62.

203. Ibid., 358.

204. Ibid.

205. Ibid., 360.

206. Wang Guangqi, "Zhengzhi Huodong yu Shehui Huodong (Jielu)" (Political Action and Social Action [Excerpt]), in WSSQDST, 1:400, dated October 1921 (published in *Young China* on March 1, 1922).

207. Ibid., 401.

208. Ibid.

209. For the documents, see WSSQDST, 1:390–535.

210. Quoted in Rankin, *Elite Activism*, 277.

211. Chen Duxiu, "Tan Zhengzhi (Yijiuerlingnian, Jiuyue Yiri)" (Talking about Politics [September 1, 1920]), in *Chen Duxiu Wenzhang Xuanbian* (Selected Articles by Chen Duxiu), 2:4. In defending his commitment to Marxism-Leninism, Yun Daiying resorted to the same line of argument (Yun Daiying, "Wei Shaonian Zhongguo Xuehui Jinyijie" [A Further Explanation to the Young China Study Society], in *Yun Daiying Wenji* (Collected Works), 328 [published in *Young China* on June 1, 1922]).

212. Mao Zedong, "Mao Zedong Gei Xiao Xudong, Cai Linbin Bing Zai Fa Zhu Huiyou)" (Letter from Mao Zedong to Xiao Xudong, Cai Linbin, and All Society Members in France), in Hunansheng Bowuguan (Hunan Museum of the Revolution), ed., *Xinmin Xuehui Ziliao* (Source Materials for the New Citizen Study Society), 149, dated December 1, 1920. Xiao Xudong and Cai Linbin are better known as Xiao Zisheng and Cai Hesen.

213. Ibid., 148–49.

214. Schram, "Mao Tse-tung's Thought to 1949," in CHOC, 13:803.

215. "Mao Zedong Gei Xiao Xudong, Cai Linbin, Bing Zai Faguo Zhu Huiyou (Yijiuerlingnian, Shieryue Yiri)" (Letter from Mao Zedong to Xiao Xudong, Cai Linbin, and All Society Members in France [December 1, 1920]), in Zhongguo Geming Bowuguan (Museum of the Chinese Revolution) et al., *Xinmin Xuehui Ziliao* (Sources for the New Citizen Study Society), 148.

216. Chen Duxiu, "Tan Zhengzhi (Yijiuerlingnian, Jiuyue Yiri)" (Talking about Politics [September 1, 1920]), in *Chen Duxiu Wenzhang Xuanbian* (Selected Articles by Chen Duxiu), 2:9.

217. Li Dazhao, "Xin Jiyuan (Yijiuyijiunian, Yuandan)" (The New Age [New Year's Day, 1919]), in *Li Dazhao Wenji* (Collected Works), 98–99.

218. "Lun Shehuizhuyi (Yijiuerlingnian, Shiyiyue Shiwuri)" (On Socialism [November 15, 1920]), in Yun Daiying, *Yun Daiying Wenji* (Collected Works), 250 (published in *Youth*, 2:5, on the date provided in the title).

219. "Geming de Jiazhi (Yijiuerlingnian, Shiyue)" (The Value of Revolution [October 1920]), in Yun Daiying, *Yun Daiying Wenji* (Collected Works), 224–25 (published in the *Study Lamp* [Xuedeng], a supplement of the *Times*, on the date provided in the title).

220. "Wei Shaonian Zhongguo Xuehui Tongren Jinyijie" (A Further Explanation to the Comrades of the Young China Study Society), in WSSQDST, 1:397.

221. Li Dazhao, "Minyi yu Zhengzhi (Yijiuyiliunian, Wuyue Shiwuri)" (The People's Will and Government [May 15, 1915]), in *Li Dazhao Wenji* (Selected Works), 164.

222. "Geming de Jiazhi (Yijiuerlingnian, Shiyue Shiri)" (The Value of Revolution [October 10, 1920]), in *Yun Daiying Wenji* (Collected Works), 225.

223. "Wei Shaonian Zhongguo Xuehui Tongren Jinyijie" (A Further Explanation to the Comrades of the Young China Study Society), in WSSQDST, 1:397.

224. Ibid., 398.

2. THE FOUNDING OF COMMUNIST CELLS AND THE FIRST CONGRESS

1. See, for example, He Ganzhi, *Zhongguo Xiandai Gemingshi* (History of the Contemporary Chinese Revolution). A more recent and more detailed treatment of the founding of the CCP is Li Xin and Chen Tiejian, *Weida de Kaiduan, 1919–1923* (The Great Beginning: 1919–1923). While incorporating much new material, Li Xin and Chen Tiejian remain within the established CCP view of its own history. They analyze the founding of the CCP as the result of the confluence of the rise of a domestic labor movement and the impact of the October Revolution, and they portray the founding of communist cells as the result of this. For a dissenting Chinese view, see Cai Hesen, "Zhongguo Gongchandangshi de Fazhan (Tigang; Yijiuerliunian) (The Historical Development of the Chinese Communist Party [Outline; 1926]), in *Cai Hesen de Shierbian Wenzhang* (Twelve Essays by Cai Hesen), 1–67. Cai Hesen, emphasizing the importance of study societies, the fragmented nature of the early CCP, and the ideological "immaturity" of its members, wrote his history in 1926 before the CCP had generated an orthodoxy about its own history, which occurred in 1945 at the Seventh CCP Congress.

The most recent treatment of the founding of the CCP outside of China is Dirlik, *Origins of Chinese Communism*. This work is discussed in this chapter. Older accounts include those of Benjamin Schwartz and James Harrison. Hatano Ken'ichi's multivolume *Chūgoku Kyōsantōshi* (History of the Chinese Communist Party) set an early standard.

2. Dirlik, *Origins of Chinese Communism*, 218–19.

3. Ibid., 172–252.

4. Ibid., 255.

5. Ibid., 155.

6. YDQH. This collection consists of three volumes. Dirlik had access only to the first two. The third was published after historians in China decried the omission of important sources and the partiality of the first two volumes.

7. For instance see Li Da, "Guanyu Zhongguo Gongchandang Jianli de Jige Wenti (Yijiuwusinian, Eryue Ershisanri)" (Some Issues concerning the Founding of the CCP [Feburary 23, 1954]), in YDQH, 2:1–5, and "Zhongguo Gongchandang de Faqi he Diyici, Dierci Daibiao Dahui Jingguo de Huiyi (Yijiuwuwunian, Bayue Erri)" (The Beginning of the CCP and Its First and Second Congresses [August 2, 1955]), in YDQH, 2:6–18. The circumstances in which Li Da's recollections were produced are not clear. However, 1954 and 1955 were years of anti-bourgeois

campaigns by the CCP, and Li was under some pressure to demonstrate his contributions to the founding of the CCP. He had left the CCP in September 1923 after a conflict with Chen Duxiu and reapplied for membership only in 1949, having accepted a string of KMT appointments. See Xiao Chaoran, *Zhongguo Dangshi Jianming Cidian* (Concise Dictionary of the Chinese Communist Party's History), 2:710. Before being granted readmission into the CCP, Li Da produced an account of his involvement in the early CCP. See "Li Da Zishu (Jielu)" (Li Da on Li Da [Excerpt]), 1–12.

8.   YDDAZL.

9.   Respectively, Zhongguo Geming Bowuguan, Hunansheng Geming Bowuguan (Museum of the Chinese Revolution, Hunan Provincial Museum of the Revolution), eds., *Xinmin Xuehui Ziliao* (Sources for the New Citizen Study Society), WSSQDST, and FFSL.

10.   Zhongguo Renmin Daxue Zhonggong Dangshixi Ziliaoshi (Materials Section, Department of CCP History, People's University), ed., *Gongchanzhuyi Xiaozu he Dang de 'Yida' Ziliao Huibian (Xiaonei Yongshu)* (Collected Source Materials for CCP Cells and the Party's "First Congress" [For University Use Only]); YDQH; Wang Jianying, ed., *Zhongguo Gongchandang Zuzhishi Ziliao Huibian* (Edited Source Materials for the Organizational History of the CCP), 15, note 1, mentions that the word *cell* emerged only some time after the founding of the CCP. The history of the word will be discussed later.

11.   "Yang Zhihua zhi Huiyi (Yijiuwuliunian Jiuyue)" (Yang Zhihua's Recollections [September 1956]), in YDQH, 2:25. Li Da, "Zhongguo Gongchandang de Faqi He Diyici, Dierci Daibiao Dahui Jingguo de Huiyi (Yijiuwuwunian, Bayue Erri)" (The Beginning of the CCP and Its First and Second Congresses [August 2, 1955]), in YDQH, 2:7; Chen Wangdao, "Huiyi Dang Chengli Shiqi de Yixie Qingkuang (Yijiuwuliunian, Liuyue Shiqiri)" (Recollections of Some Aspects of the Situation at the Time of the Founding of the Party [June 17, 1956]), in YDQH, 2:20; Shi Fuliang [Shi Cuntong], "Zhongguo Gongchandang Chengli Shiqi de Jige Wenti (Yijiuwuliunian Shieryue)" (Some Issues at the Time of the Founding of the Chinese Communist Party [December 1956]), in YDQH, 2:35. Shen Yanbing, "Huiyi Shanghai Gongchanzhuyi Xiaozu (Yijiuwuqinian Siyue)" (Remembering the Shanghai Communist Cell [April 1957]), in YDQH, 2:46.

12.   "Zhongguo Gongchandang Diyici Daibiao Dahui" (The First Congress of the Chinese Communist Party), in YDDAZL, 11. This document's first sentence stated that "the Chinese communist organization was established after the middle of last year," referring to the Shanghai cell. Therefore, it was written in 1921. The document also states that it was Nikolaevsky, a representative of the Far East Bureau at the CCP's First Congress, who suggested that the congress report to Irkutsk. This report may be the result of this proposal. Its level of detail and its exactness suggest that it was written shortly after the congress. The document is a translation of a Russian original in the Comintern Archives.

13.   For instance, Li Da, "Zhongguo Gongchandang de Faqi He Diyici, Dierci Daibiao Dahui Jingguo de Huiyi (Yijiuwuwunian, Bayue Erri)" (The Beginning of the CCP and Its First and Second Congresses [August 2, 1955]), in YDQH, 2:8; Chen Wangdao, "Huiyi Dang Chengli Shiqi de Yixie Qingkuang (Yijiuwuliunian, Liuyue Shiqiri)" (Recollections of Some Aspects of the Situation at the Time of

the Founding of the Party [June 17, 1956]), in YDQH, 2:23; Shi Fuliang [Shi Cuntong], "Zhongguo Gongchandang Chengli Shiqi de Jige Wenti (Yijiuwuliunian Shieryue)" (Some Issues in the Founding of the Chinese Communist Party [December 1956]), in YDQH, 2:35.

It is unclear to which other four people the above quote, which mentioned Chen Duxiu as the founder of the Shanghai cell, referred. Dai Jitao and Zhang Dongsun can be ruled out. Zhang Dongsun supported Russell's views and became the butt of Chen Duxiu's bile in the fall of 1920; Dai was a principled KMT supporter. Some communist authors state that Dai did not join the CCP only because of a personal loyalty to Sun Yatsen (Zhang Guotao, *Rise of the Chinese Communist Party*, 103–6). This charge probably derived from a CCP attempt to paint Dai in a negative light. As early as 1912, Dai had argued that "a political party is built on . . . a convergence of political views. Members group around an ism, around a program, and not around a person" (see "Wo zhi Jingji Zhengci" [My Economic Policies], in Chen Tianxi, ed., *Dai Jitao Xiansheng Wencun Zai Bianxu* [Second Revised Edition of Mr. Dai Jitao's Extant Writings], 64).

14.   Qiang Chonghua, ed., *Chen Duxiu Beipu Ziliao Huibian* (Compilation of Historical Materials on Chen Duxiu's Imprisonments), 5–8.

15.   Chow Tse-tsung, *May Fourth Movement*, 44–45, note d, 250–51.

16.   Zhang Guotao, *Rise of the Chinese Communist Party*, 98–102.

17.   Hatano Ken'ichi, *Chūgoku Kyōsantōshi* (History of the Chinese Communist Party), 5:620–21; "Weijingsiji Zai Hua Huodung Jishi" (Chronology of Voitinsky's Activities in China), in Yang Yunruo et al., eds., *Weijingsiji Zai Zhongguo de Youguan Ziliao* (Source Materials for Voitinsky's Activities in China), 460 n.4.

18.   Ibid., 460–61.

19.   "Zhongguo Gongchandang Xuanyan (Yijiuerlingnian Shiyiyue)" (Manifesto of the Chinese Communist Party [November 1920]), in YDDAZL, 1–5.

20.   "Deng Zhongxia Huiyi Zhongguo Gongchandang de Chengli ji Dang Lingdao de Zaoqi Gongren Yundong (Yijiusanlingnian Liuyue)" (Deng Zhongxia's Recollections of the Founding of the CCP and the Early Labor Movement Led by the Party [June 1930]), in YDQH, 2:80; Zhou Yangru, " 'Yida' Qian de Shanghai Gongchandang" (The Shanghai Communist Party before the First Congress), 55.

21.   "Deng Zhongxia Huiyi Zhongguo Gongchandang de Chengli ji Dang Lingdao de Zaoqi Gongren Yundong (Yijiusanlingnian Liuyue)" (Deng Zhongxia's Recollections of the Founding of the CCP and the Early Labor Movement Led by the Party [June 1930]), in YDQH, 2:80.

22.   Zhou Yangru, " 'Yida' Qian de Shanghai Gongchandang" (The Shanghai Communist Party before the First Congress), 54; Chow Tse-tsung, *May Fourth Movement*, 250.

23.   See the table of contents of the *New Youth*, 8:1 (September 1, 1920); 8:2 (October 1, 1920); 8:3 (November 1, 1920); 8:4 (December 1, 1920); 8:5 (January 1, 1921).

24.   Maring Archive, no. 3153/1. This is an undated sheet with handwritten notes.

25.   Xiao Chaoran, *Zhonggong Dangshi Jianming Cidian* (Concise Dictionary of the Chinese Communist Party's History), 2:686.

26.   Shen Yanbing, "Huiyi Shanghai Gongchanzhuyi Xiaozu (Yijiuwuqi-

nian)" (Recollections of the Shanghai Communist Cell [1957]), in YDQH, 2:47; Bao Huiseng, "Gongchandang Diyici Quanguo Daibiao Huiyi Qianhou de Huiyi (Yijiuwusannian, Ba, Jiuyue)" (Recollections of the Period Surrounding the First Congress of the Chinese Communist Party [August–September, 1953]), in YDQH, 2:304; Li Da, "Qiyi Huiyi (Yijiuwubanian, Qiyue Yiri)" (July 1 Recollections [July 1, 1958]), in Zhongguo Renmin Daxue Zhonggong Dangshixi Ziliaoshi (Materials Section of the Department of CCP History, People's University), ed., *Gongchanzhuyi Xiaozu He Dang de "Yida" Ziliao Huibian (Xiaonei Yongshu)* (Compilation of Materials for Communist Cells and the First Congress [Sourcebook for University Use Only]), 56–57.

27. "Weijingsiji Zai Hua Huodong Jishi" (Chronology of Voitinsky's Activities in China), in Yang Yunruo et al., eds., *Weijingsiji Zai Zhongguo de Youguan Ziliao* (Source Materials for Voitinsky's Activities in China), 464.

28. Maring, "Bericht des Genossen H. Maring für die Executive," Maring Archive no. 225. Translation by A. Saich.

29. Li Da, "Zhongguo Gongchandang de Faqi he Diyici, Dierci Daibiao Dahui Jingguo de Huiyi (Yijiuwuwunian, Bayue Erri)" (The Beginning of the CCP and Its First and Second Congresses [August 2, 1955]), in YDQH, 2:8–10. See also "Li Da Zishu (Jielu)" (Li Da on Li Da [Excerpt]), 3–5; Li Shengfu, "Wode Fuqin Li Hanjun" (My Father, Li Hanjun), 38.

30. Li Da, "Zhongguo Gongchandang de Faqi he Diyici, Dierci Daibiao Dahui Jingguo de Huiyi (Yijiuwuwunian, Bayue Erri)" (The Beginning of the CCP and Its First and Second Congresses [August 2, 1955]), in YDQH, 2:7–8.

31. Zhang Guotao, *Rise of the Chinese Communist Party*, 137.

32. Cai Hesen, "Zhongguo Gongchandangshi de Fazhan (Tigang; Yijiuyiliunian)" (The Historical Development of the Chinese Communist Party [Outline; 1926]), in *Cai Hesen de Shierbian Wenzhang* (Twelve Essays by Cai Hesen), 24.

33. Li Shengfu, "Wode Fuqin Li Hanjun" (My Father, Li Hanjun), 35–36.

34. Xiao Chaoran, *Zhongguo Gongchandang Jianming Cidian* (Concise Dictionary of the Chinese Communist Party's History), 697.

35. Li Bogang, "Huiyi Li Hanjun" (Recollections of Li Hanjun), *Dangshi Yanjiu Ziliao* (Sources for Party History Research), 4:283–84 (1983); Bao Huiseng, "Huainian Li Hanjun Xiansheng" (In Memoriam of Mr. Li Hanjun), in DSZL, 1(1980):136; Bao Huiseng, *Bao Huiseng Huiyilu* (Memoirs of Bao Huiseng), 17–18; Chen Wangdao, "Dang de Jianli Shiqi de Qingkuang" (Circumstances Surrounding the Founding of the CCP), in DSZL, 1(1980):30; Xiao Chaoran, *Zhonggong Dangshi Jianming Cidian* (Concise Dictionary of the Chinese Communist Party's History), 2:697.

36. Li Da, "Zhongguo Gongchandang de Faqi he Diyici, Dierci Daibiao Dahui Jingguo de Huiyi (Yijiuwuwunian, Bayue Erri)" (The Beginning of the CCP and Its First and Second Congresses [August 2, 1955]), in YDQH, 2:6–10. Chen Tanqiu, "Diyici Daibiao Dahui de Huiyi (Yijiusanliunian)" (Recollections of the First Congress [1936]), in YDQH, 2:286–87.

37. Li Da, "Zhongguo Gongchandang de Faqi he Diyici, Dierci Daibiao Dahui Jingguo de Huiyi (Yijiuwuwunian, Bayue Erri)" (The Beginning of the CCP and Its First and Second Congresses [August 2, 1955]), in YDQH, 2:8–10; Chen Tanqiu, "Diyici Daibiao Dahui de Huiyi (Yijiusanliunian)" (Recollections of the First Congress [1936]), in YDQH, 2:286–87; "Zhongguo Gongchandang Diyici Daibiao

Dahui de Jige Wenti (Yijiuqibanian, Bayue Shierri)" (Some Issues in the First Congress of the Chinese Communist Party [August 12, 1978]), in YDQH, 2:375–78; Chen Gongbo, "Wo yu Gongchandang (Yijiusiliunian)" (The CCP and I [1946]), in YDQHGD, 90–91.

38. Shao Weizheng, "Dang de 'Yida' Yiti Chutan" (Preliminary Examination of Disputes at the First Congress), in DSZL, 3(1980):127–39.

39. Cai Hesen, "Zhongguo Gongchandangshi de Fazhan (Tigang; Yijiuerliunian)" (The Historical Development of the Chinese Communist Party [Outline; 1926]), in *Cai Hesen de Shierbian Wenzhang* (Twelve Essays by Cai Hesen), 25; "Zai Dang de Diliuci Daibiao Dahuishang Taolun Zhengzhi Baogao Shi de Fayan (Yijiuerbanian, Liuyue Ershierri)" (Comments Made during the Discussion of the Political Report at the Sixth Congress [June 22, 1928]), in Cai Hesen, *Cai Hesen de Shierbian Wenzhang* (Twelve Essays by Cai Hesen), 136.

40. Xiao Chaoran, *Zhongguo Gongchandangshi Jianming Cidian* (Concise Dictionary of the Chinese Communist Party's History), 697.

41. Ibid., 743.

42. Cai Hesen, "Zhongguo Gongchandangshi de Fazhan (Tigang; Yijiuerliunian)" (The Historical Development of the Chinese Communist Party [Outline; 1926]), in *Cai Hesen de Shierbian Wenzhang* (Twelve Essays by Cai Hesen), 38.

43. On Huang Lingshuang, see Zhang Dainian et al., eds., *Wuzhengfu Zhuyi Sixiang Ziliaoxuan* (A Selection of Source Materials on Anarchist Thought), 350. This collection also contains many writings by Huang.

44. Ibid.

45. Scalapino, *Chinese Anarchist Movement*, 35–36.

46. "Guangzhou Gongchandang de Baogao" (Report of the Canton Communist Party), in YDDAZL, 23. On Liu Shifu, see Scalapino and Yu, *Modern China*, 507–13.

47. YDDAZL, 24.

48. "Guan Qian Guanyu Beijing Shehuizhuyi Qingniantuan yu Wuzhengfudang Huzhutuan Huodong Qingxing zhi Wang Huanqing Cheng (1921nian 3yue)" (Letter from Guan Qian to Wang Huanqing about the Activities of the Peking Socialist Youth League with the Anarchist Party and the Mutual-Aid Society [March 1921]), in Zhang Dainian et al., eds., *Wuzhengfu Zhuyi Sixiang Ziliaoxuan* (A Selection of Source Materials on Anarchist Thought), 1054.

49. "Guangzhou Gongchandang de Baogao" (The Report of the Canton Communist Party), in YDDAZL, 24.

50. Ibid.

51. Ibid.

52. Ibid., 24–25.

53. Maring, "Bericht des Genossen H. Maring für die Executive" (Report of Comrade H. Maring to the Executive), Maring Archive, 255.

54. Huang Xianmeng, "Guanyu 'Yida' de Hunan Gongchandang Xiaozu Wenti" (On the Issue of the Hunan CCP Cell at the Time of the First Congress), in Zhu Chengjia, *Zhonggong Dangshi Yanjiu Lunwenxuan* (Selection of Research Articles on CCP History), 120–26; Zhonggong Zhongyang Dangshi Yanjiushi (Party History Institute of the CCP Central Committee), *Zhonggong Dangshi Dashi Nianbiao* (Chronology of CCP History), 1–3. For the PRC historians, see

Saich, "Through the Past Darkly," 172–73. It was only after Mao Zedong came back from the First Congress that the Changsha cell was formally linked to the Shanghai cell. This is confirmed by Yi Lirong, "Dang de Chengli Shiqi Hunan de Yixie Qingkuang (Yijiuqijiunian, Jiuyue Shiyiri)" (The Circumstances in Hunan at the Time of the Founding of the Party [September 11, 1979]), in YDQH, 2:282.

55. "Xinmin Xuehui Huiwu Baogao (Dierhao)" (New Citizen Study Society Report [Number Two]," in WSSQDST, 1:597.

56. "Cai Linbin Gei Mao Zedong (Yijiuerlingnian, Bayue Shisanri)" (Letter from Cai Linbin to Mao Zedong [August 13, 1920]), in Zhongguo Geming Bowuguan (Museum of the Chinese Revolution) et al., eds., *Xinmin Xuehui Ziliao* (Source Materials for the New Citizen Study Society), 128–29.

57. "Cai Linbin Gei Mao Zedong" (Letter from Cai Linbin to Mao Zedong), in Zhongguo Geming Bowuguan (Museum of the Chinese Revolution), ed., *Xinmin Xuehui Ziliao* (Source Materials for the New Citizen Study Society), 160. (The letter was dated September 16, 1920, and published in the third volume of *Xinmin Xuehui Huiyuan Tongxinji* [The Correspondence of New Citizen Study Society Members], published in January 1921.)

58. Ibid.

59. Ibid.

60. Ibid.

61. "Cai Linbin Gei Mao Zedong (Yijiuerlingnian, Bayue Shisanri)" (Letter from Cai Linbin to Mao Zedong [August 13, 1920]), in Zhongguo Geming Bowuguan (Museum of the Chinese Revolution) et al., eds., *Xinmin Xuehui Ziliao* (Source Materials for the New Citizen Study Society), 129.

62. Ibid.

63. Ibid., 129–30.

64. Ibid., 130

65. "Cai Linbin Gei Mao Zedong" (Letter from Cai Linbin to Mao Zedong), in Zhongguo Geming Bowuguan (Museum of the Chinese Revolution), ed., *Xinmin Xuehui Ziliao* (Source Materials for the New Citizen Study Society), 161.

66. "Mao Zedong Gei Xiao Xudong, Cai Linbin, Bing Zai Fa Zhu Huiyou" (Letter from Mao Zedong to Xiao Xudong, Cai Linbin, and All Society Members in France), in Zhongguo Geming Bowuguan (Museum of the Chinese Revolution), ed., *Xinmin Xuehui Ziliao* (Source Materials for the New Citizen Study Society), 151. The letter was dated December 1, 1920.

67. "Cai Linbin Gei Mao Zedong" (Letter from Cai Linbin to Mao Zedong), in Zhongguo Geming Bowuguan (Museum of the Chinese Revolution), ed., *Xinmin Xuehui Ziliao* (Source Materials for the New Citizen Study Society), 161.

68. Li Jui, *Early Revolutionary Activities*, 170–77.

69. "Mao Zedong Gei Cai Hesen" (Letter from Mao Zedong to Cai Hesen), in Zhongguo Geming Bowuguan (Museum of the Chinese Revolution) et al., eds., *Xinmin Xuehui Ziliao* (Source Materials for the New Citizen Study Society), 163.

70. Wang Jianying, ed., *Zhongguo Gongchandang Zuzhishi Ziliao Huibian* (Edited Source Materials for the Organizational History of the Chinese Communist Party), 21.

71. "Beijing Gongchanzhuyi Zuzhi de Baogao (Yijiueryinian)" (Report of the Peking Communist Organization [1921]), in YDDAZL, 15. There has been

discussion about this date. Zhu Wushan says that there was no official cell until early 1921; "Zhonggong Chengli Qianhou Zai Beijing Gongzuo de Huiyi (Yijiu-wuliunian Liuyue)" (Recollections of Activities in Peking during the Founding of the CCP [June 1956]) in YDQH, 2:91. Liu Renjing agrees with him; "Huiyi 'Wusi' Yundong, Beijing Makesizhuyi Yanjiuhui he Dang de 'Yida' (Yijiuwuqinian Siyue)" (Recollections of the "May Fourth" Movement, the Peking Marxism Research Society, and the "First Congress" of the Party [April 1957]), in YDQH, 2:116. As the report is the earliest evidence, it should be considered the most reliable. It may be that Zhu and Liu joined later.

72. Zhang Guotao, Rise of the Chinese Communist Party, 96–114.

73. Meisner, Li Ta-chao, 114–18.

74. For a list of cell members, see Wang Jianying, ed., Zhongguo Gongchan-dang Zuzhishi Ziliao Huibian (Edited Source Materials for the Organizational History of the Chinese Communist Party), 1–2. For membership lists of the three study societies in question, see WSSQDST, 1:241–43; 2:49–52; 2:140–41. Memoirs emphasized this common background. See Zhang Guotao, Rise of the Chinese Communist Party, 109–20; Zhu Wushan, "Zhonggong Chengli Qianhou Zai Beijing Gongzuo de Huiyi (Yijiuwuliunian, Liuyue)" (Recollection of Activities in Peking at the Time of the Founding of the Chinese Communist Party), 2:89–95.

75. In addition to the above, see "Deng Zhongxia Huiyi Zhongguo Gongchan-dang de Chengli Ji Dang Lingdao de Zaoqi Gongren Yundong (Yijiusanlingnian Liuyue)" (Deng Zhongxia's Recollections of the Founding of the Chinese Com-munist Party and the Early Labor Movement under CCP Leadership), in YDQH, 2:79–85; "Yu Shude de Huiyi (Yijiuwuliunian Shieryue)" (Recollections of Yu Shude [December 1956]), in YDQH, 2:108–12; Liu Renjing, "Huiyi 'Wusi' Yun-dong, Beijing Makesizhuyi Yanjiuhui he Dang de 'Yida' (Yijiuwuqinian Siyue)" (Recollections of the May Fourth Movement, the Peking Marxism Research Soci-ety, and the First Congress of the CCP [April 1957]), in YDQH, 2:113–17; Luo Zhanglong, "Huiyi Beijing Daxue Makesi Xueshuo Yanjiuhui (Yijiuqibanian, Jiu-yue Siri)" (Recollections of the Peking University Marxist Theory Study Society [September 4, 1978]), in YDQH, 2:184–94.

76. Meisner, Li Ta-chao, 114–19; Zhang Guotao, Rise of the Chinese Com-munist Party, 117.

77. "Beijing Gongchanzhuyi Xiaozu de Baogao" (Report of the Peking Com-munist Organization), in YDDAZL, 19; "Deng Zhongxia Huiyi Zhongguo Gong-chandang de Chengli jiqi Dang Lingdao de Zaoqi Gongren Yundong (Yijiusanling-nian Liuyue)" (Deng Zhongxia's Recollections of the Founding of the Chinese Communist Party and the Early Labor Movement Led by the Party [June 1930]), in YDQH, 2:80; see also Meisner, Li Ta-chao, 114–15.

78. "Beijing Gongchanzhuyi Xiaozu de Baogao" (Report of the Peking Com-munist Organization), in YDDAZL, 19–20.

79. Ibid.

80. Ibid., 21.

81. Ibid.

82. Ibid.

83. Scalapino and Yu, Modern China, 490–500, 510–11.

84. "Zhao Shiyan Gei Chen Gongpei Xin" (Letter from Zhao Shiyan to Chen Gongpei), in FFSL, 2b:840, dated May 5, 1922.

85. "Beijing Gongchanzhuyi Xiaozu de Baogao" (Report of the Peking Communist Organization), YDDAZL, 21.

86. Ibid., 20.

87. Ibid., 15.

88. Ibid.

89. Ibid., 17–18.

90. Li Shengfu, "Wode Fuqin Li Hanjun" (My Father, Li Hanjun), 36.

91. In the 1930s, he was acting chairman of the Shen-Gan-Ning base area and was one of the CCP's negotiators with the KMT; after the Second World War, he was one of the signatories of the UN Charter. See Xiao Chaoran, *Zhongguo Gongchandang Jianming Cidian* (Concise Dictionary of the Chinese Communist Party's History), 653; ZGDSSJRWL, 653.

92. Xie Jinghua, Liao Huimin, "Dang Zai Hubei Diyige Zhibu—Wuhan Zhibu" (The First CCP Cell in Hubei—the Wuhan Cell), 237.

93. Ibid.

94. Ibid., 238.

95. For Dong Biwu, Chen Tanqiu, Bao Huiseng, and Liu Bochui, ibid., 237–39. See also Liao Huanxing, "Wuchang Liqun Shushe Shimo (Yijiuwusannian)" (History of Wuchang's Benevolence Society [1953]), in YDQH, 2:298–302; Bao Huiseng, "Gongchandang Diyici Quanguo Daibiao Huiyi Qianhou de Huiyi" (Recollections of the Time of the First CCP Congress [August and September 1953]), 311–15; Wu Defeng, "Dang Chengli Qianhou Wuhan Diqu de Yixie Qingkuang (Yijiuwuliunian)" (Circumstances in the Wuhan Area at the Time of the Founding of the Party [1956]), in YDQH, 2:356–59.

96. Published in *Ours* (Womende), vol. 7 (August 10, 1921). Quoted in Liao Huanxing, " 'Wusi' Shiqi de Wuchang Liqun Shushe" (The Benevolence Society of Wuchang during the May Fourth Period), in *Chuhui*, 1:352; this article refers extensively to primary documents.

97. It was Yi Lirong who was present at the meeting of study societies in Wuhan that led to the establishment of the Coexistence Society. Ibid.

98. "Sichuansheng Chongqing Gongchanzhuyi Zuzhi de Baogao" (Report of the Communist Organization in Chongqing, Sichuan), in YDDAZL, 27–32.

99. Ibid., 29–31.

100. Ibid., 31–32.

101. Zhou Enlai, "Qin-Gong Jianxuesheng Zai Fa Zuihou zhi Yunming" (The Recent Fate of the Diligent Work and Frugal Study Students in France), in FFSL, 1:42 (first published serially in the *Yishibao* [Benefit] of Tianjin from December 18, 1921, to January 9, 1922).

102. Ibid., 30.

103. Xiao Chaoran, *Zhongguo Gongchandang Jianming Cidian* (Concise Dictionary of the Chinese Communist Party's History), 728–29.

104. Boorman, *Biographical Dictionary*, 3:465–67.

105. See Wu Yuzhang, *Wu Yuzhang Huiyilu* (Recollections of Wu Yuzhang), 119–20, and chronology.

106. "Wu Yuzhang Tan Zai Sichuan Jianli Zhongguo Qingnian Gongchandang (Yijiuwubanian)" (Wu Yuzhang Discusses the Establishment of the Communist Party of Chinese Youth in Sichuan [1958]), in YDQH, 3:108.

107. The most important collection of sources on the work-study movement

is FFSL. Outside of China, the most comprehensive account so far is Leung, *Chinese Work-Study Movement*. Bailey, "Chinese Work-Study Movement in France," and Scalapino, *Chinese Anarchist Movement*, also provide important information on the movement.

108. Zhang Shenfu, "Zhang Shenfu Tan Lü'Ou Dang, Tuan Zuzhi Huodong Qingkuang" (Zhang Shenfu Discusses the Organization and Activities of the Party and Socialist Youth League in France), 86.

109. Ibid., 87.

110. Ibid.

111. Liu Ye and Zhu Yuhe, "Shilun Lü'Ou Zhongguo Gongchanzhuyi Zuzhi de Xingcheng" (Preliminary Discussion of the Formation of a Chinese Communist Organization in Europe), in Zhu Chengjia, *Zhonggong Yanjiu Lunwenxuan* (Selected Research Articles on CCP History), 170–90.

112. Xiao Chaoran, *Zhongguo Dangshi Jianming Cidian* (Concise Dictionary of the Chinese Communist Party's History), 2:591.

113. Zhou Enlai, "Lü'Ou Zhongguo Gongchanzhuyi Qingniantuan (Zhongguo Shehuizhuyi Qingniantuan Lü'Ou zhi Bu) Baogao Diyihao" (Report Number One of the Chinese Communist Youth League in Europe [the European Branch of the Chinese Socialist Youth League]), in FFSL, 2b:845.

114. Zhou Enlai, "Xi-Ou de 'Chi' Kuang" (The "Red" Light in Europe), in FFSL, 2b:830 (published in April 1923 in Tianjin's the *New People's Will* [Xin Minyibao]). A note by the editor of the *People's Will* mentioned that Zhou had written this article in March 1922 but that it had taken the mail almost a year to deliver it to Tianjin.

115. Zhao Shiyan, "Gei Longzhi Tongzhi de Xin" (Letter to Longzhi [Li Lisan]), in *Zhao Shiyan Xuanji* (Selected Works), 68, dated April 25, 1922.

116. Zhang Shenfu, "Zhang Shenfu Tan Lü'Ou Dang, Tuan Zuzhi Huodong Qingkuang" (Zhang Shenfu Discusses the Organization and Activities of the Party and Socialist Youth League in France), 88.

117. "Gei Longzhi Tongzhi de Xin" (Letter to Longzhi [Li Lisan]), in Zhao Shiyan, *Zhao Shiyan Xuanji* (Selected Works), 68, dated April 25, 1922.

118. "Weijingsiji Zai Hua Huodong Jishi" (Chronology of Voitinsky's Activities in China), in Yang Yunruo et al., eds., *Weijingsiji Zai Zhongguo de Youguan Ziliao* (Source Materials for Voitinsky's Activities in China), 471.

119. "Li Weihan Gei Mao Zedong" (Letter from Li Weihan to Mao Zedong), in Zhongguo Geming Bowuguan (Museum of the Chinese Revolution) et al., eds., *Xinmin Xuehui Ziliao* (Source Materials for the New Citizen Study Society), 143–44, dated August 28, 1920.

120. Li Weihan, "Huiyi Xinmin Xuehui" (Recollections of the New Citizen Study Society), in WSSQDST, 1:625–26, dated December 1978.

121. Bailey, "Chinese Work-Study Movement," 456–57.

122. Li Lisan, "Zhao Shiyan de Huiyi (Yijiuliulingnian, Jiuyue Sanri)" (Recollections of Zhao Shiyan [September 3, 1960]), in FFSL, 3:437–39; Bailey, "Chinese Work-Study Movement," 456.

123. Ibid.; Xiao San, "Qianhui Qin'gong Jianxuesheng zhi Zhenxiang" (Unearthing the Real Work-Study Student), in Xiao San, *Xiao San Wenji* (Collected Works), 250–53; Zhou Enlai, "Fa'Lü Huaren Ju Jiekuan zhu Yundong"

(The Movement of Chinese in France to Resist Loans), in FFSL, 2b:460–66 (first published in Tianjin's *Yishibao* between August 16 and 18, 1921; manuscript dated June 30); Bailey, "Chinese Work-Study Movement," 456–57.

124. Bailey, "Chinese Work-Study Movement," 456–60; Leung, *Chinese Work-Study Movement*, 176–79; Xiao San, "Qianhui Qin'gong Jianxuesheng zhi Zhenxiang" (Unearthing the Real Work-Study Student), in *Xiao San Wenji* (Collected Works), 255; Li Lisan, "Zhao Shiyan de Huiyi (Yijiuliulingnian, Jiuyue Sanri)" (Recollections of Zhao Shiyan [September 3, 1960]), in FFSL, 3:438–39; Qi Feng, "Liu'Fa Qin'gong Jianxuesheng Jingguo Jishi" (True Account of my Experiences as a Work-Study Student in France), in FFSL, 1:125–26; Li Weihan, "Huiyi Xinmin Xuehui" (Recollections of the New Citizen Study Society), in WSSQDST, 1:629. Wu Qi, "Zhou Enlai," 134–35. For a number of recollections concerning the occupation of the China Academy at Lyons, see FFSL, 2:519–71; Li Lisan, "Zhao Shiyan de Huiyi (Yijiuliulingnian, Jiuyue Sanri)" (Recollections of Zhao Shiyan [September 3, 1960]), in FFSL, 3:438–39.

125. "Zhao Shiyan Nianpu" (Chronological Biography of Zhao Shiyan), in Zhao Shiyan, *Zhao Shiyan Xuanji* (Selected Works), 576–77.

126. Zhou Enlai, "Lü'Ou Zhongguo Gongchanzhuyi Qingniantuan (Zhongguo Shehuizhuyi Qingniantuan Lü'Ou zhi Bu) Baogao Diyihao" (Report Number One of the Chinese Communist Youth League in Europe [the European Branch of the Socialist Youth League]), in FFSL, 2b:843–46, dated March 13, 1923.

127. Ibid., 845–46.

128. "Gei Wu Ming de Sanfengxin" (Three Letters to Wu Ming [Chen Gongpei]), in Zhao Shiyan, *Zhao Shiyan Xuanji* (Selected Works), 71–72. See also "Lü'Ou Zhongguo Gongchanzhuyi Qingniantuan (Zhongguo Shehuizhuyi Qingniantuan Lü'Ou zhi Bu) Baogao Diyihao" (Report Number One of the Chinese Communist Youth League in Europe [the European Branch of the Chinese Socialist Youth League]), in FFSL, 2b:843, dated March 13, 1923.

129. "Gei Wu Ming de Sanfengxin" (Three Letters to Wu Ming [Chen Gongpei]), in Zhao Shiyan, *Zhao Shiyan Xuanji* (Selected Works), 72.

130. "Gei Longzhi de Sanfeng Xin" (Letter to Comrade Longzhi [Li Lisan]), ibid., 68, dated April 25, 1922.

131. "Zhongguo Gongchandang Diyici Daibiao Dahui" (The First Congress of the Chinese Communist Party), in YDDAZL, 11.

132. For Tokyo, see "Zhou Fohai Huiyi Zhongguo Gongchandang de Chengli (Yijiusiernian Yiyue)" (Zhou Fohai's Recollections of the Founding of the CCP [January 1942]), in YDQH, 2:491–94. For Ji'nan, see Ma Baosan, "Shandong Dang Zuzhi de Fatuan (Yijiuwuyinian Qiyue)" (The Beginnings of Party Organization in Shandong [July 1951]); Jia Shiting, "Dang Chuangli Shiqi Shandong Diqu de Yixie Qingkuang (Yijiuwuqinian, Wuyue Siri)" (The Shandong Area at the Time of the Founding of the Party [May 4, 1957]); Ma Futang, "Dang Chengli Qianhou Shandong Diqu de Yixie Qingkuang (Yijiuwuqinian)" (Circumstances in Shandong at the Time of the Founding of the Party [1957]); all in YDQH, 2:392–402.

133. Lin Maosheng, *Zhongguo Xiandai Zhengzhi Sixiangshi, 1919–1949* (The History of Contemporary Chinese Political Thought, 1919–1949), 27–28.

134. See, for instance, Lin Maosheng, *History*, 27–28; Benjamin Schwartz, *Chinese Communism*, 7; Meisner, *Li Ta-chao*, 52–57.

135. Lin Maosheng, *History*, 30.

136. Zhu Wushan, "Huiyi Beida Makesi Xueshuo Yanjiuhui" (Recollections of the Peking Marxism Research Society), in WSSQDST, 2:293–94, dated June 1960.

137. See "Faqi Makesi Xueshuo Yanjiuhui Qishi" (Announcement of the Founding of the Marxism Research Society), in WSSQDST, 2:272–73 (published in *Beijing Daxue Rikan* [Peking University Daily] on November 17, 1921).

138. "Makesi Xueshuo Yanjiuhui Tonggao (Si)" (Announcement of the Marxism Research Society [4]), in WSSQDST, 2:278–80 (published in *Beijing Daxue Rikan* [Peking University Daily] on February 6, 1922). Titles are given as they appear in this source.

139. See, e.g., "Wenhua Shushe Diyici Yingye Baogao" (First Report on Business Conducted by the Culture Book Society), in WSSQDST, 1:52–55 (published in *Tongsubao* [Vernacular Gazette] on November 6, 10, 11, 1920); "Wenhua Shushe Huiwu Baogao (Jielu; Dierqi)" (Report on the Affairs of the Culture Book Society [Excerpts; Number Two]), in WSSQDST, 1:56–65 (the editor of WSSQDST notes that the report was published in April 1921); "Faqi Liu'E Qin'gong Jianxue" (Organizing Work-Study in Russia), in WSSQDST, 1:65–66 (published in Changsha's *Dagongbao* [Public Affairs] on August 22, 1920).

140. "Wenhua Shushe Huiwu Baogao (Jielu; Dierqi)" (Report on the Affairs of the Culture Book Society [Excerpts; Number Two]), in WSSQDST, 1:60 (published in April 1921).

141. "Wenhua Shushe Diyici Yingye Baogao" (First Report on Business Conducted by the Culture Book Society), in WSSQDST, 1:53–54.

142. "Wenhua Shushe Huiwu Baogao (Jielu; Dierqi)" (Report on the Affairs of the Culture Book Society [Excerpts; Number Two]), in WSSQDST 1:62–64.

143. See Liao Xinchu, " 'Wusi' Shiqi de Wuchang Liqun Shushe" (The Benevolence Society of Wuchang during the May Fourth Period), in *Chuhui*, 1:344, 351; Wu Defeng, "Dang Chengli Qianhou Wuhan Diqu de Yixie Qingkuang (Yijiuwuliunian)" (Some Aspects of the Wuhan Area during the Period of the Founding of the Party [1956]), in YDQH, 2:356–58

144. Liao Xinchu, " 'Wusi' Shiqi de Wuchang Liqun Shushe" (The Benevolence Society of Wuchang during the May Fourth Period), in *Chuhui*, 1:347–48; Liao Huanxing, "Wuchang Liqun Shushe Shimo (Yijiuwusannian)" (History of the Benevolence Society in Wuchang [1953]), in YDQH, 2:298–302

145. Liao Huanxing, "Wuchang Liqun Shushe Shimo (Yijiuwusannian)" (History of the Benevolence Society in Wuchang [1953]), in YDQH, 2:299.

146. "Zhongguo Gongchanzhuyi Diyici Daibiao Dahui" (The First Congress of the Chinese Communist Party), in YDDAZL, 11. It does not bear a date, but the opening sentence states that "communist organizations in China were established beginning last year." Hence it must have been written in 1921, after the First Congress. The document states that it was Nikolaevsky, representing the Far East Bureau of the Comintern located in Moscow, who suggested that the congress report to Irkutsk. This report may be the result of this proposal. Its level of detail and exactness in dates suggests that it was written shortly after the congress. The document is a translation of a Russian original held in Comintern archives.

147. Ibid.

148. Ibid.

149. The following representatives were present at the congress:

Hunan	Mao Zedong, He Shuheng
Wuhan	Dong Biwu, Chen Tanqiu
Guangdong	Chen Gongbo
Peking	Zhang Guotao, Liu Renjing
Shanghai	Li Da, Li Hanjun
Shangdong	Wang Jinmei, Deng Enming
Tokyo	Zhou Fohai

Bao Huiseng was the additional participant. Zhao Bu, "Zhongguo Gongchandang Zuzhi Ziliao, Yi" (Information on the Organizational History of the CCP, One), 65; and Wang Jianying, ed., *Zhongguo Gongchandang Zuzhishi Ziliao Huibian* (Edited Source Materials for the Organizational History of the Chinese Communist Party), 61.

150. "Zhongguo Gongchanzhuyi Diyici Daibiao Dahui" (The First Congress of the Chinese Communist Party), in YDDAZL, 11.

151. Li Shengfu, "Wode Fuqin Li Hanjun" (My Father, Li Hanjun), 36–38. For Wang Huiwu, see her " 'Yida' Zai Nanhu Kaihui de Qingkuang (Yijiuwujiunian, Sanyue Shiyiri)" (The Circumstances of the First Congress's Meeting at South Lake [March 31, 1959]), in YDQH, 2:56–57.

152. "Mao Zedong Gei Cai Hesen" (Letter from Mao Zedong to Cai Hesen), in Zhongguo Geming Bowuguan (Museum of the Chinese Revolution) et al., eds., *Xinmin Xuehui Ziliao* (Source Materials for the New Citizen Study Society), 162–63, dated January 21, 1921.

153. "Beijing Gongchanzhuyi Zuzhi de Baogao" (The Report of the Peking Communist Organization), in YDDAZL, 15.

154. Ibid., 12.

155. Ibid.

156. Ibid., 13.

157. Ibid., 12.

158. Ibid., 12–13.

159. Ibid., 12.

160. Ibid.

161. Ibid., 13.

162. Ibid.; Wang Huiwu, " 'Yida' Zai Nanhu Kaihui de Qingkuang (Yijiuwusannian, Sanyue Sanshiyiri)" (The Circumstances of the First Congress's Meeting at South Lake [March 31, 1953]), in YDQH, 2:56–57.

163. Maring, "Bericht des Genossen H. Maring für die Executive" (Report of Comrade H. Maring to the Executive), in Maring Archive, 255.

164. "Zhongguo Gongchanzhuyi Diyici Daibiao Dahui" (The First Congress of the Chinese Communist Party), in YDDAZL, 13.

165. Ibid.

166. "Zhongguo Gongchandang Diyige Jueyi (Yijiuerlingnian)" (The First Resolution of the Chinese Communist Party [1921]), in YDDAZL, 10. This document is also a translation of a Russian original in the Comintern Archives.

167. "Zhongguo Gongchanzhuyi Diyici Daibiao Dahui" (The First Congress of the Chinese Communist Party), in YDDAZL, 14.

168. "Zhongguo Gongchandang Diyige Jueyi (Yijiuerlingnian)" (The First Resolution of the Chinese Communist Party [1921]), in YDDAZL, 8.

169. Maring, "Bericht des Genossen H. Maring für die Executive" (Report of Comrade H. Maring to the Executive), in Maring Archive, 255.

170. "Zhongguo Gongchanzhuyi Diyici Daibiao Dahui" (The First Congress of the Chinese Communist Party), in YDDAZL, 14.

171. Zhao Bu, "Zhongguo Gongchandang Zuzhishi Ziliao, Yi" (Information on the Organizational History of the CCP, One), 65; Wang Jianying, ed., *Zhongguo Gongchandang Zuzhishi Ziliao Huibian* (Edited Source Materials for the Organizational History of the Chinese Communist Party), 3.

172. Quoted in Wang Shudi et al., "Chen Duxiu Wuci Beipu Gaishu" (A Survey of Chen Duxiu's Five Imprisonments), in Qiang Zhonghua, *Chen Duxiu Beipu Ziliao Huibian* (Compilation of Sources on Chen Duxiu's Five Imprisonments), 4.

3.   HESITANT BEGINNINGS, 1921–1925

1.   "Chen Duxiu Tongzhi Daibiao Zhonggong Zhongyang Xiang Disanci Daibiao Huiyi de Baogao (Yijiuersannian, Liuyue)" (Comrade Chen Duxiu's Report to the Third Congress on Behalf of the CCP Central Committee [June 1923]), in EDHSD, 172. The text also appears in Guangdong Geming Lishi Bowuguan (Guangdong Museum of Revolutionary History), *Zhonggong "Sanda" Ziliao* (Sources for the Third Congress), 56–62, where it carries the date August 28, 1923. According to the editor of *Zhonggong "Sanda" Ziliao*, the text is a translation of a Russian original. The date of August 28, then, may refer to the time the Russian translation was made or filed in Moscow.

2.   For the first figure, see Glunin, "The Comintern," 300. Glunin has access to Comintern archives. For the figure of 250, see Maring, "Bericht Ueber die Lage in China and unsere Arbeit fuer die Periode von 15 bis 31 Mai 1923" (Note on the Situation in China and Our Activities in the Period May 12–31, 1923), in Maring Archive 3060/1-4.

3.   "Chen Duxiu Zai Zhongguo Gongchandang Disanci Quanguo Daibiao Dahui de Baogao (Yijiuersannian Liuyue)" (Chen Duxiu's Report to the Third Congress of the Chinese Communist Party [June 1923]), in EDHSD, 168.

4.   Ibid.

5.   Maring, "Bericht des Genossen H. Maring für die Executive" (Report of Comrade H. Maring to the Executive), in Maring Archive, 225.

6.   "Zhongguo Gongchandang Diyici Xiuzheng Zhangcheng" (The First Revised Constitution of the Chinese Communist Party), in "Zhongguo Gongchandang Disanci Quanguo Daibiao Dahui Jueyian ji Xuanyan (Yijiuerernian Qiyue)" (Resolutions and Manifesto of the Third Congress of the Chinese Communist Party [June 1923]), in EDHSD, 190.

7.   The CCP organization is set out clearly in Wang Jianying, ed., *Zhongguo Gongchandang Zuzhishi Ziliao Huibian* (Edited Source Materials for the Organizational History of the Chinese Communist Party), 3–24. For the arrangements

made at the First Congress, see "Zhongguo Gongchandang Diyige Gangling (Yijiu-eryinian)" (The First Program of the Chinese Communist Party), in Zhongyang Dang'anguan (Central Committee Archives), *Zhongguo Gongchandang Diyici Daibiao Dahui Dang'an Ziliao (Zengdingben)* (Archival Sources for the First Congress of the Chinese Communist Party [Revised and Enlarged Edition]), 6–7. For the first CCP constitution, see "Zhongguo Gongchandang Zhangcheng" (The Constitution of the Chinese Communist Party), in "Zhongguo Gongchandang Dierci Quanguo Daibiao Dahui Jueyian (Yijiuerernian Qiyue)" (Resolution of the Second National Congress of the Chinese Communist Party [July 1922]), in EDHSD, 86–91. For the organization of the Central Executive Committee and the Central Bureau as decided upon by Third Congress participants, see "Zhongguo Gongchandang Zhongyang Zhixing Weiyuanhui Zuzhifa" (Regulations for the Organization of the Central Executive Committee of the Chinese Communist Party), in "Zhongguo Gongchandang Disanci Quanguo Daibiao Dahui Jueyian ji Xuanyan (Yijiuersannian Liuyue)" (Resolutions and Declaration of the Third National Congress of the Chinese Communist Party [June 1923]), in EDHSD, 187–88. For the Third Congress constitution, see "Zhongguo Gongchandang Di-yici Xiuzheng Zhangcheng" (First Revised Resolution of the Chinese Communist Party), in "Zhongguo Gongchandang Disanci Quanguo Daibiao Dahui Jueyian ji Xuanyan (Yijiuersannian Liuyue)" (Resolutions and Declaration of the Third National Congress of the Chinese Communist Party [June 1923]), in EDHSD, 188–93.

8. Cai Hesen, "Zhongguo Gongchandangshi de Fazhan (Tigang; Yijiuershi-liunian)" (The Historical Development of the Chinese Communist Party [Outline; 1926]), in *Cai Hesen de Shierbian Wenzhang* (Twelve Essays by Cai Hesen), 39–40. For Chen Gongbo, see Chen Gongbo, "Wo yu Gongchandang (Yijiusiliu-nian)" (The CCP and I [1946]), in YDQHGD, 98–108.

9. Cai Hesen, "Zhongguo Gongchandangshi de Fazhan (Tigang; Yijiuershi-liunian)" (The Historical Development of the Chinese Communist Party [Outline; 1926]), in *Cai Hesen de Shierbian Wenzhang* (Twelve Essays by Cai Hesen), 39. Chen Gongbo identifies Zhang Tailei as the Central Bureau's investigator in Chen Gongbo, "Wo yu Gongchandang (Yijiusiliunian)" (The CCP and I [1946]), in YDQHGD, 105–6.

10. Chen Gongbo, "Wo yu Gongchandang (Yijiusiliunian)" (The CCP and I [1946]), in YDQHGD, 106–7.

11. "Chen Duxiu Zai Zhongguo Gongchandang Disanci Quanguo Daibiao Dahui de Baogao (Yijiuersannian Liuyue)" (Chen Duxiu's Report to the Third National Congress of the Chinese Communist Party [June 1923]), in EDHSD, 173.

12. Cai Hesen, "Zhongguo Gongchandangshi de Fazhan (Tigang; Yijiuer-shiliunian)" (The Historical Development of the Chinese Communist Party [Outline; 1926]), in *Cai Hesen de Shierbian Wenzhang* (Twelve Essays by Cai Hesen), 40.

13. Chen Gongbo, "Wo yu Gongchandang (Yijiusiliunian; Xuan Zi Hanfeng-ji)" (The CCP and I [1946; Selected from the Cold Wind Collection]), in YDQHGD, 106. See also Chen's comments on the First Congress, ibid., 90–91.

14. "Lü'Ou Zhongguo Gongchanzhuyi Qingniantuan (Zhongguo Shehui-zhuyi Qingniantuan Lü'Ou zhi Bu) Baogao Diyihao" (Report Number One of the Chinese Communist Youth League in Europe [the European Branch of the Chinese Socialist Youth League]), in FFSL, 2b:843–44, dated March 13, 1923.

15. Ibid., 843.

16. For the latter, see Wang Jianying, ed., *Zhongguo Gongchandang Zuzhishi Ziliao Huibian* (Edited Source Materials for the Organizational History of the CCP), 62, 72. For the first, see note 18.

17. Leung, *Chinese Work-Study Movement*, 41–45.

18. "Zheng Chaolin Tan Zhao Shiyan he Lü'Ou Zhibu (Yijiuliulingnian, Shiyiyue Shisiri)" (Zheng Chaolin Discusses Zhao Shiyan and the European Branch [November 14, 1960]), in YDQH, 2:535.

19. "Lü'Ou Zhongguo Gongchanzhuyi Qingniantuan (Zhongguo Shehui-zhuyi Qingniantuan Lü'Ou zhi Bu) Baogao Diyihao" (Report Number One of the Chinese Communist Youth League in Europe [the European Branch of the Chinese Socialist Youth League]), in FFSL, 2b:844.

20. "Zheng Chaolin Tan Zhao Shiyan he Lü'Ou Zhibu (Yijiuliulingnian, Shiyiyue Shisiri)" (Zheng Chaolin Discusses Zhao Shiyan and the European Branch [November 14, 1960]), in YDQH, 2:536.

21. "Lü'Ou Zhongguo Gongchanzhuyi Qingniantuan (Zhongguo Shehui-zhuyi Qingniantuan Lü'Ou zhi Bu) Baogao Diyihao" (Report Number One of the Chinese Communist Youth League in Europe [the European Branch of the Chinese Socialist Youth League]), in FFSL, 2b:846.

22. "Zheng Chaolin Tan Zhao Shiyan he Lü'Ou Zhibu (Yijiuliulingnian, Shiyiyue Shisiri)" (Zheng Chaolin Discusses Zhao Shiyan and the European Branch [November 14, 1960]), in YDQH, 2:536.

23. "Chen Duxiu zhi Wu Tingkang de Xin (Yijiuerernian, Siyue Liuri)" (Letter from Chen Duxiu to Wu Tingkang [Voitinsky] [April 6, 1922]), in EDHSD, 36.

24. Ibid.

25. According to Maring's notes, he was back in Shanghai on August 12 (Maring Archive 3142/1. This document lacks a title.)

26. "Fuer Genosse Sinoview, Bucharin, Radek" (Letter to Comrades Zinov-iev, Bukharin, and Radek), in Maring Archive 3066/1-5, dated June 20, 1923. See also Dov Bing, "Sneevliet and the Early Years," 688.

27. "Gei Gongchan Guoji Zhu Zhongguo Tepai Daibiao de Zhishi (Yijiuerer-nian Bayue)" (Instruction to the Comintern's Special Representatives in China [August 1922]), in EDHSD, 122.

28. Wang Jianying, ed., *Zhongguo Gongchandang Zuzhishi Ziliao Huibian* (Edited Source Materials for the Organizational History of the CCP), 9; Maring Archive 3142/1. See also Maring, "Fuer Genosse Sinoview, Bucharin, Radek" (Letter to Comrades Zinoviev, Bukharin, and Radek), in Maring Archive 3066/1-5, dated June 20, 1923; Maring Archive 3142/1 (untitled, n.d.).

29. Lin Guliang, "Guanyu Zhonggong Zhongyang (Hangzhou) Xihu Huiyi" (The West Lake [Hangzhou] Meeting of the CCP Central Committee), in DSYJZL, 1:272–78 (1980). This article collects the major statements and analyses of the meeting.

30. "Chen Duxiu Tongzhi Daibiao Zhonggong Zhongyang Xiang Disanci Dang Daibiao Huiyi de Baogao (Yijiuersannian Liuyue)" (Chen Duxiu's Report to the Third Party Congress on Behalf of the CCP Central Committee [June 1923]), in EDHSD, 170.

31. Liu Renjing, "Huiyi Canjia Gongchan Guoji Disici Daibiao Dahui de

Qingkuang" (Recollections of My Participation in the Fourth Comintern Congress), in DSYJZL, 3(1982):190–215.

32. Liu Renjing, "Guanyu Zhongguo Xingshi de Baogao—Zai Gongchan Guoji Disici Daibiao Dahuishang de Fayan (Yijiuerernian, Shiyiyue Ershisanri)" (Report on the Situation in China—Speech at the Fourth Congress of the Comintern [November 23, 1922]), in EDHSD, 130, 132–33.

33. "Gongchan Guoji Zhixing Weiyuanhui Guanyu Zhongguo Gongchandang yu Guomindang de Guanxi Wenti de Jueyi (Yijiuersannian, Yiyue Shierri)" (Resolution of the Executive Committee of the Comintern about the Relationship between the CCP and the KMT [January 12, 1923]), in EDHSD, 146.

34. Ibid.

35. Maring, "Fuer Genosse Sinoview, Bucharin, Radek" (Letter to Comrades Zinoviev, Bukharin, and Radek), in Maring Archive 3066/1-5, dated June 20, 1923.

36. "Geweiyuan Baogao" (Reports from the Delegates), in "Zhongguo Gongchandang Diyici Zhongyang Zhixing Weiyuanhui Wenjian (Yijiuersannian, Shiyue Ershisiri–Ershiwuri)" (Documents of the First Central Executive Committee Meeting of the Chinese Communist Party [November 24–25, 1923]), in EDHSD, 235.

37. Ibid., 236.

38. Ibid.

39. Ibid., 237.

40. "Zhongju Baogao" (Report of the Central Bureau), in "Zhongguo Gongchandang Diyici Zhongyang Zhixing Weiyuanhui Wenjian (Yijiuersannian, Shiyue Ershisiri–Ershiwuri)" (Documents of the First Central Executive Committee Meeting of the Chinese Communist Party [November 24–25, 1923], in EDHSD, 233.

41. "Guanyu Guomin Yundong yu Guomindang Wenti de Yijuean" (Resolution on Issues in the Nationalist Movement and the KMT), in "Zhongguo Gongchandang Disanci Quanguo Daibiao Dahui Jueyian ji Xuanyan (Yijiuersannian Liuyue)" (Resolutions and Declaration of the Third National Congress of the Chinese Communist Party [June 1923]), in EDHSD, 181–83.

42. For the issues involved in the dating of the secretariat's founding, see Zeng Changqiu, "Zhongguo Laodong Zuhe Shujibu Chengli yu 'Yida' Yiqian" (The Secretariat of China's Labor Federation Was Founded before the First Congress), in *Jindaishi Yanjiu* (Modern History Research), 2 (1986):280–81. The secretariat's declaration was published in the *Chinese Communist Party Weekly*, vol. 6, which bore the date July 7, 1921, more than two weeks before the Congress; Luo Zhanglong, "Luo Zhanglong Tan Laodong Zuhe Shujibu" (Luo Zhanglong Talks about the Secretariat of China's Labor Federation), 2; Maring, "Fuer Genosse Sinoview, Bucharin, Radek" (Letter to Comrades Zinoviev, Bukharin, and Radek), in Maring Archive 3066/1-5.

43. See Chen Gongbo, "Wo yu Gongchandang (Yijiusiliunian)" (The CCP and I [1946]), in YDQHGD, 90–91; see also Cai Hesen, "Zhongguo Gongchandangshi de Fazhan (Tigang; Yijiuerliunian)" (The Development of CCP History [Outline; 1926], in *Cai Hesen de Shierbian Wenzhang* (Twelve Essays by Cai Hesen), 36–38.

44. Zhang Guotao, *Rise of the Chinese Communist Party*, 251–52.

45. Maring, "Fuer Genosse Sinoview, Bucharin, Radek" (Letter to Comrades Zinoviev, Bukharin, and Radek), in Maring Archive, 3066/1-5.

46. "Chen Duxiu Tongzhi Daibiao Zhonggong Zhongyang Xiang Disanci Daibiao Huiyi de Baogao (Yijiuersannian Liuyue)" (Comrade Chen Duxiu's Report on Behalf of the CCP Central Committee to the Third Congress [June 1923]), in EDHSD, 172.

47. Maring, "Fuer Genosse Sinoview, Bucharin, Radek" (Letter to Comrades Zinoviev, Bukharin, and Radek), in Maring Archive, 3066/1-5.

48. "Zhongyangju Baogao" (Report of the Central Bureau), in "Zhongguo Gongchandang Kuoda Zhixing Weiyuanhui Huiyi Wenjian (Yijiuersinian, Wuyue Shiri–Shiwuri)" (Documents of the Enlarged Central Executive Committee of the Chinese Communist Party [May 10–15, 1924]), in EDHSD, 283; "Zhang Guotao Gei Weijingsiji, Mu Xin de Xin (Yijiuersannian, Shiyiyue Shiliuri)" (Letter from Zhang Guotao to Voitinsky and Mu Xin [November 16, 1923]), in EDHSD, 220–31.

49. "Chen Duxiu Zai Zhongguo Gongchandang Disanci Quanguo Daibiao Dahui de Baogao (Yijiuersannian Liuyue)" (Chen Duxiu's Report to the Third National Congress of the Chinese Communist Party [June 1923]), in EDHSD, 172.

50. Zhang Guotao, *Rise of the Chinese Communist Party*, 170.

51. Chen Duxiu, "Zhongguo Gongchandang Zhongyangju Tonggao—Guanyu Jianli yu Fazhan Dang, Tuan, Gonghui Zuzhi ji Xuanchuan Gongzuo (Yijiueryinian Shiyiyue)" (Announcement of the Central Bureau of the Chinese Communist Party—Concerning Organization and Propaganda Activities for the Establishment and Development of the Party, the Youth League, and Labor Union [November 1921]), in YDDAZL, 33.

52. Zhang Guotao, *Rise of the Chinese Communist Party*, 271–72; see also Chen Duxiu, "Chen Duxiu Gei Gongchan Guoji de Baogao (Yijiuerernian, Liuyue Sanshiri)" (Chen Duxiu's Report to the Comintern [June 30, 1922]), in EDHSD, 60.

53. Zhonggong Zhongyang Dangshi Yanjiushi (CCP Central Party History Research Institute), ed., *Zhonggong Dangshi Dashi Nianbiao* (Chronology of CCP History), 4; ZGDSSJRWL, 95; see also, Chesneaux, *Chinese Labor Movement*, 183.

54. Su Zhaozheng, "Lun Haiyuan Tuanjie zhi Yiyi" (On the Significance of Seamen's Unity), in Zhonggong Guangdong Shengwei Dangshi Yanjiu Weiyuan Bangongshi (Office of the Section for Party History of the Guangdong Provincial Committee of the Chinese Communist Party) et al., eds., *Su Zhaozheng Shiliao* (Sources for Research on Su Zhaozheng), 5–6, dated 1924; Su Zhaozheng, "Zhonghua Haiyuan Gongye Lianhe Zonghui Baogao: Xiang Zhongguo Haiyuan Diyici Daibiao Dahui zhi Baogao" (Report of the General Industrial Union of Chinese Seamen: A Report to the First Congress of Chinese Seamen), ibid., 19, dated March 1926.

55. A. C. Dalin, *Zhongguo Huiyilu* (China Memoirs), 87. The CCP fliers are mentioned in "Chen Duxiu Gei Gongchan Guoji de Baogao (Yijiuerernian, Liuyue Sanshiri)" (Chen Duxiu's Report to the Comintern [June 30, 1922]), in EDHSD, 60.

56. Zhang Guotao, *Rise of the Chinese Communist Party*, 114.

57. Ling Biying, "Erqi Can'an Jingguo" (Events Leading up to the February 7 Massacre), 41.

58. Honig, *Sisters and Strangers*, 94–131; Herschatter, *Workers of Tianjin*, 140–50.

59. Li Bogang, "Wuhan Jiandang Chuqi de Huiyi" (Recollections of the Period of Founding the Party in Wuhan), 3.

60. Ling Biying, "Erqi Can'an Jingguo" (Events Leading up to the February 7 Massacre), 41; Sheridan, "The Warlord Era," in CHOC, 12:272–74.

61. For the war, see Wu's biography in Boorman, *Biographical Dictionary*, 3:446–47. For the strategic value of the line to Wu, see Zhang Guotao, " 'Erqi' Qianhou Gonghui Yundong Lueshi" (A Short History of the Union Movement at the Time of "February 7"), in *Zhongguo Gongyun Shiliao* (Historical Sources for the Chinese Labor Movement), 3:99 (1980).

62. Zhang Guotao, *Rise of the Chinese Communist Party*, 275.

63. "Chen Duxiu Tongzhi Daibiao Zhonggong Zhongyang Xiang Disanci Daibiao Huiyi de Baogao (Yijiuersannian Liuyue)" (Comrade Chen Duxiu's Report to the Third Congress on Behalf of the CCP Central Committee [June 1923]), in EDHSD, 170.

64. Zhang Guotao, *Rise of the Chinese Communist Party*, 275.

65. Li Bogang, "Wuhan Jiandang Chuqi de Huiyi" (Recollections of the Period of Founding the Party in Wuhan), 3.

66. Zhang Guotao, " 'Erqi' Qianhou Gonghui Yundong Lueshi" (A Short History of the Union Movement at the Time of "February 7"), in *Zhongguo Gongyun Shiliao* (Historical Sources for the Chinese Labor Movement), 3:96.

67. Ibid.

68. Ibid., 96–98.

69. Ibid.

70. Ibid., 98–101.

71. Ibid., 101–2.

72. Ibid., 106.

73. Li Bogang, "Wuhan Jiandang Chuqi de Huiyi" (Recollections of the Period of Founding the Party in Wuhan), 3.

74. See documents 3148/1-2, 3147/1-10, and 3179/1-36 in the Maring Archive. None are titled, but they appear to be Maring's notes of meetings at the time. Li Bogang, "Wuhan Jiandang Chuqi de Huiyi" (Recollections of the Period of Founding the Party in Wuhan), 5.

75. On the point of propaganda, see "Chen Duxiu Tongzhi Daibiao Zhonggong Zhongyang Zai Zhongguo Gongchandang Disanci Quanguo Daibiao Dahui de Baogao (Yijiuersannian Liuyue)" (Chen Duxiu's Report On Behalf of the CCP Central Committee to the Third Congress of the Chinese Communist Party [June 1923], in EDHSD, 171–72. See also "Duiyu Xuanchuan Gongzuo zhi Jueyian" (Resolution on Propaganda Work), in "Zhongguo Gongchandang Disici Quanguo Daibiao Dahui Wenjian (Yijiuerwunian Yiyue)" (Documents of the Fourth National Congress of the Chinese Communist Party [January 1925]), in ZZWX, 1:305–6; Maring Archive, 3179/1-36.

76. "Geweiyuan Baogao" (Reports from the Regional Members), in "Zhongguo Gongchandang Diyici Zhongyang Zhixing Weiyuanhui Wenjian (Yijiuersannian, Shiyiyue Ershisiri–Ershiwuri)" (Documents of the First Central Executive Committee of the Chinese Communist Party [November 24–25, 1923]), in EDHSD, 237.

77. "Funü Yundong Jueyian" (Resolution on the Women's Movement), in "Zhongguo Gongchandang Disanci Quanguo Daibiao Dahui Jueyian ji Xuanyan

(Yijiuersannian Liuyue)" (Resolutions and Declaration of the Third National Congress of the Chinese Communist Party [June 1923]), in EDHSD, 186.

78. Ibid.

79. "Duiyu Nüren Yundong zhi Jueyian" (Resolution on the Women's
Movement), in "Zhongguo Gongchandang Disici Quanguo Daibiao Dahui Wen-
jian (Yijiuerwunian Yiyue)" (Documents of the Fourth Congress of the Chinese
Communist Party [January 1925]), in ZZWX, 1:301–4.

80. Chesneaux, *Secret Societies*, 47–51; Coble, *Shanghai Capitalists*, 36–39.

81. "Geweiyuan Baogao" (Reports from the Regional Members), in "Zhongguo Gongchandang Diyici Zhongyang Zhixing Weiyuanhui Wenjian (Yijiuersannian, Shiyiyue Ershisiri–Ershiwuri)" (Documents of the First Central Executive
Committee of the Chinese Communist Party [November 24–25, 1923]), in
EDHSD, 237; see also Honig, *Sisters and Strangers*, 120–24.

82. "Geweiyuan Baogao" (Reports from the Regional Members), in "Zhongguo Gongchandang Diyici Zhongyang Zhixing Weiyuanhui Wenjian (Yijiuersannian, Shiyiyue Ershisiri–Ershiwuri)" (Documents of the First Central Executive
Committee of the Chinese Communist Party [November 24–25, 1923]), in
EDHSD, 236–37; see also "Shanghai Difang Baogao" (Report of the Shanghai
Locality), in "Zhongguo Gongchandang Kuoda Zhixing Weiyuanhui Wenjian (Yijiuersinian, Wuyue Shiri–Shiwuri)" (Documents of the Enlarged Central Executive Committee of the Chinese Communist Party [May 10–15, 1924]), in EDHSD,
285–86.

83. For the number, see Wang Jianying, ed., *Zhongguo Gongchandang Zuzhishi Ziliao Huibian* (Edited Source Materials for the Organizational History of
the CCP), 21.

84. "Xiangqu Baogao" (Report from the Hunan Region), in "Zhongguo
Gongchandang Kuoda Zhixing Weiyuanhui Huiyi Wenjian (Yijiuersinian, Wuyue
Shiri–Shiwuri)" (Documents of the Enlarged Central Executive Committee Meet-
ing [November 10–15, 1924]), in EDHSD, 296.

85. Chesneaux, *Secret Societies*, 15–16.

86. Kuhn and Mann, "Dynastic Decline," 134.

87. Ibid., 135.

88. "Li Lisan Tongzhi Tan Anyuan Gongyun" (Comrade Li Lisan Discusses
the Anyuan Labor Movement), in DSYJZL, 1(1979):224, 226.

89. Fairbank, Brand, and Schwartz, *A Documentary History of the Chinese
Communist Party*, 165–66, 179–84.

90. "Li Lisan Tongzhi Tan Anyuan Gongyun" (Comrade Li Lisan Discusses
the Anyuan Labor Movement), in DSYJZL, 1(1979):224; "Xiangqu Baogao" (Report from the Hunan Region), in "Zhongguo Gongchandang Kuoda Zhixing Weiyuanhui Huiyi Wenjian (Yijiuersinian, Wuyue Shiri–Shiwuri)" (Documents of the
Enlarged Central Executive Committee Meeting [November 10–15, 1924]), 296.

91. "Li Lisan Tongzhi Tan Anyuan Gongyun" (Comrade Li Lisan Discusses
the Anyuan Labor Movement), in DSYJZL, 1(1979):225.

92. Ibid., 226.

93. Ibid.

94. "Anyuan Lu'Kuang Gongren Julebu Zhi Pingkuang Kuangzhang Han"
(Letter from the Anyuan Railroad and Mine Club to the Mine Director of the Ping
Mines), in Changshashi Geming Jinian Difang Bangongshi / Anyuan Lu'Kuang

Gongren Yundong Jinianguan (Office of Revolutionary Monuments in Changsha, Museum of the Workers' Movement in the Anyuan Railroad and Mines), eds., *Anyuan Lu'Kuang Gongren Yundong Shiliao* (Historical Sources for the Workers' Movement in the Anyuan Railroad and Mines), 65. *Ping* was the rural district (*xiang*) where the mines were located.

95. Ibid.

96. "Anyuan Gongren Xiang Hanyeping Gongsi Fachu de Bagong Tongdian" (Telegram from the Anyuan Workers to the Hanyeping Announcing Their Strike), ibid., 66.

97. "Anyuan Lu'Kuang Gongren Julebu Tonggao" (Announcement of the Anyuan Railroad and Mine Workers Club), ibid., 67.

98. Chesneaux, *Chinese Labor Movement*, 211–33. For proof of the club's continued existence, see "Xiangqu Baogao" (Report from the Hunan Region), in "Zhongguo Gongchandang Kuoda Zhixing Weiyuanhui Huiyi Wenjian (Yijiuersinian, Wuyue Shiri–Shiwuri)" (Documents of the Enlarged Central Executive Committee Meeting [November 10–15, 1924]), 295–96.

99. "Guanyu Andi Shijian Jueyi" (Resolution concerning the Anyuan Incident), in "Zhonggong Zhongyang Kuoda Zhixing Weiyuanhui Wenjian (Yijiuerwunian Shiyue)" (Documents of the Enlarged Central Executive Committee Meeting of the CCP [October 1925]), in ZZWX, 1:430–32.

100. "Yang Zhihua Huiyi (Yijiuwuliunian Jiuyue)" (Recollections of Yang Zhihua [September 1956]), in YDQH, 2:25; Xiao Chaoran, *Zhonggong Dangshi Jianming Cidian* (Concise Dictionary of the Chinese Communist Party), 743; Li Da, "Zhongguo Gongchandang de Faqi he Diyici, Dierci Daibiao Dahui Jingguo de Huiyi (Yijiuwuwunian, Bayue Erri)" (Recollections of the Events Leading to the Founding of the Chinese Communist Party and Its First and Second Congresses), in YDQH, 2:7; Shao Weizheng, "Yaqian Nongmin Xiehui Shimo" (History of the Yaqian Peasant Association), 461.

101. Shao Weizheng, "Yaqian Nongmin Xiehui Shimo" (History of the Yaqian Peasant Association), 461.

102. Ibid., 464–65. *New Youth*, 9:4 (August 1921). The subsequent issue published Shen's article on peasant self-determination.

103. Shao Weizheng, "Yaqian Nongmin Xiehui Shimo" (History of the Yaqian Peasant Association), 465. "Chen Duxiu Gei Gongchan Guoji de Baogao (Yijiuerernian, Liuyue Sanshiri)" (Chen Duxiu's Report to the Comintern [June 30, 1922]), in EDHSD, 61.

104. Shao Weizheng, "Yaqian Nongmin Xiehui Shimo" (History of the Yaqian Peasant Association), 466–67. "Chen Duxiu Gei Gongchan Guoji de Baogao (Yijiuerernian, Liuyue Sanshiri)" (Chen Duxiu's Report to the Comintern [June 30, 1922]), in EDHSD, 61.

105. Galbiati, *P'eng P'ai*; Hofheinz, *Broken Wave*; Marks, *Rural Revolution*.

106. "Zhongju Baogao" (Report of the Central Bureau), in "Zhongguo Gongchandang Diyici Zhongyang Zhixing Weiyuanhui Wenjian (Yijiuersannian, Shiyiyue Ershisiri–Ershiwuri)" (Documents of the First Central Executive Committee of the Chinese Communist Party [November 24–25, 1923]), in EDHSD, 235.

107. Galbiati, *P'eng P'ai*, 19–20.

108. Ibid., 57–58.

109. "Lu'An Dashiji" (Chronology of Lu'An), in *Peng Pai Yanjiu Shiliao*

Bianjizu (Editorial Group for Sources for Research on Peng Pai), ed., *Peng Pai Yanjiu Shiliao* (Sources for Research on Peng Pai), 102–3. See also Galbiati, *P'eng P'ai*, 65, 73–74.

110. "Lu'An Dashiji" (Chronology of Lu'An), in *Peng Pai Yanjiu Shiliao* Bianjizu (Editorial Group for Sources for Research on Peng Pai), ed., *Peng Pai Yanjiu Shiliao* (Sources for Research on Peng Pai), 109.

111. "Guangdong Nonghui zhi Zuzhi yu Jingguo" (Organization and Activities of the Guangdong Peasant Association), in GQDTYS, 34, dated September 1923.

112. "Bi Yun Gei Ziyou Xiongmen" (Letter from Bi Yun to the Brothers Ziyou), in GQDTYS, 26. The editor dates this as late February 1923 and points out that Bi Yun is a pseudonym for Yang Sizhen, while the Ziyou brothers probably referred to the Central Committee of the Youth League.

113. "Guangdong Nonghui zhi Zuzhi yu Jingguo" (Organization and Activities of the Guangdong Peasant Association), in GQDTYS, 35, dated September 1923.

114. Marks, *Rural Revolution*, 124–27.

115. "Lu'An Dashiji" (Chronology of Lu'An), in *Peng Pai Yanjiu Shiliao* Bianjizu (Editorial Group for Sources for Research on Peng Pai), ed., *Peng Pai Yanjiu Shiliao* (Sources for Research on Peng Pai), 106–7.

116. Ibid., 104–5.

117. "Bi Yun Gei Shehuizhuyi Qingniantuan Zhongyang Zhixing Weiyuanhui de Baogao" (Bi Yun's [Yang Sizhen's] Report to the Central Executive Committee of the Socialist Youth League), in GQDTYS, 25–26, dated February 20, 1923.

118. "Guangdong Nonghui zhi Zuzhi yu Jingguo" (Organization and Activities of the Guangdong Peasant Association), in GQDTYS, 36–37, dated September 1923.

119. "Discussion on the Relation between the CPC and the Kuomintang," in Maring Archive, 3166/1, undated. In a postcongress letter to Comintern leaders, Maring set out what he had said at the congress, and this suggests that the "Discussion" was a draft speech or speaking notes. For the letter, see Maring, "Fuer Genosse Sinoview, Bucharin, Radek" (Letter to Comrades Zinoviev, Bukharin, and Radek), in Maring Archive, 3066/1-5, dated June 20, 1923.

120. Maring, "Fuer Genosse Sinoview, Bucharin, Radek" (Letter to Comrades Zinoviev, Bukharin, and Radek), in Maring Archive, 3066/1-5, dated June 20, 1923.

121. "Fu: Malin de Buchong Fayan" (Attachment: Maring's Supplementary Remark), in Guangdong Geming Lishi Bowuguan (Guangdong Museum of Revolutionary History), ed., *Zhonggong "Sanda" Ziliao* (Sources for the Third CCP Congress), 62. For the attitude with which Maring went to the congress, see "Fuer Genosse Sinoview, Bucharin, Radek" (Letter to Comrades Zinoviev, Bukharin, and Radek), in Maring Archive, 3066/1-5, dated June 20, 1923.

122. Maring, "Discussion on the Relation between the CPC and the Kuomintang," in Maring Archive, 3166/1; Maring, "Fuer Genosse Sinoview, Bucharin, Radek" (Letter to Comrades Zinoviev, Bukharin, and Radek), in Maring Archive, 3066/1-5, dated June 20, 1923.

123. "Thesis on the Relation between National and Kuomintan," in Maring Archive, undated and unnumbered.

124. Maring, "Discussion on the Relation between the CPC and the Kuomintang," in Maring Archive, 3166/1.

125. Ibid.

126. Ibid.

127. Ibid.

128. Ibid.

129. Ibid.

130. Ibid.

131. Ibid.

132. Ibid.

133. Maring, "Fuer Genosse Sinoview, Bucharin, Radek," (Letter to Comrades Zinoviev, Bukharin, and Radek), in Maring Archive, 3066/1-5, dated June 20, 1923. It is unclear how each person voted at the congress. Mao's pessimism about the possibilities of a revolution in China might indicate that he voted in favor of the bloc-within policy, but this kind of reasoning certainly does not form conclusive proof.

134. Maring, "Bericht ueber die Lage in China und unsere Arbeit fuer die Periode von 15 bis 31 Mai, 1923" (Report on the Situation in China and Our Work in the Period between 15 and 30 May, 1923), in Maring Archive, 3060/1-4, dated May 31, 1923.

135. Whiting, *Soviet Policies*, 42–58, 248–62.

136. See Zhongguo Geming Bowuguan (Museum of the Chinese Revolution), ed., *Xinmin Xuehui Ziliao* (Source Materials for the New Citizen Study Society), 42–163.

137. Wang Jianying, ed., *Zhongguo Gongchandang Zuzhishi Ziliao Huibian* (Edited Source Materials for the Organizational History of the CCP), 19; "Cai Hesen Tongzhi Shengping Nianbiao" (Chronological Biography of Comrade Cai Hesen), in *Cai Hesen Wenji* (Collected Works of Cai Hesen), 840–42.

138. FFSL, 3:3–396.

139. Wu Hao [Zhou Enlai], "Shiyue Geming" (The October Revolution), in FFSL, 3:175–80 (published in *Youth* [Shaonian] on December 1, 1922) and "Zongjiao de Jingshen yu Gongchanzhuyi" (The Religious Spirit and Communism), in FFSL, 3:279–84 (published in *Youth* on September 1, 1922). See also Zhou Enlai, "Xi'Ou de 'Chiguang' " (The "Red Light" in Europe), in FFSL, 2b:826–42.

140. Zhao Shiyan, "Elosi Geming de Jiaoxun" (The Lesson of the Russian Revolution), in FFSL, 3:181–87 (published originally in *Youth*, vol. 5, January 1, 1922). Zhao signed a letter to Chen Gongpei as "Le feu"; see Zhao Shiyan, "Gei Wu Ming de Sanfeng Xin" (Three Letters to Wu Ming), in *Zhao Shiyan Xuanji* (Selected Works), 75, dated April 30, 1922.

141. Zhao Shiyan, "Lü'Fa Zhongguo Qingnian Yinggai Juexingle" (Chinese Students in France Should Wake Up), in FFSL, 3:297–300 (published in *Youth*, vol. 5, March 1, 1923).

142. "Xin Su-E Lianbang yu Diguozhuyi," in FFSL, 3:201–2 (published in *Red Light*, vol. 3, March 1, 1923).

143. "Hu Shi Deng de Zhengzhi Zhuzhang yu Women," in FFSL, 3:294–96 (published in *Youth*, vol. 2, September 1, 1922).

144. "Zhongguo Gongchandang Diyige Jueyi (Yijiueryinian)" (The First Resolution of the Chinese Communist Party [1921]), in YDDAZL, 10.

145. Sun Wuxia, *Gongchan Guoji yu Zhongguo Geming Ziliao* (Materials for the History of the Relationship between the Comintern and the Chinese Revolution), 1:92–129.

146. Xiao Chaoran, *Zhongguo Dangshi Jianming Cidian* (Concise Dictionary of the Chinese Communist Party's History), 2:1173–74.

147. "Gongchandang de Zuzhi Jianshe, Gongzuo Fangfa, he Gongzuo Neirong" (Outline for the Organizational Establishment, Work Methods, and Contents of a Communist Party), in Sun Wuxia, *Gongchan Guoji yu Zhongguo Geming Ziliao* (Materials for the History of the Relationship between the Comintern and the Chinese Revolution), 1:94–95.

148. Ibid., 120.

149. Ibid., 123.

150. Ibid.

151. Ibid., 94.

152. Ibid.

153. Ibid., 124.

154. Ibid., 100–120.

155. Ibid., 116.

156. Ibid., 97.

157. Ibid.

158. Zhang Guotao, *Rise of the Chinese Communist Party*, 255–56.

159. See Saich, "Sneevliet (Maring) Archives," 10–12.

160. Maring Archive, 3099/1-6. Letter to Sun Yatsen, dated April 29, 1924. See also two letters by Maring to Voitinsky and Borodin of April 29, 1924, in Maring Archive, 3098/1 and 3150/1. Chiang Kai-shek wrote Maring on November 28, 1923, from Moscow—he was part of a KMT delegation—stating that he hoped Maring would come to Canton and that he would speak to Sun Yatsen about this (Maring Archive, 3089/1).

161. "Zhongguo Gongchandang Zhongyang Zhixing Weiyuanhui Zuzhifa" (Rules for the Organization of the CCP Central Executive Committee), in "Zhongguo Gongchandang Disanci Quanguo Daibiao Dahui Jueyian ji Xuanyan (Yijiuersannian Liuyue)" (Resolutions and Declaration of the Third National Congress of the Chinese Communist Party), in EDHSD, 187–88.

162. Ibid., 187.

163. Ibid.

164. In chronological order:

"Zhongguo Gongchandang Diyici Zhongyang Zhixing Weiyuanhui Wenjian (Yijiuersannian, Shiyiyue Ershisiri–Ershiwuri)" (Documents of the First Central Executive Committee of the Chinese Communist Party [November 24–25, 1923]), in EDHSD, 232–49 (first published on November 30 in the *Party Journal* [Dangbao], vol. 1).

"Tongzhimen Zai Guomindang Gongzuo ji Taidu Jueyian (Yijiuersinian Eryue)" (Resolution on the Attitude of Comrades Active in the KMT [February 1924]), in EDHSD, 263–66 (first published in the *Youth League Journal* [Tuankan], vol. 7, April 11, 1924). An editorial footnote of EDHSD, p. 263, explains that this document was probably a resolution of the February 1924 Central Executive Committee meeting, and it may have been its only one.

"Zhongguo Gongchandang Kuoda Zhixing Weiyuanhui Huiyi Wenjian (Yijiuersinian, Wuyue Shiri–Shiwuri)" (Documents of the Enlarged CCP Central Executive Committee Meeting [May 10–15, 1924]), in EDHSD, 267–303 (published in the *Party Journal,* vol. 3, May 20, 1924, and in the *Party Journal,* vol. 4, June 1, 1924).

165. "Zhongju Baogao" (Central Bureau Report), in "Zhongguo Gongchandang Diyici Zhongyang Zhixing Weiyuanhui Wenjian (Yijiuersannian, Shiyiyue Ershisiri–Ershiwuri)" (Documents of the First Central Executive Committee of the CCP [November 24–25, 1923]), in EDHSD, 233.

166. Ibid., 233–35.

167. Ibid., 233.

168. "Geweiyuan Baogao" (Reports from the Committees), ibid., 236–37.

169. Ibid., 235–36.

170. Ibid., 236.

171. "Zhang Guotao Gei Weijingsiji, Mu Xin de Xin (Yijiuersannian, Shiyiyue Shiliuri)" (Letter from Zhang Guotao to Voitinsky and Mu Xin [November 16, 1923]), in EDHSD, 228.

172. "Zhongguo Gongchandang Diyici Xiuzheng Zhangcheng" (First Revised Constitution of the Chinese Communist Party), in "Zhongguo Gongchandang Disanci Quanguo Daibiao Dahui Jueyian ji Xuanyan (Yijiuersannian Liuyue)" (Resolutions and Declaration of the Third National Congress of the Chinese Communist Party [June 1923]), in EDHSD, 190.

173. "Zhang Guotao Gei Weijingsiji, Mu Xin de Xin (Yijiuersannian, Shiyiyue Shiliuri)" (Letter from Zhang Guotao to Voitinsky and Mu Xin [November 16, 1923]), in EDHSD, 228.

174. "Guomin Yundong Jinxing Jihua Jueyian" (Resolution on Our Plan of Action in the Nationalist Movement), in "Zhongguo Gongchandang Diyici Zhongyang Zhixing Weiyuanhui Wenjian (Yijiuersannian, Shiyiyue Ershisiri–Ershiwuri)" (Documents of the First Central Executive Committee of the CCP [November 24–25, 1923]), in EDHSD, 244–45.

175. Ibid., 244.

176. Wilbur, *Nationalist Revolution,* 11–13.

177. "Zhongyangju Baogao" (Central Bureau Report), in "Zhongguo Gongchandang Kuoda Zhixing Weiyuanhui Huiyi Wenjian (Yijiuersinian, Wuyue Shiri–Shiwuri)" (Documents of the Enlarged Central Executive Committee of the Chinese Communist Party [May 10–15, 1924]), in EDHSD, 283.

178. Glunin, "Comintern," 309.

179. "Gongchandang Zai Guomindangnei de Gongzuo Wenti Yijuean" (Resolution on CCP Work within the KMT) and "Gonghui Yundong Wenti Jueyian" (Resolution on Union Movement Issues), in "Zhongguo Gongchandang Kuoda Zhixing Weiyuanhui Huiyi Wenjian (Yijiuersinian, Wuyue Shiri–Shiwuri)" (Documents of the Enlarged Central Executive Committee of the Chinese Communist Party [May 10–15, 1924]), in EDHSD, 268–75.

180. Ibid., 268.

181. Ibid.

182. "Gonghui Yundong Wenti Jueyian" (Resolution on Union Movement Issues), ibid., 274.

183. Ibid.

184. Glunin, "Comintern," 309–13.

185. "Guomindang Zuo You Pai zhi Zhenyi (Yijiuersinian, Siyue Ershisan-ri)" (The Real Meaning of the KMT Left and Right Wings [April 23, 1924]), in Chen Duxiu, *Chen Duxiu Wenzhang Xuanbian* (Selected Articles), 2:459–60.

186. "Zhongguo Gongchandang Zhongyang Zhixing Weiyuanhui Zuzhifa" (Rules for the Organization of the CCP Central Executive Committee), in "Zhong-guo Gongchandang Disanci Quanguo Daibiao Dahui Jueyian ji Xuanyan (Yijiuer-sannian Liuyue)" (Resolutions and Declaration of the Third National Congress of the Chinese Communist Party [June 1923]), in EDHSD, 187.

187. Ibid.

188. Wang Jianying, ed., *Zhongguo Gongchandang Zuzhi Ziliao Huibian* (Edited Source Materials for the Organizational History of the CCP), 18.

189. Luo Zhanglong, "Zhongguo Gongchandang Disanci Quanguo Dai-biao Dahui He Diyici Guo-Gong Hezuo (Xu)" (The Third Congress of the Chinese Communist Party and the First Period of KMT-CCP Cooperation [Continued]), 14.

190. Fairbank, "Creation of the Treaty System," in CHOC, 10:242.

191. For the statute on the number of meetings, see "Zhongguo Gongchan-dang Zhongyang Zhixing Weiyuanhui Zuzhifa" (Rules for the Organization of the CCP Central Executive Committee), in "Zhongguo Gongchandang Disanci Quanguo Daibiao Dahui Jueyian ji Xuanyan (Yijiuersannian Liuyue)" (Resolu-tions and Declaration of the Third National Congress of the Chinese Communist Party [June 1923]), in EDHSD, 187.

192. Luo Zhanglong, "Zhongguo Gongchandang Disanci Quanguo Daibiao Dahui He Diyici Guo-Gong Hezuo (Xu)" (The Third Congress of the Chinese Communist Party and the First Period of KMT-CCP Cooperation [Continued]), 13–15.

193. Ibid., 8.

194. These are numbers 19, 11, 13, 15, 17, xxx, 24, and one jointly issued with the Youth League, in ZZWX, 1:134–35, 153, 165, 223–24, 225, 240–41, 256–57, 261–62.

195. "Zhongguo Gongchandang Zhongyang Weiyuanhui Dishisanhao Tong-gao (Yijiuersannian, Shieryue Ershiwuri)" (Central Executive Committee An-nouncement 13 [December 25, 1923]), in EDHSD, 254–56.

196. "Zhonggong Tonggao Dishiqihao—Guanyu Fandui Zhejiang Junfa Douzheng Wenti (Yijiuersinian, Jiuyue Shiri)" (Central Committee Announce-ment 17—Concerning the Issue of Opposition to Zhejiang Warlord Struggle [Sep-tember 10, 1924]), in ZZWX, 1:225.

197. "Gonghui Yundong Wenti Jueyian" (Resolution on Union Movement Issues), in "Zhongguo Gongchandang Kuoda Zhixing Weiyuanhui Huiyi Wenjian (Yijiuersinian, Wuyue Shiri–Shiwuri)" (Documents of the Enlarged Central Exec-utive Committee of the Chinese Communist Party [May 10–15, 1924]), in EDHSD, 275.

198. Wilbur, *Nationalist Revolution*, 20.

199. "Zhongyang Tonggao Di xxx hao—Sun Zhongshan Beishang, Gedi Ying Zuzhi Guomin Huiyi Cuchenghui ji Zhankai Huodong (Yijiuersinian Shiyi-yue)" (Central Committee Announcement xxx—When Sun Travels to the North [to Attend the Peace Conference], All Localities Must Organize National Assembly Promotion Agencies and Begin Activities [November 1924]), in ZZWX, 1:240–41.

200. Wilbur, *Nationalist Revolution*, 20–21, 24–37.

201. "Jiaoyu Xuanchuan Wenti Jueyian" (Resolution on Education and Propaganda), in "Zhongguo Gongchandang Diyici Zhongyang Zhixing Weiyuanhui Wenjian (Yijiuersannian, Shiyiyue Ershisiri–Ershiwuri)" (Documents of the First Central Executive Committee of the Chinese Communist Party [November 24–25, 1923]), in EDHSD, 249.

202. "Zhongying (Ji Zhongyang) zhi Gequ, Difang He Xiaozu Tong-zhixin—Banfa Jiaoyu Xuanchuan Weiyuanhui Zuzhifa (Yijiuersannian, Shiyue Shiwuri)" (Letter from Zhongying [the Central Committee] to each Regional and Local Committee and to All Cells—Promulgating the Regulations for the Education and Propaganda Committee [October 15, 1923]), in Zhongguo Shehui Ke-xueyuan Xinwen Yanjiusuo (Journalism Institute of the Chinese Academy of Social Sciences), ed., *Zhongguo Gongchandang Xinwen Gongzuo Wenjian Huibian* (Compilation of Documents of CCP Journalism), 6; for the regulations, see "Jiaoyu Xuanchuan Weiyuanhui Zuzhifa (Yijiuersannian Shiyue)" (Rules for the Committee on Education and Propaganda [October 1923]), ibid., 6–11.

The date seems wrong. Given that the first issue of the *Party Journal* came out on November 30, that the above documents were the first to mention the existence of that journal, and that this was a follow-up to the November 1923 Central Executive Committee meeting to have the CCP and the Socialist Youth League form a joint Education and Propaganda Committee, the document must date from some time after the closing of the meeting on November 25 and maybe before the first issue of the *Party Journal* came out.

203. "Zhongying (Ji Zhongyang) zhi Gequ, Difang He Xiaozu Tong-zhixin—Banfa Jiaoyu Xuanchuan Weiyuanhui Zuzhifa (Yijiuersannian, Shiyue Shiwuri)" (Letter from Zhongying [the Central Committee] to Each Regional and Local Committee and to All Cells—Promulgating the Regulations for the Education and Propaganda Committee [October 15, 1923]), in Zhongguo Shehui Ke-xueyuan Xinwen Yanjiusuo (Journalism Institute of the Chinese Academy of Social Sciences), ed., *Zhongguo Gongchandang Xinwen Gongzuo Wenjian Huibian* (Compilation of Documents of CCP Journalism), 6–11.

204. Ibid., 6; "Jiaoyu Xuanchuan Weiyuanhui Zuzhifa (Yijiuersannian Shi-yue)" (Rules for the Committee on Education and Propaganda [October 1923]), ibid., 6–11.

205. "Zhongying (Ji Zhongyang) zhi Gequ, Difang He Xiaozu Tong-zhixin—Banfa Jiaoyu Xuanchuan Weiyuanhui Zuzhifa (Yijiuersannian, Shiyue Shiwuri)" (Letter from Zhongying [the Central Committee] to Each Regional and Local Committee and to All Cells—Promulgating the Regulations for the Education and Propaganda Committee [October 15, 1923]), in Zhongguo Shehui Ke-xueyuan Xinwen Yanjiusuo (Journalism Institute of the Chinese Academy of Social Sciences), ed., *Zhongguo Gongchandang Xinwen Gongzuo Wenjian Huibian* (Compilation of Documents of CCP Journalism), 9–10.

206. "Zhongguo Gongchandang Cunzai de Liyou," in EDHSD, 424–25.

207. Ibid., 424.

208. EDHSD refers to the *Party Journal* as its source for the texts of Central Executive Committee documents. The reports and resolutions of the first Central Executive Committee, originally published in the first issue of the *Party Journal*, were reprinted in EDHSD, 232–49. Those of the third were published in two

separate issues of the *Party Journal*. Its resolutions were published in the *Party Journal*, vol. 3, May 20, 1924 (referred to in EDHSD, 267–82), and the reports in the *Party Journal*, vol. 4, June 1, 1924 (referred to in EDHSD, 282–303). I have found no references to the second issue, but it is likely that it contained a copy of the February 1924 Central Executive Committee meeting's "Resolution on the Work of Comrades in the KMT, " a copy of which was published in the *League Journal* (Tuankan), the league's equivalent of the *Party Journal* (see EDHSD, 263n.). The footnote explains that this resolution was originally passed at the February 1924 CCP Central Executive Committee meeting.

The copies in my possession of the *Party Journal* are on the whole illegible except for titles and section headings. However, when one puts the EDHSD and the originals next to each other, it is clear that the texts are identical.

209.   "Dangnei Zuzhi ji Xuanchuan Jiaoyu Jueyian" (Resolution on Internal Party Organization as well as Education and Propaganda), in "Zhongguo Gongchandang Kuoda Zhixing Weiyuanhui Huiyi Wenjian (Yijiuersinian, Wuyue Shiri–Shiwuri)" (Documents of the Enlarged Central Executive Committee of the Chinese Communist Party [May 10–15, 1924]), in EDHSD, 280.

Again, the document carries the wrong date in Zhongguo Shehui Kexueyuan Xinwen Yanjiusuo (Journalism Institute of the Chinese Academy of Social Sciences), ed., *Zhongguo Gongchandang Xinwen Gongzuo Wenjian Huibian* (Compilation of Documents of CCP Journalism), 12–14.

210.   "SY Gongzuo yu CP Guanxi Jueyian" (The Work of the Socialist Youth League and Its Relationship with the CP), in "Zhongguo Gongchandang Kuoda Zhixing Weiyuanhui Huiyi Wenjian (Yijiuersinian, Wuyue Shiri–Shiwuri)" (Documents of the Enlarged Central Executive Committee of the Chinese Communist Party [May 10–15, 1924]), in EDHSD, 275–77.

211.   "Zhongguo Gongchandang Zhangcheng" (Constitution of the Chinese Communist Party), in "Zhongguo Gongchandang Dierci Quanguo Daibiao Dahui Jueyian (Yijiuerernian Qiyue)" (Resolutions of the Second National Congress of the Chinese Communist Party [July 1922]), in EDHSD, 87.

212.   "Duiyu Zuzhi Wenti zhi Jueyian" (Resolution on Organizational Problems), in "Zhongguo Gongchandang Disici Quanguo Daibiao Dahui Wenjian (Yijiuerwunian Yiyue)" (Documents of the Fourth Congress of the Chinese Communist Party [January 1925]), in ZZWX, 1:309; "Zhongguo Gongchandang Dierci Xiuzheng Zhangcheng" (The Second Revised Constitution of the Chinese Communist Party), ibid., 312.

213.   Shanghai, Jiangsu, Zhejiang Dangshi Ziliao Zhengweihui, Dang'anguan (Editorial Committees and Archives of Shanghai, Jiangsu, and Zhejiang), in "Yijiueryinian zhi Yijiuerqinian Shanghai, Jiangsu, Zhejiang Dang Zuzhi Fazhan Gaikuang" (An Overview of the Development of Party Organizations in Shanghai, Jiangsu, and Zhejiang from 1921 to 1927), 5–6. The article lists the names of the members of each cell.

214.   Ibid., 5.

215.   "Dangnei Zuzhi yu Xuanchuan Wenti Jueyian" (Resolution on Problems in Internal Party Organization and Propaganda), in "Zhongguo Gongchandang Kuoda Zhixing Weiyuanhui Huiyi Wenjian (Yijiuersinian Wuyue Shiri–Shiwuri)" (Documents of the Enlarged Central Executive Committee of the Chinese Communist Party [May 10–15, 1924]), in EDHSD, 279.

216. "Zhongyang Tonggao Diershiyihao—Jiaqiang Dangwu Gongzuo, Dui Sun Zhongshan Canjia Beifang Hehui de Taidu (Yijiuersinian, Shiyiyue Yihao)" (Central Executive Committee Announcement 21—Strengthening Party Work, Our Attitude toward Sun Yatsen's Participation in the Northern Peace Conference [November 1, 1924]), in ZZWX, 1:233–34.

217. "Guanyu Zuzhi Wenti Jueyian" (Resolution on Organization), in "Zhongguo Gongchandang Disici Quanguo Daibiao Dahui Wenjian (Yijiuerwunian Yiyue)" (Documents of the Fourth National Congress of the Chinese Communist Party [January 1925]), in ZZWX, 1:310.

218. Ibid.

219. "Guomin Yundong Jinxing Jihua Jueyian" (Resolution on Our Plan of Operating in the Nationalist Movement), in "Zhongguo Gongchandang Diyici Zhongyang Zhixing Weiyuanhui Wenjian (Yijiuersannian, Shiyiyue Ershisiri–Ershiwuri)" (Documents of the First Central Executive Committee of the Chinese Communist Party [November 24–25, 1923]), in EDHSD, 244.

220. Xiao Sheng, "Tan Jing-Han Tielu Dabagong de Lingdao Wenti" (The Issue of Leadership in the Peking-Hankow Railroad Strike), 241–42.

221. "Tongzhimen Zai Guomindang Gongzuo ji Taidu Wenti (Yijiuersinian Eryue)" (Resolution on the Attitude and Activities of Our Comrades in the KMT [February 1924]), in EDHSD, 265.

222. "Zhongyang Tonggao Diershiyihao—Jiaqiang Dangwu Gongzuo, Dui Sun Zhongshan Canjia Beifang Hehui de Taidu (Yijiuersinian, Shiyiyue Yihao)" (Central Executive Committee Announcement 21—Strengthening Party Work, Our Attitude toward Sun Yatsen's Participation in the Northern Peace Conference [November 1, 1924]), in ZZWX, 1:233–34.

223. "Zhongguo Gongchandang Duiyu Muqian Shiji Wenti zhi Jihua (Yijiuersannian Yiyue)" (Plans of the CCP concerning Concrete Present-day Problems [January 1923]), in EDHSD, 143.

224. "Gonghui Yundong Wenti Jueyian" (Resolution on Union Movement Issues), in "Zhongguo Gongchandang Kuoda Zhixing Weiyuanhui Huiyi Wenjian (Yijiuersinian, Wuyue Shiri–Shiwuri)" (Documents of the Enlarged Central Executive Committee Meeting [May 10–15, 1924]), in EDHSD, 273.

225. Ibid., 272.

226. "Laodong Yundong Jinxing Fangzhen Yijuean" (Resolution on a Program of Action for the Labor Movement), in "Zhongguo Gongchandang Diyici Zhongyang Zhixing Weiyuanhui Wenjian (Yijiuersannian, Shiyiyue Ershisiri–Ershiwuri)" (Documents of the First Central Executive Committee of the Chinese Communist Party [November 24–25, 1923]), in EDHSD, 245–46.

227. "Gonghui Yundong Wenti Jueyian" (Resolution on Union Movement Issues), in "Zhongguo Gongchandang Kuoda Zhixing Weiyuanhui Huiyi Wenjian (Yijiuersinian, Wuyue Shiri–Shiwuri)" (Documents of the Enlarged Central Executive Committee of the Chinese Communist Party [May 10–15, 1924]), in EDHSD, 271.

228. "Duiyu Zhigong Yundong zhi Jueyian" (Resolution on the Labor Movement), in "Zhongguo Gongchandang Disici Quanguo Daibiao Dahui (Yijiuerwunian Yiyue)" (Resolutions of the Fourth National Congress of the Chinese Communist Party [January 1925]), in ZZWX, 1:286–87.

229. Zhao Bu, "Zhongguo Gongchandang Zuzhishi Ziliao (San)" (Organizational History of the CCP [Three]), 60–61.

230. Ibid., 60–67. Peng Shuzhi, "Guanyu Dang de Disici Quanguo Daibiao Dahui—Peng Shuzhi Gei Zhonggong Lü'Mo Zhibu Quanti Tongzhi Xin (Yijiuerwunian, Eryue Erri)" (The Fourth National Congress of the Chinese Communist Party—Peng Shuzhi's Letter to All Comrades of the CCP's Moscow Branch [February 2, 1925]), *Zhonggong Dangshi Ziliao*, 3(1983):16–21; Zhang Bojian, "Guanyu Dang Disici Daibiao Dahui he Tuan Disanci Daibiao Dahui—Zhang Bojian Gei Dongfang Daxue Tongzhi Xin (Yijiuerwunian, Eryue Wuhao)" (The Fourth Congress of the Chinese Communist Party and the Socialist Youth League's Third Congress—Letter from Zhang Bojian to Comrades at the University of the East [February 5, 1925]), *Zhonggong Dangshi Ziliao*, 3(1983):23–25.

231. Peng Shuzhi, "Guanyu Dang de Disici Quanguo Daibiao Dahui—Peng Shuzhi Gei Zhonggong Lü'Mo Zhibu Quanti Tongzhi Xin (Yijiuerwunian, Eryue Erri)" (The Fourth National Congress of the Chinese Communist Party—Peng Shuzhi's Letter to All Comrades of the CCP's Moscow Branch [February 2, 1925]), *Zhonggong Dangshi Ziliao*, 3(1983):20.

232. Zhang Bojian, "Guanyu Dang Disici Daibiao Dahui he Tuan Disanci Daibiao Dahui—Zhang Bojian Gei Dongfang Daxue Tongzhi Xin (Yijiuerwunian, Eryue Wuhao)" (The Fourth Congress of the Chinese Communist Party and the Socialist Youth League's Third Congress—Letter from Zhang Bojian to Comrades at the University of the East [February 5, 1925]), *Zhonggong Dangshi Ziliao*, 3(1983):24.

233. "Zuzhi Wenti Jueyian" (Resolution on Organization Problems), in "Zhongguo Gongchandang Disici Quanguo Daibiao Dahui Wenjian (Yijiuerwunian Yiyue)" (Documents of the Fourth Congress of the Chinese Communist Party [January 1925]), in ZZWX, 1:308.

4.   THE CCP AS MASS PARTY

1. A basic account in English is Richard Rigby, *The May Thirty Movement*, vii–viii, 1–62. See also Wilbur, *Nationalist Revolution*, 21–23, and for warlord support expressed in telegrams, see Zhongguo Dier Lishi Dang'anguan (Number Two Archives), *Wusa Yundong yu Shenggang Bagong* (The May Thirtieth Movement and the Canton–Hong Kong Strike), 10–11, 17, 22–24, 29.

2. Rigby, *May Thirty Movement*, 63.

3. Ibid., 64–65. For contemporary Peking government documents on the nationwide response to the May Thirtieth movement, see Zhongguo Dier Lishi Dang'anguan (Number Two Archives), *Wusa Yundong yu Shenggang Bagong* (The May Thirtieth Movement and the Canton–Hong Kong Strike), 10–243.

4. Wilbur, *Nationalist Revolution*, 25–26.

5. Zhang Tinghao, "Huiyi Guomindang Shanghai Zhixingbu" (Recollections of the Shanghai Executive Branch of the KMT), 114–15.

6. Shanghai, Jiangsu, Zhejiang Dangshi Ziliao Zhengweihui, Dang'anguan (Compilation Committees of Sources for Party History and Archives in Shanghai, Jiangsu, and Zhejiang), ed., "Yijiueryinian zhi Yijiuerqinian Shanghai, Jiangsu, Zhejiang Dang Zuzhi Fazhan Gaikuang" (The Circumstances and Development of Party Organizations in Shanghai, Jiangsu, and Zhejiang between 1921 and 1927), 14–17.

7. Ibid.

8. Jiang Peinan, "Wusa Yundong Qianhou Huxi Gongren de Geming Dou-zheng" (The Revolutionary Struggle of the West Shanghai Workers at the Time of the May Thirtieth Movement), 1–12. This is Jiang's oral recollection of CCP organization in Shanghai during the May Thirtieth movement. See also contemporary newspaper reports, in Shanghai Shehui Kexueyuan Lishi Yanjiusuo (History Institute, Shanghai Academy of Social Sciences), ed., *Wusa Yundong Shiliao* (Sources for the May Thirtieth Movement), 270–76. For a club constitution, ibid., 276–80. For further recollections, ibid., 281–97.

9. Deng Zhongxia, "Shanghai Riben Shachang Bagongzhong Suodelaide Jing-yan" (Experiences Gained in the Strikes at Japanese Cotton Mills in Shanghai), in Shanghai Shehui Kexueyuan Lishi Yanjiusuo (History Institute, Shanghai Academy of Social Sciences), ed., *Wusa Yundong Shiliao* (Sources for the May Thirtieth Movement), 465 (originally published in the *Chinese Worker* [Zhongguo Gongren] in May 1925).

10. Honig, *Sisters and Strangers*, 79–93, 114–32.

11. Rigby, *May Thirty Movement*, 24–34. "Eryue Bagong de Baofa he Kuoda, Gongren de Yingyong Douzheng" (Eruption and Expansion of the February Strike, and the Courageous Struggle of Workers), in Shanghai Shehui Kexue-yuan Lishi Yanjiusuo (History Institute, Shanghai Academy of Social Sciences), ed., *Wusa Yundong Shiliao* (Sources for the May Thirtieth Movement), 297.

12. "Wusa Yundong Qijian Zhonggong Shanghai Diwei Huiyi Jilu (Xuanzai; Yijiuerwunian Wuyue)" (Minutes of Shanghai Local Committee Meetings of the CCP during the May Thirtieth Movement [selections]), in DSZL, 22(1985):3.

13. Ibid., 4.

14. Ibid.

15. "Zhongyang Tonggao Disanshisanhao: Wei Haozhao He Fazhan Fandong Riben Diguozhuyi de Da Yundong (Yijiuerwunian, Wuyue Shijiuhao)" (Central Executive Committee Announcement 33: To Arouse and Develop a Large Anti-Imperialist Movement against Japan [May 19, 1925]), in ZZWX, 1:334.

16. "Wusa Yundong Qijian Zhonggong Shanghai Diwei Huiyi Jilu (Xuanzai) (Yijiuerwunian Wuyue)" (Minutes of Shanghai Local Committee Meetings of the CCP during the May Thirtieth Movement [selections]), in DSZL, 22(1985):6–7.

17. Ibid., 8–9. Ren Wuxiong, "Guanyu Guomindang Shanghai Zhixingbu" (The Shanghai Executive Branch), 127.

18. Xu Deliang, "Wusa Yundong Yu Shanghai Daxue" (The May Thirtieth Movement and Shanghai University), 53–55.

19. "Wusa Yundong Qijian Zhonggong Shanghai Diwei Huiyi Jilu (Xuanzai; Yijiuerwunian Wuyue)" (Minutes of Shanghai Local Committee Meetings of the CCP during the May Thirtieth Movement [selections]), in DSZL, 22(1985):9–10.

20. Ibid., 7.

21. "Zhongyang Tonggao Disanshisanhao: Wei Haozhao He Fazhan Fandong Riben Diguozhuyi de Da Yundong (Yijiuerwunian, Wuyue Shijiuhao)" (Central Executive Committee Announcement 33: To Arouse and Develop a Large Anti-Imperialist Movement against Japan [May 19, 1925]), in ZZWX, 1:334.

22. "Wusa Yundong Qijian Zhonggong Shanghai Diwei Huiyi Jilu (Xuanzai) (Yijiuerwunian Wuyue)" (Minutes of Shanghai Local Committee Meetings of the CCP during the May Thirtieth Movement [selections]), in DSZL, 22(1985):7.

23. Ibid.

24. Ibid., 11.

25. Ibid.

26. Luo Suwen, "Wusa Shiqi de Shanghai Zongshanghui Chutan" (A Preliminary Investigation of the Shanghai General Chamber of Commerce during the May Thirtieth Period), 85–96. Rigby, *May Thirty Movement*, 53.

27. Zhang Weizhen, "Zhang Weizhen Tongzhi Tan Shanghai 'Wusa' Yundong" (Comrade Zhang Weizhen Talks about the May Thirtieth Movement in Shanghai), 304–5; Zhang Guotao, *Rise of the Chinese Communist Party*, 428–29.

28. Zhang Weizhen, "Zhang Weizhen Tongzhi Tan Shanghai 'Wusa' Yundong" (Comrade Zhang Weizhen Talks about the May Thirtieth Movement in Shanghai), 304–6.

29. Ibid., 308–10; "Shanghaiqu Zhigong Yundong Jueyian" (Resolution on the Labor Movement in the Shanghai Area), in "Zhonggong Zhongyang Zhigong Weiyuanhui Guanyu Quanguo Zhigong Yundong Taolun Huiyi Jueyian (Yijiuer-liunian Wuyue)" (Resolutions of a Discussion Conference of the CCP Central Committee's Labor Movement Committee on the National Labor Movement [May 1926]), in Zhonghua Quanguo Zonggonghui (National General Labor Union of China), ed., *Zhonggong Zhongyang Guanyu Gongren Yundong Wenjian Xuanbian* (Compilation of CCP Central Committee Documents on the Labor Movement), 113–14.

30. Zhang Weizhen, "Zhang Weizhen Tongzhi Tan Shanghai 'Wusa' Yundong" (Comrade Zhang Weizhen Talks about the May Thirtieth Movement in Shanghai), 306–8. "Shanghaiqu Zhigong Yundong Jueyian" (Resolution on the Labor Movement in the Shanghai Area), in "Zhonggong Zhongyang Zhigong Weiyuanhui Guanyu Quanguo Zhigong Yundong Taolun Huiyi Jueyian (Yijiuer-liunian Wuyue)" (Resolutions of a Discussion Conference of the CCP Central Committee's Labor Movement Committee on the National Labor Movement), in Zhonghua Quanguo Zonggonghui (National General Labor Union of China), ed., *Zhonggong Zhongyang Guanyu Gongren Yundong Wenjian Xuanbian* (Compilation of CCP Central Committee Documents on the Labor Movement), 113–14.

31. Zhang Weizhen, "Zhang Weizhen Tongzhi Tan Shanghai 'Wusa' Yundong" (Comrade Zhang Weizhen Talks about the May Thirtieth Movement in Shanghai), 308.

32. "Gongzei yu Gongren Ziweituan Yijuean" (Resolution on Scabs and Workers' Self-Defense Corps), in "Zhonggong Zhongyang Zhigong Weiyuanhui Guanyu Quanguo Zhigong Yundong Taolun Huiyi Jueyian (Yijiuerliunian Wuyue)" (Resolutions of a Discussion Conference of the CCP Central Committee's Labor Movement Committee on the National Labor Movement [May 1926]), in Zhonghua Quanguo Zonggonghui (National General Labor Union of China), ed., *Zhonggong Zhongyang Guanyu Gongren Yundong Wenjian Xuanbian* (Compilation of CCP Central Committee Documents on the Labor Movement), 140.

33. "Chanye Gonghui de Fazhan yu Tongyi Wenti" (Development of Industrial Unions and the Question of Unity), in "Zhonggong Zhongyang Zhigong Weiyuanhui Guanyu Quanguo Zhigong Yundong Taolunhui Jueyian" (Resolutions of a Discussion Conference of the CCP Central Committee and the Labor Movement Committee on the National Labor Movement), in Zhonghua Quanguo Zonggonghui (National General Labor Union of China), ed., *Zhonggong Zhongyang Guanyu Gongren Yundong Wenjian Xuanbian* (Compilation of CCP Central Committee Documents on the Labor Movement), 123.

34. Chen Zhiwen, "Zhongguo Gongchandang Zai Guangdong Diqu Jiandang Chuqi de Yixie Ziliao" (Some Sources for Early Party-Building Activities in the Guangdong Area), 5–7; Chen Zhiwen, "Dageming Shiqi Guangzhou Gongren Shiqi" (The Workers' Movement in Canton at the Time of the Great Revolution), 32–33; Li Xiantao, "Guang-San Tielu Gongren de Douzheng ji Zhonggong Guangdong Shengwei Chuqi de Yixie Qingkuang" (The Struggle of Canton-San-shui Railroad Workers and the Early Circumstances of the Guangdong Provincial Committee), 46–48; Vishnyakova-Akimova, *Two Years in Revolutionary China*, 233; Deng Zhongxia, "Zhongguo Zhigong Yundong Jianshi Yijiuyijiunian–Yijiu-erliunian (Yijiusanlingnian, Liuyue Shijiuri)" (A Short History of the Chinese Labor Movement, 1919–1926 [June 19, 1930]), in Deng Zhongxia, *Deng Zhongxia Wenji* (Collected Works), 610–12; Rao Weisheng, "Zhongguo Gongchandang Zai Guangdong Diqu Jiandang Chuqi Qingkuang Diandi" (Some Aspects of the Situation at the Beginning of CCP Party Construction in the Guangdong Region), 23.

35. Wilbur, *Nationalist Revolution*, 8–14, 19–20.

36. Ibid., 20.

37. Wang Jianmin, *Zhongguo Gongchandang Shigao* (Draft History of the Chinese Communist Party), 1:103; Wilbur and How, *Missionaries of Revolution*, 90–91, 101–3.

38. Wang Jianmin, *Zhongguo Gongchandang Shigao* (Draft History of the Chinese Communist Party), 1:112.

39. "Shehuizhuyi Qingniantuan Guangdong Quwei Zuzhibu Baogao (Diyi-hao)" (Report from the Organization Department of the Guangdong Regional Executive Committee of the Chinese Communist Youth League), in GQDTYS, 132, dated January 1, 1925.

40. On the strike, see Wilbur, *Nationalist Revolution*, 25–27, 69.

41. Deng Zhongxia, "Zhongguo Zhigong Yundong Jianshi Yijiuyijiu-nian–Yijiuerliunian (Yijiusanlingnian, Liuyue Shijiuri)" (Short History of the Chinese Labor Movement, 1919–1926 [June 19, 1930]), in Deng Zhongxia, *Deng Zhongxia Wenji* (Collected Works), 611.

42. Ibid., 611–12.

43. Deng Zhongxia, "Shenggang Bagong Gongren de Zuzhi" (Organization of Workers of the Canton–Hong Kong Strike), in *Shenggang Dabagong* (The Great Canton–Hong Kong Strike), 149–53 (originally published in the *Workers' Way* [Gongren zhi Lu], vols. 22, 23, July 16, 17, 1925). For further documents on the organization of the strike, ibid., 154–58; "Shenggang Bagong Jingguo Baogao" (Report on the Progress of the Canton–Hong Kong Strike), in Zhonggong Guang-dong Shengwei Dangshi Yanjiu Bangongshi (Office of the Section for Party History of the Guangdong Provincial Committee of the Chinese Communist Party) et al., eds., *Su Zhaozheng Yanjiu Shiliao* (Su Zhaozheng: Research and Historical Sources), 36–37; Chen Zhiwen, "Zhongguo Gongchandang Zai Guangdong Diqu Jiandang Chuqi de Yixie Ziliao" (Some Sources for Early Party-Building Activities in the Guangdong Area), 28.

44. Deng Zhongxia, "Zhongguo Zhigong Yundong Jianshi—Yijiuyijiu-nian–Yijiuerliunian" (Short History of the Chinese Labor Movement—1919–1926), in *Deng Zhongxia Wenji* (Collected Works), 615–26. Deng lists origins of donations to the Strike Committee, the greatest part coming from the Canton Government.

45. "Shenggang Bagong Weiyuanhui Zhi Guomindang Zhongyang Zhengzhi Weiyuanhui Han" (Letter from the Hong Kong Strike Committee to the Political Council of the KMT), in Zhonggong Guangdong Shengwei Dangshi Yanjiu Bangongshi (Office of the Section for Party History of the Guangdong Provincial Committee of the Chinese Communist Party) et al., eds., *Su Zhaozheng Yanjiu Shiliao* (Su Zhaozheng: Research and Historical Sources), 147–52. The letter contains reports on the delegate congresses and was published in a special edition of the *Workers' Way*, on August 13, 1925.

46. Deng Zhongxia, "Yinianlai Shenggang Bagong de Jingguo (Yijiuerliunian Bayue)" (The Canton–Hong Kong Strike in the Last Year [August 1926]), in Deng Zhongxia, *Deng Zhongxia Wenji* (Collected Works), 273.

47. Ibid., 268–72. For challenges to CCP leadership from within the union, see "Shenggang Bagong Weiyuanhui Zhi Guomindang Zhongyang Zhengzhi Weiyuanhui Han" (Letter from the Hong Kong Strike Committee to the Political Council of the KMT), in Zhonggong Guangdong Shengwei Dangshi Yanjiu Bangongshi (Office of the Section for Party History of the Guangdong Provincial Committee of the Chinese Communist Party) et al., eds., *Su Zhaozheng Yanjiu Shiliao* (Su Zhaozheng: Research and Historical Sources), 147–52 (first published in the *Workers' Way* on August 13, 1925).

48. Deng Zhongxia, "Yinianlai Shenggang Bagong de Jingguo (Yijiuerliunian Bayue)" (The Canton–Hong Kong Strike in the Last Year [August 1926]), in Deng Zhongxia, *Deng Zhongxia Wenji* (Collected Works), 268–72; "Shenggang Bagong Jingguo Baogao" (Report on the Progress of the Canton–Hong Kong Strike), in Zhonggong Guangdong Shengwei Dangshi Yanjiu Bangongshi (Office of the Section for Party History of the Guangdong Provincial Committee of the Chinese Communist Party) et al., eds., *Su Zhaozheng Yanjiu Shiliao* (Su Zhaozheng: Research and Historical Sources), 36.

49. Chen Zhiwen, "Dageming Shiqi Guangzhou Gongren Yundong" (The Workers' Movement in Canton at the Time of the Great Revolution), 15–18.

50. "Kaipi Huangpu Shangfu Gejie Huiyi Qingxing" (Meeting of Various Circles to Discuss the Construction of a Harbor at Whampoa), in Zhonggong Guangdong Shengwei Dangshi Yanjiu Bangongshi (Office of the Section for Party History of the Guangdong Provincial Committee of the Chinese Communist Party) et al., eds., *Su Zhaozheng Yanjiu Shiliao* (Su Zhaozheng: Research and Historical Sources), 173–74 (first published on November 30, 1925, in the *Workers' Way*, vol. 157). See also a piece by the same title, also in *Su Zhaozheng Yanjiu Shiliao*, 176 (published originally on December 7, 1925, in the *Workers' Way*, vol. 164).

51. "Guangdong Gongren Yundong Baogao (Jielu)" (Report on the Guangdong Labor Movement [Excerpt]), in GQDTYS, 159–63, undated; according to the editors of GQDTYS, produced in 1925.

52. "Zuzhi Wenti Jueyian" (Resolution on Organizational Problems), in "Zhonggong Zhongyang Kuoda Zhixing Weiyuanhui Wenjian (Yijiuerwunian Shiyue)" (Documents of the Enlarged Central Executive Committee Meeting of the Chinese Communist Party [October 1925]), in ZZWX, 1:406.

53. "Zhongguo Gongchandang de Zhiren" (Tasks of the Chinese Communist Party), ibid., 403.

54. "Jingqu Baogao Jueyian" (Resolution on the Report of the Peking Region), "Yuequ Baogao Jueyian" (Resolution on the Report of the Guangdong

Region), "Xiangqu Baogao Jueyian" (Resolution on the Report of the Hunan Region), "Henan Baogao Jueyian" (Resolution on the Report from Henan), "Shandong Baogao Jueyian" (Resolution on the Report from Shandong), "Hubei Baogao Jueyian" (Resolution on the Report from Hubei), ibid., 421–27.

55. "Yuequ Baogao Jueyian" (Resolution on the Report of the Guangdong Region), ibid., 422.

56. Wilbur, *Nationalist Revolution*, 30

57. Qu Qiubai, "Zhongguo Guomin Geming yu Dai Jitao-zhuyi (Yijiuerwu-nian Jiuyue)" (The Chinese National Revolution and Dai Jitao-ism [September 1925]), in ZZWX, 1:381–95; Chen Duxiu, "Gei Dai Jitao de Yifeng Xin (Yijiuer-wunian Jiuyue Shisiri)" (Letter to Dai Jitao [September 11, 1925]), in Chen Duxiu, *Chen Duxiu Wenzhang Xuanbian* (Selected Articles), 2:85–95 (published in the *Guide*, vols. 129, 130, on the date in the title).

58. Zhao Bu, "Zhongguo Gongchandang Zuzhishi Ziliao (Wu)" (Information on the Organizational History of the CCP [Five]), 90.

59. "Zuzhi Wenti Jueyian" (Resolution on Organizational Issues), in "Zhong-gong Zhongyang Kuoda Zhixing Weiyuanhui Wenjian (Yijiuerwunian Shi-yue)" (Documents of the Enlarged Central Executive Committee Meeting of the Chinese Communist Party [October 1925]), in ZZWX, 1:407.

60. "Xuanchuan Wenti Jueyian" (Resolution on Propaganda Issues), ibid., 410.

61. "Zuzhi Wenti Jueyian" (Resolution on Organizational Issues), ibid., 409. See also Zhao Bu, "Zhongguo Gongchandang Zuzhishi Ziliao (Si)" (Information on the Organizational History of the CCP [Four]), 82.

62. "Zuzhi Wenti Jueyian" (Resolution on Organizational Problems), in "Zhonggong Zhongyang Kuoda Zhixing Weiyuanhui Wenjian (Yijiuerwunian Shiyue)" (Documents of the Enlarged Central Executive Committee Meeting of the Chinese Communist Party [October 1925]), in ZZWX, 1:408.

63. Ibid., 407–8.

64. Chen Duxiu, "Chen Duxiu Zai Zhongguo Gongchandang Diwuci Quan-guo Daibiao Dahuishang de Baogao (Yijiuerqinian, Siyue Ershijiuri)" (Chen Duxiu's Report at the Fifth National Congress of the Chinese Communist Party [April 29, 1927]), 31.

65. "Zhongguo Gongchandang de Renwu Jueyian" (Resolution on the Tasks of the Chinese Communist Party), in "Zhonggong Zhongyang Kuoda Zhixing Weiyuanhui Wenjian (Yijiuerwunian Shiyue)" (Documents of the Enlarged Cen-tral Executive Committee of the Chinese Communist Party [October 1925], in ZZWX, 1:404–5.

66. Ibid.

67. Zhao Bu, "Zhongguo Gongchandang Zuzhishi Ziliao (Si)" (Information on the Organizational History of the CCP [Four]), 82–86; "Zhongguo Gongchan-dang Zuzhishi Ziliao (Liu)" (Information on the Organizational History of the CCP [Six]), 40.

68. Renmin Chubanshe (People's Press), ed., *Diyici Guonei Geming Zhan-zheng Shiqi de Nongmin Yundong Ziliao* (Sources for the Peasant Movement during the Period of the First Internal Revolutionary War), 65–66.

69. Wilbur, *Nationalist Revolution*, 8.

70. Peng Jianhua, "Yijiuersinian Dong Baoluoting Zai Beijing Zhaojide Yici Huiyi" (A Meeting Convened by Borodin in the Winter of 1924), 22–23.

71. "Zhongyang Tonggao Diqishijiuhao—Guanyu Zhongyang Tebie Huiyi (Yijiuerliunian, Sanyue Shisihao)" (Central Executive Committee Announcement 79—concerning the Special Central Executive Committee Meeting [March 14, 1926]), in ZZWX, 2:47–48.

72. Ibid., 48.

73. "Guanyu Xianshi Zhengju yu Gongchandang de Zhuyao Renwu Jueyian" (Resolution on the Present Political Situation and the Tasks of the Chinese Communist Party), in "Zhongyang Tebie Huiyi (Yijiuerliunian, Eryue Ershiyiri–Ershisiri)" (The Special Meeting of the Central Executive Committee [February 21–24, 1926]), in ZZWX, 2:28–29.

74. Ibid., 29–32. See also "Zhongyang Tonggao Diqishijiuhao—Guanyu Zhongyang Tebie Huiyi (Yijiuerliunian, Sanyue Shisihao)" (Central Executive Committee Announcement 79—concerning the Special Central Executive Committee Meeting [March 14, 1926]), in ZZWX, 2:47–48.

75. Hofheinz, *Broken Wave*; Marks, *Rural Revolution*; Galbiati; *P'eng P'ai.*

76. "Guangdong Nongmin Yundong Baogao (Yijiuerliunian Liuyue)" (Report on the Guangdong Peasant Movement [June 1926])," in Guangzhou Nongmin Yundong Jiangxisuo Jiuchi Jinianguan (Museum of the Original Site of the Canton Peasant Movement Training Institute), ed., *Guangdong Nongmin Yundong Ziliao Xuanbian* (Compilation of Sources of the Guangdong Peasant Movement), 16–110. The editors of the compilation date the report as written in May or June 1926, during and after the peasant-association conference. It was printed in October.

77. "Guangdong Nongmin Yundong Baogao (Yijiuerliunian Liuyue)" (Report on the Guangdong Peasant Movement [June 1926]), in Guangzhou Nongmin Yundong Jiangxisuo Jiuchi Jinianguan (Museum of the Original Site of the Canton Peasant Movement Training Institute), ed., *Guangdong Nongmin Yundong Ziliao Xuanbian* (Compilation of Sources of the Guangdong Peasant Movement), 20–32.

78. Ibid.

79. Ibid., 22–23.

80. Ibid., 26–29.

81. Ibid., 31–32. On the Triads, see also Kuhn and Mann, "Dynastic Decline," 135–36.

82. "Guangdong Nongmin Yundong Baogao (Yijiuerliunian Liuyue)" (Report on the Guangdong Peasant Movement [June 1926]), in Guangzhou Nongmin Yundong Jiangxisuo Jiuchi Jinianguan (Museum of the Original Site of the Canton Peasant Movement Training Institute), ed., *Guangdong Nongmin Yundong Ziliao Xuanbian* (Compilation of Sources of the Guangdong Peasant Movement), 31–32.

83. "Tuan Yue Quwei Dierci Daibiao Dahui Guanyu Guangdong Nongmin Yundong Jueyian (Yijiuersinian Liuyue)" (Resolution on the Guangdong Peasant Movement, Second Guangdong Regional Congress of the Socialist Youth League [June 1924]), ibid., 5–7.

84. Sources for the 1921–1925 period contained in GQDTYS suggest that in Guangdong the Youth League was the institution through which most communist activity was channeled in the region. On January 1, 1925, the league's Guangdong Regional Executive Committee instructed that members be divided between the party and the league on the basis of age, but its implementation seems to have been very gradual. See "Shehuizhuyi Qingniantuan Guangdong Quwei Zuzhibu

Baogao (Diyihao)" (Report from the Organization Department of the Guangdong Regional Executive Committee of the Chinese Communist Youth League), in GQDTYS, 131. See also Yuan Bangjian, "Dageming Shiqi Dang, Tuan Zuzhi Guanxi de Bianhua" (Changes in the Organizational Relations of the Party and the Youth League in Guangdong at the Time of the Great Revolution), 215–17.

85. See "Nongmin Yundong Jueyian" (Resolution on the Peasant Movement), in "Zhongguo Gongchandang Disanci Zhongyang Kuoda Zhixing Weiyuanhui (Yijiuerliunian Qiyue)" (The Third Enlarged Central Executive Committee of the Chinese Communist Party [July 1926]), in ZZWX, 2:142–49.

86. "Tuan Yue Quwei Dierci Daibiao Dahui Guanyu Guangdong Nongmin Yundong Jueyian (Yijiuersinian Liuyue)" (Resolution on the Guangdong Peasant Movement, Second Guangdong Regional Congress of the Socialist Youth League [June 1924]), in Guangzhou Nongmin Yundong Jiangxisuo Jiuchi Jinianguan (Museum of the Original Site of the Canton Peasant Movement Training Institute), ed., *Guangdong Nongmin Yundong Ziliao Xuanbian* (Compilation of Sources of the Guangdong Peasant Movement), 7.

87. Ibid.

88. Ibid., 5.

89. "Guangdong Nongmin Yundong Baogao (Yijiuerliunian Liuyue)" (Report on the Guangdong Peasant Movement [June 1926]), ibid., 33–34.

90. "Tuan Yue Quwei Dierci Daibiao Dahui Guanyu Guangdong Nongmin Yundong Jueyian (Yijiuersinian Liuyue)" (Resolution on the Guangdong Peasant Movement, Second Guangdong Regional Congress of the Socialist Youth League [June 1924]), ibid., 5.

91. "Guangdong Nongmin Yundong Baogao (Yijiuerliunian Liuyue)" (Report on the Guangdong Peasant Movement [June 1926]), ibid., 67.

92. Ibid., 62–69.

93. Ibid., 72.

94. Ibid., 76–89.

95. Ibid., 84–85.

96. Wang Yongju, "Youguan Zhou Enlai Dageming Shiqi de Liangjian Shishi de Dingzheng" (A Verification of Two Historical Facts concerning Zhou Enlai at the Time of the Great Revolution), 308–13. Wang argues that Zhou could not have been director of the Political Department of the Command Department of the First Eastern Campaign since it did not exist yet, but that he was in charge of political work.

97. "Xuanchuandui Chufa Lufeng Qijian zhi Jingguo ji Diaocha Zhuangkuang" (Events Surrounding the Departure to Lufeng of the Propaganda Team and the Circumstances of Its Investigations), in Peng Pai Yanjiu Shiliao Bianjibu (Editorial Department for Historical Sources for Research on Peng Pai), ed., *Peng Pai Yanjiu Shiliao* (Historical Sources for Research on Peng Pai), 139 (published on May 11, 1925, in the *Lu'an Daily*).

98. Ibid., 137–39. See also "Lufeng Xianzhang Juhuo Sitiao" (Fearing Trouble Because of Malfeasance, the Lufeng Magistrate Runs Away) and "Dijiuqu Nongmin Xiehui Kai Chengli Hui" (Peasants in Ward Nine Convene an Opening Meeting), ibid., 136 and 137, respectively (the first article appeared on May 7 in the *Lu'an Daily*, the second a day later).

99. "Gongchanzhuyi Qingniantuan Guangdong Quwei Zuzhibu Gongzuo

Jinxing ji Ge Fenxiao Jinkuang Shuyao" (Progress in the Work of the Organization Department of the Guangdong Regional Executive Committee of the Chinese Communist Youth League and Recent Developments in the Situation at Branch Schools), in GQDTYS, 172 ("branch schools" referred to branches), dated November 20, 1925.

100. "Gongchanzhuyi Qingniantuan Shantou Diwei Baogao (Diliuhao)" (Report of the Swatow Local Committee of the Chinese Communist Youth League), in GQDTYS, 185–87, dated December 10, 1925; "Gongchanzhuyi Qingniantuan Shantou Diwei Guanyu Disanci Difang Dahui Jingguo zhi Baogao" (Report on the Proceeding of the Third Local Congress by the Swatow Local Committee of the Chinese Communist Youth League), 194, dated December 24, 1925. Lai Xiansheng, "Zai Guangdong Geming Hongliuzhong—Huiyi 1922–1927nian de Douzheng" (In the Torrent of the Guangdong Revolution—Recollections of the Struggle 1922–1927), in GDDSZL, 1:122–25.

101. "Dierci Nongmin Yundong Daibiao Dahuihou Guangdong Nongyun Qingkuang—Yijiuerliunian, Qiyue Ershierri Jiyuan zai Quwei Baogao" (The Guangdong Peasant Movement after the Second Peasant Congress—Luo Qiyuan's Report to the Regional Committee of July 22, 1926), in GQDTYS, 383.

102. Ibid., 383–87.

103. Guan Dongqu [pseudonym for Guangdong Regional Committee of the Socialist Youth League], "Sun Wen Zhuyi Xuehui Zai Yue Huodong Zhuangkuang" (The Activities of the Sun Yatsen-ism Study Society in Guangdong), in GQDTYS, 206–7, dated January 4, 1926; "Gongchanzhuyi Qingniantuan Guangzhou Diwei Zhengzhi Baogao (Dierhao)" (Political Report of the Canton Local Committee of the Communist Youth League [Number Two]), in GQDTYS, 208, dated January 5, 1926; Wilbur and How, *Missionaries of Revolution*, 192–93; "Document 37," ibid., 662–63.

104. Lai Xiansheng, "Zai Guangdong Geming Hongliuzhong—Huiyi Yijiuerernian–Yijiuerqinian de Douzheng" (In the Torrent of the Revolution in Guangdong—Recollections of the Struggle 1922–1927), in GDDSZL, 1:125.

105. "Stepanov's Report [to a Meeting of the Soviet Group at Canton]" (brackets by Wilbur and How), Wilbur and How, *Missionaries of Revolution*, 712, dated April 10, 1926.

106. "Gongchanzhuyi Lu-Feng Tezhi Baogao" (Report of the Special Socialist Youth League Branch of Haifeng and Lufeng), in GQDTYS, 269, dated May 25, 1926; "Gongchanzhuyi Qingniantuan Guangzhou Diwei Zhengzhi Baogao (Dierhao)" (Political Report of the Canton Local Committee of the Communist Youth League [Number Two]), in GQDTYS, 208. On the society, see also Vishnyakova-Akimova, *Two Years in Revolutionary China*, 170–71.

107. "Gongchanzhuyi Qingniantuan Guangzhou Diwei Zhengzhi Baogao (Dierhao)" (Political Report of the Canton Local Committee of the Communist Youth League [Number Two]), in GQDTYS, 208, dated January 5, 1926.

108. Hofheinz, *Broken Wave*, 67–136.

109. Guan Dongqu [pseudonym for Guangdong Regional Committee of the Socialist Youth League], "Sun Wen Zhuyi Xuehui Zai Yue Huodong Zhuangkuang" (The Activities of the Sun Yatsen-ism Study Society in Guangdong), in GQDTYS, 206; "Gongchanzhuyi Qingniantuan Guangzhou Diwei Zhengzhi Baogao (Dierhao)" (Political Report of the Canton Local Committee of the Communist Youth League [Number Two]), in GQDTYS, 208–11.

110. Ibid.

111. Wilbur, *Nationalist Revolution*, 47–49.

112. "Guangdong Nongmin Yundong Baogao (Yijiuerliunian Liuyue)" (Report on the Guangdong Peasant Movement [June 1926]), in Guangzhou Nongmin Yundong Jiangxisuo Jiuchi Jinianguan (Museum of the Original Site of the Canton Peasant Movement Cadre Training Institute), ed., *Guangdong Nongmin Yundong Ziliao Xuanbian* (Compilation of Sources of the Guangdong Peasant Movement), 99–104.

113. "Zhongyang Dierci Kuoda Huiyi Duiyu Guangdong Nongmin Yundong Jueyian (Yijiuerliunian Qiyue)" (Resolution of the Second Enlarged Central Executive Committee Meeting on the Guangdong Peasant Movement [July 1926]), ibid., 111–29. The quote can be found on p. 119. This resolution does not appear among the July 1926 Central Executive Committee's documents included in ZZWX. It may not be in the Central Committee Archives. It may not have obtained approval of the majority, or the Central Committee Archives may have decided against distribution of the document, for which there could be many reasons.

114. Wilbur, *Nationalist Revolution*, 30–32.

115. Ibid., 47–48.

116. "Guangdong Nongmin Yundong Baogao (Yijiuerliunian Liuyue)" (Report on the Guangdong Peasant Movement [June 1926]), in Guangzhou Nongmin Yundong Jiangxisuo Jiuchi Jinianguan (Museum of the Original Site of the Canton Peasant Movement Training Institute), ed., *Guangdong Nongmin Yundong Ziliao Xuanbian* (Compilation of Sources of the Guangdong Peasant Movement), 98.

117. "Qu Qiubai You Yue Huilai Baogao—Guangdong Zhengzhi Zhuangkuang, Zuo, You Pai Zhanzheng ji Dang de Gongzuo Deng" (Report from Qu Qiubai after Returning from Guangdong—the Political Situation in Guangdong, the Struggle between the Left and Right Wings, and Party Activities, etc.), in GQDTYS, 415–16 (published on September 28, 1926, in *Central Political Information* [Zhongyang Zhengzhi Tongxun], an internal CCP publication that continued *The Party Journal*.)

118. "Zhonggong Guangdong Quwei Zhengzhi Baogao (Er)—Guomin Zhengfu Qianyi ji Sheng Zhengfu Gaizu Hou Guangdong Zhengju yu Women de Zhengce" (Political Report of the Guangdong Regional Committee of the CCP—the Move of the Nationalist Government [from Canton to Wuhan], the Reconstitution of the Provincial Government, and Our Policies), in GQDTYS, 483, 486, dated November 23, 1926.

119. Boorman, *Biographical Dictionary*, 2:292–93.

120. Jacobs, *Borodin*, 200–203.

121. Wilbur, *Nationalist Revolution*, 48–49; "Stepanov's Report [to a Meeting of the Soviet Group at Canton]," in Wilbur and How, *Missionaries of Revolution*, 708–9.

122. "Stepanov's Report on the March 20 Incident," "Stepanov's Report [to a Meeting of the Soviet Group at Canton]," "Summary Report by 'Seifulin' on the Political Developments in Canton in May 1926," in Wilbur and How, *Missionaries of Revolution*, 703–20, respectively dated April 2, April 13, and June 3, 1926.

123. "Zhongyang Tonggao Dierhao—Guanyu Sheng-Gang Bagong (Yijiuerliunian, Qiyue Ershiyiri)" (Central Executive Committee Announcement 2—Con-

cerning the Canton–Hong Kong Strike [July 31, 1926]), in Zhonghua Quanguo Zonggonghui (National General Labor Union of China), ed., *Zhonggong Zhongyang Guanyu Gongren Wenjian Xuanbian* (Compilation of CCP Central Committee Documents on the Labor Movement), 152–53; Deng Zhongxia, "Zhongguo Zhigong Yundong Jianshi" (Short History of the Chinese Labor Movement), in Deng Zhongxia, *Deng Zhongxia Wenji* (Collected Works), 627–39.

124. Chen Zhiwen, "Dageming Shiqi Guangzhou Gongren Yundong" (The Workers' Movement in Canton at the Time of the Great Revolution), 38–39.

125. Ibid., 39–40.

126. Li Xiantao, "Guang-San Tielu Gongren de Douzheng ji Zhonggong Guangdong Shengwei Chuqi de Yixie Qingkuang" (The Struggle of Canton-Sanshui Railroad Workers and the Early Circumstances of the Guangdong Provincial Committee), 54–56.

127. See chapter 5.

128. "Zhongyang Tonggao Diyibailingyihao—Zuijin Zhengju Guancha ji Women Jinhou Gongzuo Yuanze (Yijiuerliunian, Wuyue Qiri)" (Central Executive Committee Announcement 101—Review of the Recent Political Situation and Principles for Our Activities from Now On [May 7, 1926]), in ZZWX, 2:81.

129. "Zuzhi Wenti Jueyian" (Resolution on Organizational Issues), in "Zhongguo Gongchandang Disanci Zhongyang Kuoda Zhixing Weiyuanhui (Yijiuerliunian Qiyue)" (The Third Enlarged Central Executive Committee Meeting of the Chinese Communist Party [July 1926]), in ZZWX, 2:133–34.

130. "Zhongyang Tonggao xxx Hao—Jieshao Meige Tongzhi Bidu de Xiao Cezi *Women Jinhou Yingdang Zemmayang Gongzuo*" (Central Executive Committee Announcement xxx—Introducing the Booklet to Be Read by All Comrades *How Should We Work from Now On?* [April 1926]), in ZZWX, 2:63–71.

131. Ibid., 64.

132. Ibid., 70.

133. Ibid., 68–69.

134. Ibid., 66–71.

135. Ibid., 67–68.

136. "Shanghaiqu Zhigong Yundong Jueyian" (Resolution on the Labor Movement in the Shanghai Area), in "Zhonggong Zhongyang Zhigong Weiyuanhui Guanyu Quanguo Zhigong Yundong Taolun Huiyi Jueyian (Yijiuerliunian Wuyue)" (Resolutions of the Discussion Conference of the Central CCP Labor Movement Committee on the National Labor Movement [May 1926]), in Zhonghua Quanguo Zonggonghui (National General Labor Union of China), ed., *Zhonggong Zhongyang Guanyu Gongren Yundong Wenjian Xuanbian* (Compilation of CCP Central Committee Documents on the Labor Movement), 128.

137. "Shanghaiqu Zhigong Yundong Jueyian" (Resolution on the Labor Movement in the Shanghai Area), ibid., 111–15.

138. "Gongzei yu Gongren Ziweituan Jueyian" (Resolution on Scabs and Workers' Pickets), ibid., 140–42.

139. Wang Jianying, ed., *Zhongguo Gongchandang Zuzhishi Ziliao Huibian* (Edited Source Materials for the Organizational History of the CCP), 34.

140. Ibid.

141. "Zhongyang Dierci Kuoda Huiyi Duiyu Guangdong Nongmin Yundong Jueyian (Yijiuerliunian Qiyue)" (Resolution of the Second Enlarged Central Exec-

utive Committee Meeting on the Guangdong Peasant Movement [July 1926]), in Guangzhou Nongmin Yundong Jiangxisuo Jiuchi Jinianguan (Museum of the Original Site of the Canton Peasant Movement Cadre Training Institute), ed., *Guangdong Nongmin Yundong Ziliao Xuanbian* (Compilation of Sources of the Guangdong Peasant Movement), 111–29.

142. "Nongmin Yundong Jueyian" (Resolution on the Peasant Movement), in "Zhongguo Gongchandang Disanci Zhongyang Kuoda Zhixing Weiyuanhui (Yijiuerliunian Qiyue)" (The Third Enlarged Central Executive Committee Meeting of the Chinese Communist Party [July 1926]), in ZZWX, 2:144.

143. Ibid., 142–49.

144. "Zhongyang Zhengzhi Baogao" (Central Executive Committee Report), ibid., 118.

145. Walder, *Communist Neo-Traditionalism*.

146. Wilbur, *Nationalist Revolution*, 56.

147. "Lun Guomin Zhengfu de Beifa (Yijiuerliunian, Liuyue Qiri)" (On the Northern Expedition of the Nationalist Government [June 7, 1926]), in Chen Duxiu, *Chen Duxiu Wenzhang Xuanbian* (Selected Articles), 3:250–52.

148. Zhao Bu, "Wuci Dahui Dao Liuci Dahui Yinianzhong Dang de Zuzhi Zhuangkuang (Yi)" (Party Organization in the Year between the Fifth and the Sixth Congresses [One]), 63.

149. "Zhongguo Gongchandang Zhongyang Weiyuanhui Guanyu Ruokan Lishi Wenti de Jueyi" (Resolution of the CCP Central Committee on Several Historical Issues), in Zhonggong Zhongyang Shujichu (Secretariat of the CCP Central Committee, ed., *Liuda Yilai* (Since the Sixth Party Congress), 1179–80.

150. In the early and middle 1980s, mainland historians attempted a reevaluation of the party's judgment on Chen Duxiu. For the results, see Zhang Shuichun, "'Jindai Zhongguo Bainianshi Cidian' Shengao Yijian Zhailu" (Excerpts of Suggestions Made on the Review Copy of *Dictionary of a Century of Modern Chinese History*), in *Bianji zhi You* (Companion for Editing), March 1986, 87; Du Weihua, "'Zhonggong Dangshi Dashi Nianbiao' Fanyingde Bufen Xin Guannian" (Some New Standpoints as Reflected in *Chronology of CCP History*), in *Shehui Kexue Cankao* (Social Science Review), March 1983, 23–28.

151. Brandt, *Stalin's Failure*, viii, 79.

152. Meisner, *Mao's China*, 29.

153. Wilbur, *Nationalist Revolution*, 53–55.

154. Tang Shengzhi, "Cong Xinhai Geming Dao Beifa Zhanzheng—Tang Shengzhi Huiyilu Pianduan" (From the 1911 Revolution to the Northern Expedition—Some Recollections of Tang Shengzhi), 174–75.

155. "Hunan Nongmin Yundong Zhenshi Qingxing—Hunan Minzhong Tuanti Qingyuan Daibiaotuan de Baogao" (The Real Conditions of the Hunan Peasant Movement—Report by a Delegation of the Hunan People), in Renmin Chubanshe (People's Press), ed., *Diyici Guonei Geming Zhanzheng Shiqi de Nongmin Yundong Ziliao* (Sources for the Peasant Movement during the First Period of the Civil War), 381 (originally published in the *Guide*, vol. 199, June 22, 1927).

156. "Hunan Nongmin Geming de Zhuishu" (An Account of the Hunan Peasant Revolution), ibid., 374–75 (originally published on January 2 in the *Bolshevik*, vols. 13, 14).

157. "Fuyi: Xiangqu Shuji Baogao (Yijiuerliunian, Shiyiyue Ershierri)" (En-

closure: Report of the Secretary of the Hunan Regional Executive Committee [November 22, 1926]), in ZZWX, 2:302. "Duiyu Muqian Shiju de Jige Zhongyao Wenti" (Some Central Issues of the Present Day [November 9, 1926]), in ZZWX, 2:292–97.

158. "Fusi: Guanyu Xiangqu CP yu KMT Guanxi Jueyian (Yijiuerliunian, Shiyue Xiangqu Daibiao Dahui Jueyi)" (Enclosure 4: Resolutions Concerning the Relationship Between the CCP and the KMT in the Hunan Area [Resolution of the October 1926 Hunan Regional Congress]), in ZZWX, 2:306. The enclosure was attached to "Duiyu Muqian Shiju de Jige Zhongyao Wenti" (Some Central Issues of the Present Day [November 9, 1926]), in ZZWX, 2:292–97.

159. Ibid., 308.

160. "Fuyi: Xiangqu Shuji Baogao (Yijiuerliunian, Shiyiyue Ershierri)" (Enclosure: Report of the Secretary of the Hunan Regional Executive Committee [November 22, 1926]), ibid., 302.

161. Ibid.

162. "Fuer: Hunan Nongmin Yundong Xin Qushi yu Women Dui Zuopai Zhengci (Yijiuerliunian, Shiyiyue Shiwuri Xiangqu Baogao)" (Enclosure 2: The New Situation in the Hunan Peasant Movement and Our Policy toward the Left Wing [November 15, 1926]), in ZZWX, 2:324. This was an enclosure to "Zhongyang Zhengzhiju yu Guoji Daibiao Taolun Duifu Muqian Shiju zhi Jielun (Yijiuerliunian, Shiyiyue Ershiyiri)" (Conclusions of a Discussion by the Central Politburo and the Comintern Representatives about the Current Situation [November 21, 1926]), in ZZWX, 2:319–21.

163. "Fuyi: Hunan (Shiyuefen) Minxiao Yundong Baogao (Fabiao yu Yijiuerliunian Shiyiyue)" (Enclosure 1: Report on Our KMT Campaign in Hunan [October; published in November 1926]), in ZZWX, 2:321. This was an enclosure to "Zhongyang Zhengzhiju yu Guoji Daibiao Taolun Duifu Muqian Shiju zhi Jielun (Yijiuerliunian, Shiyiyue Ershiyiri)" (Conclusions of a Discussion by the Central Politburo and the Comintern Representatives about the Current Situation [November 21, 1926]), in ZZWX, 2:319–21.

164. "Fusan: Xiangqu Baogao (Er): Dui Tang Shengzhi ji Hunan Zhengzhi de Duici" (Enclosure 2: Our Response toward Tang Shengzhi and the Hunan Political Situation), in ZZWX, 2:305, dated November 14 and published in *Central Political News*. This was attached to "Duiyu Muqian Shiju de Jige Zhongyao Wenti" (Some Central Issues of the Present Day [November 9, 1926]), in ZZWX, 2:292–97.

165. Wu Jianren, "Dageming Shiqi de Jianghua Nongyun" (The Peasant Movement in Jianghua during the Great Revolution), 62–81.

166. Fairbank, Brandt, Schwartz, eds., *Documentary History*, 80–93. See also Schram, "Mao Tse-tung's Thought," in CHOC, 13:817.

167. "Mao Zedong Guanyu Gongchan Guoji Daibiao Baogao de Fayan" (Mao Zedong's Speech concerning the Report of the Comintern Representative), in Zhonggong Zhongyang Dangshi Ziliao Zhengji Weiyuanhui (CCP Central Compilation Committee for Sources for Party History) et al., eds., *Baqi Huiyi* (The August 7 Conference), 57. This is Mao's response to Lominadze's report at the conference.

168. Mao Zedong, "Zhongguo Shehui Gejieji de Fenxi (Yijiuerliunian Sanyue)" (Class Analysis of Chinese Society [March 1926]), in LDYQ, 430–31.

169. Mao Zedong, "Hunan Nongmin Yundong Kaocha Baogao (Yijiuerqinian Sanyue)" (Report on an Investigation of the Hunan Peasant Movement [March 1927]), in LDYQ, 742. The translation is from *Selected Works of Mao Tse-tung*, 1:32–33.

170. "Mao Zedong Guanyu Gongchan Guoji Daibiao Baogao de Fayan" (Mao Zedong's Speech concerning the Report of the Comintern Representative), in Zhonggong Zhongyang Dangshi Ziliao Zhengji Weiyuanhui (CCP Central Compilation Committee for Sources for Party History) et al., eds., *Baqi Huiyi* (The August 7 Conference), 57.

171. "Mao Zedong Guanyu Gongchan Guoji Daibiao Baogao de Fayan" (Mao Zedong's Speech concerning the Report of the Comintern Representative), in Zhonggong Zhongyang Dangshi Ziliao Zhengji Weiyuanhui (CCP Central Compilation Committee for Sources for Party History) et al., eds., *Baqi Huiyi* (The August 7 Conference), 58.

172. Wilbur, *Nationalist Revolution*, 127–29.

173. Wu Jianren, "Dageming Shiqi de Jianghua Nongyun" (The Peasant Movement in Jianghua during the Great Revolution), 78–81.

174. Wilbur, *Nationalist Revolution*, 59.

175. For these figures, see Zeng Chenggui, "Shilun Dageming Shiqi Dang Lingdao Nongmin Yundong de Jingyan yu Jiaoxun" (Preliminary Discussion of the Experiences and Lessons of the Party's Leadership of the Peasant Movement in Hubei during the Period of the Great Revolution), 36, 41.

176. Ibid., 39.

177. Ibid., 40–41. See also "Yijiuerqinian, Wu Liu Yuefen Hubei Gexian Nongmin Xiehui Huiyuan Tongji" (Statistics for County Peasant Associations in Hubei, May–June 1927), in Renmin Chubanshe (People's Press), ed., *Diyici Guonei Geming Zhanzheng Shiqi de Nongmin Yundong Ziliao* (Sources for the Peasant Movement during the First Period of Civil War), 461. (These statistics were first published in November 1927 in "Zhonggong Hubei Shengwei Guanyu Hubei Nongmin Baodong Jingguo de Baogao" [Report of the Hubei Provincial CCP Committee on the Peasant Uprising in Hubei].)

178. "Zuijin Hubei Nongming Yundong Gaikuang" (Survey of the Recent Peasant Movement in Hubei), in Renmin Chubanshe (People's Press), *Diyici Guonei*, 515. (These statistics were first published in November 1927 in "Zhonggong Hubei Shengwei Guanyu Hubei Nongmin Baodong Jingguo de Baogao" [Report of the Hubei Provincial CCP Committee on the Peasant Uprising in Hubei].)

179. Ibid., 518.

180. Ibid.

181. "Jiangxi Nongmin Yundong Zhuangkuang" (The Situation of the Kiangsi Peasant Movement), ibid., 523. (These statistics were first published in November 1927 in "Zhonggong Hubei Shengwei Guanyu Hubei Nongmin Baodong Jingguo de Baogao" [Report of the Hubei Provincial CCP Committee on the Peasant Uprising in Hubei].)

182. Wilbur, *Nationalist Revolution*, 59–60.

183. "Guanyu Xiang, E, Gan Sansheng Nongyun Yijuean" (Resolution on the Peasant Movement in Hunan, Hubei, and Kiangsi), in "Zhongyang Tebie Huiyi (Yijiuerliunian Shieryue)" (The Special Central Executive Committee Meeting [December 1926]), in ZZWX, 2:395.

184. Wilbur, *Nationalist Revolution*, 51, 59–60.

185. Ibid., 72–94.

186. "Zhongyang, Qu Dangtuan Lianxi Huiyi Jueyi—Guanyu Tingzhi Baodonghou de Ruokan Zhengce Wenti Bing Zuzhi Tewei Zhidao Gongzuo (Yijiuerqinian, Eryue Ershisanri)" (Resolutions of the Joint Meeting of the Central Executive Committee and the Shanghai Regional Committee [February 23, 1927]), in DSZL, 11(1982):10–11.

187. "Zhongyangju Guanyu Quanguo Zhengzhi Qingxing ji Dang de Celue de Baogao—Shi, Shiyiyuefen (Yijiuerliunian, Shieryue Wuri)" (Report on the Contemporary Political Situation in the Country and the Party's Policies—October, November [December 5, 1926]), in ZZWX, 2:366–67.

188. "Zhongyang, Qu Dangtuan Lianxi Huiyi Jueyi—Guanyu Tingzhi Baodonghou de Ruokan Zhengce Wenti Bing Zuzhi Tewei Zhidao Gongzuo (Yijiuerqinian, Eryue Ershisanri)" (Resolutions of the Joint Meeting of the Central Executive Committee and the Shanghai Regional Committee [February 23, 1927]), in DSZL, 11(1982):10–11.

189. "Zhongyangju Guanyu Quanguo Zhengzhi Qingxing ji Dang de Celue de Baogao—Shi, Shiyiyuefen (Yijiuerliunian, Shieryue Wuri)" (Report on the Contemporary Political Situation in the Country and the Party's Policies—October, November [December 5, 1926]), in ZZWX, 2:365–67.

190. For the assembly's constitution, see "Shanghai Tebieshi Linshi Gongyue Caoan (Yijiuerqinian Siyue)" (Draft Provisional Covenant of the Shanghai Special Municipality [April 1927]), in Shanghaishi Dang'anguan (Shanghai Municipal Archives), ed., *Shanghai Gongren Sanci Wuzhuang Qiyi Dang'an Shiliao Huibian* (Compilation of Archival Sources for the Three Armed Uprisings of Shanghai Workers), 440–43. For the organization of the Shanghai government the CCP proposed, see "Shanghai Tebieshi Shimin Daibiao Huiyi Zhengfu Zuzhi Tiaoli Caoan (Yijiuerqinian Sanyue)" (Draft Regulations for the Shanghai Municipal Assembly and the Municipal Government [March 1927]), 430–35. See also "Tewei Huiyi Jilu—Wuzhuang Qiyi de Zhunbei Gongzuo, Zhihui Renyuan ji Shimin Huiyi, Shi Zhengfu Mingdan (Yijiuerqinian, Sanyue Wuri Wan Jiushi)" (Minutes of a Special Committee Meeting—Preparations for the Armed Uprising, Leadership and the Citizens' Assembly, and the Slate for the Municipal Government [March 5, 1927]), in DSZL, 11(1982):17–18.

191. "Tewei Huiyi Jilu—Wuzhuang Qiyi de Zhunbei Gongzuo, Zhihui Renyuan ji Shimin Huiyi, Shi Zhengfu Mingdan (Yijiuerqinian, Sanyue Wuri Wan Jiushi)" (Minutes of a Special Committee Meeting—Preparations for the Armed Uprising, Leadership and the Citizens' Assembly, and the Slate for the Municipal Government [March 5, 1927]), in DSZL, 11(1982):13–14.

192. "Zhongyang, Qu Dangtuan Lianxi Huiyi Jueyi—Guanyu Tingzhi Baodonghou de Ruokan Zhengce Wenti Bing Zuzhi Tewei Zhidao Gongzuo (Yijiuerqinian, Eryue Ershisanri)" (Resolutions of the Joint Meeting of the Central Executive Committee and the Shanghai Regional Committee [February 23, 1927]), in DSZL, 11(1982):10.

193. "Tewei Huiyi Jilu—Wuzhuang Qiyi de Zhunbei Gongzuo, Zhihui Renyuan ji Shimin Huiyi, Shi Zhengfu Mingdan (Yijiuerqinian, Sanyue Wuri Wan Jiushi)" (Minutes of a Special Committee Meeting—Preparations for the Armed Uprising, Leadership and the Citizens' Assembly, and the Slate for the Municipal Government [March 5, 1927]), in DSZL, 11(1982):13.

194. "Tewei Huiyi Jilu—Xue Yue Jundui Liu Hu, Zhao Bing, Junxie Baozang, Jiaochadui Xiuzheng, Dui Niu Tisheng, Zhao Jing Taidu Deng Wenti (Yijiuerqinian, Sanyue Ershisanri Wan Jiushi)" (Minutes of the Special Committee Meeting—Issues Such as Keeping Xue Yue in Shanghai, Mobilizing Troops, Stocking Military Equipment, the Rectification of Pickets, and Our Attitude toward Niu Tisheng and Zhao Jing [March 23, 1927]), in DSZL, 11(1982):23.

195. Wilbur, *Nationalist Revolution*, 100–117.

196. Ibid., 109.

197. "Tewei Huiyi Jilu—Wuzhuang Qiyi de Zhunbei Gongzuo, Zhihui Renyuan ji Shimin Huiyi, Shi Zhengfu Mingdan (Yijiuerqinian, Sanyue Wuri Wan Jiushi)" (Minutes of a Special Committee Meeting—Preparations for the Armed Uprising, Leadership and the Citizens' Assembly, and the Slate for the Municipal Government [March 5, 1927]), DSZL, 11(1982):14.

198. "Tewie Huiyi Jilu—Taolun Zhongyang Dui Hu Qu Gongzuo de Jueyian (Yijiuerqinian, Siyue Shibari Xiawu Sanshi)" (Minutes of the Special Committee Meeting—Discussion of the Central Executive Committee's Meeting about Work in Shanghai [April 18, 1927]), in Shanghaishi Dang'anguan (Shanghai Municipal Archives), ed., *Shanghai Gongren Sanci Wuzhuang Qiyi Dang'an Shiliao Huibian* (Compilation of Archival Sources for the Three Armed Uprisings of Shanghai Workers), 466–67.

199. Zhao Bu, "Wuci Dahui Dao Liuci Dahui Yinianzhong Dang de Zuzhi Zhuangkuang (Yi)" (Party Organization in the Year between the Fifth and Sixth Congresses [One]), 63.

200. Ibid.

201. Cai Yichen, "Hubei Nongyun zhi Kunnan ji Zuijin Celüe—Zhaodai Xinwen Jizhe zhi Baogao" (Difficulties in the Hubei Peasant Movement and Recent Policies—Report at a News Conference), in Renmin Chubanshe (People's Press), ed., *Diyici Guonei Geming Zhanzheng Shiqi de Nongmin Yundong Ziliao* (Sources for the Peasant Movement during the First Period of Civil War), 519 (first published in the *Hankow Republican Daily* on June 12 and 13, 1927).

202. Chen Duxiu, "Chen Duxiu Zai Zhongguo Gongchandang Diwuci Quanguo Daibiao Dahuishang de Baogao (Yijiuerqinian, Siyue Ershijiuri)" (Chen Duxiu's Report at the Fifth Congress [April 29, 1927]), 49.

203. Zhao Bu, "Wuci Dahui Dao Liuci Dahui Yinianzhong Dang de Zuzhi Zhuangkuang (Yi)" (Party Organization in the Year between the Fifth and Sixth Congresses [One]), 63.

204. For data on CCP membership growth between 1925 and 1927, see Zhao Bu, "Zhongguo Gongchandang Zuzhishi Ziliao (Si)" (Sources for the Organizational History of the CCP [Four]), 82–87; "Zhongguo Gongchandang Zuzhishi Ziliao (Wu)" (Sources for the Organizational History of the CCP [Five]), 90–91; "Zhongguo Gongchandang Zuzhishi Ziliao (Liu)" (Organizational History of the CCP [Six]), 40.

205. Wilbur, *Nationalist Revolution*, 147–49.

206. Selden's *Yenan Way* argued that the mass line was a Maoist product in which the CCP's egalitarian social and economic policies mobilized the population and CCP cadres were attuned to the population, participating in production and learning from the masses. For the mass line, see also Schram, "Mao Tse-tung's Thought to 1949," in CHOC, 13:821–22. In *China's Art of Revolution*, Ristaino argued that the mass line had become a reality by the Sixth Congress of June 1928.

207. Schram, "Mao Tse-tung's Thought to 1949," in CHOC, 13:821–22.

208. Duara, *Culture, Power, and the State*.

5. THE PARTY ARISES

1. Jowitt, *Leninist Response*, 41–43.

2. Ibid., 39.

3. Ibid.

4. Zhongguo Gongchandang Zhongyang Zhixing Weiyuanhui (Central Executive Committee of the Chinese Communist Party), "Gao Quandang Dangyuan Shu" (Letter of Warning to All Party Members), in Zhonggong Zhongyang Dangshi Ziliao Zhengji Weiyuanhui (CCP Central Compilation Committee for Sources for Party History) et al., eds., *Baqi Huiyi* (The August 7 Conference), 9.

5. Ibid., 6–9.

6. Lieberthal and Oksenberg, *Policy Making in China*, 58–62; Nathan, "A Factionalism Model for CCP Politics," *China Quarterly* 103 (1973): 34–66; Tsou Tang, "Prolegomenon to the Study of Informal Groups in CCP Politics," in *Cultural Revolution*, 95–111; Pye, *Asian Power and Politics*, 182–214.

7. For the makeup of the committee, see Wang Jianying, ed., *Zhongguo Gongchandang Zuzhishi Ziliao Huibian* (Edited Source Materials for the Organizational History of the CCP), 35–36.

8. Huang Ping, *Wangshi Huiyi* (Recollections of Past Affairs), 25–26.

9. "Guanyu Xianshi Zhengju yu Gongchandang de Zhuyao Renwu Jueyian" (Resolution on the Present Political Situation and the Tasks of the Chinese Communist Party), in "Zhongyang Tebie Huiyi (Yijiuerliunian, Eryue Ershiyiri–Ershisiri)" (The Special Meeting of the Central Executive Committee [February 21–24, 1926]), in ZZWX, 2:28–32.

10. "Zhongyang Tonggao Diqishijiuhao—Guanyu Zhongyang Tebie Huiyi (Yijiuerliunian, Sanyue Shisihao)" (Central Executive Committee Announcement 79—concerning the Special Central Executive Committee Meeting [March 14, 1926]), in ZZWX, 2:46.

11. "Zhongyangju Guanyu Zuijin Quanguo Zhengzhi Qingxing yu Dang de Fazhan de Baogao (Yijiuerliunian, Jiuyue Ershihao)" (The Central Bureau's Report on Recent Political Developments in the Nation and the Growth of the Party [September 20, 1926]), in ZZWX, 2:254.

12. "Lun Guomin Zhengfu de Beifa (Yijiuerliunian, Liuyue Qiri)" (On the Northern Expedition of the Nationalist Government [June 7, 1926]), in *Chen Duxiu Wenzhang Xuanbian* (Selected Articles), 3:250–52.

13. "Gei Jiang Jieshi de Yifeng Xin (Yijiuerliunian, Liuyue Siri)" (Letter to Chiang Kai-shek [June 4, 1926]), ibid., 226–32 (originally published in *The Guide*, vol. 47, on the date in the title); "Zhongguo Gongchandang Wei Shiju yu ji Guomindang Lianhe Zhanxian Zhi Zhongguo Guomindang Shu (Yijiuerliunian, Liuyue Siri)" (Letter from the CCP to the KMT on the Present Situation and the Joint United Front with the KMT [June 4, 1926]), in ZZWX, 2:97–99. See also Xiang Qing, "Gongchan Guoji, Sulian, He Zhongshanjian Shijian" (The Comintern, the Soviet Union, and the Naval Vessel *Zhongshan* Incident), 106–9.

14. "Zhonggong Zhongyang Gei Guangdong Xin—Wang Jiang Wenti Zuihou de Jueyi" (Letter from the CCP Central Committee to Guangdong—the Final

Resolution on the Issue of Wang Jingwei and Chiang Kai-shek), in GQDTYS, 411–13, dated September 22, 1926; "Zhonggong Zhongyang Zhi Yuequ de Xin—Zhiding Zuopai Zhenggang, Cucheng Wang, Jiang Hezuo" (Letter from the CCP Central Committee to the Guangdong Region—Determining a Platform for the Left Wing and Encouraging Cooperation between Wang and Chiang), in GQDTYS, 422–26, dated September 16, 1926; "Zhongguo Gongchandang yu Guomindang Guanxi Jueyian" (Resolution on the Issue of the Relationship between the CCP and the KMT), in "Zhonggong Zhongyang Disanci Kuoda Zhixing Weiyuanhui (Yijiuyiliunian Qiyue)" (The Third Enlarged Central Executive Committee Meeting of the Chinese Communist Party [July 1926]), in ZZWX, 2:120; Qu Qiubai, "Zhongguo Gongchandang Diliuci Daibiao Dahui Zhengzhi Jueyian (Yijiuerbanian, Qiyue Jiuri)" (Resolution on Politics of the Sixth Congress of the Chinese Communist Party [August 9, 1928]), in *Qu Qiubai Xuanji* (Selected Works), 418–19; "Weijingsiji Zai Hua Huodong Jishi" (Chronology of Voitinsky's Activities in China), in Yang Yunruo et al., eds., *Weijingsiji Zai Zhongguo de Youguan Ziliao* (Source Materials for Voitinsky's Activities in China), 486.

15. "Zhongyang Zhengzhi Baogao" (Report of the Central Executive Committee), in "Zhongguo Gongchandang yu Guomindang Guanxi Wenti Jueyian" (Resolution on the Problem of the Relation between the CCP and the KMT), in "Zhongguo Gongchandang Disanci Kuoda Zhixing Weiyuanhui (Yijiuerliunian Qiyue)" (The Third Enlarged Central Executive Committee Meeting of the Chinese Communist Party [July 1926]), in ZZWX, 2:111–22.

16. "Zhonggong Zhongyang Zhi Yuequ de Xin: Zhiding Zuopai Zhenggang, Cucheng Wang, Jiang Hezuo" (Letter from the Central Bureau to the Guangdong Region: Stipulating a Political Platform for the Left Wing and Encouraging Cooperation between Wang and Chiang), in GQDTYS, 422, dated September 17, 1926.

17. "Weijingsiji Zai Hua Huodong Jishi" (Chronology of Voitinsky's Activities in China), in Yang Yunruo et al., eds., *Weijingsiji Zai Zhongguo de Youguan Ziliao* (Source Materials for Voitinsky's Activities in China), 483–87. See also reports by Stepanov in Wilbur and How, *Missionaries of Revolution*, 703–16.

18. "Stepanov's Report on the March Twentieth Incident," in Wilbur and How, *Missionaries of Revolution*, 705.

19. "Weijingsiji Zai Hua Huodong Jishi" (Chronology of Voitinsky's Activities in China), in Yang Yunruo et al., eds., *Weijingsiji Zai Zhongguo de Youguan Ziliao* (Source Materials for Voitinsky's Activities in China), 483.

20. Brandt, *Stalin's Failure*, 103, 156–57.

21. "Zhongyang Zhengzhiju Duiyu Guoji Diqici Kuodahui Zhongguo Wenti Jueyian de Jieshi" (The Central Politburo's Understanding of the Resolutions on the China Question of the Seventh Enlarged Comintern Plenum), in ZZWX, 3:12.

22. "Weijingsiji Zai Hua Huodong Jishi" (Chronology of Voitinsky's Activities in China), in Yang Yunruo et al., eds., *Weijingsiji Zai Zhongguo de Youguan Ziliao* (Source Materials for Voitinsky's Activities in China), 486.

23. Lai Xiansheng, "Zai Guangdong Geming Hongliuzhong—Huiyi 1922nian–1927nian de Douzheng" (In the Revolutionary Tide in Guangdong—Recollection of the Struggle in the 1922–1927 Period), in GDDSZL, 1:126–28.

24. Ibid., 138–139.

25. For Zhang, see Zhang Guotao, *Rise of the Chinese Communist Party*, 494, and "Weijingsiji Zai Hua Huodong Jishi" (Chronology of Voitinsky's Activities in China), in Yang Yunruo et al., eds., *Weijingsiji Zai Zhongguo de Youguan Ziliao* (Source Materials for Voitinsky's Activities in China), 486. For Peng, see Xiang Qing, "Gongchan Guoji, Sulian, He Zhongshanjian Shijian" (The Comintern, the Soviet Union, and the Naval Vessel *Zhongshan* Incident), 106–7.

26. "Zhonggong Zhongyang Gei Guangdong de Xin—Wang Jiang Wenti Zuihou de Jueyi" (Letter from the CCP Central Committee to the Guangdong Region—the Final Resolution on the Issue of Wang Jingwei and Chiang Kai-shek), in GQDTYS, 411; "Zhonggong Zhongyang Zhi Yuequ de Xin—Zhiding Zuopai Zhenggang, Cucheng Wang, Jiang Hezuo" (Letter from the CCP Central Committee to the Guangdong Region—Determining a Platform for the Left Wing and Encouraging Cooperation between Wang and Chiang), ibid., 422–26, dated September 16, 1926.

27. "Qu Qiubai You Yue Huilai Baogao: Guangdong Zhengzhi Qingkuang, Zuo, You Pai Douzheng ji Dang de Gongzuo Deng" (Qu Qiubai's Report after Returning from Guangdong: The Political Situation in Guangdong, the Struggle between the Left and Right Wings, Party Work, etc.), in GQDTYS, 415–19.

28. Ibid., 418.

29. Ibid., 419.

30. See GQDTYS, 411–95; ZZWX, 2:278–87.

31. "Zhonggong Zhongyang Zhi Yuequ de Xin—Zhiding Zuopai Zhenggang, Cucheng Wang, Jiang Hezuo" (Letter from the CCP Central Committee to the Guangdong Region—Determining a Political Platform for the Left Wing and Encouraging Cooperation between Wang and Chiang), in GQDTYS, 421–26, dated September 17, 1926.

32. Ibid., 425–26.

33. Ibid., 424.

34. "Zhonggong Zhongyang Zhi Yuequ de Xin: Guanyu Dui Guomindang Zuopai de Zhengce" (Letter from the CCP Central Bureau to the Guangdong Region: Concerning Our Policy toward the Left-Wing KMT, etc.), in GQDTYS, 449–52, undated, but according to the editor of GQDTYS, it was published in *Zhongyang Zhengzhi Tongxun* (Central Political News) on October 4, 1926.

35. "Zhonggong Zhongyang Gei Yuequ de Xin—Shiju Biandong yu Women Dui Wang, Jiang Wenti zhi Xin Jueding" (Letter from the CCP Central Committee—Changes in the Situation and Our New Decision on the Question of Wang and Chiang), in GQDTYS, 448–49, dated November 3; for an explanation of the dating, see the footnote on p. 448.

36. "Zhonggong Zhongyang zhi Yuequ Xin—Guanyu Dui Guomin Zuopai de Zhengci Deng" (Letter from the CCP Central Committee to the Guangdong Region—concerning Our Policy toward the KMT and Other Matters), in GQDTYS, 449–52; for the dating see footnote 1 on p. 449.

37. "Zhonggong Zhongyang Zhi Yuequ Xin: Guanyu Dui Guomindang Zuopai de Zhengci Deng" (Letter from the CCP Central Executive Committee to the Guangdong Region: Concerning Our Policy toward the Right-Wing KMT and Other Issues), in GQDTYS, 451; the editor of GQDTYS notes that the letter was published in the October 4, 1926, issue of *Central Executive Committee Political News* (Zhongyang Zhengzhi Tongxun).

38. Ibid.

39. Ibid., 449–52.

40. "Zhonggong Guangdong Quwei Dafu Shiyue Siri Lai Xin" (The Guangdong Regional Committee Responds to the CCP Central Bureau's Letter of October 4), in GQDTYS, 457.

41. Ibid.

42. Ibid., 458–59.

43. One document termed this a Politburo meeting, even though no CCP regulations for such an office had yet been issued (see ZZWX, 2:278 n.1). It may be that something like a Politburo had grown up informally.

44. "Fu: Yuequ Duiyu Zuopai Wenti zhi Taolun (Yijiuerliunian Shiyue)" (Supplement: A Discussion by the Guangdong Region about the Left Wing [October 1926]), in ZZWX, 2:285; in ZZWX this is a supplement to "C Tongzhi Guanyu KMT Wenti Baogao (Yijiuerliunian, Shiyue Siri)" (Comrade C's Report on the KMT Issue [November 4, 1926]), 278–84. It may have been published originally together with Chen Duxiu's statement in *Discussion of the KMT Issue*, which came out in December (see ZZWX, 2:278 n.1).

45. "C Tongzhi Guanyu KMT Wenti Baogao (Yijiuerliunian, Shiyue Siri)" (Comrade C's Report on the KMT Issue [November 4, 1926]), in ZZWX, 2:278.

46. "Zhonggong Guangdong Quwei Dafu Dang Zhongyang Shiyue Siri Lai Xin" (The Guangdong Region's Reply to the Central Bureau's Letter of October Fourth), in GQDTYS, 459, dated October 21, 1926. The Guangdong Regional Committee explained the presence of Guangdong members in Jiangxi as due to the fact that these were active within Northern Expedition forces.

47. "C Tongzhi Guanyu KMT Wenti Baogao (Yijiuerliunian, Shiyue Siri)" (Comrade C's Report on the KMT Issue [November 4, 1926]), in ZZWX, 2:278.

48. Wang Jianying, ed., *Zhongguo Gongchandang Zuzhishi Ziliao Huibian* (Edited Source Materials for the Organizational History of the CCP), 31. See also Boorman, *Biographical Dictionary*, 3:73–74.

49. Zhang Guotao, *Rise of the Chinese Communist Party*, 408–12, 486–88.

50. Wang Jianying, ed., *Zhongguo Gongchandang Zuzhishi Ziliao Huibian* (Edited Source Materials for the Organizational History of the CCP), 34.

51. "Guanyu Zhengzhi Baogao Jueyian" (Resolution on the Political Report), in "Zhongyang Tebie Huiyi (Yijiuerliunian Shieryue)" (The Special Central Executive Committee Meeting [December 1926]), in ZZWX, 2:389–90.

52. Chen Duxiu, "Zhengzhi Baogao (Yijiuerliunian, Shieryue Shisanri)" (Political Report [December 13, 1926]), in "Zhongyang Tebie Huiyi (Yijiuerliunian Shieryue)" (The Special Central Executive Committee Meeting [December 1926]), in ZZWX, 2:384.

53. Ibid., 384–85.

54. Ibid., 384.

55. Ibid.

56. Wilbur, *Nationalist Revolution*, 48.

57. Chen Duxiu, "Zhengzhi Baogao (Yijiuerliunian, Shieryue Shisanri)" (Political Report [December 13, 1926]), in "Zhongyang Tebie Huiyi (Yijiuerliunian Shieryue)" (The Special Central Executive Committee Meeting [December 1926]), in ZZWX, 2:384.

58. Ibid., 385–86.

59. "Zhonggong Zhongyang Zhi Yuequ Xin—Guanyu Guomin Zhengfu Qian Han Hou Yingfu Yuequ de Celüe" (Letter from the CCP Central Committee to the Guangdong Region—on Our Strategy in Response to the Situation in Guangdong after the Nationalist Government Moves to Wuhan), in GQDTYS, 487.

60. Ibid., 488.

61. Brandt, *Stalin's Failure*, 103–4.

62. "Gongchan Guoji Diqici Kuoda Zhixing Weiyuanhui Huiyi Zhongguo Wenti Jueyian" (Resolution on the China Question of the Seventh Enlarged Meeting of the Executive Committee of the Comintern), in ZZWX, 2:327. I have used this text on the assumption that it is the one preserved in CCP archives and therefore was the one seen by CCP members at the time.

63. Ibid., 331.

64. Ibid., 332–33. The resolutions were actually passed on December 16 (Degras, *Communist International*, 2:336–48).

65. "Gongchan Guoji Diqici Kuoda Zhixing Weiyuanhui Huiyi Zhongguo Wenti Jueyian" (Resolution on the China Question of the Seventh Enlarged Meeting of the Executive Committee of the Comintern), in ZZWX, 2:334–35.

66. Ibid., 335.

67. Ibid., 334.

68. Ibid., 336.

69. Ibid., 338.

70. "Zhongyang Zhengzhiju Duiyu Guoji Diqici Kuodahui, Zhongguo Wenti Jueyian de Jieshi" (The Central Bureau Interpretation of the "Resolution on the China Question" Passed by the Seventh Enlarged Central Executive Committee Meeting of the Comintern), in ZZWX, 3:12.

The exact timing of the arrival of the Comintern's resolutions and the formulation of the Central Bureau response is unclear. The editor of ZZWX explains in a note that the official CCP response was released somewhere between December 16 (the day the Comintern's meeting closed) and April 24 (a few days before the opening of the Fifth Congress); ZZWX, 3:12. Qu Qiubai mentioned the CCP's response in an article issued in February 1927, Qu Qiubai, "Zhongguo Gemingzhong zhi Gongchandang Dangnei Wenti (Yijiuerqinian Eryue)" (Internal Problems in the CCP during the Chinese Revolution [February 1927]), in *Qu Qiubai Xuanji* (Selected Works), 331–32. Hence, the Comintern resolutions must have arrived after December 16 but before the end of February.

71. Schwartz, *Chinese Communism*, 65–68.

72. Ibid., 59. See also Brandt, *Stalin's Failure*, ix, 87–111.

73. " 'Qu Qiubai Lunwenji' Zixu (Yijiuerqinian, Eryue Shiqiri)" (Preface to *Collected Essays of Qu Qiubai* [February 17, 1927]), in Qu Qiubai, *Qu Qiubai Xuanji* (Selected Works), 310.

74. Ibid., 311.

75. "Zhongguo Gemingzhong zhi Gongchandang Dangnei Wenti (Yijiuerqinian Eryue)" (Internal Problems in the CCP during the Chinese Revolution [February 1927]), in Qu Qiubai, *Qu Qiubai Xuanji* (Selected Works), 332.

76. E.g., Brandt, *Stalin's Failure*, 149; Schwartz, *Chinese Communism*, 71; see also *Qu Qiubai Xuanji* (Selected Works), 331, editorial footnote.

77. "Zhongguo Gemingzhong zhi Gongchandang Dangnei Wenti (Yijiuer-

qinian Eryue)'' (Internal Problems in the CCP during the Chinese Revolution [February 1927]), in *Qu Qiubai Xuanji* (Selected Works), 333.

78. Ibid., 334.

79. Ibid., 335.

80. Ibid.

81. Ibid.

82. Ibid., 336–37.

83. Ibid., 339.

84. Schwartz, *Chinese Communism*, 97–108.

85. ''Tewei Huiyi Jilu—Taolun Zhongyang Dui Huqu de Jueyian (Yijiuerqinian, Siyue Ershibari Xiawu Sanshi)'' (Minutes of the Special Committee Meeting—Discussion of the Central Committee Resolution on the Shanghai Area [April 18, 1927], in Shanghaishi Dang'anguan (Shanghai Municipal Archives), ed., *Shanghai Gongren Sanci Wuzhuang Qiyi Dang'an Shiliao Huibian* (Compilation of Archival Sources for the Three Armed Uprisings of Shanghai Workers), 467.

86. Ibid.

87. Ibid., 466.

88. ''Tewei Huiyi Jilu—Chuangda Zhongyang Dui Shanghai Wenti de Jueding ji Taolun Zhi Dian Wuhan Fan Chiang Wenti (Yijiuerqinian, Siyue Shiliuri)'' (Minutes of the Special Committee—Transmitting the Central Committee's Decisions on the Shanghai Issue and Discussion of the Telegram to Wuhan about the Question of Opposing Chiang [April 16, 1927]), ibid., 458.

89. ''Tewei Huiyi Jilu—Taolun Zhongyang Dui Huqu de Jueyian (Yijiuerqinian, Siyue Ershibari Xiawu Sanshi)'' (Minutes of the Special Committee Meeting—Discussion of the Central Committee Resolution on the Shanghai Area [April 18, 1927]), ibid., 466–67.

90. Ibid., 466.

91. Ibid., 466–69.

92. ''Mao Zedong Guanyu Gongchan Guoji Daibiao Baogao de Fayan'' (Mao Zedong's Speech concerning the Report of the Comintern Representative), in Zhonggong Zhongyang Dangshi Ziliao Zhengji Weiyuanhui (CCP Central Compilation Committee for Sources for Party History) et al., eds., *Baqi Huiyi* (The August 7 Conference), 57.

93. Mao Zedong, ''Hunan Nongmin Yundong Kaocha Baogao (Yijiuerqinian Sanyue)'' (Report on an Investigation of the Hunan Peasant Movement [March 1927]), in LDYQ, 737.

94. Qu Qiubai, *''Hunan Nongmin Geming Xu* (Yijiuerqinian, Siyue Shiyiri)'' (Foreword to *The Hunan Peasant Revolution* [April 11, 1927]), in *Qu Qiubai Xuanji* (Selected Works), 345–48; see editorial footnote on p. 345 for publication history of Mao Zedong's Hunan Report.

95. Schwartz, *Chinese Communism*, 75–78.

96. Qu Qiubai, *''Hunan Nongmin Geming Xu* (Yijiuerqinian, Siyue Shiyiri)'' (Foreword to *The Hunan Peasant Revolution* [April 11, 1927]), in *Qu Qiubai Xuanji* (Selected Works), 346.

97. Schwartz, *Chinese Communism*, 78.

98. ''Zuzhi Wenti Jueyian'' (Resolution on Organizational Questions), in ''Zhongguo Gongchandang Diwuci Quanguo Daibiao Dahui (Yijiuerqinian, Siyue zhi Wuyue)'' (The Fifth National Congress of the Chinese Communist Party

[April–May 1927]), in Zhongyang Dang'anguan (Central Committee Archives), ed., *Zhongguo Gongchandang Dierci zhi Diliuci Quanguo Daibiao Dahui Wenjian Huibian* (Compilation of Documents of the Second to Sixth National Congresses of the Chinese Communist Party), 154.

99.   Ibid.

100.   Ibid., 154–55.

101.   "Zhongguo Gongchandang Disanci Xiuzheng Zhangcheng Juean (Yijiu-erqinian, Liuyue Yiri Zhongyang Zhengzhiju Huiyi Jueyian)" (The Third Revised Party Constitution of the Chinese Communist Party [Resolution of the June 1, 1927, Meeting of the Central Politburo]), in Zhongyang Dang'anguan (Central Committee Archives), *Zhongguo Gongchandang Dierci zhi Diliuci Quanguo Daibiao Dahui Wenjian Huibian* (Compilation of Documents of the Second to Sixth Party Congresses of the Chinese Communist Party), 204.

102.   Ibid.

103.   Ibid., 199.

104.   Ibid.

105.   Wang Jianying, ed., *Zhongguo Gongchandang Zuzhishi Ziliao Huibian* (Edited Source Materials for the Organizational History of the CCP), 30.

106.   Ibid., 31.

107.   Ibid., 59–60.

108.   Ibid., 59.

109.   Ibid., 60.

110.   Ibid.

111.   Ibid.

112.   "Zhongguo Gongchandang Disanci Xiuzheng Zhangcheng Juean (Yijiu-erqinian, Liuyue Yiri Zhongyang Zhengzhiju Huiyi Jueyian)" (The Third Revised Party Constitution of the Chinese Communist Party [Resolution of the June 1, 1927, Meeting of the Central Politburo]), in Zhongyang Dang'anguan (Central Committee Archives), *Zhongguo Gongchandang Dierci zhi Diliuci Quanguo Daibiao Dahui Wenjian Huibian* (Compilation of Documents of the Second to Sixth Party Congresses), 203.

113.   Ibid., 197–99.

114.   Ibid., 198.

115.   Meisner, *Li Ta-chao*, 257–61.

116.   Li Weihan, *Huiyi yu Yanjiu* (Recollections and Studies), 1:158.

117.   Ibid.; Wang Jianying, ed., *Zhongguo Gongchandang Zuzhishi Ziliao Huibian* (Edited Source Materials for the Organizational History of the CCP), 67.

118.   Zhonggong Zhongyang Dangshi Ziliao Zhengji Weiyuanhui / Zhongyang Dang'anguan (CCP Central Compilation Committee for Sources for Party History / Central Committee Archives), "Guanyu Baqi Huiyi Ruokan Qingkuang Diaocha Baogao (Yijiubaliunian Eryue)" (Report on Investigations concerning Several Issues Related to the August 7 Conference), in Zhonggong Zhongyang Dangshi Ziliao Zhengji Weiyuanhui (CCP Central Compilation Committee for Sources for Party History) et al., eds., *Baqi Huiyi* (The August 7 Conference), 201.

119.   Li Weihan, *Huiyi yu Yanjiu* (Recollections and Studies), 1:158, 164–66.

120.   Three of the instructions the Comintern sent to the CCP in May 1927 survive. They all say more or less the same thing. See "Gongchan Guoji Guanyu Zhongguo Geming Wenti de Jige Zhishi (Jielu)" (Some Instructions of the Comin-

tern concerning the Question of the Chinese Revolution), "Gongchan Guoji Zhi-xing Weiyuanhui Jiji Zhishi (Yijiuerqinian Wuyue)" (An Urgent Instruction of the Executive Committee of the Comintern [May 1927]), in *Gongchan Guoji yu Zhongguo Geming Ziliao Xuanji (Yijiuerwunian–Yijiuerqinian)* (The Communist International and the Chinese Revolution: Selected Sources [1925–1927]), 416–17, 465, respectively.

121. "Chen Duxiu Genju Zhengzhiju Yijian zhi Gongchan Guoji Dian (Yijiu-erqinian Liuyue)" (A Telegram from Chen Duxiu to the Comintern Based on the Opinion of the Politburo [June 15, 1927]), in *Gongchan Guoji yu Zhongguo Geming Ziliao Xuanji (Yijiuerwunian–Yijiuerqinian)* (The Communist International and the Chinese Revolution: Selected Sources [1925–1927]), 508.

122. "Zhongguo Gongchandang Disanci Xiuzheng Zhangcheng Juean (Yijiu-erqinian, Liuyue Yiri Zhongyang Zhengzhiju Huiyi Jueyian)" (The Third Revised Party Constitution of the Chinese Communist Party [Resolution of the June 1, 1927, Meeting of the Central Politburo]), in Zhongyang Dang'anguan (Central Committee Archives), *Zhongguo Gongchandang Dierci zhi Diliuci Quanguo Daibiao Dahui Wenjian Huibian* (Compilation of Documents of the Second to Sixth Party Congresses), 199.

123. Wilbur, *Nationalist Revolution*, 113–49.

124. Li Weihan, *Huiyi yu Yanjiu* (Recollections and Studies), 1:158–61.

125. Ibid., 160; Zhang Guotao, *Rise of the Chinese Communist Party*, 659–63; Wang Zhixin, *Zhongguo Gongchandang Lici Zhongyao Huiyiji* (History of Several Important Meetings of the Chinese Communist Party), 81–83; Wilbur, *Nationalist Revolution*, 147–49.

126. For the Autumn Harvest uprising, see "Zhongyang Duiyu Wuhan Fan-dong Shiju zhi Tonggao (Yijiuerqinian, Qiyue Ershiqiri)" (Resolution of the Central Committee on the Reactionary Situation in Wuhan [July 24, 1927]), in ZZWX, 3:190–92, and "Zhonggong Zhongyang Guanyu Xiang-E-Yue-Gan Sisheng Nong-min Qiushou Baodong Dagang (Yijiuerqinian, Bayue Sanri)" (CCP Central Executive Committee Outline for the Autumn Harvest Peasant Uprisings of Peasants in the Four Provinces of Hunan, Hubei, Guangdong, and Jiangxi [August 3, 1927]), in ZZWX, 3:220–22; see also Nanchang Baqi Jinianguan (Museum of the August 1 Nanchang Uprising), ed., *Nanchang Qiyi* (The Nanchang Uprising).

127. "Gongchan Guoji Guanyu Zhongguo Geming Zhishi de Jige Zhishi (Jielu)" (Some Comintern Directives concerning Issues in the Chinese Revolution [Summary]), in Sun Wuxia, *Gongchan Guoji yu Zhongguo Geming Ziliao* (Sources for the Comintern and the Chinese Revolution), 2:416–17; "Extracts from the Resolution of the Eighth ECCI [Executive Committee of the Comintern] Plenum on the Chinese Question," in Degras, *Communist International*, 2:387–88. The resolutions were passed on May 30, 1927; "Gongchan Guoji Zhi-xing Weiyuanhui Jinji Zhishi (Yijiuerqinian Wuyue)" (Urgent Directive from the Executive Committee of the Comintern [May 1927]), in Sun Wuxia, *Gongchan Guoji yu Zhongguo Geming Ziliao* (Sources for the Comintern and the Chinese Revolution), 2:465–66.

128. "Zhongguo Gongchandang Zhongyang Weiyuanhui Dui Zhengju Xuan-yan (Yijiuerqinian, Qiyue Shisanri)" (CCP Central Executive Committee Views on the Current Situation [July 13, 1927]), in ZZWX, 3:180–81.

129. Ibid., 182.

130. "Guomin Geming de Muqian Xingdong Zhenggang Caoan (Yijiuerqinian, Qiyue Zhongguo Gongchandang Tichu)" (Draft for a Present Political Platform for the National Revolution [Raised by the CCP in July 1927]), in ZZWX, 3:190–92.

131. "Extracts from an ECCI [Executive Committee of the Communist International] Resolution on the Present Stage of the Chinese Revolution," in Degras, *Communist International*, 2:396.

132. "Luo Yinong Guanyu Gongchan Guoji Daibiao Baogao de Fayan" (Luo Yinong's Speech concerning the Report of the Representative of the Comintern), in Zhonggong Zhongyang Dangshi Ziliao Zhengji Weiyuanhui (CCP Central Compilation Committee for Sources for Party History) et al., eds., *Baqi Huiyi* (The August 7 Conference), 63.

133. "Gongchan Guoji Daibiao Luomingnazi de Jielun" (Concluding Remarks by the Representative of the Comintern, Lominadze), ibid., 67.

134. Zhang Guotao, *Rise of the Chinese Communist Party*, 664–69.

135. "Li Weihan, *Huiyi yu Yanjiu* (Recollections and Studies), 1:166.

136. Ibid.

137. "Cai Hesen Guanyu Gongchan Guoji Daibiao Baogao de Fayan" (Cai Hesen's Speech concerning the Report of the Representative of the Comintern), in Zhonggong Zhongyang Dangshi Ziliao Zhengji Weiyuanhui (CCP Central Compilation Committee for Sources for Party History) et al., eds., *Baqi Huiyi* (The August 7 Conference), 61–62.

138. Ibid., 61.

139. Ibid., 61–62.

140. "Deng Zhongxia Guanyu Gongchan Guoji Daibiao Baogao de Fayan" (Deng Zhongxia's Speech concerning the Report of the Comintern's Representative), ibid., 59. For similar statements by Luo Yinong and Ren Bishi, ibid., 63–64, 65–66.

141. "Cai Hesen Guanyu Gongchan Guoji Daibiao Baogao de Fayan" (Cai Hesen's Speech concerning the Report of the Representative of the Comintern), ibid., 62.

142. Chen Qiaonian served as head of the Organization Department of the Peking Regional Executive Committee and later served as vice-head of the Central Organization Department (Wang Jianying, ed., *Zhongguo Gongchandang Zuzhishi Ziliao Huibian* [Edited Source Materials for the Organizational History of the CCP], 23, 41, 61). In Guangdong, Chen Yannian was the secretary of the Guangdong Regional Executive Committee.

143. Yang Shaolian et al., "Chen Yannian," 177.

144. "Ren Bishi Guanyu Gongchan Guoji Daibiao Baogao de Fayan" (Ren Bishi's Speech concerning the Report of the Representative of the Comintern), in Zhonggong Zhongyang Dangshi Ziliao Zhengji Weiyuanhui (CCP Central Compilation Committee for Sources for Party History) et al., eds., *Baqi Huiyi* (The August 7 Conference), 66.

145. "Mao Zedong Guanyu Gongchan Guoji Baogao de Fayan" (Mao's Speech concerning the Report of the Representative of the Comintern), ibid., 57.

146. "Luo Yinong Guanyu Gongchan Guoji Daibiao Baogao de Fayan" (Luo Yinong's Speech concerning the Report of the Representative of the Comintern), ibid., 63.

147. "Zhongguo Gongchandang Zhongyang Zhixing Weiyuanhui Gao Quandang Dangyuanshu" (Letter of Warning to All Members of the Party from the Central Executive Committee of the Chinese Communist Party), ibid., 9.

148. Ibid., 10.

149. Ibid., 13.

150. Ibid., 8.

151. Ibid., 9.

152. Ibid.

153. "Zuijin Nongmin Douzheng de Yijuean" (Resolution on the Struggle of the Peasantry), ibid., 39.

154. Ibid.

155. "Zuijin Zhigong Yundong Yijuean" (Resolution on the Recent Labor Movement), ibid., 41.

156. "Dang de Zuzhi Wenti Jueyian" (Resolution on Organizational Issues in the Party), ibid., 46.

157. Ibid.

158. "Gongchan Guoji Daibiao Luomingnazi de Baogao" (The Report of the Representative of the Comintern, Lominadze), ibid., 49–50.

159. "Dang de Zuzhi Wenti Jueyian" (Resolution on Organizational Issues in the Party), ibid., 44.

160. "Mao Zedong Guanyu Nongmin Douzheng Jueyi de Fayan" (Mao Zedong's Speech concerning the Resolution on the Peasant Struggle), ibid., 73.

161. "Gongchan Guoji Daibiao Luomingnazi Guanyu Nongmin Douzheng Jueyian de Fayan" (Speech of Lominadze concerning the Resolution on the Peasant Struggle), ibid., 74.

162. Zhonggong Zhongyang Dangshi Ziliao Zhengji Weiyuanhui / Zhongyang Dang'anguan (CCP Central Compilation Committee for Sources for Party History / Central Committee Archives), "Guanyu Baqi Huiyi Ruokan Qingkuang Diaocha Baogao (Yijiubaliunian Eryue)" (Report on Investigations concerning Several Issues Related to the August 7 Conference), ibid., 200.

163. "Hunan Zhi Zhongyang Han (Yijiuerqinian, Bayue Ershiri)" (Communication from Hunan to the Central Committee [August 20, 1927]), supplement to "Zhongyang Fu Hunan Shengwei Han (Yijiuerqinian, Bayue Ershisanri)" (The Central Committee Replies to a Communication of the Hunan Provincial Committee [August 23, 1927]), in ZZWX, 3:303.

164. Schapiro, *Communist Party*, 54–70. This was a time of infighting among Russian communists, the Social Democrats divided between Menshevik and Bolshevik camps.

165. "Zhongyang Fu Hunan Shengwei Han (Yijiuerqinian, Bayue Ershisanri)" (The Central Committee Replies to a Communication of the Hunan Provincial Committee [August 23, 1927]), in ZZWX, 3:301.

166. Ibid., 302.

Selected Bibliography

Action Bolchevik à Shanghai (Bolshevism in Shanghai). Shanghai: French Consulate-General, 1926–?.

Alitto, Guy. *The Last Confucian: Liang Shu-ming and the Chinese Dilemma of Modernity*. Berkeley: University of California Press, 1979.

Averill, Stephen. "Party, Society, and Local Elite in the Jiangxi Communist Movement." *Journal of Asian Studies* 46 (May 1987): 279–304.

Bakulin, A. B. *Zhongguo Dageming Wuhan Shiqi Jianwenlu: (Yijiuerwunian–Yijiuerqinian Zhongguo Dageming Zhaji)* (Diaries and Impressions of Wuhan during the Great Chinese Revolution: [Notes and Writings during the Great Chinese Revolution, 1925–1927]), tr. Zheng Haoan et al. Bejing: Chinese Academy of Social Sciences Press, 1985.

Bailey, Paul. "The Chinese Work-Study Movement in France." *China Quarterly* 115 (September 1988): 441–61.

Bao Huiseng. *Bao Huiseng Huiyilu* (Memoirs of Bao Huiseng). Beijing: People's Press, 1981.

Beijing Daxue Shehui Kexuechu (Social Sciences Group, Peking University), ed. *Beijing Daxue Jinian Gongchandang Chengli Liushi Zhounian Lunwenji* (Articles in Commemoration of the Sixtieth Anniversary of the Founding of the Chinese Communist Party). Beijing: Peking University Press, 1981.

Berlin, Isaiah. *Karl Marx: His Life and Environment*. New York: Oxford University Press, 1959.

Bianco, Lucian. *Origins of the Chinese Revolution, 1915–1949*, tr. Muriel Bell. Stanford: Stanford University Press, 1971.

———. "Peasant Movements." In CHOC, 13:270–328.

Bing, Dov. "Sneevliet and the Early Years of the CCP." *China Quarterly* 48 (October-November 1971): 677–97.

Boorman, H., et al., eds. *Biographical Dictionary of Republican China*. 5 vols. New York: Columbia University Press, 1967–1971.

Brandt, Conrad. *Stalin's Failure in China: 1924–1927*. Cambridge: Harvard University Press, 1958.

Brandt, Conrad, Benjamin Schwartz, and John K. Fairbank, eds. *A Documentary History of Chinese Communism*. New York: Atheneum, 1971.

Cai Hesen. *Cai Hesen de Shierbian Wenzhang* (Twelve Essays by Cai Hesen). Beijing: People's Press, n.d. (editorial postscript dated 1979).

———. *Cai Hesen Wenji* (Collected Works of Cai Hesen), ed. Liang Dawei. Beijing: People's Press, 1980.

———. "Wudang Chansheng de Beijing ji qi Lishi Shiming: (Yijiuerliunian)" (The Background of the Birth of Our Party and Its Historical Mission: [1926]). In YDQHGD, 28–70.

Cai Yuanpei. *Cai Yuanpei Quanji* (Collected Works of Cai Yuanpei). Taibei: Wang-jia Press, 1975.

Carr, E. H. *The Russian Revolution: From Lenin to Stalin*. New York: Free Press, 1979.

Chan, Gilbert. *China at the Cross-Roads: Nationalists and Communists, 1927–1949*. Boulder, Colo.: Westview Press, 1980.

Chang Hao. *Liang Ch'i-ch'ao and Intellectual Transition in China, 1890–1907*. Cambridge: Harvard University Press, 1971.

———. *Chinese Intellectuals in Crisis: The Search for Meaning and Order*. Berkeley: University of California Press, 1987.

———. "Intellectual Change and the Reform Movement: 1890–1898." In CHOC, 11:274–338.

Chang Kuo-t'ao: see Zhang Guotao.

Chang P'eng-yuan. "The Constitutionalist." In M. C. Wright, *China in Revolution*, 143–84.

Changshashi Geming Jinian Difang Bangongshi/Anyuan Lukuang Gongren Yundong Jinianguan (Changsha Office of Memorial Sites for the Revolution/Memorial Museum for the Labor Movement of Anyuan Railroad and Mine Workers), ed. *Anyuan Lukuang Gongren Yundong Shiliao* (Historical Sources for the Labor Movement of Anyuan Railroad and Mine Workers). Changsha: Hunan People's Press, 1980.

Chen Baoting, ed. *Zhonggong Dangshi Renwu Bieminglu* (Pseudonyms of People in CCP Party History). Beijing: Red Flag Press, 1985.

Chen Duxiu. *Chen Duxiu Xiansheng Jiangyanlu* (Chen Duxiu's Lectures). Guang-zhou: Dingbu Press, 1923.

———. *Chen Duxiu Zuihou Duiyu Minzhu Zhengzhi de Jianjie* (Chen Duxiu's Final Views on Democratic Government). Hong Kong: Free China Press, 1950.

———. *Ziyi Leili* (An Illustrated Classification of Characters and Their Meaning). Shanghai: East Asian Press, 1925; repr. Hong Kong: Shixian Press, 1970.

———. "Chen Duxiu Zai Zhongguo Gongchandang Diwuci Quanguo Daibiao Dahuishang de Baogao: (Yijiuerqinian, Siyue Ershijiuri)" (Chen Duxiu's Report at the Fifth National Congress of the Chinese Communist Party: [April 29, 1927]). In *Zhonggong Dangshi Ziliao* (Sources for CCP Party History) 3 (1982): 26–59.

———. "Jinfenlei Wushiliushou" (Golden Tears: 56 Poems). In DSZL 16 (1983): 122–51.

———. *Chen Duxiu Wenzhang Xuanbian* (Selected Articles by Chen Duxiu), ed. Lin Maosheng et al. 3 vols. Beijing: Sanlian Press, 1984.

Chen Gongbo [Ch'en Kung-po]. *The Communist Movement in China*, ed. Martin Wilbur. New York: East Asian Studies Institute, Columbia University, 1960.

———. "Wo yu Gongchandang: (Yijiusiliunian)" (The Communist Party and I: [1946]). In YDQHGD, 80–112.

Chen Honglu. *Zhongguo Jindaishi Ziliao Gaishu* (Overview of Materials for Modern Chinese History). Beijing: Zhonghua Shuju, 1982.

Chen, Jeromeh. "The Chinese Communist Movement to 1927." In J. K. Fairbank, ed., *The Cambridge History of China*. Vol. 12, *Republican China (1912–1949), Part 1*. Cambridge: Cambridge University Press, 1983, 505–26.

Chen Min, ed. *Zhongguo Zhigongdang* (Chinese Party for Justness). Beijing: Wenshi Ziliao (Sources for History and Civilization) Press, 1981.

Chen Shaokang. "Jieshao 'Xin Shidai Congshu' She he 'Xin Shidai Congshu' " (An Introduction to the Society for the "New Age Collection of Writings" and the "New Age Collection of Writings"). DSYJZL 5 (1985): 451–57.

Chen Shiping. "Zhonggong Chongqing Diwei de Jianli" (The Founding of the Chongqing Local Committee). In DSYJZL 4 (1983): 221–33.

Chen Tianxi, ed. *Dai Jitao Xiansheng Wencun Zaixubian* (Second Revised Edition of Dai Jitao's Extant Writings). Taibei: Taiwan Commercial Press, 1968.

Chen Wangdao. *Chen Wangdao Wenji* (Collected Works of Chen Wangdao), ed. Fudan Daxue Yuyan Yanjiushi (Linguistics Institute, Fudan University). Shanghai: People's Press, 1981.

Ch'en Yung-fa. "Rural Elections in Wartime Central China: The Democratization of the Sub-Bureaucracy." *Modern China* 6:2 (July 1980): 267–310.

———. *Making Revolution: The Communist Movement in Eastern and Central China, 1937–1945*. Berkeley: University of California Press, 1986.

Chen Zhiwen. "Zhongguo Gongchandang Zai Guangdong Diqu Jiandang Chuqi de Yixie Ziliao" (Some Sources for Early Party-Building Activities in the Guangdong Area). In *Guangzhou Wenshi Ziliao* (Sources for History and Culture in Guangzhou) 17 (1979):1–19.

———. "Dageming Shiqi Guangzhou Gongren Yundong" (The Workers' Movement in Guangzhou at the Time of the Great Revolution). *Guangzhou Wenshi Ziliao Xuanji* (Compiled Sources for the History and Culture of Guangzhou) 21 (December 1980): 1–45.

Ch'eng I-fan. "Kung as Ethos in Late Nineteenth Century China: The Case of Wang Hsien-ch'ien (1842–1918)." In Cohen and Schrecker, eds., *Reform in Nineteenth Century China*, 170–80.

Cherapanov, A. *Notes of a Military Advisor in China*, tr. Alexander Smith. Taibei: Office of Military History, 1970.

Chesneaux, Jean. *The Chinese Labor Movement*. Stanford: Stanford University Press, 1968.

———. *Secret Societies in China*, tr. G. Nettle. Ann Arbor: University of Michigan Press, 1971.

Ch'i Hsi-sheng. *Nationalist China at War*. Ann Arbor: University of Michigan Press, 1982.

Chow Tse-tsung. *The May Fourth Movement: Intellectual Revolution in Modern China*. Stanford: Stanford University Press, 1967.

Chuhui (Hubei's Light): Hubei People's Press.

Clifford, Nicholas. *Shanghai, 1925: Urban Nationalism and the Defense of Foreign Privilege*. Ann Arbor: Center for Chinese Studies, University of Michigan, 1979.

Clopton, Robert, and Tsuin-chen Ou. *John Dewey: Lectures in China, 1919–1920*. Honolulu: East-West Center, 1973.

Coble, Parks. *The Shanghai Capitalists and the Nationalist Government, 1927–1933*. Cambridge: Harvard University Press, 1980.

Cohen, Paul. *Discovering History in China: American Historical Thinking on the Chinese Past*. New York: Columbia University Press, 1984.

———. "The Post-Mao Reforms in Historical Perspective." *Journal of Asian Studies* 47 (August 1988): 518–40.

Cohen, Paul, and John Schrecker, eds. *Reform in Nineteenth Century China*. Cambridge: Harvard University Press, 1976.

Dai Maolin. *Wuzhengfuzhuyizhe Canjia Beijing Gongchanzhuyi Xiaozu de Yuanyin* (The Reasons for the Participation of Anarchists in the Peking Communist Cell). In DSYJ 3 (May 1986): 50–54.

Dalin, A. C. *Zhongguo Huiyilu, 1921–1927* (Recollections of China, 1921–1927), tr. Li Yuzhen. Foreword dated 1980, date and place of publication unknown; Russian original published in 1975.

Dangbao (The Party Journal).

Dangshi Xinxi (News in Party History). Shanghai: Shanghaishi Dangshi Xuehui (Shanghai Study Society for Party History) and Kongjun Zhengzhi Xueyuan (Political Academy of the Air Force).

Dangshi Yanjiu (Party History Research). Zhonggong Zhongyang Dangxiao *Dangshi Yanjiu* Bianjibu (Central Party School, Editorial Board of *Dangshi Yanjiu*).

Dangshi Yanjiu Ziliao (Source Materials for and Research on Party History). Zhongguo Geming Bowuguan Dangshi Yanjiushi (Party History Section of the Museum of the Chinese Revolution).

Dangshi Ziliao (Source Materials for Party History). *Dangshi Ziliao* Bianjibu (Editorial Board for *Dangshi Ziliao*).

de Bary, Wm. Theodore, ed. *The Unfolding of Neo-Confucianism*. New York: Columbia University Press, 1975.

Degras, Jane, ed. *The Communist International, 1919–1943: Documents*. London: Oxford University Press, 1960.

Deng Zhongxia. *Deng Zhongxia Wenji* (Collected Works of Deng Zhongxia). Beijing: People's Press, 1983.

Ding Shouhe and Yin Xuyi. *Cong Wusi Qimeng Yundong Dao Makesizhuyi de Chuanbo* (From the May Fourth Enlightenment Movement to the Dissemination of Marxism). Beijing: Sanlian Press, 1983.

Dirlik, Arif. *The Origins of Chinese Communism*. Oxford: Oxford University Press, 1989.

———. *Revolution and History: The Origins of Marxist Historiography in China, 1919–1937*. Berkeley: University of California Press, 1978.

———. "Culture, Society, and Revolution: A Critical Discussion of American Studies of Modern Chinese Thought." In *Working Papers in Asian/Pacific Studies*. Duke, 1985.

Dittmer, Lowell. *China's Continuous Revolution: The Post-Liberation Epoch, 1949–1981*. Berkeley: University of California Press, 1987.

Dong Biwu. "Guanyu 'Yida' De Huiyi—Dong Biwu Gei He Shuheng de Xin: (Yijiuerjiunian, Shieryue Sanshiyiri)" (Recollections Concerning the First Congress—a Letter from Dong Biwu to He Shuheng: [December 31, 1929]). In *Zhonggong Dangshi Ziliao* (Sources for CCP Party History) 3 (1982): 1–2.

———. *Dong Biwu Xuanji* (Selected Works of Dong Biwu). Beijing: Xinhua Shuju, 1985.

Du Weihua. *Zhou Enlai Tongzhi Shengping Huodong Nianbiao: 1898 Nian–1976 Nian* (Chronology of Activities of Comrade Zhou Enlai: 1898–1976). Beijing: Zhongguo Geming Bowuguan (Museum of the Chinese Revolution), 1980.

Du Weihuan. *"Zhonggong Dangshi Dashi Nianbiao* Fanying de Pufen Xin Guandian" (Some New Standpoints as Reflected in *A Chronology of CCP History*). *Shehui Kexue Cankao* (Social Science Review) (March 1983): 23–28.

Du Zhonglin et al. "Yijiuerlingnian Zhi Yijiuerjiunian Hubei Dang Zuzhi Gaikuang" (Survey of Party Organization in Hubei from 1920 to 1929), DSYJ 3 (1981), 70–72.

Duara, Prasenjit. *Culture, Power, and the State: Rural North China, 1900–1942*. Stanford: Stanford University Press, 1988.

Eastman, Lloyd E. *The Abortive Revolution: China under Nationalist Rule, 1927–1937*. Cambridge: Harvard University Press, 1974.

———. *Seeds of Destruction: Nationalist China in War and Revolution, 1937–1949*. Stanford: Stanford University Press, 1984.

Elman, Benjamin. *From Philosophy to Philology: Intellectual and Social Aspects of Change in Late Imperial China*. Cambridge: Council on East Asian Studies, Harvard University, 1984.

Elvin, Mark. *The Pattern of the Chinese Past*. Stanford: Stanford University Press, 1973.

Esherick, J. *Reform and Revolution in China: The 1911 Revolution in Hunan and Hubei*. Berkeley: University of California Press, 1976.

E-tu Zen-sun. "The Growth of the Academic Community." In CHOC, 13:361–420.

Fairbank, John, ed. *Cambridge History of China*, vols. 10–14. Cambridge: Cambridge University Press, 1978–1987.

———. "The Creation of the Treaty System." In CHOC, 10:213–63.

Feigon, Lee. *Chen Duxiu: Founder of the Chinese Communist Party*. Lawrenceville: Princeton University Press, 1983.

Feng Shoucai. "Shanghai Gongren Disanci Wuzhuang Qiyi de Zuzhi Lingdao Jiguang Gaikuang" (Survey of Organization and Leadership of the Third Shanghai Armed Uprising). DSZL 24 (1985): 73–76.

Fidlon, David, tr. *Soviet Volunteers in China*. Moscow: Progress Publishers, 1980.

Fincher, John. "Provincialism and National Revolution." In Mary Wright, ed., *China in Revolution*, 186–226.

Fogel, Joshua. *Ai Ssu-ch'i's Contribution to the Development of Chinese Marxism*. Harvard Contemporary China Series, 4. Cambridge: Harvard University Press, 1987.

Friedman, Edward. *Backward Toward Revolution: The Chinese Revolutionary Party*. Berkeley: University of California Press, 1974.

Fung Yu-lan. *A History of Chinese Philosophy*, tr. Derk Bodde. Princeton: Princeton University Press, 1953.

Furth, Charlotte, ed. *The Limits of Change*. Cambridge: Harvard University Press, 1976.

———. *Ting Wen-chiang: Science and China's New Culture*. Cambridge: Harvard University Press, 1970.

Galbiati, Fernando. *P'eng P'ai and the Hai-Lu-Feng Soviet*. Stanford: Stanford University Press, 1985.

Gamble, Sidney. *Ting Hsien: A North China Rural Community*. Stanford: Stanford University Press, 1968.

Gasster, Michael. "The Republican Revolutionary Movement." In CHOC, 11:463–534

Geertz, Clifford. "Ideology as a Cultural System." In *The Interpretation of Cultures*. New York: Basic Books, 1973.

Ge Gongzhen. "Zhongguo Baozhi Jinhua zhi Gaiguan" (An Overview of the Modernization of Chinese Periodicals). In Zhang Jinglu, 4:10–21.

Gemingshi Ziliao (Sources for the History of the Revolution): Shanghai People's Press.

Glunin. "The Comintern and the Rise of the Communist Movement in China: (1920–1927)." In R. A. Ulyanovsky, *The Comintern and the East*, 280–344.

Gongchan Guoji yu Zhongguo Geming Ziliao Xuanji: (Yijiuererwunian–Yijiuerqinian) (The Comintern and the Chinese Revolution: Selected Sources [1925–1927]). Bejing: People's Press, 1985.

Gongchandang Yijiuerliunian–Yijiusanyinian Nei Wenji (Collection of Discussions of the Chinese Communist Party, 1926–1931). Zhongguo Kexue Yanjiuyuan (Chinese Academy of Social Sciences)?, Foreword 1932. KMT Archives 200.4 2900/57947.

Gongchandang Yuekan (The Communist Party Monthly).

Gongdang Wenti Yanjiu (Studies in Communism), ed. *Gongdang Wenti Yanjiu Zazhishe Bianji Weiyuanhui* (Editorial Committee of the Society for Magazine *Studies in Communism*). Taibei: Investigation Department, Ministry of Justice.

Grieder, Jeromeh. *Hu Shih and the Chinese Renaissance: Liberalism and the Chinese Revolution, 1917–1933*. Cambridge: Harvard University Press, 1970.

———. *Intellectuals and the State in Modern China: A Narrative History*. New York: Free Press, 1981.

Gu Shigu. "Gu Shigu Tongzhi Huiyi Ershiniandai de Geming Jingli" (Comrade Gu Shigu Remembers the Revolutionary Events of the Twenties). In *Sichuan Wenshi Ziliao Xuanji* (Compiled Sources for History and Culture in Sichuan), vol. 34. Chengdu: Sichuan People's Press, 1983.

Guangdong Dangshi Ziliao (Source Materials for Party History in Guangdong) vols. 1, 2. Zhonggong Guangdong Shengwei Dangshi Ziliao Zhengji Weiyuanhui (Editorial Committee for Source Materials for Party History, Guangdong Provincial Committee of the CCP), Zhonggong Guangdong Shengwei Dangshi Yanjiu Weiyuanhui (Research Committee for Party History, Guangdong Provincial Committee of the CCP).

Guangdong Geming Lishi Bowuguan (Guangdong Museum of Revolutionary History). *Guangzhou Qiyi Ziliao* (Materials concerning the Canton Uprising). Guangzhou: Guangdong People's Press, 1985.

Guangdong Qunbao (The Guangdong Masses), ed. Zhonggong Guangdongsheng Dangshi Yanjiu Weiyuanhui Bangongshi (Office of the Party History Research Committee of the CCP Guangdong Provincial Committee). (Undated manuscript.)

Guangdong Zhexue Shehui Kexue Yanjiusuo Lishi Yanjiushi (Department of History, Guangdong Institute for Philosophy and Social Science). *Shenggang Dabagong Ziliao* (Sources for the Great Canton–Hong Kong Strike). Guangzhou: Guangdong People's Press, 1980.

Guangdongsheng Dang'anguan (Guangdong Provincial Archives) and Guangdong Shengwei Dangshi Yanjiu Weiyuanhui Bangongshi (Office of the Party History Research Committee of the Guangdong Provincial Committee), eds. *Guangdongqu Dang, Tuan Yanjiu Shiliao (1921–1926)* (Source Materials for Research on the History of the Party and the Socialist Youth League in the Guangdong Region [1921–1926]). Guangzhou: Guangdong People's Press, 1983.

Guangzhou Nongmin Yundong Jiangxisuo Jiuchi Jinianguan (Museum of the Original Site of the Peasant Movement Training Institute in Canton), ed. *Guangdong Nongmin Yundong Ziliao Xuanbian* (A Compilation of Sources of the Guangdong Peasant Movement). Beijing: People's Press, 1986.

Guillermaz, Jacques. *A History of the Chinese Communist Party, 1921–1949.* London: Methuen, 1968.

Guo Chengxiang. "Diyici Guo-gong Hezuo Dashiji" (Chronology of the First Period of CCP and KMT Cooperation). In *Guangdong Dangshi Tongxun* (Guangdong Party History News), 42–67. N.p.

Guo Hualun. *Zhonggong Shilun* (On the History of the Chinese Communist Party). Taibei: Zhengzhi Daxue (Public Administration University) Press, 1982.

"Guomindang Shanghai Zhishibu Shiliao Xuanji" (Selected Historical Sources for the Shanghai Executive Branch of the KMT). DSZL 18 (1984): 129–39.

Guy, R. Kent. *The Emperor's Four Treasures: Scholars and the State in the Late Ch'ien-lung Era.* Cambridge: Harvard University Press, 1987.

Harrison, James. *The Long March to Power: A History of the Chinese Communist Party, 1921–1977.* New York: Praeger, 1972.

Hatano Ken'ichi. *Chūgoku Kyōsantō Shi.* Tokyo: Jiji Press, 1961.

He Boli. "Huzhou Chuannan Shifan Shihua" (Historical Anecdotes concerning the South Sichuan Normal School in Huzhou). In *Sichuan Wenshi Ziliao Xuanji* (Compilation of Materials for History and Culture in Sichuan) 33 (1984): 170–74.

He Chunxi. "Mao Zedong Zai Lingdao Qiushou Qiyizong Dui Dang de Sixiang Lilun Gongxian" (Mao Zedong's Contributions to Party Thought and Theory during the Autumn Harvest Uprising). DSYJ 6 (December 1983): 17–23.

He Ganzhi. *Zhongguo Xiandai Gemingshi* (History of the Contemporary Chinese Revolution). Beijing: People's Press, 1956.

He Guilin. "Guanyu 'Sida' Pingjiazhong Liangge Juti Wenti de Tantao" (Inquiry into Two Concrete Issues in Evaluations of the "Fourth Congress"). DSYJ 1 (February 1983): 49–54.

He Mengxiong. *He Mengxiong Wenji* (Collected Works of He Mengxiong), ed. Lu Zunwang et al. Beijing: Xinhua Shuju, 1980.

He Mianzhou and Sha Dongxun. "Guangdong Zuichu Gongchandang Zuzhi zhi Yanjiu" (Research on the First Party Organization in Guangdong). In Zhu Chengjia, 157–69.

Hebeisheng Zhengxie Wenshi Ziliao Yanjiu Weiyuanhui / Baodingshi Zhengxie Wenshi Ziliao Yanjiu Weiyuanhui (Committee on Research and Sources for History and Civilization, Hebei Political Consultative Conference / Committee on Research and Sources for History and Civilization, Baoding Political Consultative Conference), eds. *Baoding Lujun Junguan Xuexiao* (The Baoding Army Officers Academy). Shijiazhuang: Hebei People's Press, 1987.

Herschatter, Gail. *The Workers of Tianjin, 1900–1949*. Stanford: Stanford University Press, 1986.

Hersey, John. *The Call*. New York: Viking (Penguin Books), 1986.

Ho Pingti and Tang Tsou, eds. *China in Crisis*. Vol. 1, *China's Heritage and the Communist Political System*. Chicago: University of Chicago Press, 1968.

Hofheinz, Roy. *The Broken Wave: The Chinese Communist Peasant Movement*. Cambridge: Harvard University Press, 1977.

Honig, Emily. *Sisters and Strangers: Women in the Shanghai Cotton Mills*. Stanford: Stanford University Press, 1986.

How, Julie Lien-ying. "Soviet Advisors with the Kuominchun, 1925–1926: A Documentary Study." *Chinese Studies in History* 19:1–2 (Fall–Winter 1985–1986).

Hsia Tsi-an. *The Gate of Darkness: Studies on the Leftist Literary Movement*. Seattle: University of Washington Press, 1968.

Hsiung, James. *Ideology and Practice: The Evolution of Chinese Communism*. New York: Praeger, 1972.

Hu Daojing. *Shanghai Xinwen Shiye Shiliao Jiyao* (Compilation of Important Historical Sources for the Shanghai News Profession), ed. Fang Shiduo. Taibei: Tianyi (Universal Unity) Press, n.d.

Hu Hua, ed. *Zhonggong Dangshi Renwuzhuan* (Biographies of Outstanding People in the History of the Chinese Communist Party). Xi'an: Shenxi People's Press. (Many volumes forthcoming.)

———. *Zhongguo Xinminzhuzhuyi Gemingshi* (History of the Chinese New Democratic Revolution). Beijing: People's Press, 1950.

Hu Qiaomu. *Zhongguo Gongchandang de Sanshinian* (Thirty Years of the Chinese Communist Party). Beijing: People's Press, 1951.

Hu Qingyun. "Hunan Gongchanzhuyizhe de Jiandang Huodong" (How the Hunan Communists Founded the Party). DSYJ 1 (1980): 60–62.

Hu Shengming. "Dui 'Zhonggong Chongqing Diwei de Jianli' Yiwen de Puyun" (Addendum to "The Founding of the Chongqing Local Committee"). DSYJZL 5 (1985): 357–65.

Huang, Philip. *Liang Ch'i-ch'ao and Modern Chinese Liberalism*. Seattle: University of Washington Press, 1972.

Huang Ping. *Wangshi Huiyi* (Recollections of Past Affairs). Beijing: People's Press, 1981.

Huang Xianmeng. "Guanyu 'Yida' Qian de Hunan Gongchandang Xiaozu Wenti" (The Hunan CCP Cell before the First Congress). In Zhu Chengjia, *Zhonggong Dangshi Yanjiu Lunwenxuan* (Selected Research Articles on the History of the Chinese Communist Party), 1:120–26.

Hubeisheng Shehui Kexueyuan Lishi Yanjiusuo (History Institute, Hubei Provincial Academy of Sciences), ed. *Hankou, Jiujiang Shouhui Yingzujie Ziliao Xuanbian* (Compilation of Sources for the Repossession of the British Concessions in Hankou and Kiukiang). Wuhan: Hubei People's Press, 1982.

Hunansheng Zhexue Shehui Kexue Yanjiusuo Xiandaishi Yanjiushi (Contemporary History Research Section, Hunan Provincial Research Institute for Philosophy and Social Science), ed. *Wusi Shiqi Hunan Renmin Geming Douzheng Shiliao Xuanbian* (Compilation of Historical Sources for Revolutionary Struggles of the People in Hunan during the May Fourth Period). Changsha: Hunan People's Press, 1979.

Iriye, Akira. *The Chinese and the Japanese: Essays in Political and Cultural Interaction.* Princeton: Princeton University Press, 1980.

Isaacs, Harold. *The Tragedy of the Chinese Revolution.* 2d ed. Stanford: Stanford University Press, 1961.

Jacobs, Daniel. *Borodin: Stalin's Man in China.* Cambridge: Harvard University Press, 1981.

Jiang Changren. *San.Yiba Can'an Ziliao Huibian* (Compilation of Sources for the March Eighteenth Incident). Beijing: Peking Press, 1985.

Jiang Peinan. "Wusa Yundong Qianhou Huxi Gongren de Geming Douzheng—Zhonen Niko Changshi Xuanzai" (The Revolutionary Struggle of the West Shanghai Workers at the Time of the May Thirtieth Movement—Selected Documents Concerning the History of the Number Two Shanghai Factory). *Wenshi Ziliao Xuanbian* (Compilation of Sources for History and Culture) 22 (1978): 1–52.

Jiang Weixin. "Cong Eryue Bagong Dao Wusa Yundong" (From the February Strike to the May Thirtieth Movement). *Wenshi Ziliao Xuanji* (Selection of Sources for History and Culture) 3 (1980, Shanghai): 41–50.

Jiang Yongjing. *Bao Luoting yu Wuhan Zhengquan* (Borodin and the Wuhan Government). Taibei: Zhuanji Wenxue Chubanshe (Biographical Literature Press), 1972.

———, ed. *Beifa Shiqi de Zhengzhi Shiliao—Yijiuerqinian de Zhongguo* (Historical Sources for Politics in the Period of the Northern Expedition—China in 1927). Taibei: Zhongzheng Press, 1981.

Jindaishi Yanjiu (Research on Modern History). *Jindaishi Yanjiu* Bianji Weiyuanhui (Editorial Committee for *Research on Modern History*).

Jindaishi Ziliao (Materials for Modern History). Zhongguo Shehui Kexue Yanjiuyuan Jindaishi Yanjiusuo (Institute of Modern History, Chinese Academy of Social Sciences).

Johnson, Chalmers. *Peasant Nationalism and Communist Power: The Emergence of Revolutionary China, 1937–1945.* Stanford: Stanford University Press, 1962.

———, ed. *Ideology and Politics in Contemporary China.* Seattle: University of Washington Press, 1973.

Jowitt, K. *The Leninist Response to National Dependency.* Berkeley: University of California Press, 1978.

Juewu (The Awakening). Supplement of *Minguo Ribao* (The Republican Daily).

Kagan, Richard. *The Chinese Trotskyist Movement and Ch'en Tu-hsiu: Culture, Revolution and Party.* Ph.D. diss., University of Pennsylvania, 1969.

———. "Chen Tu-hsiu's Unfinished Biography." *The China Quarterly* 50 (1972): 295–314.

Kautsky, Karl. *The Class Struggle,* tr. William Bohm. New York: Norton, 1971.

Klein, Donald, and Ann Clark, eds. *Biographical Dictionary of Chinese Communism, 1921–1965.* Cambridge: Harvard University Press, 1971.

Kuang Shanji. "Makesizhuyi de Chuanbo yu Sichuan Renmin de Juewu" (The Spread of Marxism and the Awakening of the Sichuanese). *Sichuan Daxue Xuebao, Zhexue Shehui Kexueban* (Journal of Sichuan University, Philosophy and Social Science Issue) 2 (1983): 6–10.

Kuhn, Philip A. *Rebellion and Its Enemies in Late Imperial China: Militarization and Social Structure, 1796–1864.* Cambridge: Harvard University Press, 1970.

―――. "Origins of the Taiping Vision: Cross-Cultural Dimensions of a Chinese Rebellion." *Comparative Studies in Society and History* 19:3 (July 1977): 350–66.

―――. "Local Self-Government under the Republic." In Wakeman and Grant, eds., *Conflict and Control in Late Imperial China*, 257–98.

―――. "The Development of Local Government." In CHOC, 13:329–60.

Kuhn, Philip A., and Susan Mann Jones. "Dynastic Decline and the Roots of Rebellion." In CHOC, 10:107–62.

Kundera, Milan. *The Book of Laughter and Forgetting*. New York: Knopf, 1980.

Kuo, Thomas. *Chen Tu-hsiu (1879–1942) and the Chinese Communist Movement*. South Orange, N.J.: Seton Hall University Press, 1975.

Kwok, Danny. *Scientism in Chinese Thought, 1900–1950*. New Haven: Yale University Press, 1965.

Lai Xiansheng. "Zai Guangdong Geming Hongliuzhong—Huiyi Yijiuerer–Yijiuerqinian de Douzheng" (In the Torrent of the Revolution in Guangdong—Recollections of the Struggle in the 1922–1927 Period). In GDDSZL, 1:89–151.

―――. "Zai Guangdong Geming Hongliuzhong—Huiyi Yijiuersinian zhi Yijiuerqinian de Geming Douzheng (Zhi Er)" (In the Torrent of the Revolutionary Struggle in Guangdong—Recollections of the Revolutionary Struggle in the 1924–1927 Period [Two]). In GDDSZL, 2:100–128.

Le Tianyu. "Wo Suo Zhidaode Zhonggong Beijing Diwei Zaoqi de Geming Huodong" (The Early Revolutionary Activities of the CCP Peking Local Committee of Which I Possess Knowledge). *Wenshi Ziliao Xuanbian* (Compilation of Sources for History and Culture) 11 (1981, Peking): 1–44.

Lee Chong-sik. *Revolutionary Struggle in Manchuria: Chinese Communism and Soviet Interest, 1922–1945*. Berkeley: University of California Press, 1983.

Lee, Leo Ou-fan. *The Romantic Generation of Modern Chinese Writers*. Cambridge: Harvard University Press, 1973.

―――. *Lu Xun and His Legacy*. Berkeley: University of California Press, 1985.

Lenin, V. I. *Selected Works*. Moscow: Foreign Languages Publishing House, 1952.

―――. *Collected Works*. Moscow: Foreign Languages Publishing House, 1961.

―――. *What Is to Be Done?*, tr. Joe Fineberg and George Hanna. London: Penguin Books, 1988.

Leonard, Jane. *Wei Yuan and China's Rediscovery of the Maritime World*. Cambridge: Harvard University Press, 1984.

Leung, John. *The Chinese Work-Study Movement: The Social and Political Experience of Chinese Students and Student-Workers in France, 1913–1925*. Ph.D. diss., Brown University, 1982.

Levenson, Joseph. *Confucian China and Its Modern Fate: A Trilogy*. Berkeley: University of California Press, 1968.

―――. *Liang Ch'i-ch'ao and the Mind of Modern China*. Berkeley: University of California Press, 1970.

Lewin, Moshe. *Lenin's Last Struggle*, tr. Sheridan Smith. New York: Monthly Review Press, 1968.

Li Bogang. "Wuhan Jiandang Chuqi de Huiyi" (Recollections of Early Party-Building Efforts in Wuhan). *Wuhan Wenshi Ziliao Xuanbian* (Compilation of Sources for History and Culture in Wuhan) 3 (1981): 1–5.

————. "Huiyi Li Hanjun" (Recollections of Li Hanjun). DSYJZL 4 (1983): 283–88.

Li Da. *Li Da Wenji* (Collected Works of Li Da). Beijing: People's Press, 1980.

————. "Li Da Zishu" (Li Da on Li Da). DSYJZL, 2 (1981): 1–12.

Li Dazhao. *Li Dazhao Xuanji* (Selected Works of Li Dazhao), ed. Zhonggong Zhongyang Makesi, Engesi, Liening, Sidalin Zhuzuo Bianyiju Yanjiushi (Research Section of the Central Committee's Bureau for the Editing and Translation of the Works of Marx, Engels, Lenin, and Stalin). Beijing: People's Press, 1962.

————. *Li Dazhao Wenji* (Collected Works of Li Dazhao), ed. Yuan Qian. 2 vols. Beijing: People's Press, 1984.

Li Jiannong. *Zhongguo Jinbainian Zhengzhishi* (Political History of China in the Last Century). Shanghai: Commercial Press, 1947.

Li Jiazhong. "Wo Zai Dageming Shiqi de Yiduan Jingli" (An Episode I Experienced in the Period of the Great Revolution). *Sichuan Wenshi Ziliao Xuanji* (Selected Source Materials for the History and Culture in Sichuan) 31 (1983): 20–21.

Li Jui. *The Early Revolutionary Activities of Comrade Mao Zedong*, tr. Anthony Sariti. White Plains, N.Y.: M. E. Sharpe, 1977. (See also Li Rui.)

Li Liangming. "Yun Daiying Shi Zouzhe Wuzhengfuzhuyi Daolu Ma" (Did Yun Daiying Travel the Anarchist Road?). DSYJ 1 (January 1986): 45–49.

Li Ling. "Dang de Diwuci Quanguo Daibiao Dahui Kaihui Riqikao" (An Investigation into the Dates for the Fifth CCP Congress). DSYJ 2 (April 1983): 47–49.

————. Zhongguo Gongchandang Diyici Quanguo Daibiao Dahui Jige Wenti de Kaozheng" (Evidential Research of Some Problems concerning the First CCP Congress). DSYJ 5 (October 1983): 64–66.

————. "Zhonggong Zhongyang Junshibu de Chengli ji qi Zuichu de Gongzuo" (The Formation of the Military Department of the CCP Central Committee and Its Earliest Activities). DSYJ 3 (May 1986): 55–56.

Li Rui. *Mao Zedong de Zaoqi Geming Huodong* (Early Revolutionary Activities of Mao Zedong). Changsha: Hunan People's Press, 1980.

Li Shengfu. "Wode Fuqin Li Hanjun" (My Father, Li Hanjun). *Wuhan Wenshi Ziliao Xuanbian* (Compilation of Sources for History and Culture in Wuhan) 3 (1981): 35–41.

Li Weihan. *Huiyi yu Yanjiu* (Recollections and Studies). Beijing: Zhonggong Dangshi Ziliao Chubanshe (Publishing House for Materials for the History of the Chinese Communist Party), 1986.

Li Xiantao. "Guang-San Tielu Gongren de Douzheng ji Zhonggong Guangdong Shengwei Chuqi de Yixie Qingkuang" (The Struggle of Canton-Sanshui Railroad Workers and the Early Circumstances of the Guangdong Provincial Committee). *Guangzhou Wenshi Ziliao Xuanji* (Selected Sources for the History and Culture of Canton) 21 (1980): 46–60.

Li Xin and Chen Tiejian. *Zhongguo Xinminzhuzhuyi Gemingshi: Weida de Kaiduan, 1919–1923* (History of China's New Democratic Revolution: The Great Beginning, 1919–1923). Beijing: Chinese Academy of Social Sciences Press, 1983.

Li Yibin. *Zhongguo Qingniandang* (China Youth Party). Beijing: Chinese Academy of Social Sciences Press, 1982.

Li Yun-han. *Cong Ronggong Dao Qingdang* (From Cooperation with the CCP to the Party Purge). Taibei: Committee on Contributions to Chinese Scholarship, 1966.

———. "A Re-appraisal of the Party Purification Movement." *Chinese Studies in History* (Spring 1988): 51–75.

Li Zeping. "Sanshiwunian Lai zhi Zhongguo Chubanye: (Yibajiuqinian–Yijiusanyinian)" (Chinese Publishing in the Last Thirty-five Years: [1897–1931]). In Zhang Jinglu, 4:381–94.

Li Zhaonian and Dong Tianjia. " 'Wu'an' Shi Shimma Yihuishi" (What was the "Case of Wu?"). DSYJZL, 5 (1985): 727–29.

Liang Qichao. "Lun Xuehui" (On Study Societies). In *Bianfa Tongyi* (General Discussion of Institutional Reforms), dated 1896, in *Liang Qichao Yinbinshi Wenji* (Collected Works), 1:31–34.

———. *Yinbinshi Wenji* (Collected Works from the Ice Cream Parlor). Shanghai: n.d.

Liao Huanxing. "Wuchang Liqun Shushe Shimo" (History of the Benevolence Society in Wuchang). WSSQDST, 1:202–7.

Liao Xinchu. "Hubei Dang Zuzhi de Jianli ji Qi Shiqi de Huodong" (The Founding of a Party Organization in Hubei and its Activities). In Zhu Chengjia, 127–43.

———. " 'Wusi' Shiqi de Wuchang Liqun Shushe" (The Benevolence Society in Wuchang during the May Fourth Period). In *Chuhui* (Hubei's Light), 1:341–52.

Liao Zhongkai. *Liao Zhongkai Ji (Zengdingben)* (A Collection of Liao Zhongkai's Writings [Revised], ed. Guangdongsheng Shehui Kexueyuan Lishi Yanjiushi (Institute of History, Guangdong Academy of Social Sciences). Beijing: China Press, 1983.

Lieberthal, K. *Revolution and Tradition in Tsientsin, 1949–1952.* Stanford: Stanford University Press, 1980.

Lieberthal, K., and M. Oksenberg. *Policy Making in China: Leaders, Structures, and Process.* Princeton: Princeton University Press, 1988.

Lin Maosheng et al., eds. *Zhongguo Xiandai Zhengzhi Sixiangshi, 1919–1949* (The History of Contemporary Chinese Political Thought, 1919–1949). Harbin: Heilongjiang People's Press, 1984.

Lin Nengshi and Hu Pingsheng, eds. *Zhongguo Xiandaishi Lunwen Xuanji* (Compilation of Articles on Contemporary Chinese History). Taibei: Huashi Press, 1982.

Lin Wunong. "Peng Pai yu Hailufeng Nongmin Yundong de Jiujian Shi" (Nine Events Concerning Peng Pai and the Hailufeng Peasant Movement). *Guangdong Wenshi Ziliao* (Sources for History and Culture in Guangdong) 30 (1981): 35–53.

Lin Yu-sheng. *The Crisis of Chinese Consciousness: Radical Anti-Traditionalism in the May Fourth Era.* Madison: University of Wisconsin Press, 1979.

Ling Biying. " 'Er.qi' Can'an Jingguo" (The February 7 Massacre). *Wenshi Ziliao Xuanbian* (Selected Sources for History and Culture) 9 (1981): 40–52.

Liu Jingfang. "Ping 'Baqi' Huiyi Guanyu Zhigong Yundong de Celue" (A Critique of the Labor Movement Policy of the "August 7" Emergency Conference). DSYJ 3 (May 1986): 57–59.

Liu Linsong. "Peng Pai Lieshi Rudang Shijian Wenti Shangque" (A Discussion of the Time When the Hero Peng Pai Joined the Party). DSYJZL (1980): 323–33.

————, ed. *Ruan Xiaoxian Yanjiu* (Studies on Ruan Xiaoxian). Guangzhou: Guangdong People's Press, 1985.

Liu Qingyang. "Huiyi Jiandang Chuqi Dang Lingdao Beifang Renmin Jinxing de Yingyong Douzheng" (My Recollections of the Heroic Struggles of the People in North China under Party Leadership). *Hebei Wenshi Zialiao* (Sources for History and Civilization in Hebei) 2 (1981): 1–22.

Liu Ye et al. "Shilun Lü'Ou Zhongguo Gongchanzhuyi Zuzhi de Xingcheng" (Preliminary Discussion of the Formation of a Chinese Communist Organization in Europe). In Zhu Chengjia, 170–90.

Liu Zhaiquan. "Yuebei Nonggonghui Liangjian Shishi Zhi Bianzheng" (Rectification of Two Historical Facts Relating to the Yuebei Peasant Association). DSYJZL 6 (1985): 118–21.

Liu Zhongmin. "Shanghai Dangwu Baogao" (Report on Shanghai [KMT] Party Affairs. DSZL 18 (1984): 119–23.

Lu Xun. *Selected Stories of Lu Xun*, tr. Yang Hsien-yi and Gladys Yang. Beijing: Foreign Languages Press, 1972.

"Lü'Ou Dang-Tuan Huodong Wenxian Ziliao Xuan" (A Selection of Materials concerning the Activities of the Party and Youth League in Europe). DSYJZL 3 (1982): 10–27.

Luo Suwen. "Wusa Shiqi de Shanghai Zongshanghui Chutan" (A Preliminary Investigation of the Shanghai General Chamber of Commerce during the May Thirtieth Period). DSZL 24 (1985): 85–96.

Luo Zhanglong. "Luo Zhanglong Tan Zhongguo Laodong Zuhe Shujibu" (Luo Zhanglong Discusses the All-China Labor Secretariat). In Zhongguo Geming Bowuguan (Museum of the Chinese Revolution), ed., *Beifang Diqu Gongren Yundong Ziliao Xuanbian* (A Selection of Sources for the Labor Movement in the North), 2–21.

————. "Zhongguo Gongchandang Disanci Quangguo Daibiao Dahui He Diyici Guogong Hezuo" (The Third Congress of the Chinese Communist Party and the First Cooperation between the KMT and the CCP). DSZL 16 (1983): 4–11.

————. "Zhongguo Gongchandang Disanci Quangguo Daibiao Dahui He Diyici Guogong Hezuo (Xu)" (The Third Congress of the Chinese Communist Party and the First Cooperation between the KMT and the CCP [Continued]). DSZL 17 (1983): 8–21.

Ma Guifan, tr. "Sulian Xin Fabiaode Gongchan Guoji Youguan Zhongguo Geming de Dang'an Wenjian (Zhiyi)" (Archival Documents Relating to the Chinese Revolution Recently Published in the Soviet Union [One]). *Zhonggong Dangshi Yanjiu* (CCP Party History Research) 73 (1988): 73–79.

Ma Junling. "Guanyu Zhongguo Gongchandang Zuzhishi Yanjiu de Jige Wenti" (Some Issues in Research concerning the Organizational History of the CCP). DSYJ 4 (July 1986): 80–81.

Ma Lianru. "Cai Hesen yu Diyici Guogong Hezuo" (Cai Hesen and the First KMT-CCP Cooperation). In *Guangdong Dangshi Tongxun* (Guangdong Party History News), November 1983.

McCord, Edward. "*The Emergence of Modern Chinese Warlordism: Military Power and Politics in Hunan and Hubei.*" Ph. D. diss., University of Michigan, 1985.

McDonald, A. "Mao Tse-tung and the Hunan Self-Government Movement, 1920." *China Quarterly* 68 (February 1976): 751–77.

Maeder, Eric. *Trois Textes de Chen Duxiu: Contribution a l'Etude des Origines Intellectuelles de la Révolution Chinoise* (Three Texts Written by Chen Duxiu: A Contribution to the Study of the Intellectual Origins of the Chinese Revolution). Vevey: Imprimerie Delfa, 1981.

Malreaux, Andre. *Het Menselijk Tekort* (The Human Condition), tr. E. du Perron. Utrecht: Het Spectrum, n.d.

Mann, Susan. *Local Merchants and the Chinese Bureaucracy, 1750–1950*. Stanford: Stanford University Press, 1987.

Mao Lei et al. "Wuhan Guomin Zhengfu Dashiji" (Chronology for the Wuhan Nationalist Government). In *Chuhui* (Southern Light), 1:246–89, n.p., n.d.

Mao Zedong. *Selected Works of Mao Zedong*. Beijing: Foreign Languages Press, 1967.

———. *Mao Zedong Nongcun Diaocha Wenxuan* (Mao Zedong's Peasant Village Investigations: Selected Writings). Beijing: People's Press, 1982.

———. *Mao Zedong Shuxin Xuanji* (Selection of Mao Zedong's Letters). Beijing: People's Press, 1983.

———. *Mao Zedong Zhuzuo Xuandu* (Reader in Mao Zedong's Major Works), ed. Zhonggong Zhongyang Wenxian Bianji Weiyuanhui (Editorial Committee of Documents of the CCP-CC). Beijing: People's Press, 1986.

———. *Mao Zedong Xinwen Gongzuo Wenxuan* (Mao Zedong's Journalistic Activities: Selected Writings). Beijing: Xinhua Press, n.d.

———. "Mao Zedong Gei Li Jinxi de Liufeng Xin" (Six Letters from Mao Zedong to Li Jinxi). In *Zhonggong Dangshi Cankao Ziliao* (Historical Documents for CCP History), 1:497–500.

Maring Archive: Unpublished documents preserved at the Institute of Social History, Amsterdam.

Maring, Hendrik. *Bericht des Genossen H. Maring für die Executive* (Memorandum from Comrade H. Maring to the Executive [of the Comintern]). Arrondissementsparket in Amsterdam (District Court of Amsterdam), archive no. 797/33.

Marks, Robert. *Rural Revolution in South China*. Madison: University of Wisconsin Press, 1984.

Mast, Herman. "Tai Chi-t'ao, Sunism, and Marxism during the May Fourth Movement in Shanghai." *Modern Asian Studies* 3 (1971): 227–49.

Meisner, Maurice. *Li Ta-chao and the Origins of Chinese Marxism*. New York: Atheneum, 1977.

———. *Mao's China: A History of the People's Republic*. New York: Free Press, 1977.

Metzger, Thomas. *Escape from Predicament: Neo-Confucianism and China's Evolving Political Culture*. New York: Columbia University Press, 1970.

Miff, Pavel. *Heroic China: Fifteen Years of the Communist Party of China*. New York: Worker's Library, 1937.

Moore, Barrington. *Social Origins of Dictatorship and Democracy: Lord and Peasant in the Making of the Modern World*. Harmondsworth, Penguin Books, 1984.

Mote, F. "Confucian Eremitism in the Yuan Period." In A. F. Wright, *The Confucian Persuasion*, 202–40.

Nanchang Bayi Jinianguan (Memorial Museum for the August 1 Nanchang Uprising). *Nanchang Qiyi* (The Nanchang Uprising). Beijing: CCP Historical Sources Press, 1987.

Nanchang "Bayi" Qiyi Jinianguan (Memorial Museum for the "August First" Nanchang Uprising), ed. "Guanyu Zuochu Nanchang Qiyi Jueding de Qing-kuang" (Circumstances Surrounding the Decision to Undertake the Nanchang Uprising). *Zhonggong Dangshi Ziliao* (Sources for CCP Party History) 10 (1984): 245–54.

Nathan, Andrew. "A Factionalism Model for CCP Politics." *China Quarterly* 103 (1973): 34–36.

―――. *Peking Politics, 1918–1923: Factionalism and the Failure of Constitution-alism.* Berkeley: University of California Press, 1976.

―――. *Chinese Democracy.* Berkeley: University of California Press, 1986.

Nihon Kokusai Mondai Kenkyūjo (Japanese Institute of Internal Affairs), ed. *Chū-goku Kyōsantō Shi Shiryō Shū* (Compilation of Materials on the History of the Chinese Communist Party). Tokyo: Chūgoku Bukai, 1970–1975.

Nivison, David. "Ho-shen and His Accusers." In Nivison and Wright, eds., *Con-fucianism in Action.* Stanford: Stanford University Press, 1959.

Nivison, D., and A. F. Wright, eds. *Confucianism in Action.* Stanford: Stanford University Press, 1959.

North, R., and X. Eudin. *M. N. Roy's Mission to China: The Communist-Kuo-mintang Split of 1927.* Berkeley: University of California Press, 1963.

Parsons, Talcott. *Politics and Social Structure.* New York: Free Press, 1969.

"Peasant Strategies in Asian Societies: Moral and Rational Economic Ap-proaches—a Symposium." *Journal of Asian Studies* 42:4 (1983): 747–868.

Peng Jianhua. "Yijiuersinian Qiu Li Dazhao Chuxi Gongchan Guoji Wuda Hou Dui Beifangqu Gongzuo de Bushu" (Measures for Work in the North Adopted after Li Dazhao Participated in the Fifth Comintern Congress in the Fall of 1924). DSZL 15 (1983): 110.

―――. "Yijierwunian Qiu Zai Beijing Zhaokai de Zhongyang Kuoda Huiyi" (The Enlarged Central Executive Committee Held in the Fall of 1925 in Peking). DSZL 15 (1983): 120–23.

―――. "Yijiuersinian Dong Baoluoting Zai Beijing Zhaojide Yici Huiyi" (A Meeting Convened by Borodin in Peking in the Winter of 1924). DSZL 17 (1983): 22–24.

Peng Ming. *Wusi Yundongshi* (History of the May Fourth Period). Beijing: Peo-ple's Press, 1984.

Peng Pai Yanjiu Shiliao Bianjibu (Editorial Department for *Historical Sources for Research on Peng Pai*), ed. *Peng Pai Yanjiu Shiliao* (Historical Sources for Research on Peng Pai). Guangzhou: Guangdong People's Press, 1981.

Peng Shuzhi. *The Chinese Communist Party in Power.* New York: Monad Press 1980.

―――. "Guanyu Dangde Disici Quanguo Daibiao Dahui—Peng Shuzhi Gei Zhonggong Lü'Mo Zhibu Quanti Tongzhi Xin: (Yijiuerwunian, Eryue Erri)" (On The Fourth CCP Congress—Peng Shuzhi's Letter to All Comrades of the CCP Moscow Cell). *Zhonggong Dangshi Ziliao* (Sources for CCP Party His-tory) 3 (1982): 16–22.

Perry, Elizabeth. *Rebels and Revolutionaries in North China.* Stanford: Stanford University Press, 1980.

————. "Social Banditry Revisited: The Case of Bai Lang, a Chinese Brigand." *Modern China* 9:3 (1983): 355–79.

Pickowicz, Paul. *Marxist Literary Thought in China: The Influence of Ch'ü Ch'iu-pai*. Berkeley: University of California Press, 1981.

Pye, Lucian. *Asian Power and Politics: The Cultural Dimensions of Authority*. Cambridge: Harvard University Press, 1985.

Qiang Zhonghua, ed. *Chen Duxiu Beipu Ziliao Huibian* (Compilation of Sources on Chen Duxiu's Imprisonments). Henan People's Press, 1982.

Qinghua Daxue Zhonggong Dangshi Jiaoyanzu (Teaching and Research Group for CCP History at Qinghua University), ed. *Fu'Fa Qin'gong Jianxue Yundong Shiliao* (Source Materials for the Work-Study Movement to France). Beijing: Beijing Press, 1979.

Qiu Jun. "Makesizhuyi Zai Zhongguo De Chuangbo" (The Dissemination of Marxism in China). DSYJ 2 (April 1983): 19–30.

Qu Qiubai. *Qu Qiubai Xuanji* (Selected Works of Qu Qiubai), ed. Qu Qiubai Xuanji Bianjizu (Editorial Committee for the Selected Works of Qu Qiubai). Beijing: People's Press, 1985.

————. *Zhongguo Gemingzhong zhi Zhenglun Wenti* (Controversial Issues in the Chinese Revolution). Party Organ Committee of the CCP, 1928.

Rankin, Mary. *Early Chinese Revolutionaries: Radical Intellectuals in Shanghai and Che-chiang, 1902–1919*. Cambridge: Harvard University Press, 1971.

————. *Elite Activism and Political Transformation in China: Zhejiang Province, 1865–1911*. Stanford: Stanford University Press, 1986.

Rao Weihua. "Zhongguo Gongchandang Zai Guangdong Diqu Jiandang Chuqi Qingkuang Diandi" (Remarks on Early Party-Building Efforts of the CCP in the Guangdong Region). *Guangzhou Wenshi Ziliao* (Sources for History and Culture in Canton) 17 (1979): 20–24.

Ren Jianshu, et al. "Chen Duxiu he *Anhui Suhuabao*" (Chen Duxiu and *The Anhui Colloquial*). DSZL 2 (1980): 69–77.

————. "Wuhan Guomin Zhengfu de Chengli, Tuibian, Xiaoshi—Cong Wang Fuzhi zhi Wang-Jiang Heliu (Shang)" (The Erection, Transformation, and Elimination of the Wuhan Republican Government—from Wang [Jingwei]'s Resumption of Function to the Reunification of Wang and Chiang Kai-shek). DSZL 20 (1984): 84–96.

————, eds. "Chen Duxiu Zhuzuo Xuan (1903.5–1915.7): Fu: Chen Duxiu Zhu, Yi, Xin Mulu (1903.5–1915.7)" (Selected Writings of Chen Duxiu [May 1903–July 1915]: Supplement: Index of Chen Duxiu's Writings, Translations, and Letters [May 1903–July 1915]). DSZL 5 (1980): 56–191.

————, eds. *Chen Duxiu Zhuzuo Xuan* (Selected Writings of Chen Duxiu), vol. 1. Shanghai: People's Press, 1984.

Ren Wuxiong. "Guanyu Dangde 'Erda' he 'Sanda' " (Concerning the "Second" and "Third" Congresses of the Party). *Wenshi Ziliao Xuanbian* (Compilation of Sources for History and Culture) 3 (1980): 1–11.

————. "Guanyu Guomindang Shanghai Zhixingbu" (The Shanghai Executive Branch of the KMT). DSZL 18 (1984): 124–28.

————, et al. "Yun Daiying" (Yun Daiying). In Hu Hua, ed., *Zhonggong Dangshi Renwuzhuan* (Biographies of Eminent People in the History of the Chinese Communist Party), 5:1–47.

————. "Yun Daiying Yanjiuzhong de Jige Wenti" (Some Issues in Research on Yun Daiying). DSYJ 1 (January 1980): 78–81.

Renmin Chubanshe (People's Press), ed. *Diyici Guonei Geming Zhanzheng Shiqi de Nongmin Yundong Ziliao* (Sources for the Peasant Movement during the First Period of Civil War). Beijing: People's Press, 1983.

Rigby, Richard. *The May 30 Movement: Events and Themes.* Folkestone: Dawson, 1980.

Ristaino, M. *China's Art of Revolution: The Mobilization of Discontent, 1927 and 1928.* Durham: Duke University Press, 1987.

Rozman, Gilbert, ed. *The Modernization of China.* New York: Free Press, 1982.

Saich, Tony. "The Sneevliet (Maring) Archives." *CCP Research Newsletter* 1 (Fall 1988): 10–20.

————. "Through the Past Darkly: Some New Sources on the Founding of the Party." *International Review of Social History* 30:2 (1985): 167–82.

Scalapino, Robert. *The Chinese Anarchist Movement.* Berkeley: University of California Press, 1961.

————. "The Evolution of a Young Revolutionary: Mao Zedong in 1919–1921." JAS 42:1 (November 1982): 29–62.

Scalapino, Robert, and George T. Yu. *Modern China and Its Revolutionary Process.* Berkeley: University of California Press, 1985.

Schapiro, Leonard. *The Communist Party of the Soviet Union.* New York: Vintage Books, 1960.

Schoppa, K. *Chinese Elites and Political Change.* Cambridge: Harvard University Press, 1982.

Schram, Stuart. *Mao Tse-tung.* New York: Simon and Schuster, 1967.

————. *The Political Thought of Mao Tse-tung.* Rev. ed. New York: Praeger, 1969.

————. "From 'The Great Union' to the 'Great Alliance.' " *China Quarterly* 41 (January 1972): 88–105.

————. "Mao Tse-tung's Thought to 1949." In CHOC 13:796–870.

————, tr. "The Great Union of the Popular Masses." *China Quarterly* 41 (January 1972): 76–87.

Schurmann, Franz. *Ideology and Organization in Communist China.* Berkeley: University of California Press, 1966.

Schurmann, Franz, and Orville Schell, eds. *Republican China: Nationalism, War and the Rise of Communism, 1911–1949.* New York: Vintage Books, 1967.

Schwarcz, Vera. *The Chinese Enlightenment Intellectuals and the Legacy of the May Fourth Movement of 1919.* Berkeley: University of California Press, 1986.

Schwartz, Benjamin. "Chen Tu-hsiu and the Acceptance of the Modern West." *Journal of the History of Ideas* (January 1951): 61–72.

————. *Chinese Communism and the Rise of Mao.* Cambridge: Harvard University Press, 1951.

————. *In Search of Wealth and Power.* Cambridge: Harvard University Press, 1964.

————. "A Personal View of Some Thoughts of Mao Zedong." In Chalmers Johnson, ed., *Ideology and Politics in Contemporary China.* Seattle: University of Washington Press, 1973.

————, ed. *Reflections on the May Fourth Movement.* Cambridge: Harvard University Press, 1972.

Scott, James. *The Moral Economy of the Peasant: Rebellion and Subsistence in Southeast Asia.* New Haven: Yale University Press, 1979.

Selden, Mark. *The Yenan Way in Revolutionary China.* Cambridge: Harvard University Press, 1974.

Sha Dongxun. "Guangdong Shehuizhuyi Qingniantuan Shishi" (Historical Facts Concerning the Guangdong Socialist Youth League). *Qingyunshi Ziliao yu Yanjiu* (Materials for and Research on the History of the Youth Movement), n.d., 1–14

————, ed. *Laodongzhe* (The Worker). Guangzhou: Guangdong People's Press, 1984.

"Shanghai Gongren Sanci Wuzhuang Qiyi Dang'an Shiliao Xuanzai" (Selected Historical Sources for the Three Armed Uprisings of Shanghai Workers). DSZL 11 (1982): 5–28.

Shanghai, Jiangsu, Zhejiang Dangshi Ziliao Zhengweihui, Dang'anguan (Compilation Committees and Archives of Sources for Party History in Shanghai, Jiangsu, and Zhejiang), ed. "Yijiueryinian zhi Yijiuerqinian Shanghai, Jiangsu, Zhejiang, Dang Zuzhi Fazhan Gaikuang" (An Overview of the Development of Party Organizations in Shanghai, Jiangsu, and Zhejiang). DSZL 19 (1984): 3–47.

Shanghai Shehui Kexueyuan Lishi Yanjiusuo (History Institute, Shanghai Academy of Social Sciences), ed. *Wusa Yundong Shiliao* (Historical Materials for the May Thirtieth Movement). Shanghai: Shanghai People's Press, 1981.

Shanghai Zhonggong Dangshi Ziliao Zhengji Weiyuanhui, Dang'anguan (Shanghai Compilation Committee for Materials Concerning CCP History) et al., ed. "Yijiueryinian zhi Yijiuerqinian Shanghai, Jiangsu, Zhejiang Dang Zuzhi Fazhan Gaikuang" (The Development of Party Organizations in Shanghai, Jiangsu, and Zhejiang between 1921 and 1927). *Zhonggong Dangshi Ziliao* (Source Materials for CCP History) 10 (1984): 181–244.

Shanghaishi Dang'anguan (Shanghai Municipal Archives), ed. *Shanghai Gongren Sanci Wuzhuang Qiyi Dang'an Shiliao Huibian* (Compilation of Archival Sources for the Three Armed Uprisings of the Shanghai Workers). Shanghai: People's Press, 1983.

Shao Lizi. *Shao Lizi Wenji* (Collected Works of Shao Lizi), ed. Chuan Xuewen. Beijing: Zhonghua Shuju, 1985.

Shao Weizheng. "Guangyu Zhongguo Gongchandang Diyici Quanguo Daibiao Dahui Zhaokai Riqi Chubu Kaozheng" (Preliminary Investigation concerning the Dates of the First Congress of the CCP). DSZL 1 (1979): 127–39.

————. "Dang de 'Yida' Yiti Chutan" (Preliminary Examination of Disputes at the "First Congress"). DSZL 3 (1980): 126–140.

————. "Jiandang Qianhou de Shanghai Gongren Yundong" (The Shanghai Labor Movement at the Time of the Party's Founding). DSZL 12 (1982): 64–84.

————. "Shilun Zhongguo Gongchandang Jiandang Tese" (Preliminary Discussion of the Special Characteristics of the CCP's Party Building). DSZL 4 (1985): 25–45.

————. "Yaqian Nongming Xiehui Shimo" (The History of the Yaqian Peasant Association). DSYJZL 5 (1985): 458–69.

Shao Weizheng and Xu Shihua. " 'Erda' de Zhaokai he Minzhu Geming Gangling de Zhiding" (The Second Congress and the Determination of the Guiding Principle of the Democratic Revolution). DSYJ 5 (1980): 15–21.

Shen Yunlong. *Zhongguo Gongchandang zhi Laiyuan* (The Origins of the Chinese Communist Party). Taibei: Wenhai Press, 1978.

———. *Zhongguo Qingniandang de Guoqu yu Xianzai* (The Past and Present of the China Youth Party). Taibei: Zhongguo Qingniandang Zhongyang Dangbu (Central Department, China Youth Party), 1983.

Sheng Yueh. *The Sun Yatsen University in Moscow and the Chinese Revolution: A Personal Account.* Lawrence: University of Kansas Press, 1972.

Shenggang Dabagong (The Guangzhou–Hong Kong Strike). Guangzhou: People's Press, 1980.

Sheridan, James E. *China in Disintegration: The Republican Era in Chinese History, 1912–1949.* New York: Free Press, 1975.

———. *Chinese Warlord: The Career of Feng Yu-hsiang.* Stanford: Stanford University Press, 1966.

Shi Guang, Zhou Cheng'en et al., eds. *"Erda" he "Sanda": Zhongguo Gongchandang Dier-san Daibiao Dahui Ziliao Xuanbian* (The Second Congress and the Third Congress: An Edited and Selected Compilation of Sources for the Second and Third Congresses of the Chinese Communist Party). Beijing: Chinese Academy of Social Sciences Press, 1985.

Shi Yisheng. "Huiyi Zhonggong Lü'Ou Zhibu Guanghui Yeji" (Recollections of the Glorious Achievements of the CCP Branch in Europe). *Tianjin Wenshi Ziliao Xuanji* (Compilation of Sources for History and Culture in Tianjin) 15 (1981): 114–30.

Sima Lu. *Zhonggong Dangshi Ji Wenxian Xuancui, Diyibu: Makesizhuyi Zai Zhongguo de Chuangbo* (Documented History of the Chinese Communist Party, Part I: The Spread of Marxism in China). Hong Kong: Zilian Press, 1973.

———. *Zhonggong Dangshi Ji Wenxian Xuancui, Dierbu: Zhonggong de Chengli yu Chuqi Huodong* (Documented History of the Chinese Communist Party, Part II: The Founding of the CCP and Its Early Activities). Hong Kong: Zilian Press, 1973.

Skocpol, Theda. *States and Social Revolutions.* Cambridge: Harvard University Press, 1979.

Snow, Edgar. *Red Star over China.* New York: Random House, 1938.

Solomon, R. *Mao's Revolution and the Chinese Political Culture.* Berkeley: University of California Press, 1971.

Spence, Jonathan. *The Gate of Heavenly Peace: The Chinese and Their Revolution, 1895–1980.* Harmondsworth, U.K.: Penguin Books, 1982.

Sulian Yinmou Wenzheng Huibian (Compilation of Documentary Evidence of the Soviet Conspiracy), ed. Zhang Guochen. Beijing: Metropolitan Police Headquarters, 1928.

Sun Wuxia et al., eds. *Gongchan Guoji yu Zhongguo Geming Ziliao* (Materials for the History of the Relationship between the Comintern and the Chinese Revolution). Vol. 1, 1919–1924, vol. 2, 1925–1927. Beijing: People's Press, 1985.

Takeuchi Minoru. *Mao Zedong Ji* (Collected Writings of Mao Zedong). Tokyo: Hokubosha, 1970–1972. (Sososha is updating this under the title *Mao Zedong Ji, Bujuan* [Collected Writings of Mao Zedong, Supplementary Volumes].)

Tang Shengzhi. "Cong Xinhai Geming Dao Beifa Zhanzheng—Tang Shengzhi Huiyilu Pianduan" (From the 1911 Revolution to the Northern Expedition—Some Recollections of Tang Shengzhi). *Wenshi Ziliao Xuanji* (Selections of Sources for History and Culture) 105 (1985): 161–81.

Thaxton, Ralph. *China Turned Rightside Up: Revolutionary Legitimacy in the Peasant World.* New Haven: Yale University Press, 1983.

Thompson, Roger. *Visions of the Future, Realities of the Day: Local Administrative Reform, Electoral Politics, and Traditional Chinese Society on the Eve of the 1911 Revolution.* Ph.D. diss., Yale University, 1985.

Tianjinshi Renmin Tushuguan (People's Library of Tianjin City), ed. *Zhou Enlai Tongzhi Lü'Ou Wenji* (Collection of Comrade Zhou Enlai's European Writings). Beijing: Wenwu Press, 1979.

Tichelman, F. *Henk Sneevliet: Een Politieke Biografie* (Henk Sneevliet: A Political Biography). Amsterdam: Kritiese Bibliotheek van Gennep, 1974.

———. *Socialism in Indonesia: De Indische Sociaal Democratische Beweging, Deel 1897–1917* (Socialism in Indonesia: The Indian Social Democratic Movement, 1897–1917). Dordrecht: Foris, 1985.

Trotsky, Leon. *Problems of the Chinese Revolution,* tr. Max Schachtman. 2d ed. New York: Paragon Book Gallery, 1962.

———. *1905,* tr. Anya Bostoch. New York: Vintage Books, 1972.

Tsou Tang. *The Cultural Revolution and Post-Mao Reforms.* Chicago: Chicago University Press, 1986.

Tsou Tang and Ho Ping-ti, eds. *China in Crisis.* Vol. 1, *China's Heritage and the Political System.* Chicago: Chicago University Press, 1968.

Ulyanovsky, R. A., ed. *The Comintern and the East: The Struggle for the Leninist Strategy in National Liberation Movements.* Moscow: Progress, 1979.

Vishnyakova-Akimova, Vera V. *Two Years in Revolutionary China, 1925–1927,* tr. Steven Levine. Cambridge: Harvard University Press, 1971.

Wakeman, Frederic. "The Price of Autonomy: Intellectuals in Ming and Ch'ing Politics." *Daedalus* 102:2 (1972): 35–70.

———. *History and Will.* Berkeley: University of California Press, 1973.

———. "Rebellion and Revolution: The Study of Popular Movement in Chinese History." *Journal of Asian Studies* 36:2 (1977): 201–37.

———. *The Great Enterprise: The Manchu Reconstruction of Imperial Order in Seventeenth-Century China.* Berkeley: University of California Press, 1985.

Wakeman, Frederic, and Carolyn Grant, eds. *Conflict and Control in Late Imperial China.* Berkeley: University of California Press, 1975.

Walder, Andrew. *Communist Neo-Traditionalism: Work and Authority in Chinese Industry.* Berkeley: University of California Press, 1986.

Wales, Nym. *Red Dust: Autobiographies of Chinese Communists.* Stanford: Stanford University Press, 1952.

Wang Erh-min. *Wan'Qing Zhengzhi Sixiangshi Lun* (On the History of Political Thought of the Late Qing). Taibei, Huashi Press, 1980.

Wang Jianmin. *Zhongguo Gongchandang Shigao* (Draft History of the Chinese Communist Party). Taibei, 1965.

Wang Jianying. "Wodang Gongyun Lingdao Jigou de Yange" (The Evolution of Our Party's Labor Movement Leadership Institutions). DSYJZL 5 (1985): 327–31.

———, ed. *Zhongguo Gongchandang Zuzhishi Ziliao Huibian* (Edited Source

Materials for the Organizational History of the CCP). Beijing: Red Flag Press, 1982.

Wang Laidi. "Guanyu Zhongguo Gongchandang Zaoqi Zuzhi zhi Jige Wenti" (Some Issues in the Early Organization of the Chinese Communist Party). In Zhu Chengjia, 211–16.

———. "Lun Chen Duxiu Zai Jiandangzhong de Zuoyong" (On Chen Duxiu's Endeavors During the Founding of the Party). In Beijing Daxue Shehui Kexuechu (Social Science Section, Peking University), ed., *Beijing Daxue Jinian Gongchandang Chengli Liushi Zhounian Lunwenji* (Articles in Commemoration of the Sixtieth Anniversary of the Founding of the Chinese Communist Party), 119–41.

Wang Ruofei. "Guanyu Dageming Shiqi de Zhongguo Gongchandang" (The Chinese Communist Party at the Time of the Great Revolution). *Jindaishi Yanjiu* (Modern History Research) 1 (1981): 39–60.

Wang Yongju. "Youguan Zhou Enlai Zai Dageming Shiqi de Liangjian Shishi de Dingzheng" (A Verification of Two Historical Facts concerning Zhou Enlai at the Time of the Great Revolution). DSYJZL 3 (1982): 308–15.

Wang Zhixin. *Zhongguo Gongchandang Lici Zhongyao Huiyiji (Shang)* (History of Several Important Meetings of the Chinese Communist Party [One]). Shanghai: People's Press, n.d.

Weigelin-Schwiedrzick, Susanne. *Parteigeschichtsschreibung in der VR China: Typen, Methoden, und Funktionen* (Historiography of the Party in the People's Republic of China: Types, Methods, and Functions). Wiesbaden: Otto Harrassowitz, 1984.

Weishenniyakewa-Ajimowa [Vishniakova-Akimova, Vera]. *Zhongguo Dageming Jianwen—Sulian Zhuhua Guwentuan Yiyuan de Huiyi* (Memoirs of China's Great Revolution—the Recollections of a Translator for Soviet Advisors in China), tr. Wang Chi. Beijing: Chinese Academy of Social Sciences Press, 1985. Translated from the original Russian into English by Steven Levine as *Two Years in Revolutionary China, 1925–1927*. Cambridge: Harvard University Press, 1971.

Whiting, A. S., *Soviet Policies in China, 1917–1924*. Stanford: Stanford University Press, 1968.

Wilbur, C. Martin. *The Nationalist Revolution*. Cambridge: Cambridge University Press, 1983.

Wilbur, C. Martin, and Julie Lien-ying How, eds. *Documents on Communism, Nationalism, and Soviet Advisors in China (1918–1927): Papers Seized in the 1927 Peking Raid*. New York: Columbia University Press, 1956.

Wilbur, C. Martin, and Julie L. How. *Missionaries of Revolution: Soviet Advisors and Nationalist China, 1920–1927*. Cambridge: Harvard University Press, 1984.

Wittfogel, Karl. "The Legend of Maoism." *China Quarterly* 1 (1960): 72–86.

———. "The Legend of Maoism (Conclusion)." *China Quarterly* 2 (1960): 16–34.

Wohl, Robert. *French Communism in the Making*. Palo Alto, Calif.: Stanford University Press, 1966.

Womack, Brantley. *The Foundations of Mao Zedong's Political Thought, 1917–1935*. Honolulu: University Press of Hawaii, 1982.

Wright, M. C. *China in Revolution: The First Phase, 1900–1913*. New Haven: Yale University Press, 1968.

Wright, Timothy. *Coal Mining in China's Economy and Society*. Cambridge: Cambridge University Press, 1984.

Wu, Eugene. "Divergence in Strategic Planning: Chiang Kai-shek's Mission to Moscow, 1923." Delivered at the Conference on Chiang Kai-shek and Modern China, Taibei, 1986.

Wu Jianren. "Dageming Shiqi de Jianghua Nongyun" (The Peasant Movement in Jianghua During the Great Revolution). *Gemingshi Ziliao* (Sources for Revolutionary History) 13 (1984): 62–81.

Wu Qi. "Zhou Enlai Tongzhi Qingnian Shidai Zai Fa-De Liangguo Geming Huodong" (Comrade Zhou Enlai's Revolutionary Activities in France and Germany as a Youth). *Tianjin Wenshi Ziliao Xuanji* (Selected Sources for History and Culture in Tianjin) 15 (1981): 131–45.

Wu Shihao. "Chen Wangdao de 'Gongchandang Xuanyan' Chuban Shijian Luekao" (Preliminary Consideration of the Publication Date of Chen Wangdao's [translation of] 'The Communist Manifesto'). DSZL 1 (1981): 156–65.

Wu Yu. *Wu Yu Ji* (Collected Works of Wu Yu), ed. Zhao Qing. Chengdu: Sichuan People's Press, 1985.

Wu Yuzhang. *Wu Yuzhang Huiyilu* (Recollections of Wu Yuzhang). Beijing: China Youth Press, 1978.

"Wusa Yundong Qijian Zhonggong Shanghai Diwei Huiyi Jilu (Xuanzai)" (Minutes of Shanghai Local Committee Meetings during the May Thirtieth Movement [Selections]). DSZL 22 (1985): 3–12.

Wylie, Raymond. *The Emergence of Maoism: Mao Tse-tung, Ch'en Po-ta, and the Search for Chinese Theory, 1935–1945*. Stanford: Stanford University Press, 1980.

Xiang Qing. "Chen Duxiu Deng Tichu Gongchandangren Tuichu Guomindang Shishi Kaoding" (A Verification of the Historical Truth of Whether Chen Duxiu and Others Proposed CCP Members to Withdraw from the KMT). DSYJZL 6 (1985): 104–8.

Xiang Qing et al. "Gongchan Guoji Daibiaodeng Renwu Jieshao (Er)" (Introduction to the Comintern's Representatives [Two]). DSZL 3 (1980): 127–47.

———. "Zhonggong Daibiaodeng Zai Gongchan Guoji de Huodong Jieshao (Yi)" (Introduction to the Activities of CCP Representatives with the Comintern [One]). DSZL 7 (1981): 158–71.

———. "Zhonggong Daibiaodeng Zai Gongchan Guoji de Huodong Jieshao (Er)" (Introduction to the Activities of CCP Representatives with the Comintern [Two]). DSZL 8 (1981): 144–60.

———. "Zhonggong Daibiaodeng Zai Gongchan Guoji de Huodong Jieshao (San)" (Introduction to the Activities of CCP Representatives with the Comintern [Three]). DSZL 9 (1981): 148–70.

———. "Guanyu Gongchan Guoji He Zhongguo Geming Jianli Lianxi de Tantao" (Investigation and Discussion of the Comintern's Efforts to Establish Contact with the Chinese Revolution). DSYJZL 3 (1982): 122–30.

———. "Gongchan Guoji, Sulian, He Zhongshanjian Shijian" (The Comintern, the Soviet Union, and the Naval Vessel *Zhongshan* Incident). DSZL 14 (1983): 94–113.

Xiangdao Zhoubao (The Guide Weekly), referred to in this text as the *Guide*; the characters for *Xiangdao* on the original are large, while those for *Zhoubao* are small.

Xiao Chaoran et al., eds. *Zhonggong Dangshi Jianming Cidian* (A Concise Dictionary of the Chinese Communist Party's History). Beijing: Liberation Army Press, 1986.

———."Xin Minzhu Zhuyi Shiqi Mao Zedong Dui Maliezhuyi Jiandang Xueshu de Gongxian" (Mao Zedong's Contributions to the Marxist-Leninist Theory of Party Building During the New Democratic Period). In Beijing Daxue Shehui Kexuechu (Social Science Section, Peking University), ed., *Beijing Daxue Jinian Gongchandang Chengli Liushi Zhounian Lunwenji* (Articles in Commemoration of the Sixtieth Anniversary of the Founding of the Chinese Communist Party), 1–23.

———. "Zhongguo Gongchandang de Chuangli yu Beijing Daxue" (The Founding of the Chinese Communist Party and Peking University), ibid., 98–105.

Xiao San. *Xiao San Wenji* (Collected Works of Xiao San). Beijing: New China Press, 1983.

Xiao Sheng. "Ye Tan Jing-Han Tielu de Lingdao Wenti" (An Additional Discussion of the Leadership Issues of the Great Peking-Hankow Railroad Strike). DSYJZL 3 (1982): 241–46.

Xiao Yanzhong. "Mao Zedong Zaoqi Hunan Gongheguo Sixiang Chuyi" (Preliminary Discussion of Mao Zedong's Hunanese Republicanism). *Jindaishi Yanjiu* (Modern History Research) 3 (May 1986): 132–50.

Xie Jinghua and Liao Huimin. "Dang Zai Hubei Diyige Zhibu—Wuhan Zhibu" (The First CCP Cell in Hubei—the Wuhan Cell). In *Chuhui* (Southern Light), 1:231–45.

Xin Qingnian (The New Youth), subtitle *La Jeunesse*; began as *Qingnian Zazhi* (Youth Magazine).

Xin Qingnianshe Bianjibu (Editorial Department, The New Youth Society), ed. *Shehuizhuyi Taolunji* (A Collection of Discussions of Socialism). Canton: New Youth Society, 1922.

Xin Shidai (The New Age), ed. *Hunansheng Tushuguanxiao* (Library School of Hunan). Changsha: Hunan People's Press, 1980.

Xingqi Pinglun (Weekly Critic), repr. People's Press, Beijing, 1981.

Xu Deliang. "Wusa Yundong yu Shanghai Daxue" (The May Thirtieth Movement and Shanghai University). In *Wenshi Ziliao Xuanji* (A Selection of Sources for History and Culture) 22 (1978): 53–64.

Xu Meikun. "Jiangzhe Quwei Chengli Qianhou de Pianduan Huiyi" (Some Recollections of the Time of the Founding of the Regional Committee for Zhejiang and Jiangsu). DSZL 7 (1981): 24–28.

Xu Xingzhi. "Dang Chengli Shiqi Zhejiang de Gongnong Yundong" (The Peasant Movement in Zhejiang during the Founding Period of the Party). In YDQH, 2:38–44.

Yang Shaolian. "Chen Yannian." In *Guangdong Dangshi Ziliao* (Source Materials for Party History in Guangdong), 1:171–80.

Yang Shusheng et al., eds. "Li Dazhao Nianpu, 1889–1927." *Hebei Wenshi Ziliao Xuanji* (A Selection of Sources for History and Culture in Hebei) 3 (1981): 1–247.

Yang Tianshi et al., eds. *Nanshe* (The Southern Society). Beijing: Zhonghua Shuju, 1980.

Yang Youjiong. *Zhongguo Zhengdangshi* (History of Political Parties in China). Taibei: Taiwan Commercial Press, 1979.

Yang Yunruo. *Gongchan Guoji He Zhongguo Geming Guanxi Jishi, 1919–1943* (Chronology of CCP-Comintern Relations, 1919–1943). Beijing: Chinese Academy of Social Sciences Press, 1983.

Yang Yunruo et al., eds. *Weijingsiji Zai Zhongguo de Youguan Ziliao* (Source Materials for Voitinsky's Activities in China). Beijing: Chinese Academy of Social Sciences Press, 1982.

Yang Yuqing. "Dageming Shidai de Wuhan Suojian Suowen" (Memoirs of Wuhan during the Period of the Great Revolution). *Wuhan Wenshi Ziliao Xuanbian* (Compilation of Sources for History and Culture in Wuhan) 3 (1981): 43–56.

Yang Zhihua. "Yang Zhihua zhi Huiyi" (Recollections of Yang Zhihua). In YDQH, 2:25–31.

Yao Tianyu. "Peiyang Geming Ganbu de Honglu—Shanghai Daxue" (The Factory for Revolutionary Cadres—Shanghai University). DSZL 2 (1980): 72–80.

Ye Lei and Qiu Zuojian. "Waiguoyu Xueshe" (Foreign Languages Study Society). DSZL 1 (1980): 174–76.

" 'Yida' Qianhou" *Xiudingben Zengbu de Ziliao* (The Additional Sources in the Revised Edition of *The Founding of the Party*). DSYJZL 3 (1982): 28–121.

Young, Ernest. "Politics in the Aftermath of the Revolution: The Era of Yuan Shikai." In CHOC, 12:209–55.

Yu Guolin. "Yi Wuchang Zhongyang Nongjiangsuo de Xuexi" (Recollections of My Study at the Central Peasant Movement Cadre Institute in Wuchang). *Wuhan Wenshi Ziliao Xuanbian* (Compilation of Sources for History and Culture in Wuhan) 3 (1981): 17–31.

Yu Yingbin. "Cai Hesen yu Zhonggong Dangshi Yanjiu" (Cai Hesen and Research on Party History). DSYJ 4 (1986): 28–34.

Yuan Bangjian. "Dageming Shiqi Guangdong Dang, Tuan Zuzhi Guanxi de Bianhua" (Changes in the Organizational Relations of the Party and the Youth League in Guangdong at the Time of the Great Revolution). DSYJZL 4 (1983): 170–83.

Yuan Zhongxiu. "Guanyu Peng Pai Tongzhi Kaishi Congshi Nongmin Yundong He Rudang de Shijian" (Concerning the Date When Comrade Peng Pai Began His Involvement in the Peasant Movement and Joined the Party). DSYJZL 1 (1980): 319–22.

Yun Daiying. *Lai Hong Qu Yan Lu* (Record of Arriving Geese and Departing Swallows). Beijing: Beijing Press, 1981.

———. *Yun Daiying Riji* (Diary of Yun Daiying), ed. Zhongyang Dang'anguan and Zhongguo Geming Bowuguan (Central Committee Archives and Museum of the Chinese Revolution). 1981.

———. *Yun Daiying Wenji* (Collected Works of Yun Daiying), ed. Zhang Zhuhong. Beijing: People's Press, 1984.

Zelin, Madeleine. *The Magistrate's Tael.* Berkeley: University of California Press, 1984.

Zeng Changqiu. "Zhongguo Laodong Zuhe Shujibu Chengli yu 'Yida' Yiqian" (The General Chinese Labor Secretariat was Established before the "First Congress"). In *Jindaishi Yanjiu* (Research on Modern History), 2 (March 1986), 280–81.

Zeng Chenggui. "Guomindang Zhongyang Geshengqu Lianxi Huiyi Shulue"

(Overview of the KMT Joint Conference of the Central, Provincial and Regional Committees). DSYJZL 6 (1985): 88–95.

———. "Shilun Dageming Shiqi Dang Lingdao Hubei Nongmin Yundong de Jingyan yu Jiaoxun" (Preliminary Discussion of the Experiences and Lessons of the Party's Leadership of the Peasant Movement in Hubei during the Period of the Great Revolution). DSYJ 4 (July 1986): 35–41, 71.

Zeng Leshan, ed. *Wusi Shiqi Chen Duxiu Sixiang Yanjiu* (Studies of Chen Duxiu's Thought during the May Fourth Period). Fuzhou: Fujian People's Press, 1983.

Zhang Bojian. "Guanyu Dang de Disici Daibiao Dahui he Tuan Disanci Quanguo Daibiao Dahui—Zhang Bojian Gei Dongfang Daxue Tongzhi de Xin: (Yijiuer-wunian, Eryue Wuri)" (Concerning the Fourth Congress of the Party and the Third Congress of the Socialist Youth League—Zhang Bojian's Letter to Comrades at the University of the Toilers of the East: [February 5, 1925]). *Zhonggong Dangshi Ziliao* (CCP Party History Research) 3 (1982): 23–25.

Zhang Dainian et al., eds. *Wuzhengfuzhuyi Sixiang Ziliao Xuan* (A Selection of Source Materials for Anarchist Thought). Beijing: Peking University Press, 1983.

Zhang Guotao [Chang Kuo-t'ao]. *The Rise of the Chinese Communist Party, 1921–1927: Volume One of the Autobiography of Chang Guo T'ao.* Lawrence: Kansas University Press, 1971.

Zhang Hao. "Wusi Shiqi Yun Daiying Tongzhi Huodong de Diandi Huiyi" (A Few Recollections concerning Comrade Yun Daiying's Activities during the May Fourth Period). In WSSQDST, 1:208–10.

Zhang Jinglu, ed. *Zhongguo Xiandai Chubanshe Ziliao* (Source Materials on Publishing in Contemporary China). Beijing: China Press, 1959.

Zhang Jingru et al., eds. *Li Dazhao Shengping Shiliao Biannian* (Chronological Compilation of Source Materials for Li Dazhao's Biography). Shanghai: Shanghai People's Press, 1984.

———. *Zhongguo Gongchandang de Chuangli* (The Founding of the Chinese Communist Party). Shijiazhuang: Hebei People's Press, 1981.

Zhang Shenfu. "Zhang Shenfu Tan Lü'Ou Dang, Tuan Zuzhi Huodong Qingkuang" (Zhang Shenfu Discusses the Activities and Organization of the CCP and Socialist Youth League). In *Tianjin Wenshi Ziliao Xuanbian* (Compilation of Sources for History and Culture in Tianjin), 86–92.

Zhang Shuichun. " 'Jindai Zhongguo Bainianshi Cidian' Shengao Yijian Zhailu" (Excerpts of Suggestions Made on the Review Copy of *A Dictionary of a Century of Modern Chinese History*). *Bianji zhi You* (Companion for Editors) 3 (1986): 87.

Zhang Tailei. *Zhang Tailei Wenji* (Collected Works of Zhang Tailei). Beijing: People's Press, 1981.

Zhang Tailei [?]. "Zhongguo Gongchandang De Diyici Daibiao Dahui" (The First Congress of the CCP). In YDQH, 1:20–23.

Zhang Tinghao. "Huiyi Guomindang Shanghai Zhixingbu" (Recollections of the Shanghai Executive Branch of the KMT). DSZL 18 (1984): 114–18.

Zhang Weiping. "Lun Mao Zedong Jiandang Xueshuo Chubu Xingcheng de Zhuyao Biaozhi he Lishi Tedian" (On the Hallmarks and Historical Characteristics of the Initial Formation of Mao Zedong's Theories of Party Building). DSYJ 5 (1986): 37–44.

Zhang Weizhen. "Zhang Weizhen Tongzhi Tan Shanghai Gongren Sanci Wu-zhuang Qiyi" (Comrade Zhang Weizhen Talks about the Three Shanghai Armed Uprisings). DSYJZL 1 (1980): 313–17.

———. "Zhang Weizhen Tongzhi Tan Shanghai 'Wusa' Yundong" (Comrade Zhang Weizhen Talks about the "May Thirtieth" Movement in Shanghai). DSYJZL 1 (1980): 304–12.

Zhang Yunhou et al., eds. *Liu'Fa Qingong Jianxue Yundong* (The Work Study Movement to France). Shanghai: Shanghai People's Press, 1979.

———. *Wusi Shiqi de Shetuan* (The Societies and Leagues of the May Fourth Period). 4 vols. Beijing: Three Unity Press, 1979.

Zhang Zhong and Chen Zhibao. "Zhonggong 'Yida' Yiqian de Dangyuan Mingdan Chutan" (A Preliminary Investigation of the CCP Membership List before the First Congress). DSYJZL 3 (1982): 148–65.

Zhang Zhuhong. "Zhongguo Xiandai Gemingshi Ziliaoxue Gaiyao" (Essential Bibliography of Primary Sources for the History of the Contemporary Chinese Revolution), vols. 3–6. N.p., n.d.

Zhang Zhuhong and Yang Yunruo, eds. *Bao Luoting Zai Zhongguo de Youguan Ziliao* (Materials concerning Borodin's Activities in China). Beijing: Chinese Academy of Social Sciences Press, 1982.

Zhang Zurong et al. "Guanyu Zhonggong 'Yida' Daibiao Renshu de Jige Xueshuo" (Various Theories concerning the Number of Representatives at the First Congress). DSZL 1 (1979): 139–43.

Zhao Bu. "Wuci Dahui Dao Liuci Dahui Yinianzhong Dang de Zuzhi Zhuang-kuang (1)" (Party Organization in the Year between the Fifth and the Sixth Congresses [Part One]). DSYJ 5 (September 1986): 63–68.

———. "Wuci Dahui Dao Liuci Dahui Yinianzhong Dang de Zuzhi Zhuangkuang (2)" (Party Organization in the Year between the Fifth and the Sixth Congresses [Part Two]). DSYJ 6 (November 1986): 44–48.

———. "Zhongguo Gongchandang Zuzhishi Ziliao, 1" (Information on the Organizational History of the Party, Part One). DSYJ 2 (1981): 62–75.

———. "Zhongguo Gongchandang Zuzhishi Ziliao (1)" (Information on the Organizational History of the CCP [One]). In Zhongguo Renmin Daxue Dang'anxi (Archival Section, People's University), ed., *Zhongguo Gongchandang Jiguan Fazhanshi Cankao Ziliao* (Sources for the History of the Institutional Development of the Chinese Communist Party), 31–34. A reprint of the above.

———. "Zhongguo Gongchandang Zuzhishi Ziliao (2)" (Information on the Organizational History of the CCP [Two]). In Zhongguo Renmin Daxue Dang'anxi (Archival Section, People's University), ed., *Zhongguo Gongchandang Jiguan Fazhanshi Cankao Ziliao* (Sources for the History of the Institutional Development of the Chinese Communist Party), 42–59.

———. "Zhongguo Gongchandang Zuzhishi Ziliao (3)" (Information on the Organizational History of the CCP [Three]). In Zhongguo Renmin Daxue Dang'anxi (Archival Section, People's University), ed., *Zhongguo Gongchandang Jiguan Fazhanshi Cankao Ziliao* (Sources for the History of the Institutional Development of the Chinese Communist Party), 60–67.

———. "Zhongguo Gongchandang Zuzhishi Ziliao (4)" (Information on the Organizational History of the CCP [Four]). In Zhongguo Renmin Daxue

Dang'anxi (Archival Section, People's University), ed., *Zhongguo Gongchandang Jiguan Fazhanshi Cankao Ziliao* (Sources for the History of the Institutional Development of the Chinese Communist Party), 78–89.

———. "Zhongguo Gongchandang Zuzhishi Ziliao (5)" (Information on the Organizational History of the CCP [Five]). In Zhongguo Renmin Daxue Dang'anxi (Archival Section, People's University), ed., *Zhongguo Gongchandang Jiguan Fazhanshi Cankao Ziliao* (Sources for the History of the Institutional Development of the Chinese Communist Party), 90–106.

———. "Zhongguo Gongchandang Zuzhishi Ziliao (6)" (Information on the Organizational History of the CCP [Six]). DSYJ 2 (April 1983): 38–46.

———. "Zhongguo Shehuizhuyi Qingniantuan Diyici Quanguo Daibiao Dahui ji Qi Qianhou Ruokan Wenti" (The First National Congress of the Chinese Socialist Youth League and Some Related Issues of the Time). In *Zhongguo Shehuizhuyi Qingniantuan Chuangzao Wenti Lunwenji* (Essays on the Founding of the Chinese Socialist Youth League), 26–39.

Zhao Jing et al. *Zhongguo Jindai Jingji Sixiangshi* (History of Modern Chinese Economic Thought). Beijing: Zhonghua Shuju, 1982.

Zhao Shiyan. *Zhao Shiyan Xuanji* (Selected Works of Zhao Shiyan). Chengdu: Sichuan People's Press, 1984.

Zheng Bangxing. "Wusi Qianhou Mao Zedong Gaizao Zhongguo Tujing" (Mao Zedong's Approach to the Transformation of China during the May Fourth Period). DSYJ 6 (December 1983): 11–16.

Zheng Chaolin. "Zhongguo Shaonian Gongchandang de Ruokan Shishi" (Some Historical Facts concerning the Communist Party of Young Chinese). *Wenshi Ziliao Xuanji* (Compilation of Sources for History and Culture) (Shanghai) 3 (1981): 13–26.

Zheng Guang. "Zhongguo Shehuizhuyi Qingniantuan de Chuangzao" (The Founding of the Chinese Socialist Youth League). In *Zhongguo Shehuizhuyi Qingniantuan Chuangzao Wenti Taolunji* (Essays on the Founding of the Chinese Socialist Youth League), 12–25.

Zheng Peigang. "Zheng Peigang de Huiyi" (Recollections of Zheng Peigang). In YDQH, 2:482–86.

Zheng Wenguang. *Zhonggong Jiandang Yundongshi Zhu Wenti (Chugao)* (Various Questions concerning the History of the Party-Building Campaign [First Draft]). Hong Kong: Green Horse Publishing Service, 1976.

Zhengxie Anhuisheng Weiyuanhui Wenshi Ziliao Gongzuozu (Work Group for Source Materials for Culture and History, Political Consultative Committee of Anhui Province). "Xinhaiqian Anhui Wenjiaojie de Geming Huodong" (Revolutionary Activities in Cultural and Educational Circles before the 1911 Revolution). In Zhongguo Renming Xieshang Huiyi Quanguo Weiyuanhui Wenshi Ziliao Yanjiu Weiyuanhui (Research Committee for Source Materials for Culture and History, National Committee of the Chinese Political Consultative Conference), ed., *Xinhai Geming Huiyilu* (Recollections of the 1911 Revolution), 4:379–84.

Zhengzhi Shenghuo (Political Life), repr. People's Press, Beijing, 1982.

Zhi Min. "Wodang Heshi Kaishi Zai Guomindang He Qunzhong Tuantizhong Sheli Dangtuan" (When Began Our Party to Form Party Blocs in the KMT and in Mass Organization?). DSYJZL 4 (1983): 342–46.

Zhishi Chubanshe (Knowledge Press), ed. *Yida Huiyilu* (Memoirs of the First Congress). Beijing: Knowledge Press, 1980.

"Zhonggong Anhui Diwei de Jianli ji qi Huodong" (The Founding of the Anhui Local Committee and Its Activities). *Anhui Dangshi Tongxun* (Anhui Party History Bulletin) (1985): 22–26.

Zhonggong Dangshi Jiaoxue Cankao Ziliao (Reader for Courses on CCP History). Beijing: People's Press, 1979.

Zhonggong Dangshi Ziliao (Source Materials for CCP History), Central CCP Editorial Committee for Sources Concerning Party History and CCP Central Party History Research Institute. The CCP Central Party School Press.

Zhonggong Gongchandang Diyici Quanguo Daibiao Dahui Huichi Jinianguan (Memorial Museum for the Site of First National Congress of the Chinese Communist Party), ed. *Zhongguo Gongchandang de Tansheng Tupianji* (Pictures of the Birth of the Chinese Communist Party). Shanghai: Shanghai Educational Press, 1979.

Zhonggong Guangdong Shengwei Dangshi Yanjiu Bangongshi/Zhongguo Zhuhai Shiwei Dangshi Bangongshi (Office of the Section for Party History of the Guangdong Provincial Committee of the Chinese Communist Party / Office of Party History of the Zhuhai Municipal Committee of the Chinese Communist Party), eds. *Su Zhaozheng Yanjiu Shiliao* (Sources for Research on Su Zhaozheng). Guangzhou: Guangdong People's Press, 1985.

Zhonggong Guangdong Shengwei Dangshi Yanjiu Weiyuanhui, Guangdongsheng Dang'anguan (Research Committee for Party History of the Guangdong Provincial Committee of the Chinese Communist Party, Guangdong Provincial Archives), eds. *"Yida" Qianhou Guangdong de Dang Zuzhi* (The Guangdong Party Organization at the Time of the First Congress). 1981.

Zhonggong Henan Dangshi Ziliao (Source Materials for the History of the CCP in Henan). Zhonggong Henan Shengwei Dangshi Ziliao Zhengji Bianzuan Weiyuanhui (Committee for the Editing and Compilation of Source Materials for Party History, Henan Provincial Committee of the CCP).

Zhonggong Wuhan Shiwei Dangshi Bangongshi / Wuhanshi Wenwu Guanlichu (Party History Office, Wuhan Municipal CCP Committee / Cultural Relics Department of Wuhan City), eds. "Yijiuerqinian Zhonggong Zhongyang Jiguan You Shanghai Qian Wuhan de Jingguo ji Zai Han Qingkuang" (The Move From Shanghai to Wuhan of the Central Institutions of the Chinese Communist Party in 1927 and Its Circumstances in the City). GDDSZL 21 (1987): 113–27.

Zhonggong Zhongyang Dangshi Yanjiushi (CCP Central Party History Research Institute), ed. *Zhonggong Dangshi Dashi Nianbiao* (Chronology of CCP History). Beijing: People's Press, 1981.

Zhonggong Zhongyang Dangshi Ziliao Zhengji Weiyuanhui / Zhongyang Dang'anguan (Editorial Committee for Sources for Party History of the CCP Central Committee / Central Committee Archives), eds. *Baqi Huiyi* (The August 7 Conference). Beijing: Publishing House for Sources for CCP Party History, 1986.

———. "Guangyu Baqi Huiyi Ruokan Qingkuang de Diaocha Baogao (Yijiubaliunian Eryue)" (A Report on Research Concerning Some Aspects of the August 7 Conference [February 1986]). Ibid., 195–201.

Zhonggong Zhongyang Dangshi Ziliao Zhengji Weiyuanhui / Zhonggong Zhong-yang Dangxiao Dangshi Yanjiushi (Editorial Committee for Source Materials for Party History of the CCP Central Committee / Party History Institute of the Central Party School), eds. *Zhonggong Dangshi Ziliao* (Source Materials for Party History). Beijing: Central Party School Press.

Zhonggong Zhongyang Dangxiao Dangshi Yanjiushi (Party History Institute of the Central Party School), ed. *Zhonggong Dangshi Cankao Ziliao* (Reference Materials for CCP History). Beijing: People's Press, 1979.

Zhonggong Zhongyang Dangxiao Dangshi Yanjiushi Ziliaozu (Central Party School, Materials Section of the Party History Institute), ed. *Zhongguo Gong-chandang Lici Zhongyao Huiyi Ji* (Chronological Selection of Important CCP Meetings). Shanghai: Shanghai People's Press, n.d.

Zhonggong Zhongyang Shujichu (Secretariat of the CCP Central Committee), ed. *Liuda Yilai—Dangnei Mimi Wenjian* (Since the Sixth Congress—Secret Internal Party Documents). Beijing: People's Press, 1980.

———. *Liuda Yiqian—Dangde Lishi Cailiao* (Before the Sixth Congress: Histori-cal Documents for the Party's History). Beijing: People's Press, 1980.

Zhonggong Zhongyang Wenxian Yanjiushi (Documents and Research Institute, Central Committee of the CCP), ed. *Guanyu Jianguo Yilai Ruokan Lishi Wenti Jueyi: Zhushiben (Xiuding)* (Resolution on Several Historiographical Issues since the Establishment of the Nation: Annotated Edition [Revised]). Beijing: People's Press, 1985.

Zhongguo Dier Lishi Dang'anguan (Number Two Archives), ed. *Wusa Yundong Yu Shenggang Bagong* (The May Thirtieth Movement and the Canton–Hong Kong Strike). Jiangsu: Guji Press, 1985.

———. *Zhongguo Guomindang Diyi, Dier Quanguo Daibiao Dahui Huiyi Wen-jian* (Congress Documents of the First and Second National Congresses of the KMT). Nanjing: Jiangsu Guji Press, 1986.

Zhongguo Geming Bowuguan (Museum of the Chinese Revolution), ed. *Beifang Diqu Gongren Yundong Ziliao Xuanbian, 1921–1923* (A Compilation of Mate-rials for the Labor Movement in the North, 1921–1923). Beijing: Beijing Press, 1981.

Zhongguo Geming Bowuguan, Hunansheng Bowuguan (Museum of the Chinese Revolution, Hunan Provincial Museum), eds. *Mari Shibian Ziliao* (Sources for the Horse Day Incident). Beijing: People's Press, 1983.

Zhongguo Geming Bowuguan, Hunansheng Geming Bowuguan (Museum of the Chinese Revolution and Hunan Provincial Museum of the Revolution), eds. *Xinmin Xuehui Ziliao* (Source Materials for the New Citizen Study Society). Beijing: People's Press, 1980.

Zhongguo Gongchandang (CCP), ed. *Zhongguo Gongchandang Wunianlai zhi Zhengzhi Zhuzhang* (Political Positions of the Chinese Communist Party in the Last Five Years). 1926.

Zhongguo Gongchandang Diyici Quanguo Daibiao Dahui Huichi Jinianguan (Me-morial Museum of the Original Site of the First National Congress of the Chinese Communist Party). *Zhongguo Gongchandang de Tansheng Tupianji* (Pictures of the Birth of the Chinese Communist Party). Shanghai: Shanghai Educational Press, 1979.

Zhongguo Jin-xiandaishi Dashiji (1840–1980) (Chronology for Modern and Con-temporary Chinese History [1840–1980]). Shanghai: Zhishi Press, 1984.

Zhongguo Kexueyuan Jindaishi Yanjiusuo, Zhongguo Minguoshizu (Section for Republican History, Modern History Institute of the Chinese Academy of Sciences), ed. *Zhonghua Minguoshi Ziliao Conggao* (Draft Documentary Collections for Republican History).

Zhongguo Renmin Daxue Dang'anxi (Archival Section, People's University), ed. *Zhongguo Gongchandang Jiguan Fazhanshi Cankao Ziliao* (Sources for the History of the Institutional Development of the Chinese Communist Party). Foreword 1983.

Zhongguo Renmin Daxue Zhonggong Dangshixi Ziliaoshi (Materials Section of the Department of CCP History, People's University), ed. *Gongchanzhuyi Xiaozu de Dang de "Yida" Ziliao Huibian (Xiaonei Yongshu)* (Collection of Sources for the Communist Cells and the Party's "First Congress" [Textbook for use at People's University]). N.p., n.d.

Zhongguo Renmin Zhengzhi Xieshang Huiyi Quanguo Weiyuanhui, Wenshi Ziliao Yanjiu Weiyuanhui (Research Committee for Materials on History and Culture, National Committee of the Chinese People's Consultative Conference), ed. *Diyici Guogong Hezuo Shiqi de Huangpu Junxiao* (The Whampoa Military Academy during the First Period of CCP-KMT Cooperation). Beijing: Materials for Culture and History Press, 1984.

Zhongguo Renming Xieshang Huiyi Quanguo Weiyuanhui Wenshi Ziliao Yanjiu Weiyuanhui (Research Committee for Source Materials for Culture and History, National Committee of the Chinese Political Consultative Conference), ed. *Xinhai Geming Huiyilu* (Recollections of the 1911 Revolution). Beijing: Zhonghua Shuju, 1961–1962.

Zhongguo Shehui Kexueyuan Jindaishi Yanjiusuo / Anyuan Gongren Yundong Jinianguan (Modern History Institute of the Chinese Academy of Social Sciences / Memorial Museum for the Anyuan Workers Movement), eds. *Liu Shaoqi yu Anyuan Gongren Yundong* (Liu Shaoqi and the Anyuan Workers Movement). Beijing: Chinese Academy of Social Sciences Press, 1981.

Zhongguo Shehui Kexueyuan Jindaishi Yanjiusuo / Zhongguo Dier Lishi Dang'anguan Shiliao Bianjibu (Modern History Institute of the Chinese Academy of Social Sciences / Editorial Department for Historical Sources, Number Two Chinese Archives), eds. *Wusi Aiguo Yundong Dang'an Ziliao* (Archival Materials Concerning the May Fourth Movement). Beijing: Chinese Academy of Social Sciences Press, 1980.

Zhongguo Shehui Kexueyuan, Jingji Yanjiusuo, Zhongguo Xiandai Jingjishi Zu (Contemporary Chinese Economic History Section, Economy Institute, Chinese Academy of Social Sciences), ed. *Diyi, Erci Guonei Geming Zhanzheng Shiqi Tudi Douzheng Shiliao Xuanji* (Compilation of Historical Sources for the Land Struggle during the First and Second Periods of Internal Revolutionary Struggle). Beijing: People's Press, 1981.

Zhongguo Shehui Kexueyuan Xiandaishi Yanjiushi / Zhongguo Geming Bowuguan Dangshi Yanjiushi (Contemporary History Section of the Chinese Academy of Social Sciences / Party History Section of the Museum of the Chinese Revolution), eds. *"Yida" Qianhou: Zhongguo Gongchandang Diyici Daibiao Dahui Qianhou Ziliao Xuanbian* (The Period of the Founding of the Party: Selected Source Materials for the Period of the First National Congress of the Chinese Communist Party). 3 vols. Beijing: People's Press, 1980 (the third volume was published in 1984).

Zhongguo Shehui Kexueyuan Xinwen Yanjiusuo (Institute of Journalism of the Chinese Academy of Social Sciences), ed. *Zhongguo Gongchandang Xinwen Gongzuo Wenjian Huibian* (A Compilation of Documents for the Activities in Journalism of the Chinese Communist Party). 3 vols. Beijing: New China Press, 1980.

Zhongguo Shehuizhuyi Qingniantuan Chuangzao Wenti Lunwenji (Essays on the Founding of the Chinese Socialist Youth League). N.p., n.d.

Zhonghua Quanguo Zonggonghui (National General Labor Union of China), ed. *Zhonggong Zhongyang Guanyu Gongren Yundong Wenjian Xuanbian* (A Compilation of CCP Central Committee Documents on the Labor Movement). Beijing: Archive Press, 1985.

Zhongyang Dang'anguan (Central Committee Archives), ed. *Zhonggong Zhongyang Wenjian Xuanji* (Selected Documents of the CCP Central Committee). 3 vols. Beijing: Central Party School Press, 1982, 1983, ?. Six volumes of a public edition of this collection of Central Committee documents, covering the period 1921–1930, have been issued.

———. *Zhonggong Zhongyang Zhengzhi Baogao Xuanji* (Compilation of CCP Central Committee Political Reports). Vol. 1, *1922–1926*; vol. 2, *1927–1933*. Beijing: Zhonggong Zhongyang Dangxiao Chubanshe (Central Party School Press), 1981.

———. *Zhongguo Gongchandang Dierci zhi Diliuci Quanguo Daibiao Dahui Wenjian Huibian* (Compilation of Documents of the Second to Sixth National Congresses of the Chinese Communist Party). Beijing: People's Press, 1981.

———. *Zhongguo Gongchandang Diyici Daibiao Dahui Dang'an Ziliao: Zengdingben* (Archival Sources for the First Congress of the CCP: Revised and Enlarged Edition). Beijing: People's Press, 1984.

Zhongyang Dang'anguan, Zhongguo Geming Bowuguan, Zhongyang Dangxiao Chubanshe (CCP Central Committee Archives, Museum of the Chinese Revolution, and the Central Party School Press), eds. *Yun Daiying Riji* (Diaries of Yun Daiying). Beijing: CCP Central Party School Press, 1981.

Zhou Qisheng. *Zhonggong Dangshi Shijian Renwulu* (List of Important Events and People in Party History). Shanghai: Shanghai People's Press, 1983.

Zhou Yangru. " 'Yida' Qian de Shanghai Gongchandang" (The CCP in Shanghai before the First Congress). DSYJ 1 (1980): 53–55.

Zhou Yongxiang. "Beijing Gongchandang Xiaozu" (The Peking CCP Cell). DSYJ 1 (1980): 56–60.

———. "Shandong Gongchandang Xiaozu" (The Shandong CCP Cell). DSYJ 2 (1980): 52–56. (Also in Zhu Chengjia, 144–56.)

———. *Qu Qiubai Nianpu* (Chronology for Qu Qiubai). Guangzhou: Guangdong People's Press, 1983.

———. Xishan Huiyipai Zhaokaide Liangci Fandong Huiyi" (Two Reactionary Meetings of the Western Hills Faction). DSYJZL 6 (1985): 96–103.

Zhu Chengjia, ed. *Zhonggong Dangshi Yanjiu Lunwen Xuan* (Selection of Research Articles on CCP History). Changsha: Hunan People's Press, 1983.

Zhu Zhixin. *Zhu Zhixin Ji* (Collected Works of Zhu Zhixin), ed. Guangdongsheng Zhexue Shehui Kexue Yanjiusuo Lishi Yanjiushi (History Institute, Guangdong Academy for Philosophy and Social Sciences). Beijing: Zhonghua Shuju, 1979.

Index

Democratic centralism, 128–129;
Fifth Congress limits
democratic element of,
223–224

Deng Zhongxia: and
Canton–Hong Kong strike,
157, 202; criticized at Third
Congress, 110; criticizes
leadership at August 7
emergency conference, 231; in
KMT's Shanghai Executive
Committee's Department for
Workers and Peasants, 150; at
Nanjing Conference of Young
China Study Society, 48–49;
and Shanghai Labor Movement
during May Thirtieth
Movement, 150; and Shanghai
Uprising, 191–192

Dewey, John: influence on Chen
Duxiu, 19; popular in Hunan,
83

Dirlik, Arif: criticizes Meisner
and Schwartz, 9; critique of,
57–58; on importance of
Marxism-Leninism to CCP,
82; on importance of October
Revolution for CCP, 243; on
significance of proletariat for
CCP founding, 54; sources
used by, 58; on study societies,
38

Dogma, as understood by Lenin,
37

Dong Biwu, and Wuhan cell, 72

"Draft Provisional Regulations
for the Punishment of Local
Bullies and Evil Gentry," 189

Du Yuesheng, 116, 192

Duan Qirui, 14, 17–18, 27

Duara, Prasenjit, 197–198

Dynastic order, core concepts of,
12

Examination system, abolished,
12–13

Factionalist conflict: between
Chen Duxiu and Guangdong
Regional Executive Committee
(1926), 201–213; deepening of
(spring 1927), 220–222; and
Mao Zedong, 221–223; nature
of, 237; and Qu Qiubai,
215–219; reignited by Stalin's
intervention, 215–219

February 7 incident (1923),
111–114

Feng Yuxiang, 29

Fifth Congress of the CCP
(April–May 1927): Chen
Duxiu's report to, 162,
194–195; proceedings,
223–226

First Congress of the CCP
(July–August 1921): account
of, 3, 85–90; disputes at,
86–88; elections at, 88; list of
participants at, 275 n. 149

First Eastern Expedition (1925),
and peasant movement in
Hailufeng, 170

Foreign Languages School, of
Shanghai cell, 62

Foreman (*gongtou*): and *bang*,
112; in Peking, 70; and
workers in Shanghai, 150,
154–155. *See also* Native labor
unions

Fourth Congress of the CCP
(January 1925): attended by
twenty CCP representatives,
224; on labor movement, 143;
proceedings, 143–146;
"Resolution on Organization,"
141; and women's liberation,
115

French syndicalist strike, 47, 54

Text: 10/12 Aldus
Display: Aldus
Compositor: Maryland Composition Co.
Printer: Braun-Brumfield, Inc.
Binder: Braun-Brumfield, Inc.